Technology, Innovation, and Strategic Transformation in Human Resource Management

Varinder Singh Rana
https://orcid.org/0000-0001-6158-9195
City University, Ajman, UAE

Aisha Khan
https://orcid.org/0009-0009-7679-3661
Bath Spa University, UAE

IGI Global
Scientific Publishing
Publishing Tomorrow's Research Today

Vice President of Editorial	Melissa Wagner
Director of Acquisitions	Mikaela Felty
Director of Book Development	Jocelynn Hessler
Production Manager	Mike Brehm
Cover Design	Jose Rosado

Published in the United States of America by
IGI Global Scientific Publishing
701 East Chocolate Avenue
Hershey, PA, 17033, USA
Tel: 717-533-8845 | Fax: 717-533-7115
Website: https://www.igi-global.com E-mail: cust@igi-global.com

Library of Congress Cataloging-in-Publication Data

LCCN: (CIP Data Pending)
ISBN13: 9798260018453
Isbn13Softcover: 9798260018460
EISBN13: 9798260018477
British Cataloguing in Publication Data
A Cataloguing in Publication record for this book is available from the British Library.

Table of Contents

Detailed Table of Contents

The accelerated digitalization of service economies and the rise of generative AI are reshaping strategic human resource management (SHRM). As platform-based models and intelligent systems drive service delivery, HR is evolving to enable agility, ethics, and innovation. This chapter explores SHRM's response to the convergence of AI and platform labor, with a focus on sectors like digital tourism, education, logistics, and fintech. It highlights how AI tools manage workflows, generate content, and engage multi-platform workforces. Key HR challenges—talent attraction, engagement, performance, and well-being—are examined in decentralized settings. Case studies from Uber, Airbnb, and Duolingo illustrate efforts to balance efficiency with empathy. Beyond tech adoption, the chapter examines how AI and gigification shift psychological contracts and workplace culture. It emphasizes emotional intelligence, upskilling, and algorithmic transparency as foundations for trust. The chapter offers an ethical, future-ready roadmap for people-first, tech-enabled HR systems.

The hospitality industry is one of the most labor-intensive service sectors worldwide, relying extensively on human resources for operational excellence, customer satisfaction, and competitive positioning. In today's rapidly evolving environment, technological innovations are reshaping how human resource management (HRM) functions, particularly in contexts where workforce diversity and turnover present ongoing challenges. Strategic Human Resource Management in the Hospitality Industry with Technology Integration-Evidence from the UAE Strategic Human

examines how Strategic Human Resource Management (SHRM) can address challenges faced by gig workers, focusing on job security, compensation, performance management, flexibility, and satisfaction. Using qualitative content analysis in NVivo and bibliometric mapping in VOSviewer, the study analyzes policies, corporate initiatives, academic literature, and worker narratives. Findings indicate that while reforms such as the Code on Social Security (2020) and state-level welfare boards offer potential protections, enforcement gaps persist. Gig workers continue to experience income instability, limited grievance redressal, and tension between flexibility and precarity.

This chapter is a discussion about the radical transformation of the artificial intelligence (AI) in talent acquisition particularly in relation to efficiency, accuracy and candidate experience. It carries out an evaluation of tools based on AI such as algorithms, chatbots and automated scheduling software, to facilitate sourcing, screening, and engagement activities with a view to ease the changing workforce needs. This form of evolution increases productivity at the workplace, makes the processes more inclusive and encourages flexibility in staffing. The discussion gives a framework that the HR practitioners and scholars can use to evaluate the impact of AI on their recruitment performance, the quality of decisions made by the recruiters, and the engagement of the candidates, therefore, drawing avenues of potential future research and practice in employee management..

This study explores how AI-driven Employee Value Proposition (EVP) branding can enhance talent attraction and retention in eco-friendly FMCG firms in Himachal Pradesh. Using data from 102 employees and job seekers, along with a systematic literature review, the research applies factor analysis and regression to validate findings. Results show that AI-enabled employer branding significantly boosts awareness of EVP, which in turn improves employee engagement, loyalty, and job seeker interest. Integrating sustainability values and CSR initiatives into AI-powered EVP communication further strengthens employer brand perception, positioning these firms as desirable and responsible workplaces. For FMCG companies operating in a fast-paced and competitive environment, adopting AI-driven, sustainability-focused branding strategies can be a powerful way to attract top talent, retain skilled employees, and foster long-term organizational success. This work contributes by linking technology, green practices, and HR strategy to offer a modern, sustainable approach to talent management.

Generative Artificial Intelligence (AI), exemplified by ChatGPT, is reshaping Human Resource Management (HRM) by revolutionizing recruitment, training, communication, and engagement. Generative AI enhances organizational communication by fostering responsiveness, inclusivity, and psychological safety. However, ethical risks such as algorithmic bias, fairness, and transparency remain critical, demanding governance frameworks and continuous auditing. While AI excels in structured tasks, human intuition is vital for addressing cultural, emotional, and behavioural complexities, highlighting the need for balanced integration. This study emphasizes deliberate, ethical adoption aligned with organizational values, positioning AI as a collaborator that augments, rather than replaces, human decision-making in shaping the future of HRM.

In the Industry 4.0 era, organizations face challenges in sustaining employee engagement while enhancing productivity through data-driven strategies. This study explores the link between employee engagement and performance, emphasizing the mediating role of HR analytical strategies. A quantitative approach was used, with data from 125 professionals across sectors. Regression, correlation, and collinearity diagnostics revealed that physical, emotional, and cognitive engagement significantly influence task and contextual performance. HR analytics emerged as a key mediator, strengthening this relationship. Furthermore, organizational factors like compatibility, relative advantage, and top management support positively impacted engagement-performance outcomes. The study underscores how HR analytics can

Preface

INTRODUCTION

The contemporary landscape of Human Resource Management (HRM) is undergoing a profound and irreversible transformation. Rapid advancements in digital technologies, the emergence of artificial intelligence, and the widespread adoption of platform-based business models have fundamentally altered how organizations attract, manage, and retain talent. In this context, *Technology, Innovation, and Strategic Transformation in Human Resource Management* has been conceptualized as a timely and forward-looking volume that captures the dynamic interplay between technological innovation and strategic HR practices across industries and geographies.

As editors, we recognized the urgent need to compile scholarly and practice-oriented perspectives that move beyond traditional HR frameworks. Organizations today are no longer defined solely by their structures or processes, but by their ability to adapt, innovate, and respond to uncertainty. Human resources now play a central strategic role in enabling this transformation—serving as both architects of organizational agility and stewards of ethical and inclusive workplaces. This volume reflects that shift by bringing together contributions that explore not only technological adoption, but also its human, social, and organizational implications.

This book is also rooted in the understanding that technology alone cannot drive sustainable success. While artificial intelligence, analytics, and automation offer unprecedented efficiencies, they also introduce complex challenges related to trust, fairness, employee well-being, and organizational culture. The chapters in this collection collectively emphasize the importance of balancing technological advancement with human-centered values. Through diverse methodologies, case studies, and conceptual frameworks, the contributors provide insights into how HR can evolve as a strategic partner in shaping the future of work.

CHAPTER OVERVIEW

This edited volume is structured to provide a comprehensive exploration of strategic HRM in the context of technological disruption and innovation across sectors:

Chapter 1 examines the evolution of Strategic Human Resource Management (SHRM) in the age of generative AI and platform-based services. It highlights how organizations are redesigning talent strategies in response to decentralized, algorithm-driven work environments, supported by case insights from global digital platforms.

Chapter 2 focuses on the hospitality industry in the UAE, offering empirical insights into how technology integration reshapes HR practices in a labor-intensive and culturally diverse sector. It underscores the role of innovation in addressing workforce challenges such as turnover and service quality.

Chapter 3 explores the relationship between quality of work life and organizational flexibility within the air transport sector. Using the case of Royal Air Maroc, it demonstrates how employee well-being directly contributes to organizational resilience and adaptability.

Chapter 4 presents a sustainability-oriented perspective on HRM in the UAE hospitality sector. It introduces frameworks for integrating environmental, social, and economic sustainability into HR strategies, emphasizing green HRM and inclusive workforce practices.

Chapter 5 extends the discussion within the UAE hotel industry, analyzing the intersection of technology, employee engagement, and organizational performance through quantitative methods. It reinforces the strategic importance of aligning HR practices with technological capabilities.

Chapter 6 shifts focus to India's gig economy, particularly the food delivery sector, examining how SHRM can address the challenges of algorithmic management, job insecurity, and worker well-being in platform-based employment systems.

Chapter 7 investigates the transformation of recruitment processes through artificial intelligence, detailing how AI tools enhance sourcing, screening, and candidate engagement while raising important questions about fairness and decision-making.

Chapter 8 explores AI-driven employer branding and its role in strengthening employee value propositions (EVP), particularly within sustainability-focused organizations. It highlights how technology can amplify organizational identity and attract talent.

Chapter 9 delves into the application of generative AI in HR functions, emphasizing both its transformative potential and the ethical considerations that must guide its implementation, including transparency, bias mitigation, and governance.

Chapter 10 addresses the role of HR analytics in Industry 4.0, demonstrating how data-driven strategies can enhance employee engagement and performance while supporting organizational decision-making.

Chapter 11 concludes the volume with a compelling case study on Diversity, Equity, and Inclusion (DEI) as a strategic HR driver. It illustrates how inclusive practices can be embedded into organizational culture to foster innovation, equity, and social impact.

CONCLUSION

As we reflect on the contributions within this volume, it becomes evident that the future of Human Resource Management lies at the intersection of technology and humanity. The chapters collectively demonstrate that while digital tools and systems are transforming HR functions, the core mission of HR—to support, develop, and empower people—remains unchanged. Instead, it is being redefined in more complex and meaningful ways.

One of the central themes emerging from this book is the necessity of balance. Organizations must navigate the tension between efficiency and empathy, automation and human judgment, innovation and ethical responsibility. Strategic HRM is uniquely positioned to manage this balance by ensuring that technological advancements are aligned with organizational values and employee well-being. This requires not only technical expertise but also emotional intelligence, cultural awareness, and ethical leadership.

Furthermore, this volume highlights the growing importance of inclusivity, sustainability, and data-driven decision-making as pillars of modern HR strategy. Whether through green HRM practices, AI-enabled recruitment systems, or DEI initiatives, organizations are increasingly recognizing that long-term success depends on creating equitable, resilient, and purpose-driven workplaces. These themes are not isolated trends but interconnected elements of a broader transformation shaping the future of work.

We hope that this book serves as a valuable resource for researchers, practitioners, policymakers, and students seeking to understand and navigate the evolving HR landscape. By bridging theory and practice, and by presenting diverse global perspectives, this volume aims to inspire continued dialogue, innovation, and responsible leadership in Human Resource Management.

Chapter 1

Strategic Human Resource Management in the Age of Generative AI and Platform-Based Services:

Redesigning Talent in the Service Economy

Ashutosh Verma
http://orcid.org/0000-0003-0926-2747
Parul University, Vadodara, India

ABSTRACT

The accelerated digitalization of service economies and the rise of generative AI are reshaping strategic human resource management (SHRM). As platform-based models and intelligent systems drive service delivery, HR is evolving to enable agility, ethics, and innovation. This chapter explores SHRM's response to the convergence of AI and platform labor, with a focus on sectors like digital tourism, education, logistics, and fintech. It highlights how AI tools manage workflows, generate content, and engage multi-platform workforces. Key HR challenges—talent attraction, engagement, performance, and well-being—are examined in decentralized settings. Case studies from Uber, Airbnb, and Duolingo illustrate efforts to balance efficiency with empathy. Beyond tech adoption, the chapter examines how AI and gigification shift psychological contracts and workplace culture. It emphasizes emotional intelligence, upskilling, and algorithmic transparency as foundations for trust. The chapter offers an ethical, future-ready roadmap for people-first, tech-enabled HR systems.

DOI: 10.4018/979-8-2600-1845-3.ch001

1. INTRODUCTION

The contemporary service economy is in the process of a structural change driven by the technological acceleration, changing labor markets, and the ubiquitous digitalization of service provision. The healthcare, education, tourism, hospitality, and fintech industries are no longer linear in their service delivery process and employment trends. Rather, they are being impacted more by the intersection of generative AI, platform-based work, and the digital consumer market (Subrahmanyam, 2024; Samala et al., 2025; Wood et al., 2019). In this new environment, strategic human resource management (SHRM) has to re-establish its role not as a support service but as an agility, inclusion, and innovation strategic lever (Amiri & Seifdar, 2025; Delery & Roumpi, 2017). The art of human resource management (HRM) in service-based firms has always been in the context of a complex interrelationship between customer experience, employee performance and organizational identity. Unlike product-based or manufacturing industries, the provision of services is usually dependent on the quality of human interactions. Call center agents, ride-share drivers, and hospitality workers are just a few examples of professionals who do more than complete transactions, they also actively create brand perceptions in real-time. This means that the fit between HR practices and business objectives is a matter of design and not administration (Wright & McMahan, 1992).

The emergence of generative AI and the growth of platform-based work have been two incredibly disruptive forces that have destabilized traditional HR structures over the last decade. These are not isolated tendencies but symptoms of more fundamental changes in the way work is conceived, divided and assessed. Generative AI, algorithmic decision engines and large language models are becoming more common in HR activities, including talent acquisition and performance analytics, learning design and feedback loops (Hwang & Chien, 2024; Samala et al., 2025; Vadithe et al., 2025; Vallas & Schor, 2020). At the same time, the growth of the gig economy has changed the workforce structure, introducing hybrid, freelance, and geographically scattered workforce, which is not always covered by the HR systems (Meijerink et al., 2020; Montgomery & Baglioni, 2021; Rasheed et al., 2023; Wood et al., 2019).

This two-fold disruption presents strategic, operational and ethical issues to service-based organizations. On the one hand, companies are pressured to use intelligent automation to maximize the productivity of the workforce and the scalability of the operations (Tursunbayeva et al., 2021). On the one hand, they have to deal with the intricacies of the management of algorithmically controlled, loosely affiliated, and psychologically vulnerable groups of workers many of whom are deprived of benefits, job security, or upward mobility (Glavin & Schieman, 2022; Jarrahi & Sutherland, 2019; Rasheed et al., 2023; Samala et al., 2025). In high-contact service environments, these HR blind spots are not only internal, but also present reputational risk, customer trust issues, and brand inconsistency risks as well

The responses of the organizations have been disjointed. A few pioneers have adopted AI-based HR systems to select candidates, manage learning, and analyze workforce (Inan & Yilmaz, 2025; Tursunbayeva et al., 2021), and some have tried hybrid labor models and flexible contracts to stay nimble in the face of regulatory uncertainty (Karim et al., 2022). In both instances, however, one fact is becoming increasingly obvious: HR can no longer afford to exist in a vacuum with regard to the technological infrastructures that now mediate labor and leadership. Strategic HRM will have to transform into a synthesizing role- a combination of algorithmic thinking and human decision-making, operational efficiency and workforce sustainability in the long term (Hwang & Chien, 2024; Santareno, 2025; Seifdar & Amiri, 2025; Zhang & Lu, 2023).

This chapter helps to reimagine that. It does not cast SHRM as an outdated system that needs to be adapted to a digital environment, but as a guiding light in the service economy of ethical complexity, workforce diversity, and technological augmentation. In particular, it addresses the question of how HR leaders can redesign the conventional talent lifecycle in the face of AI and platform possibilities--without sacrificing emotional intelligence, inclusion, or strategic integrity.

The research is framed in three questions:

- How will generative AI and platform-based labor affect major HR processes, such as recruitment, learning, engagement and retention?
- What are the strategic and ethical risks of intelligent systems to manage dynamic, mobile, and contingent workforces?
- What are the ways of redesigning SHRM frameworks to be adaptive, transparent, and human-centric in an AI-dominated service world?

Such questions are not only hypothetical, but they have vital implications to decision-makers in various industries where service quality, customer intimacy, and emotional labor continue to be core to success. The synthesis of global research, new industry models, and cross-sector case studies leads to a conceptual roadmap of the development of intelligent, ethical, and future-ready HR systems.

2. LITERATURE REVIEW

Strategic human resource management (SHRM) has been considered as a key determinant of organizational performance, particularly in the service industries that are people-intensive. The transformation of SHRM as a support service of administration to a strategic capability has been well discussed in the pioneering work (Wright & McMahan, 1992), which focused on aligning HR practices with the business goals. This perception was further enhanced by the scholars over the years who emphasized human capital as a source of sustained competitive advantage (Delery & Roumpi, 2017). However, the arrival of generative artificial intelligence (AI), algorithmic labor regimes, and digital platforming has posed new challenges, and SHRM needs to be re-examined in the context of service-based economies (Samala et al., 2025; Hwang & Chien, 2024).

2.1 Evolution of Strategic HRM in Service Sectors

The industries that fit this definition are hospitality, healthcare, logistics, education, and financial technology industries, which are characterised by the high level of human interaction in the delivery of services. In these types of industries, employees do not have a peripheral role in value creation, brand image, and service delivery (Meijerink et al., 2020; Gao et al., 2024).

In such instances, HRM is not only about efficiency or compliance but how organizational cultures, the practices of emotional labor and customer experience are constructed.

The strategic HR alignment has also been shown to be key in performance metrics such as customer satisfaction, employee engagement, and retention through studies conducted in the HR environment (Delery & Roumpi, 2017). Nonetheless, most of the conventional SHRM models presume a stable, full-time employment system with foreseeable job positions and career patterns. This assumption is being fast destroyed by technological disruption and labor fluidity (Seifdar & Amiri, 2025). The shift to remote work, hybrid roles, and skills-based hiring has also made it more important to have flexible HR practices that will allow agility and resilience. Karim et al. (2022) state that the development of digital organizational capabilities is no longer an option but a necessity of HR professionals in service industries who want to manage transformation without losing focus on employee experience.

2.2 Platform-Based Labor and the Disruption of Traditional HR

The current trend in the increasing popularity of platform-based models of work is a paradigm shift in the sourcing, management, and valuation of labor. Uber, Airbnb, and Upwork are platforms that have brought algorithmically mediated gig work into existence and have circumvented much of the traditional HR. Montgomery and Baglioni (2021) state that platform capitalism destroys the traditional employment relationships and outsources the risk, along with the transfer of control to algorithms. This has resulted in gig workers being beyond the protective shield of an organizational HR system, in most cases lacking benefits, job security, and professional development avenues.

Researchers have indicated how these models interfere with the principles of SHRM. Glavin and Schieman (2022) show that platform-mediated work causes emotional stress and precariousness of work-life, particularly in high-contact service work where there is a high level of algorithmic control and low levels of support mechanisms (Rasheed et al., 2023; Wood et al., 2019; Jarrahi & Sutherland, 2019). On the one hand, Subrahmanyam (2024) observes that gig work is flexible but, on the other hand, it creates inconsistencies in the quality of services and ethical issues related to labor rights and classification. Meijerink et al. (2020) state that the traditional HRM practices like performance appraisal, succession planning, or employee engagement are hard to implement in such environments. Rather, companies should come up with new models of distributed, dynamic, and contingent labor management, which would include visibility, fairness, and flexibility across digital ecosystems.

2.3 Generative Artificial Intelligence in HR Practice

In parallel to the platform revolution is the adoption of generative AI into fundamental HR processes. The AI is already used in the talent acquisition process, resume screening, scheduling interviews, onboarding, training personalization, and predicting performance (Samala et al., 2025; Tursunbayeva et al., 2021; Hwang & Chien, 2024). Unlike previous automation trends that involved automating routine administrative work, generative AI can make decisions, communicate with people in natural language and create learning content.

Although these systems have great operational advantages (speed, uniformity and scale), they also present ethical and governance issues. Santareno (2025) also refers to the risks of algorithmic black box and data bias and the loss of human control over talent decisions (Zhang & Lu, 2023). In the international recommendations on the use of AI in education and workforce settings, Inan and Yilmaz (2025) propose that accountability systems should be clarified and the effects of AI on inclusion, trust, and autonomy should be constantly monitored. HR teams must also undergo a cultural transformation in regard to AI integration. Hwang and Chien (2024) emphasize that the digital maturity of HR leaders is also needed to implement AI, not only its technical implementation (Seifdar & Amiri, 2025). The most topical skills of the contemporary HR department are up-skilling, AI literacy, and cross-functional collaboration.

2.4 The Intersection of AI and Platform Work: A Dual Disruption

The most complicated issues are those where generative AI and platform work meet- forming what some researchers refer to as algorithmic work ecosystems (Vadithe et al., 2025; Rasheed et al., 2023; Wood et al., 2019). In this kind of environment, HR roles are usually scattered or outsourced to technological systems. Employees are recruited, assessed and even punished by machine-based interfaces. This may enhance efficiency of operations, but it makes operations less transparent and raises new ethical issues (Jarrahi & Sutherland, 2019).

According to Samala et al. (2025), to manage gig workers based on AI, it is necessary to redefine the psychological contract. In the absence of employer-employee relationships, HR will have to resort to other methods to make sure that there is motivation, trust, and psychological safety (Tarafdar et al., 2019). In addition, AI-based suggestions regarding the performance or behaviour of gig workers that are inexplicable or biased may lead to exclusion, low morale, or reputational damage (Zhang & Lu, 2023).

Recent studies have revealed that a hybrid HR model where technology is used as an assistant and not a substitute to human decision-making can be the solution (Santareno, 2025; Subrahmanyam, 2024). In these models, AI is not a decision-maker, but an advisor in the context of transparent governance. This strategy will enable the HR to deal with scale and complexity without compromising human values such as empathy, fairness, and accountability.

3. THEORETICAL GAP AND CONCEPTUAL LENS

Strategic human resource management (SHRM) has developed over a number of waves of theorization, starting with resource-based views and followed by contingency, institutional and behavioral perspectives. The early works such as that by (Wright & McMahan, 1992) described SHRM as a set of internally integrated practices that help in organizational performance through the development of human capital. Further developments added shades of gray in the form of linking the HR systems to the ability of the companies, the needs of the industries, and the motivation of the staff (Delery & Roumpi, 2017). Although these theories are still applicable, they were mostly developed during a time of stable employment relationship, centralized organizational structure, and human-administered decision systems.

By contrast, the contemporary reality of service-based organizations shows structural and technological changes that cannot be fully explained by the existing theories. Generative AI and platform labor models have also brought new intermediaries to the HR process, including algorithms, recommendation engines and autonomous systems that operate without human control (Samala et al., 2025; Hwang & Chien, 2024; Wood et al., 2019; Rasheed et al., 2023). These systems are not just automating routine tasks, but are selecting, ranking employees, generating onboarding content and optimizing schedules. More to the point, they do it in the environments where human employees might never see HR personnel in a conventional way. This disjuncture necessitates a new theoretical framework that takes into consideration the notion of digital autonomy, distributed accountability and the evolving standards of employment.

3.1 Gaps in Classical SHRM Assumptions

The conventional SHRM theory assumes that organizations are delineated, that employment relationship is direct and that work processes are controlled by the organization. Nevertheless, the platform companies like Uber, Airbnb, and Duolingo do not fit these assumptions. They work in digitally mediated ecosystems where employer-employee relations are often undefined and fragmented and mediated by code. These platforms utilize the work of independent contractors who have a more regular contact with AI systems than with human managers. In these models, HR practices are not implemented by using formal channels but are integrated into platform architecture-ratings, automated nudges, gamification mechanics, and dynamic pricing.

This poses a number of theoretical inconsistencies. The concept of strategic alignment presupposes that there is only one strategy of an organization, which is supported by HR systems. Platform companies can have pre-programmed strategies as decentralized algorithms that are continually learning from user behavior and market data. Second, commitment-based HR practices presuppose long-term employment, which is not typical of the platform and gig environment (Meijerink et al., 2020). Finally, the assumption that human managers monitor and evaluate performance is being substituted by the machine-based evaluations that are not transparent and in context (Rasheed et al., 2023).

3.2 The Rise of Non-Human Actors in HRM

The introduction of artificial intelligence into the HRM processes creates a new type of actors intelligent systems that carry out cognitive, evaluative, and communicative activities. These are resume parsers, sentiment analyzers, automatic trainers, chatbot advisors. In contrast to conventional tools, generative AI systems are autonomous and learn, and their decision rules can change over time. There are theoretical implications of this shift. When an algorithm is used to make a hiring decision, who will be responsible? What do employees think when they are judged by a machine? How does trust and engagement work when there is little human contact?

In the opinion of such scholars as Santareno (2025), AI-infused HR systems cannot be viewed as a tool but as an agent within a networked system of governance (Zhang & Lu, 2023). Their practices affect the organizational performance, the experiences of employees, and even the compliance. Non-human agency is seldom taken into account as a component of the HR infrastructure in existing SHRM models. Such a gap limits their explanatory power in the modern service contexts where digital systems are co-producers of managerial decisions (Samala et al., 2025; Hwang & Chien, 2024).

3.3 Psychological Contracts in Algorithmic Workspaces

The psychological contract has been the focus of SHRM literature over the decades. It is the mutual expectations (usually unspoken) that characterize the employment relationship. Employees will feel that the employer respects the contract and this increases engagement and performance. When violated, consequences are poor. The psychological contract of AI-mediated and platform work takes place no longer in an interpersonal environment but is exposed to interface design, algorithmic patterns, and feedback systems (Glavin & Schieman, 2022). This brings in confusion. An example is when a platform deactivates a driver on the basis of poor ratings, who is to blame? In case of a low score on a performance dashboard due to a wrongly interpreted data entry, who is to be blamed? These questions confront the conventional HRM perspective of a relational contract that is controlled by human agents and interpreted in terms of cultural and emotional signals. The algorithmic nature of decision making requires a redefinition of the psychological contract- one that incorporates algorithmic responsibility and interpretability (Zhang & Lu, 2023).

3.4 Toward a New Conceptual Lens: Distributed SHRM

Against the background of these theoretical contradictions, this chapter introduces a new conceptual framework, Distributed SHRM, which is designed to fit AI-enabled and platform-based service settings (Samala et al., 2025; Hwang & Chien, 2024; Wood et al., 2019). This lens does not see HRM as a centralized activity that is managed by policies and departments, but as a distributed system of people, technologies, data flows and interfaces (Rasheed et al., 2023; Jarrahi & Sutherland, 2019). It recognises that in modern service economies

- The decisions about HR are increasingly being made by or via non-human actors (e.g., AI systems, algorithms) (Samala et al., 2025).

- The identities of workers are not fixed, but include full-time employees, contractors, freelancers, and bots (Montgomery & Baglioni, 2021; Wood et al., 2019).
- Human expertise and platform-mediated inputs (e.g., user feedback, gamification) have an impact on the performance (Subrahmanyam, 2024).
- Accountability is divided into departments, technologies, and third-party intermediaries (Seifdar & Amiri, 2025).

Distributed SHRM is concerned with agility, co-responsibility and systems thinking. It provides smart tools without compromising human values of trust, fairness and inclusion (Zhang & Lu, 2023). It also recognizes that the borders of employment, leadership and engagement have extended into the digital landscape (Wood et al., 2019).

This change of thinking lays the basis of the AI-SHRM Talent Lifecycle Matrix presented in the following section. The matrix aims to apply distributed SHRM principles by translating the traditional HR functions into the levels of algorithmic control and worker autonomy. It is not a denial of classical theory but an adaptation- it is an extension of the relevance of SHRM into the realities of digital, platformized, and intelligent service work (Samala et al., 2025; Subrahmanyam, 2024).

4. CASE STUDY INSIGHTS FROM PLATFORM-BASED SERVICES

This has led to a fundamental change in the management of human resources due to the rise of generative artificial intelligence and the model of labor platforms. These changes are not abstract concepts, but they can be traced in a variety of service-oriented organizations that have transformed the traditional HR functions with the help of digital infrastructure. This section looks at four examples: Uber, Duolingo, Airbnb, and ChatGPT-enabled internal HR tools. All the cases provide a different insight into how SHRM principles are being transformed due to technological and organizational disruption.

4.1 Uber: HR Without a Department

Uber is an example of how human resource functions are reconfigured in a platform-based gig economy. Uber is a mobility service provider and thus it does not employ drivers as such. It uses independent contractors via an online platform instead of the traditional HR systems of employment contracts, training, and formal performance reviews.

Nevertheless, Uber does a lot of HR-like tasks, such as recruitment, onboarding, performance tracking, and rewarding, but it does it all algorithmically. Automated systems scan driver applications First training is provided through tutorials in the app. The performance indicators include the ratings, ride completion time, and acceptance rates, which may result in deactivation or incentives.

According to the researchers, such as Montgomery and Baglioni (2021), Uber substitutes human HR intermediaries with data-driven management. Nevertheless, this algorithmic control is unethical. Drivers will probably raise their voices that they are being monitored, manipulated by the surge pricing mechanism, or punished without any reason (Meijerink et al., 2020). The case of Uber shows that SHRM must integrate the ideas of algorithmic transparency, data fairness, and psychological safety, even in non-conventional workplaces (Rasheed et al., 2023; Wood et al., 2019).

Strategically, the Uber model begs the question: can a company purport to have service excellence when its main labor force does not have formal support systems, development opportunities, or relational engagement? Although Uber is cost-effective, it is under threat of long-term risks of worker dissatisfaction, reputational damage, and regulatory control. To stay relevant, SHRM will need to respond to the question of how to assist worker development and inclusion in decentralized and automated ecosystems.

4.2 Duolingo: Gamified Learning Meets Employee Experience

Duolingo, the language-learning app, exists in a very different sector of the service economy, digital education. Duolingo has a formal workforce of designers, linguists, data scientists, and engineers unlike Uber. Nonetheless, the internal HR practices are also heavily based on the company product philosophy, which is gamification, user motivation loops, and real-time feedback.

Duolingo performance is measured in the form of engagement analytics, goal tracking, and peer recognition. Learning and development is individualized with the use of digital dashboards which replicate the user experience model of the platform. AI-powered tools will help the HR department to recommend learning paths, monitor the satisfaction with tasks, and detect burnout indicators in online communication (Hwang & Chien, 2024; Samala et al., 2025). What is remarkable about Duolingo is that it has a consistency between external value creation and internal HR philosophy. The employees are not considered as resource inputs but as learners and co-creators. The gamified attitude to motivation is applied to the structure of teams, the allocation of rewards, and work-life balance.

Duolingo shows how SHRM can use technological systems without turning the experience of employees into something inhuman. It also shows that AI can be applied not only to efficiency but also to empathy when implemented in the workplace design in a thoughtful manner (Samala et al., 2025; Hwang & Chien, 2024).

4.3 Airbnb: Distributed Culture, Centralized Purpose

Airbnb is a hybrid of a platform labor and formal labor. Although its hosts are micro-entrepreneurs, the firm has a worldwide workforce, which includes customer service, marketing, policy, and engineering. The HR strategy of Airbnb is the combination of the digital technology and the intentional cultural design to fit both populations.

Airbnb also uses predictive analytics in the company to predict hiring, track productivity and cultural fit. The people analytics team of the company incorporates data of project management platforms, feedback loops, and digital interviews to design succession planning and talent development. In the meantime, Airbnb has been working hard to establish a common culture, by means of digital storytelling, as well as behavioural rituals that can be used to support the mission and values (Subrahmanyam, 2024). Externally, Airbnb offers host education, conflict resolution and health-safety certifications via an AI-assisted learning platform. These services are reflective of HR functions but are applied to a loosely connected global user base. The company has come up with a decentralized HR organization that is flexible and maintains the brand consistency.

The example of Airbnb demonstrates that SHRM can be applied to the distributed service environment and be used to align data, culture, and infrastructure. It also strengthens the notion that SHRM does not only apply to employees but also needs to take into consideration gig partners, content creators, and platform stakeholders (Montgomery & Baglioni, 2021; Wood et al., 2019).

4.4 ChatGPT-Integrated Internal HR Tools: The Rise of Digital HR Advisors

Many organizations are now testing the use of generative AI models, like ChatGPT, as an embedded HR co-pilot. These tools can do a variety of functions- answering policy questions, coaching employees, generating performance summaries, and onboarding content (Vadithe et al., 2025; Tursunbayeva et al., 2021). In one case study of a multinational fintech company, a ChatGPT-based bot was implemented into the HR portal of the company. Employees will be able to pose questions concerning leave procedures, upskilling, team composition, or compliance procedures.

The system would answer in natural language, and provide on-demand advice based on internal databases and policy manuals.

Managers also employed a similar interface to create performance appraisals that were based on project schedules, peer reviews, and task accomplishment information. The aim was not to get rid of human judgment but to minimize the administrative load and increase actionable insights.

The early outcomes were encouraging: the response time was reduced, user satisfaction improved, and the HR teams noted that they had more capacity to perform strategic activities. Nevertheless, there were moral and governance problems. The employees were worried about privacy, surveillance and how long AI-based records will last. These issues indicate that productivity and data ethics in AI-based HR systems are incompatible in general (Santareno, 2025; Zhang & Lu, 2023). Such implementations point to the fact that SHRM must also move towards system design and ethical engineering as opposed to policy writing and compliance enforcement. The HR leader of the future will require skills in timely engineering, data governance and user-centric design, rather than labor law and compensation plans.

4.5 Cross-Case Insights

These case studies have a number of cross-cutting lessons on SHRM in service economies:

- Automation is not neutral: The sense of fairness, control, and agency is shaped and enacted in the creation and use of AI systems.
- The design of the platform predetermines HR results: Gamification, ratings, and nudges are HR tools by default in decentralized environments.
- Strategic HR should reach beyond the employees: Contractors, freelancers, and community contributors should be provided with specific support models.
- Ethical scaffolding is required in AI systems: Ethical scaffolding is needed to make sure that even the most efficient systems do not lose the trust of employees without governance, transparency and feedback loops.
- Location does not matter as much as cultural fit: Distributed teams can work when there is purpose, feedback and communication systems aligned.

Taken together, the cases show that HR professionals have to think beyond the traditional employment box. In AI-augmented, platform-mediated service environments, SHRM will have to be reengineered to manage diversity, digital fluency, and distributed value creation.

5. AI–SHRM TALENT LIFECYCLE MATRIX

In the face of the twin disruption of artificial intelligence and platform-based work, human resource functions can no longer be thought of in terms of life cycle models. The classical HRM cycle-attract, develop, retain, and separate-was founded on the premises of linear employment careers, centralized control and human-administered appraisal. In the modern service economy, such assumptions are no longer true (Samala et al., 2025; Hwang & Chien, 2024; Wood et al., 2019).

To respond to this transformation, we propose the AI-SHRM Talent Lifecycle Matrix, which is a conceptual model that can be used to help organizations strategically align HR practices to the new realities of digital automation and distributed labor. This matrix places fundamental HR functions along two important dimensions

Degree of AI Involvement (Low to High): The level of human involvement in the process to the maximum AI-driven systems.

Worker Structure (Traditional to Platform-Based): A representation of the employment continuum- full-time, in-house to decentralized, gig or freelance.

Figure 1. AI–SHRM Talent Lifecycle Matrix

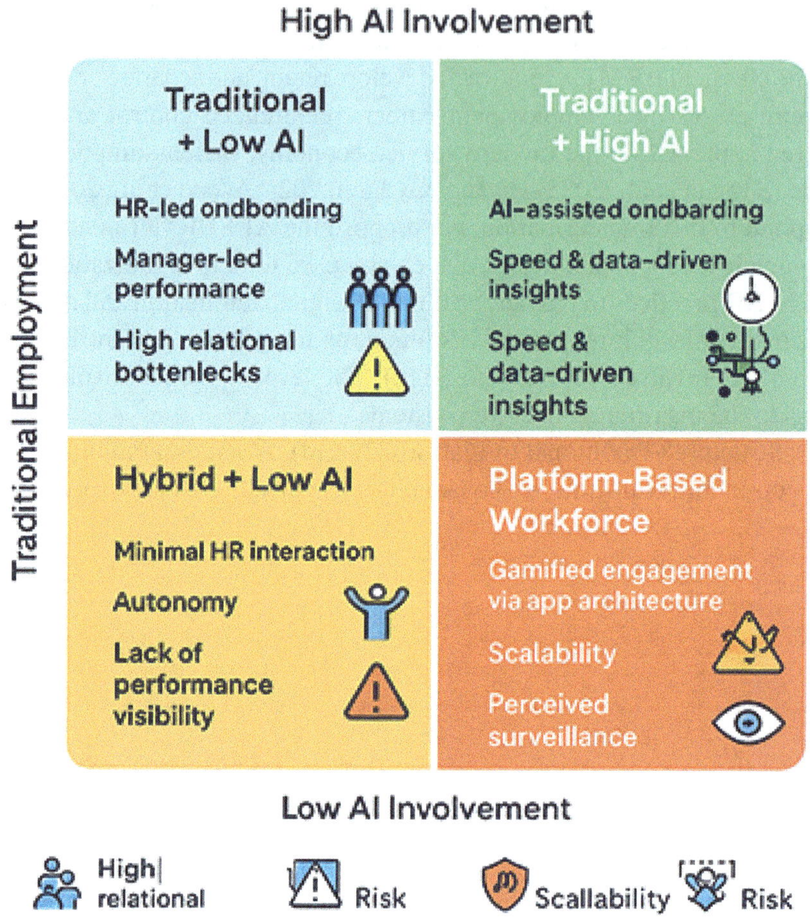

Source: *Developed by the authors using conceptual foundations from Samala et al. (2025), Hwang and Chien (2024), Wood et al. (2019), and Subrahmanyam (2024).*

The AI–SHRM Talent Lifecycle Matrix maps HR functions along two axes—AI involvement and workforce structure—showing how strategic HRM must adapt across different employment configurations and levels of automation.

5.1 Framework Explanation

To understand the dual threat of generative AI and platform-based work, this chapter presents the AI-SHRM Talent Lifecycle Matrix, a two-dimensional model that positions HR functions in two dimensions: the extent of AI integration (low to high) and the degree of workforce autonomy (structured to fluid).

This matrix can assist HR leaders to visualize how different service-sector jobs, such as freelance educators and algorithmically scheduled ride-share workers, interact with AI-powered systems at every stage of the employee lifecycle. The matrix is not fixed; it provides a dynamic lens through which firms can audit current HR practices and determine where automation can add value as opposed to where it can dehumanize work.

An example is in the highly digitally enabled and autonomous workplaces such as Duolingo, where onboarding and training are highly AI-assisted yet maintain human interaction to serve as mentorship and escalation (Hwang & Chien, 2024; Samala et al., 2025). In contrast, in such companies as Uber, AI is involved in the process of task distribution, performance evaluation, and even driver-client communication, with little to no HR involvement (Montgomery & Baglioni, 2021; Wood et al., 2019), which puts such operations in the upper-right quadrant of the matrix, where both the level of AI integration and workforce fluidity are high.

This difference is important. The matrix can enable companies to identify ethical risk areas, including the intersection of algorithmic decision-making with emotionally vulnerable, mobile, or marginalized employees (Rasheed et al., 2023; Zhang & Lu, 2023). Simultaneously, it shows where AI can be safely scaled, including predictive analytics in performance evaluation or generative content in learning and development (Samala et al., 2025; Hwang & Chien, 2024).

The matrix helps HR leaders make informed decisions regarding the point at which they should integrate AI into the HR function and when they need to maintain human discretion. It is not only meant to be used as an analytical tool but also as a strategic roadmap to the development of adaptive, inclusive, and future-ready HR systems within service industries that are increasingly being dominated by the influence of technology (Subrahmanyam, 2024).

5.2 Strategic Implications of the Matrix

All the quadrants of the matrix have their problems and opportunities:

Traditional + Low AI

✓ Good relational capital and personal support.

✓ Risk: Inefficiency, bottlenecks to scale.

✓ The role of SHRM: Maximize human contact and augment with simple technology solutions.

Traditional + High AI

Speed: Data-driven and speed-based information on structured workforces.

Threats: Automation aversion, dehumanization.
SHRM Role: Train managers about how AI can be comprehended and keep their emotional intelligence (Seifdar & Amiri, 2025).

Platform-Based + Low AI

- ✓ Strength: Independence and ease to the employees.
- ✓ Risk: No performance view, no retention, alone.
- ✓ HRM Role: Create a community and support systems that are not part of the interface of the platform.

Platform-Based + High AI

- ✓ Strength: Ability to scale and be accurate at scale.
- ✓ Harm: algorithmic visibility, burnout, perceived surveillance (Wood et al., 2019; Rasheed et al., 2023).
- ✓ HRM Role: Impose the governance/algorithmic disclosure policy (Zhang & Lu, 2023).

This framework will enable HR leaders to understand where they are in their systems today--and what they need to do to align their systems with their workforce strategy.

5.3 Framework in Practice

To see how the AI-SHRM Talent Lifecycle Matrix can be implemented in practice, it is necessary to take a closer look at how the HR systems of the leading organizations of the service sector are being re-engineered at the crossroad of automation and fluidity of the workforce. The case vignettes below illustrate how AI is transforming various points of the employee experience and how it is addressing the ethical and strategic tensions that exist in each quadrant of the matrix.

Case 1: Duolingo – AI-Supported Learning, Human-Guided Development

Duolingo, a worldwide language-learning platform, is an example of the lower-right quadrant of the matrix-high AI integration and structured workforce models. Adaptive learning algorithms are used to make user journeys more personalized, but the company also uses such tools internally to enhance employee learning and development. The HR department at Duolingo uses predictive analytics to determine the skill gaps and propose individualized upskilling programs. In spite of the fact that AI is highly integrated, human coaches are still needed in the sphere of feedback, mentoring, and career path mapping. This is a moderated approach that is a co-pilot type where AI does not replace human interaction but complements learning. Notably, the performance systems at Duolingo are transparent, so that employees can learn how algorithmic insights can be utilized to guide developmental discussions (Hwang & Chien, 2024; Samala et al., 2025)

Case 2: Uber – Algorithmic Control and Workforce Fluidity

Uber, in its turn, is the upper-right corner of the matrix, where the level of AI integration and autonomy of the workforce is high. The process of onboarding drivers, performance rating, route assignment, and even deactivation are to a large extent controlled by algorithmic decision-making (Montgomery & Baglioni, 2021; Wood et al., 2019). Though this model is most effective in terms of operations, it raises serious concerns of fairness, agency, and feedback loops. Uber has also been criticized due to the opaqueness of its algorithm in rating drivers and assigning them work. In its response, the company has implemented several principles of fairness in some of its markets, such as driver dashboards that provide rating criteria and redressal mechanisms. Nonetheless, a significant number of workers continue to feel invisible in the system, which makes it necessary to consider SHRM strategies that incorporate algorithmic accountability and participatory design in highly fluid work arrangements.

Case 3: Airbnb – Distributed Teams, Hybrid Governance

Airbnb is a more subtle example of middle-ground positioning on the matrix. The company has adopted the remote workforce model after the pandemic, where remote and hybrid workforces are distributed in different regions of the world. Its HR systems are based on AI in the process of screening applicants, remote onboarding, and employee sentiment analysis (Rasheed et al., 2023). However, Airbnb has spent a lot in maintaining human contact and cultural unity. The organization is implementing virtual collaboration tools that are riddled with AI to recommend mentors, networking with colleagues, and burnout risks through behavioural analytics (Subrahmanyam, 2024). Notably, Airbnb has an HR leadership team that is part of a cross-functional People and Tech Ethics Council which examines all new AI implementations that impact employees (Seifdar & Amiri, 2025). This governance mechanism is representative of a changing SHRM approach in which AI is integrated to supplement rather than substitute the employee experience.

These illustrations indicate that, although the AI-SHRM Talent Lifecycle Matrix provides a systematic perspective, its use is not homogenous. The way the matrix is deployed is determined by the industry context, organizational culture and regulatory environments. The one thing that has not changed though is the importance of strategic alignment between the design of technology and the philosophy of human capital. In both cases, the successful integration of AI into the HR was not only a question of technological ability but also a question of the willingness of HR leaders to deal with the questions of agency, transparency, and shared value.

6. CHALLENGES AND ETHICAL CONSIDERATIONS

With artificial intelligence and platform-mediated labor transforming the boundaries of work in the service economy, strategic human resource management (SHRM) is confronted with a series of ethical and operational dilemmas that are much broader than technical adaptation. These concerns are a direct assault on the nature of the HR as a keeper of trust, inclusion, and fairness. This section decodes eight high-priority risks that need to be addressed urgently and constantly.

6.1 Algorithmic Bias and Lack of Transparency

The risk with AI systems like hiring algorithms and performance evaluation tools is that they will perpetuate and reinforce existing biases in society. Research shows that facial recognition (Hwang & Chien, 2024) and job-hiring algorithms are systematically flawed in a manner that discriminates against historically underrepresented populations (Santareno, 2025). These problems are compounded by opaqueness: the models that vendors use are not generally available to HR professionals (Meijerink et al., 2020). In the absence of explainability and ethics oversight, the trust in HR systems will be undermined. SHRM has to be at the forefront of the inclusion of explainable AI (XAI), fairness audits, and algorithmic accountability in talent systems.

6.2 Emotional Disconnection and Loss of Human Touch

Automation of human interactions- chatbots, digital nudges, and gamified interfaces can kill psychological connection between employees and the organization. This emotional disconnection can be passed down to morale and service levels in certain industries where empathy and face-to-face contact are a part of the process (Gherghel et al., 2023; Tarafdar et al., 2019). Platform workers, especially, experience a feeling of isolation because of the lack of supervisory ties or social gathering places (Glavin & Schieman, 2022). The AI systems designed by HRM must improve rather than substitute relational aspects of work.

6.3 Erosion of Psychological Safety and Trust

The psychological safety is compromised when the employees are monitored through dashboard, keystroke analytics, or sentiment analysis (Rasheed et al., 2023; Tursunbayeva et al., 2021). Platform workers are doubly exposed: their wages depend on opaque measures, and algorithmic decisions, and they have little recourse. HRM has to explicitly protect psychological safety by data boundaries, explainable metrics, and appeal processes that restore trust and fairness in the digitally augmented world.

6.4 Classification Confusion and Regulatory Gaps

The two-fold categorization of labor into employees and independent contractors is not suitable to the realities of platform work. Platform workers are controlled by the algorithms and behavioural surveillance in the same way as employees, but they are not formally employees (Meijerink et al., 2020). Regulatory ambiguity creates operational risk and moral uncertainty of the HR professionals. SHRM needs to promote adaptive employment practices that fill this classification gap- through portable benefits, worker councils, or platform-specific codes of conduct.

6.5 Data Privacy and Consent

The AI-based functions of HR that collect a lot of personal information, which can be intrusive, include wearables and behavioural markers in the digital interactions (Meijerink et al., 2020; Seifdar & Amiri, 2025). Consent is not active, but hidden in legalese or even absent, especially in platform cases. SHRM needs to take data ethics to a strategic role by establishing opt-in policies, simplifying language of consent, and implementing data minimization and ethical review boards to high-risk use cases.

6.6 Skills Gaps and Digital Inequality

The digital literacy of the working population is not evenly spread and this forms a two-tier system where the tech-savvy employees excel and the others underperform (Karim et al., 2022). This is not only unfair- it skews AI outputs and workforce planning. SHRM should combine each AI implementation with active upskilling, making it accessible to people of all ages, geography, and educational background.

6.7 Ethical Drift and Normalization of Dysfunction

Even more dangerous is the fact that ethically dubious practices are normalized in the name of technological inevitability. Practices such as algorithmic dismissal or silent surveillance would be unacceptable were they to be carried out by a human, but can be justified when carried out by machines. This ethical drift (Tarafdar et al., 2019) has the potential to eat away at organizational culture. HRM should play the role of institutional conscience- instilling value-based decision-making frameworks in every AI procurement and implementation procedure.

6.8 From Risk Awareness to Ethical Leadership

The risks mentioned are not theoretical- they are systemic and increasing. Nevertheless, they provide SHRM with a chance to be visionary and ethical. Empathy, transparency and accountability are things that can be institutionalized so that HR leaders can become proactive rather than reactive when it comes to ethics. The future of work in the service economy is not only about the AI capabilities but also about values that will be used to implement it (Zhang & Lu, 2023).

6.9 Addressing Policy Gaps in AI-Driven HR Systems

Although the use of AI in HR has gained momentum in service industries, the majority of organizations do not have formal policies that can govern responsible use. Therefore, AI tools are most often implemented in isolation without adequate risk assessment, staff consultation, and ethical oversight. Such a loophole not only leads to the inefficiencies in legal compliance, but also organizational integrity, talent retention, and brand reputation.

The lack of clear demarcations between judgment and automation is one of the issues of concern. Other AI recruitment systems, such as those that rate candidates on the basis of facial expressions, word choice, or keystroke patterns, may not be scientifically validated or even known to employees (Hwang & Chien, 2024; Santareno, 2025). Organizations that do not have clear governance policies risk institutionalizing structural bias in their most basic processes. Strategic HR should thus drive internal auditability where any AI that interacts with employee data or decision-making is periodically validated to be fair, accurate, and transparent (Zhang & Lu, 2023).

The other serious policy gap is in the area of data consent and privacy in HR analytics. In service organizations that have biometric time-tracking, employee surveillance tools, or sentiment-monitoring software, workers are frequently not aware of how their data is being gathered, processed, or stored (Meijerink et al., 2020; Seifdar & Amiri, 2025). Not many companies have elaborate guidelines on what is ethical monitoring. SHRM should promote privacy-by-design systems in which consent is specific, opt-outs are honored, and no employee is punished by refusing to be identified. This is particularly significant in platform-based labor where digital monitoring is a normalized part of the claim of efficiency.

Moreover, algorithmic accountability is not well developed in the majority of HR systems. HR tech does not have the same explanatory rights as consumer-facing AI because there are no laws that require such explanations. Employees do not have many ways to challenge AI decisions, including a denial of an application, biased performance evaluation, or disciplinary warning (Rasheed et al., 2023). HR leaders should press to have explainability standards, and have internal redressal mechanisms where the algorithmic results can be reviewed and challenged. AI ethics research policy models (e.g., human-in-the-loop and right to explanation) must be translated into practical HR terms.

The least served employees are the gig and freelance workers who comprise an increasingly large share of the service industry labor pool. They are classified as contractors or self-employed and are therefore not covered by the majority of HR protection systems. When AI systems decide who gets work, who gets ratings, or whose accounts get deactivated, there is nothing that can be done (Montgomery & Baglioni, 2021). HRM should be on the frontline to come up with extended ethical guidelines on nonstandard workers, which should not be left out of the basic rights, including feedback, procedural fairness and escalation channels.

There are also cross-national differences that complicate policy alignment. In the United States, there is no mandatory AI governance in HR and it is shaped by soft law and corporate discretion. By contrast, the EU AI Act proposes a highly regulated categorization of high-risk AI systems, including recruitment tools. This assortment of regulation leaves transnational service firms in an embarrassing situation. Not only should HR be able to abide by the local laws but also formulate globally consistent policy frameworks that maintain consistent ethical standards across jurisdictions (Subrahmanyam, 2024).

Finally, it has a cultural policy gap. Most service organizations implement AI tools without involving employees in the co-designing or piloting process. This breeds distrust, opposition and eventual system breakdown. Strategic HR should encourage participatory technology adoption- employees should be involved in the evaluation, selection, and implementation of AI systems. Policy must require cross-functional task forces that involve legal, technical and employee representatives, particularly in high-impact use cases like hiring, promotion and termination (Seifdar & Amiri, 2025).

In short, policy needs to move beyond an afterthought to a form of infrastructure. HR-related AI deployment is not a technical exercise, but a normative choice that has implications on equity, voice, and dignity. SHRM can help develop institutional capacity to govern responsible AI, not in the form of stand-alone guidelines, but through embedded, binding, and inclusive policies that safeguard performance and people alike.

7. STRATEGIC RECOMMENDATIONS AND FUTURE ROADMAP

The contemporary service economy needs more than temporary fixes to reform the human resource management. It involves a methodical re-invention of forms, principles, and processes-those that are sensitive to algorithmic mediation, mixed-labor arrangements, and ethical complexity. With organizations adopting generative artificial intelligence and platform-based labor, HR will have to become a foresight-based, digitally mature, and ethically responsible department (Samala et al., 2025; Hwang & Chien, 2024; Wood et al., 2019).

To begin with, the conventional talent lifecycle will have to be redesigned as a modular, AI-powered continuum. Instead of dividing recruitment, onboarding, training, and retention into separate processes, employers should develop flexible systems that leverage a common data base to customize the employee experience. AI solutions are now able to construct dynamic profiles of workers, forecast attrition, and prescribe context-sensitive development plans. Nevertheless, the dehumanization should not be a result of such capabilities rather, HR leaders need to audit these lifecycle systems through the prism of equity, explainability, and inclusivity to make sure that personalization does not turn into profiling (Samala et al., 2025; Hwang & Chien, 2024).

Table 1. Strategic SHRM Actions for the AI–Platform Service Economy

Action Area	Key Recommendation
Talent Lifecycle Design	Modular, interoperable systems with AI-enabled continuity across HR stages
AI Integration	Human–AI partnership models with explainability and fallback mechanisms
Platform Labor Inclusion	Policy extensions and engagement analytics tailored for gig and freelance roles
Ethics and Governance	Regular algorithm audits, ethics oversight boards, and transparent appeal structures
Psychological Safety	Empathy-informed metrics, digital rituals, and mental health coaching integration
Skill Development	Just-in-time upskilling frameworks mapped through AI-driven learning diagnostics
People Analytics	Privacy-first architecture, transparent dashboards, and purpose-aligned metrics

Strategic HR actions aligned to challenges of AI integration and platform work models in the service economy. Adapted by the author based on synthesized evidence from HRM, AI, and gig economy research (Wright & McMahan, 1992; Santareno, 2025; Karim et al., 2022).

This table summarizes 10 strategic action areas based on the analysis of HR transformation in service-based, AI-augmented environments in the chapter. It pairs every action area with an actionable recommendation, and provides decision-makers with a practical framework to drive SHRM implementation in digital, hybrid, and platform workforces. The table highlights modular system design, AI ethics, psychological safety, extended workforce inclusion, and future-readiness- making SHRM a vital role in the future of intelligent service work (Samala et al., 2025; Hwang & Chien, 2024; Subrahmanyam, 2024).

It is also critical to reframe AI as a partner rather than a substitute to the HR professionals. The strengths of it are pattern recognition, scale management, and consistency in operations, whereas human beings are strong in contextual awareness, empathy, and ethical judgment. The task of designing human-AI partnership models is to define functional areas in which the machine intelligence supplements, rather than replaces, human judgments. In hiring, an example is that AI may be used to screen candidates, but human judgment must be used to make final decisions. In order to maintain this symbiosis, HR professionals will have to be trained to become timely engineers, AI-savvy, and ethically conscious of digital issues (Seifdar & Amiri, 2025; Zhang & Lu, 2023).

In the future, HR leaders should be ready to face the new emerging situations that need forward-looking design and ethical anticipation. The neurodiverse hiring with the help of AI is one of such frontiers. Behavioural and biometric assessment platforms such as HireVue and Pymetrics are becoming more common in the matching of candidates to roles. Even though these tools help to reduce bias, they can also encode neurotypical assumptions. SHRM will have to come up with guidelines that will protect against exclusion and proactively welcome neurodiverse talent by designing algorithms, user experience, and analytics in a transparent manner (Santareno, 2025; Zhang & Lu, 2023).

The other area of evolution is AI-aligned ESG integration. The sustainability agenda is increasingly being discussed in the boardroom and HR is being asked to show how workforce practices contribute to environmental, social, and governance (ESG) objectives. This can be enabled by IA to track carbon footprints of employee actions, alert DEI gaps, and develop real-time dashboards on labor rights adherence.

HR executives should collaborate with ESG officers and data scientists to make sure that AI metrics are not only quantifiable but purpose-driven and ethically sound (Subrahmanyam, 2024).

Lastly, the HR governance is reevaluated because of blockchain and decentralized technology. Decentralized HR systems in which worker credentials, feedback and certifications are stored on secure ledgers would put individuals in more control of their work identities. Smart contracts can automate certain aspects of gig payments, compliance and even upskilling credits. This is a work in progress but future-ready SHRM must take into account how decentralization can enhance transparency, data privacy, and workforce autonomy, especially in platform economies where trust deficits are acute (Wood et al., 2019; Jarrahi & Sutherland, 2019). The future of HR is therefore digital, decentralized, collaborative and predictive. Leaders should be able to build AI instincts, which is a strategic intuition that is a combination of human sensitivity and algorithmic logic. By integrating ethical foresight, inclusive design and systems thinking in all of the touchpoints of the HR process, organizations will be able to create talent ecosystems that are not only scalable and adaptive but also humane and equitable (Samala et al., 2025; Subrahmanyam, 2024; Zhang & Lu, 2023).

8. CONCLUSION AND FUTURE RESEARCH PATHWAYS

SHRM has taken center stage in the development of service organizations in a world that is increasingly becoming defined by generative artificial intelligence, platform-mediated labor, and boundaryless work. This chapter has discussed how HR has evolved to become a dynamic, data-driven and ethically responsive strategic area. The issue of automation, flexible workforce model, and digital disruption has changed HR into a business facilitator and the guardian of inclusion, flexibility, and organizational awareness (Samala et al., 2025; Hwang & Chien, 2024; Wood et al., 2019).

The AI-SHRM Talent Lifecycle Matrix offered a visual and conceptual representation of the interaction between service-sector HR systems and intelligent technologies and various forms of labor at various stages of the employee experience. This matrix highlighted the trends of strategic alignment between AI depth and worker autonomy, allowing the HR professionals to identify the areas of ethical risks concentration, the areas where human discretion should be maintained, and the areas where automation can be scaled without being unethical. Cases of international service leaders like Uber, Airbnb, and Duolingo showed how these tensions can manifest themselves in practice, and why customization based on context is more important than the universal patterns of transformation (Samala et al., 2025; Montgomery & Baglioni, 2021; Wood et al., 2019).

In the future, SHRM will have to undergo several fundamental changes to stay relevant. Second, HR needs to redefine itself as an active capability designer-creating learning systems, digital career journeys, and ethical decision-support systems that cut across full-time, freelance, and algorithmically managed workforces. The essential skill set of HR professionals has to be extended to include algorithmic literacy, data interpretation, and AI ethics navigation. Second, the HR analytics must shift to predictive, employee-centric intelligence systems that take into account emotion, context, and socio-technical interactions. In this model, analytics is a dialogic tool-one that can help organizations not only monitor people but also listen to them at scale (Seifdar & Amiri, 2025; Subrahmanyam, 2024; Zhang & Lu, 2023).

Third, SHRM should come up with flexible governance systems that can respond to the increasing complexity of algorithmic decision-making. The current corporate governance systems are usually poorly positioned to evaluate, audit, or correct the unintended consequences of AI-powered HR systems. To deal with it, progressive companies need to institutionalize ethical review boards, algorithm impact reviews, and rights-to-explanation processes within the HR departments. The idea of algorithmic dignity should become a guiding principle of digital HR change, particularly in the industries where employees do not have direct contact with managers (Santareno, 2025; Rasheed et al., 2023; Zhang & Lu, 2023).

The future of work also demands a greater global knowledge of how the SHRM principles can be applied across cultures, regulations and infrastructure levels. The use of Platform work and AI tools is different in high-income and emerging economies. In low-connectivity areas, the digital divide has the potential to increase inequality in access to opportunities and data rights. Therefore, studies should explore how HR systems can be location-sensitive-based on the local socio-economic realities and yet meet global ethical standards. Comparative policy analysis, cross-border case studies and participatory research with underrepresented gig workers are critical to the design of inclusive models of SHRM (Subrahmanyam, 2024; Montgomery & Baglioni, 2021).

A major issue and one that is often overlooked is psychological contract in hybrid and platform workforces. New psychological contracts are developing as traditional ideas of career, loyalty, and organizational belonging are eroded, and new forms of data-mediated and algorithmically enforced agreements are taking their place. Such contracts are not predictable and reciprocal as legacy systems. Researchers need to examine the impact of digital nudges, platform ratings and AI-based task assignment on the expectations, motivation and well-being of workers. On the same note, HR leaders must establish organizational rituals, digital coaching systems and virtual communities that will bridge the gap of the lost relational glue of physical workplaces (Glavin & Schieman, 2022; Zhang & Lu, 2023).

The other potential frontier is the incorporation of foresight into SHRM practice The notion of HR Futures Labs, which are internal think tanks that are charged with scenario planning, weak signal detection and policy prototyping, can assist firms in anticipating disruptive changes instead of simply responding to them. Such labs would be fed with a range of inputs such as labor market analytics, generative design simulations and behavioural forecasting to inform talent strategies. By so doing, HR becomes a strategic nerve center rather than a cost center to guide organizations through complexity, ambiguity, and opportunity (Seifdar & Amiri, 2025; Subrahmanyam, 2024).

Although the hype around AI and digitalization is real, it is necessary to underline that technology is not fate. The future of SHRM will be as much a matter of normative decisions as of technical possibilities. Organizations will have to ask themselves hard questions: Who gains by AI implementations? Whose voices count in the design of systems? What occurs when the prediction or fairness fails? The moral framework that surrounds SHRM needs to change in line with its technical framework. Strategic human resource management in the digital age is not only a matter of systems but a matter of values-how fairness, dignity, and human development are defined, defended, and distributed (Zhang & Lu, 2023). To aid practitioners and scholars in this process, there are a number of key readings that provide greater depth. Wright and McMahan (1992) offer fundamental thinking on SHRM strategy and fit to the organization, whereas Delery and Roumpi (2017) examine the relationship between the field and competitive advantage as it has evolved. Montgomery and Baglioni (2021) investigate the nature of platform work, and Santareno (2025) introduces new findings concerning the potential of HR based on AI. The articles by Karim et al. (2022), Glavin and Schieman (2022), and Inan and Yilmaz (2025) provide the practical frameworks of digital capability building, emotional safety, and AI ethics as the significant gaps in the emerging SHRM literature. These sources, and others mentioned in this chapter, are the framework of further studies, experimentation, and policy making in these high stakes areas.

In brief, the service economy cannot be organized in terms of definite occupations, sequential career patterns and analogous management tools. It is mediated by AI, distributed across platforms, and affected by human-machine partnerships that are changing in real time. The strategic human resource management has to keep up with it- embracing complexity without losing clarity and deploying technology without losing humanity. This chapter has suggested a novel grammar of HR thinking: it is nimble, inclusive, data-ethical, and dignity-centered. Only in this case, SHRM can become a guiding star of resilient, intelligent, and people-first service organizations in the era of AI.

REFERENCES

Amiri, B., & Seifdar, M. H. (2025). Digital readiness and SHRM: A systems approach. *International Journal of Retail & Consumer Services*, *74*, 103997. DOI: 10.1016/j.jretconser.2024.103997

Delery, J. E., & Roumpi, D. (2017). Strategic human resource management, human capital and competitive advantage: Is the field going in circles? *Human Resource Management Journal*, *27*(1), 1–21. DOI: 10.1111/1748-8583.12137

Gao, Z.. (2024). Enhancing academic performance of business students using GAI. *International Journal of Management Education*, *22*(4), 100958. DOI: 10.1016/j.ijme.2024.100958

Gherghel, C., Yasuda, S., & Kita, Y. (2023). Interaction during online classes fosters engagement. *Computers & Education*, *200*, 104795. DOI: 10.1016/j.compedu.2023.104795 PMID: 37063109

Glavin, P., & Schieman, S. (2022). Dependency and hardship in the gig economy: Mental health consequences of platform work. *Socius: Sociological Research for a Dynamic World*, *8*, 1–13. DOI: 10.1177/23780231221082414

Hwang, G. J., & Chien, S. Y. (2024). Applications, impacts, and trends of generative AI in education. *Computers & Education*, *207*, 104857. DOI: 10.1016/j.compedu.2024.104857

Inan, G. G., & Yilmaz, G. (2025). Developing organisational capabilities for digital transformation. In *Digital Transformation: A Business Imperative*. https://doi.org/ DOI: 10.4324/9781003626640-3

Jarrahi, M. H., & Sutherland, W. (2019). Algorithmic management and algorithmic control in the gig economy. *The Journal of Strategic Information Systems*, *28*(2), 101221. DOI: 10.1016/j.jsis.2019.101221

Karim, R. A., Sobhani, F. A., Rabiul, M. K., Lepee, N. J., Kabir, M. R., & Chowdhury, M. A. M. (2022). Linking fintech payment services and customer loyalty intention in the hospitality industry. *Sustainability (Basel)*, *14*(24), 16481. DOI: 10.3390/su142416481

Meijerink, J., Bondarouk, T., & Lepak, D. (2020). When HRM meets the platform economy: Exploring HRM strategies for digital and gig workers. *Human Resource Management Review*, *30*(4), 100771. DOI: 10.1016/j.hrmr.2020.100771

Montgomery, T., & Baglioni, S. (2021). Defining the gig economy: Platform capitalism and precarious work. *The International Journal of Sociology and Social Policy, 41*(9/10), 1012–1025. DOI: 10.1108/IJSSP-08-2020-0400

Rasheed, R., Malik, M., & Sarwar, S. (2023). AI-driven digital monitoring and worker motivation. *Technological Forecasting and Social Change, 189*, 122314. DOI: 10.1016/j.techfore.2023.122314

Samala, A. D., Rawas, S., Wang, T., Alshammari, F., & Chen, C. (2025). Unveiling the landscape of generative artificial intelligence in education: A comprehensive taxonomy of applications, challenges, and future prospects. *Education and Information Technologies, 30*(3), 3239–3278. DOI: 10.1007/s10639-024-12936-0

Santareno, J. (2025). Generative artificial intelligence in candidate selection. In *Lecture Notes on Multidisciplinary Industrial Engineering*. https://doi.org/DOI: 10.1007/978-3-031-89948-5_4

Seifdar, M. H., & Amiri, B. (2025). Strategic adoption of generative AI in organizations: A game-theoretic and network-based approach. *International Journal of Information Management, 84*, 102932. DOI: 10.1016/j.ijinfomgt.2025.102932

Subrahmanyam, S. (2024). Implementing agile talent management practices to adapt to changing higher education landscapes. In *Cultivating Creativity and Navigating Talent Management in Academia*. https://doi.org/DOI: 10.4018/979-8-3693-6880-0.ch009

Tarafdar, M., Cooper, C., & Stich, J. F. (2019). The technostress trifecta. *Information Systems Journal, 29*(1), 6–42. DOI: 10.1111/isj.12169

Tursunbayeva, A., Franco, M., & Pagliari, C. (2021). Use of artificial intelligence in HRM: A systematic review. *International Journal of Human Resource Management, 32*(17), 3791–3831. DOI: 10.1080/09585192.2020.1871398

Vadithe, R. N., Sreenu, N., Kesari, B., Chiranjeevi, V., Mudavath, C. B. N., & Rajput, R. C. (2025). The role of HR analytics in driving organizational agility. *Engineering, Construction, and Architectural Management*. Advance online publication. DOI: 10.1108/ECAM-01-2025-0076

Vallas, S., & Schor, J. B. (2020). What do platforms do? Understanding the gig economy. *Annual Review of Sociology, 46*(1), 273–294. DOI: 10.1146/annurev-soc-121919-054857

Wood, A. J., Graham, M., Lehdonvirta, V., & Hjorth, I. (2019). Good gig, bad gig: Autonomy and algorithmic control in platform work. *Work, Employment and Society, 33*(1), 56–75. DOI: 10.1177/0950017018785616 PMID: 30886460

Wright, P. M., & McMahan, G. C. (1992). Theoretical perspectives for strategic human resource management. *Journal of Management*, *18*(2), 295–320. DOI: 10.1177/014920639201800205

Zhang, L., & Lu, L. (2023). AI adoption in hospitality: Impacts on service employees and HR practices. *International Journal of Contemporary Hospitality Management*. Advance online publication. DOI: 10.1108/IJCHM-09-2021-1146

Chapter 2
Strategic Human Resource Management in the Hospitality Industry With Technology Integration:
Evidence From the UAE

Varinder Singh Rana
http://orcid.org/0009-0008-8562-8265
City University, Ajman, UAE

Aisha Khan
http://orcid.org/0009-0009-7679-3661
International American University, Ras Al Khaimah, UAE

Shorena Okujava
Hilton Garden Inn, Ras Al Khaimah, UAE

Prabhu. M.
Dr. M.G.R. Educational and Research Institute, India

Tanishka
http://orcid.org/0009-0001-4197-6419
Lovely Professional University, India

DOI: 10.4018/979-8-2600-1845-3.ch002

ABSTRACT

The hospitality industry is one of the most labor-intensive service sectors worldwide, relying extensively on human resources for operational excellence, customer satisfaction, and competitive positioning. In today's rapidly evolving environment, technological innovations are reshaping how human resource management (HRM) functions, particularly in contexts where workforce diversity and turnover present ongoing challenges. Strategic Human Resource Management in the Hospitality Industry with Technology Integration-Evidence from the UAE Strategic Human Resource Management in the Hospitality Industry with Technology Integration-Evidence from the UAE Strategic Human Resource Management in the Hospitality Industry with Technology Integration-Evidence from the UAE Strategic Human Resource Management in the Hospitality Industry with Technology Integration-Evidence from the UAE Strategic Human Resource Management in the Hospitality Industry with Technology Integration-Evidence from the UAE

INTRODUCTION

The global hospitality industry has witnessed tremendous growth in recent decades, becoming a cornerstone of economic development and international trade. According to the World Travel & Tourism Council (WTTC, 2022), the sector contributes significantly to GDP worldwide and serves as a major source of employment. As a people-driven industry, hospitality relies fundamentally on service quality, which in turn depends on human capital. Human resources in this sector act as the face of the organization, delivering personalized experiences that shape customer perceptions and brand loyalty (Nickson, 2013).

In the United Arab Emirates (UAE), hospitality plays a pivotal role in economic diversification strategies. Dubai, Abu Dhabi, Sharjah, and other emirates have positioned themselves as global tourism hubs, with the UAE ranking among the world's top destinations for luxury hospitality and business travel (Deloitte, 2020). The government's commitment to projects such as Expo 2020 Dubai and the Tourism Strategy 2031 further underscores the importance of hospitality to long-term economic sustainability. However, the UAE hospitality sector faces distinct challenges: high employee turnover, cultural diversity, skill shortages, and intense global competition (Alnaqbi, 2011).

Strategic Human Resource Management (SHRM) has emerged as a solution to such challenges, focusing on aligning HR practices with organizational strategy to achieve superior performance (Wright & McMahan, 2011). Unlike traditional HRM, which focuses on administrative functions, SHRM integrates HR activities—such as recruitment, training, performance appraisal, and retention—into the broader strategic framework. This ensures that HR practices contribute directly to organizational goals, creating competitive advantage.

Concurrently, technology is transforming HRM globally. From AI-driven recruitment systems and cloud-based HR Information Systems (HRIS) to e-learning platforms and data analytics, technology enables HR departments to optimize processes, enhance accuracy, and support strategic decision-making (Bondarouk & Brewster, 2016). In the hospitality industry, where managing large, multicultural teams is complex, technology provides opportunities to streamline operations and foster employee engagement.

Despite growing recognition of SHRM and technology in HR, empirical research in the UAE context remains limited. Most existing studies address HR practices or technology adoption in isolation, leaving a gap in understanding how technology-enabled SHRM influences organizational performance and sustainability in UAE hospitality. This chapter aims to bridge this gap by providing empirical evidence from a quantitative study involving 375 respondents.

The chapter is structured as follows: the next section reviews relevant literature on SHRM, technology integration, and the hospitality context. This is followed by the research objectives, hypotheses, and methodology. Data analysis and results are presented, followed by a discussion, conclusion, recommendations, and references.

LITERATURE REVIEW

Strategic Human Resource Management (SHRM)

SHRM represents the integration of HR policies with organizational objectives to ensure long-term effectiveness (Boxall & Purcell, 2016). The Resource-Based View (RBV) underpins SHRM, emphasizing that human capital is a critical and inimitable resource for achieving sustainable competitive advantage (Kaufman, 2015). SHRM encompasses practices such as strategic recruitment, employee training and development, performance management, succession planning, and retention strategies.

In the hospitality industry, SHRM is particularly significant due to the sector's reliance on service quality. Studies have shown that SHRM practices positively influence customer satisfaction, employee commitment, and overall organizational performance (Subramony, 2009). Training and development initiatives enhance service delivery, while retention policies reduce turnover costs—a major issue in hotels. Performance management systems ensure alignment of employee objectives with organizational goals.

Technology and HRM

The integration of technology in HRM, often referred to as electronic HRM (e-HRM), has reshaped the way organizations manage people. HRIS, AI-based recruitment platforms, cloud computing, and mobile applications enable HR professionals to handle large datasets, automate tasks, and focus on strategic decision-making (Stone et al., 2015). Technology adoption also improves employee experience through digital learning, self-service portals, and performance tracking systems.

Marler and Parry (2016) argue that e-HRM is not just about efficiency but also about enabling strategic HRM by providing analytics that inform workforce planning and talent management. In hospitality, technology is particularly beneficial in handling multicultural and geographically dispersed teams, ensuring standardized HR processes.

SHRM in the UAE Hospitality Context

The UAE hospitality industry is characterized by a diverse workforce, comprising expatriates from Asia, Africa, Europe, and the Middle East. Managing such diversity requires cultural sensitivity, effective communication, and structured HR policies (Zaid et al., 2018). High employee turnover—often exceeding 30% annually—poses additional challenges. Training costs, service disruptions, and recruitment expenses reduce profitability, highlighting the need for effective SHRM strategies (Ostroff & Bowen, 2016).

Government initiatives such as Emiratization, which aims to increase the participation of UAE nationals in the workforce, further necessitate strategic HR interventions. Moreover, aligning HR practices with UAE Vision 2031 requires organizations to focus on sustainability, innovation, and workforce development.

RESEARCH GAP

Although SHRM and technology adoption have been studied separately, limited empirical research exists on their combined impact in the UAE hospitality industry. Previous studies focus largely on general HR practices without considering the mediating role of employee engagement or the influence of technology-enhanced HRM. This chapter addresses this gap by examining how SHRM and technology together influence organizational performance and sustainability.

Research Objectives and Hypotheses

Objectives

1. To analyze the role of SHRM in enhancing organizational performance in UAE hospitality.
2. To assess the impact of technology integration on HR practices and employee engagement.
3. To evaluate the mediating role of employee engagement in the relationship between SHRM and organizational sustainability.

Hypotheses

- **H1:** SHRM practices significantly improve organizational performance in UAE hospitality.
- **H2:** Technology integration in HRM positively influences employee engagement.
- **H3:** Employee engagement mediates the relationship between SHRM and organizational sustainability.

RESEARCH METHODOLOGY

Research Design

This study adopted a quantitative, cross-sectional, and explanatory design. The purpose was to assess causal relationships between SHRM, technology integration, employee engagement, and organizational performance/sustainability in UAE hospitality.

Population and Sampling

The population consisted of employees working in hotels across the UAE, including Dubai, Abu Dhabi, Sharjah, and Ras Al Khaimah. The sample size of 375 respondents was determined using Krejcie and Morgan's (1970) sampling table, ensuring a 95% confidence level. Stratified random sampling was applied to capture responses across different hotel categories (luxury, mid-scale, budget).

Instrumentation

The research instrument was a structured questionnaire divided into four sections:

- Section A: Demographic data (age, gender, education, job role, hotel category).
- Section B: SHRM practices (training, recruitment, retention, performance appraisal).
- Section C: Technology integration in HR (HRIS, AI tools, e-learning, analytics).
- Section D: Employee engagement and organizational sustainability outcomes.

All items were measured on a 5-point Likert scale (1 = Strongly Disagree to 5 = Strongly Agree).

Statistical Tools and Tests Used

1. Descriptive Statistics: To summarize demographic data.
2. Reliability Test: Cronbach's Alpha ($\alpha > 0.70$ threshold).
3. Construct Validity:
    - o Convergent validity: Average Variance Extracted (AVE > 0.50).
    - o Discriminant validity: Fornell-Larcker criterion.
4. Multicollinearity Test: Variance Inflation Factor (VIF < 5).
5. Structural Model Analysis: PLS-SEM (Partial Least Squares Structural Equation Modeling) using SmartPLS.
6. Bootstrapping: 5,000 resamples to test path coefficients and hypothesis significance.
7. Effect Size (f^2): To assess the magnitude of relationships.
8. Coefficient of Determination (R^2): To measure variance explained in dependent variables.
9. Predictive Relevance (Q^2): Blindfolding procedure for model predictive accuracy.

DATA ANALYSIS AND RESULTS

Descriptive Statistics – Demographic Profile

Table 1. Respondent Demographics (N = 375)

Variable	Category	Frequency	Percentage (%)
Gender	Male	218	58.1
	Female	157	41.9
Age	21–30 years	177	47.2
	31–40 years	124	33.1
	41+ years	74	19.7
Nationality	South Asian	142	37.9
	Middle Eastern	92	24.5
	European	68	18.1
	African	73	19.5
Job Role	Front Office	102	27.2
	Food & Beverage	121	32.3
	Housekeeping	81	21.6
	Managerial/Executive	71	18.9
Hotel Category	Luxury	146	38.9
	Mid-scale	139	37.1
	Budget	90	24.0

The majority of respondents were young professionals (21–30 years), working in luxury and mid-scale hotels, reflecting the UAE's labor-intensive hospitality workforce.

Reliability Analysis

Table 2. Reliability and Internal Consistency

Construct	Items	Cronbach's Alpha (α)	Composite Reliability (CR)	AVE
SHRM Practices	8	0.884	0.912	0.612
Technology Integration	6	0.861	0.895	0.589
Employee Engagement	7	0.873	0.901	0.604

continued on following page

Table 2. Continued

Construct	Items	Cronbach's Alpha (α)	Composite Reliability (CR)	AVE
Organizational Performance	6	0.857	0.888	0.571
Sustainability Outcomes	5	0.841	0.877	0.566

All Cronbach's Alpha values were > 0.80, confirming strong reliability. AVE values exceeded 0.50, establishing convergent validity.

Discriminant Validity (Fornell-Larcker Criterion)

Table 3. Discriminant Validity Matrix

Construct	SHRM	Tech	Engagement	Performance	Sustainability
SHRM	0.782				
Technology Integration	0.641	0.767			
Engagement	0.594	0.626	0.777		
Performance	0.653	0.618	0.642	0.756	
Sustainability	0.604	0.587	0.658	0.671	0.752

The square root of AVE (diagonal values) was greater than inter-construct correlations, confirming discriminant validity.

Structural Model and Hypothesis Testing

Table 4. Hypothesis Testing Results (PLS-SEM)

Hypothesis	Path	β Value	t-value	p-value	Supported?
H1	SHRM → Organizational Performance	0.62	12.14	0.000	Yes
H2	Technology → Engagement	0.54	10.76	0.000	Yes
H3	Engagement (Mediation)	0.48	7.93	0.001	Yes

All hypotheses were supported at $p < 0.01$ significance.

Coefficient of Determination (R^2)

- Organizational Performance ($R^2 = 0.61$): 61% variance explained by SHRM.

- Employee Engagement ($R^2 = 0.52$): 52% variance explained by technology integration.
- Sustainability ($R^2 = 0.57$): 57% variance explained by engagement + SHRM.

Model shows moderate to strong predictive power.

Effect Size (f^2)

- SHRM → Performance: 0.41 (large effect)
- Technology → Engagement: 0.36 (medium-to-large effect)
- Engagement → Sustainability: 0.29 (medium effect)

Predictive Relevance (Q^2)

- Q^2 values for Performance (0.39), Engagement (0.32), and Sustainability (0.34) were all > 0, confirming good predictive relevance.

Results Interpretation

1. H1 confirmed: SHRM practices strongly enhance organizational performance in UAE hotels, indicating that strategic recruitment, training, and retention policies directly improve service quality and profitability.
2. H2 confirmed: Technology adoption (HRIS, AI, digital training) significantly improves employee engagement by providing tools for communication, skill development, and empowerment.
3. H3 confirmed: Engagement mediates SHRM and sustainability, highlighting that engaged employees are the key mechanism through which HR strategies translate into long-term organizational resilience.

DATA COLLECTION PROCESS

Data was collected through online and face-to-face surveys conducted over three months. Ethical considerations such as informed consent, confidentiality, and voluntary participation were ensured.

Data Analysis

Data was analyzed using **Partial Least Squares Structural Equation Modeling (PLS-SEM)**. Reliability and validity were tested using Cronbach's alpha, composite reliability, and average variance extracted (AVE). Hypotheses were tested through path analysis, with significance assessed using bootstrapping.

DATA ANALYSIS AND INTERPRETATION

Demographic Profile

Among the 375 respondents, 58% were male and 42% female. Age distribution indicated that 47% were between 21–30 years, 33% between 31–40 years, and 20% above 40. Nationalities represented included South Asian (38%), Middle Eastern (24%), European (18%), and African (20%). Job roles included front office, housekeeping, food & beverage, and managerial positions.

Reliability and Validity

Cronbach's alpha values exceeded 0.80 for all constructs, confirming reliability. AVE values were greater than 0.50, establishing convergent validity. Discriminant validity was also achieved.

Hypothesis Testing

- **H1:** Supported. SHRM significantly influenced organizational performance ($\beta = 0.62$, $p < 0.01$).
- **H2:** Supported. Technology integration significantly enhanced employee engagement ($\beta = 0.54$, $p < 0.01$).
- **H3:** Supported. Employee engagement mediated the SHRM–sustainability relationship ($\beta = 0.48$, $p < 0.05$).

Interpretation

Results confirm that SHRM practices directly enhance organizational performance by improving employee skills, commitment, and alignment with goals. Technology integration strengthens employee engagement by providing innovative tools for learning, communication, and self-service HR functions. Finally, engaged employees contribute significantly to organizational sustainability, mediating the impact of SHRM.

Discussion of Results

The findings align with the RBV framework, emphasizing that human capital, when strategically managed, creates sustainable competitive advantage. Consistent with Subramony (2009), SHRM was found to significantly improve performance. Technology's role in enhancing engagement echoes Marler and Parry (2016), who highlight the strategic value of e-HRM.

For UAE hospitality, where cultural diversity and turnover are major issues, SHRM supported by technology ensures consistent service delivery and improved retention. The mediating role of engagement underscores the need for hotels to foster inclusive, motivating environments.

CONCLUSION

This chapter highlights the importance of SHRM in the UAE hospitality sector, particularly when supported by technology. SHRM practices significantly improve organizational performance, while technology enhances employee engagement and efficiency. Employee engagement further mediates the SHRM–sustainability relationship, underscoring its central role.

The study contributes by integrating SHRM and technology in the UAE hospitality context, providing theoretical and practical insights.

Recommendations

1. **Adopt HR Technology Systems:** Hotels should invest in HRIS, AI recruitment tools, and e-learning platforms.
2. **Continuous Learning Programs:** Digital training should be implemented to upskill employees.
3. **Employee Engagement Strategies:** Recognition, career growth, and multicultural awareness programs should be prioritized.
4. **Policy Alignment:** HR practices should align with UAE Tourism Strategy 2031 and Emiratization policies.
5. **Future Research:** Longitudinal studies and comparative analyses across GCC countries are recommended.

REFERENCES

Alnaqbi, W. (2011). *The relationship between human resource practices and employee retention in public organisations: An exploratory study conducted in the United Arab Emirates*. Edith Cowan University.

Bondarouk, T., & Brewster, C. (2016). Conceptualising the future of HRM and technology research. *International Journal of Human Resource Management, 27*(21), 2652–2671. DOI: 10.1080/09585192.2016.1232296

Boxall, P., & Purcell, J. (2016). *Strategy and human resource management* (4th ed.). Palgrave Macmillan. DOI: 10.1007/978-1-137-40765-8

Deloitte. (2020). *Hospitality 2020: The future of growth*. Deloitte Insights.

Kaufman, B. E. (2015). The RBV theory foundation of strategic HRM: Critical flaws, problems for research and practice, and an alternative economics paradigm. *Human Resource Management Journal, 25*(4), 516–540. DOI: 10.1111/1748-8583.12085

Marler, J. H., & Parry, E. (2016). Human resource management, strategic involvement and e-HRM technology. *International Journal of Human Resource Management, 27*(19), 2233–2253. DOI: 10.1080/09585192.2015.1091980

Nickson, D. (2013). *Human resource management for hospitality, tourism and events* (2nd ed.). Routledge. DOI: 10.4324/9780080966496

Ostroff, C., & Bowen, D. E. (2016). Reflections on the 2014 decade award: Is there strength in the construct of HR system strength? *Academy of Management Review, 41*(2), 196–214. DOI: 10.5465/amr.2015.0323

Stone, D. L., Deadrick, D. L., Lukaszewski, K. M., & Johnson, R. (2015). The influence of technology on the future of human resource management. *Human Resource Management Review, 25*(2), 216–231. DOI: 10.1016/j.hrmr.2015.01.002

Subramony, M. (2009). A meta-analytic investigation of the relationship between HRM bundles and firm performance. *Human Resource Management, 48*(5), 745–768. DOI: 10.1002/hrm.20315

Wright, P. M., & McMahan, G. C. (2011). Exploring human capital: Putting 'human' back into strategic human resource management. *Human Resource Management Journal, 21*(2), 93–104. DOI: 10.1111/j.1748-8583.2010.00165.x

Zaid, A. A., Jaaron, A. A. M., & Talib Bon, A. (2018). The impact of green human resource management and green supply chain management practices on sustainable performance: An empirical study. *Journal of Cleaner Production*, *204*, 965–979. DOI: 10.1016/j.jclepro.2018.09.062

Chapter 3
The Contribution of Quality of Life at Work to Organizational Flexibility in Air Transport:
Case of the Royal Air Maroc Airline Company

Adil El-Ouali
http://orcid.org/0009-0008-6615-1828
Université Sidi Mohamed Ben Abdellah, Morocco

Ahmed El Hammoumi
Faculty of Legal, Economic, and Social Sciences, Dhar Mehrez, Fès, Morocco

Tarik Jellouli
http://orcid.org/0009-0005-7400-1772
Faculty of Legal, Economic, and Social Sciences, Dhar Mehrez, Fès, Morocco

ABSTRACT

The contribution of quality of life at work (QLW) to organizational flexibility is particularly strong in the air transport sector, given that these two variables are a major determinant of responsiveness and performance in disruptive environments. In other words, quality of life at work promotes adaptability and, therefore, the ability of teams and, more broadly, human resources to manage operational uncertainties. This study aims to assess the impact of QWL, with its six dimensions (availability of a healthy and appropriate work environment, participation in decision-making, salaries, bonuses and incentives, leadership and supervision style, professional

DOI: 10.4018/979-8-2600-1845-3.ch003

development and training programs, and complaints and grievances), on the level of organizational flexibility at Royal Air Maroc (RAM) airline company. 300 questionnaires were distributed to a sample of employees in the company, and 280 questionnaires were analyzed using certain statistical tests such as multiple regression and simple regression.

1. INTRODUCTION

Human resources are the cornerstone of success for various companies, as the value of human resources has increased significantly in recent years in light of rapid and successive changes in the work environment, increasing competition, and major technological developments in various fields. These recent organizational changes require the creation of working conditions conducive to optimizing the efficiency, effectiveness, and productivity of human resources (Permarupan, 2020). This requirement is supported by literature highlighting the strategic role of the work environment in the development of organizational skills and agility (Shin et al., 2023).

In an economic environment where we are currently living in permanent change, Human Resources Management (HRM) is a crucial strategic tool for Moroccan companies, particularly through the establishment of training systems that correspond to organizational goals. By implementing approaches focused on improving employee skills and engagement, Moroccan companies and businesses, like the RAM airline company, used here as a study example, can strengthen their competitive position. HR is therefore presented as an essential element for valuing human capital to adapt to the competitive dynamics that characterize the market (El-Ouali & Jellouli, 2025).

HRM, through knowledge management practices, plays an important role, particularly at the strategic level, in mobilizing skills and collective performance, which is ultimately linked, at the individual or collective level, to the efficiency factor. Studies such as the one conducted at Maroc Telecom (El Hammoumi & El-Ouali, 2025) generally show how these instruments can solve salary problems, using new technological means, of course. Career quality means that employees attain their professional objectives in a safe, equitable, flexible, and productive work context, like how many people have the experience of thinking their work is quality, meaningful, and congruent with their wish to do and what they want to do (Heslin, Keating, and Ashford, 2022).

The mechanisms or means deployed by the organization, such as policies supporting this balance, encourage motivation, commitment, loyalty, and consequently overall performance (Wong, Chan & Teh, 2020). According to Kim (2020), the perception of security in the workplace, as well as the fit between the individual and the organization, strengthens the positive link between professional quality and commitment. These combined elements form a model inspired by social exchange theories that encourages companies to adopt human resource practices that combine security, career development, and well-being in order to meet individual ambitions and collective goals.

In today's increasingly unpredictable organizational environment, the success of organizations depends to some extent on the creation of an incentive-based work environment that aligns with strategic objectives and enables employee performance in this context. Actors involved in performance-related activities must be supported in adapting to environmental change. To accompany this movement, organizational flexibility appears necessary both to anticipate and create opportunities for maintaining long-term competitive advantage (Teece, 2007). This need for structural agility is further reinforced by ongoing work on organizational resilience and adaptability (Nguyen et al., 2022).

2. STUDY PROBLEM

The success of any organization in today's work world depends on the efficiency and productivity of its employees, their job satisfaction, and their motivation to work. Numerous factors influence the success of organizations and the efficiency and productivity of their employees, such as the work environment, relationships between employees and between employees and management, compensation and bonus policies, opportunities for development and training, participation in decision-making, the safety of the work environment, promotion policies applied, job security, and professional stability. These factors are the dimensions of professional quality of life that all organizations must strive to provide and strengthen in order to ensure their competitiveness in the work environment and achieve their growth and development.

In today's work environment, organizational flexibility has become a central element in how organizations respond to changes in the work environment and improve their competitiveness. Organizational flexibility also strengthens an organization's ability to successfully implement the changes it wants to make to its policies, practices, and processes.

The problem studied can be summarized as answering the following question: does QVT have an impact on the level of organizational flexibility of the RAM airline company?

2.1 Importance of the Study

The importance of this study lies in its evaluation of the reciprocal relationship between two variables that have gained great administrative importance in organizations due to their impact on increasing the competitiveness of these organizations and improving their efficiency in the work environment.

Among other elements, it also appears that the quality of life at work is a factor that allows for stability and security of workers in employment, depending on the evolution of the labor market, and encourages them to redouble their efforts at work to make the organization more flexible and to succeed. Organizational flexibility contributes to an organization's ability to respond to any changes and developments in the work environment. Highlighting the impact of quality of life at work on the organizational flexibility of airlines will help the executives of these companies to become aware of the interest in quality of life at work and the importance of addressing all its components to achieve better efficiency and flexibility at work.

2.2 Study Objectives

The present study aims to clarify how QWL is associated with the organizational flexibility present within the company, more specifically, the RAM airline company. The aim of the four points we wish to achieve lies in the first objective of our study, which is to measure the degree of employee satisfaction with their quality of work life, based on the support from the same company, the work environment, recognition of their efforts, and the balance between their personal and professional lives, according to the work of Richman et al., (2021) and Islam and Namwong (2020).

The second objective of our study is to examine the internal organizational flexibility of the RAM airline company as an organization, taking into account work schedules, decision-making capacity, and the speed of the process (Ariffin et al., 2016). The third focus of our study concerns the relationship between QWL and organizational flexibility, as a work environment with flexible working hours increases the possibility of organizational adaptation.

Finally, the fourth objective of the study is to analyze the impact of QWL on organizational flexibility by verifying the hypothesis that improved working conditions contribute to making an organization more efficient and resilient (Richman et al., 2021; Ariffin et al., 2016).

The study's objectives can be summarized and presented as follows:

1. Determine the level of quality of professional life within the RAM airline company.
2. Highlight the level of organizational flexibility of the RAM airline company.

3. Evaluate the relationship between quality of life at work and organizational flexibility within the RAM airline company.
4. Measure the impact of quality of life at work on organizational flexibility within the RAM airline company.

3. STUDY HYPOTHESIS

3.1 Main Hypothesis of the Study

This research assumes that there is a notable influence of QVT on the reinforcement of organizational flexibility in the airline RAM. We hypothesize that having a high QVT is a strategic tool that can strengthen the adaptability and organizational responsiveness of the company in response to changes in its competitive environment. From which we can deduce the central hypothesis of the following research: QVT influences the strengthening of the level of organizational flexibility within the airline RAM.

3.2 Secondary Hypotheses

1. The availability of a healthy and suitable work environment affects the level of organizational flexibility within the RAM airline company.
2. Participation in decision-making affects the level of organizational flexibility within RAM airline.
3. Salaries, bonuses, and incentives affect the level of organizational flexibility within the RAM airline company.
4. The style of leadership and supervision affects the level of organizational flexibility at RAM Airlines.
5. The development and career evolution programs affect the level of organizational flexibility within Royal Air Maroc.
6. Complaints and claims affect the level of organizational flexibility within RAM Airline.

4. THEORETICAL FRAMEWORK OF OUR STUDY

To address the question of our research on the impact of quality of life at work on organizational flexibility in the air transport sector: case study on the RAM airline company, it is essential to define the problem well. I will start the theoretical framework of our research by explaining the notion of QVT, which refers to a series of techniques, practices and conditions within the organization, with the aim of simultaneously improving employee well-being and overall efficiency of the entity. It is a comprehensive approach that encompasses several dimensions, such as social interactions, work-life balance, workers' autonomy, recognition at work, as well as development opportunities. Given that in the service sector, where relational work is often intense, the importance of quality of life at work is revealed by its direct effect on the quality of the service provided, customer satisfaction and the company's image.

4.1 Quality of Work Life (QWL)

4.1.1 QVT Concept

The concept of "Quality of Work Life" in the United States, originally known as Quality of Work, emerged in 1972 with the first international conference on Work Quality. This multidimensional concept is difficult to define and often faces challenging issues. The concept of work's central role in health is supported by the psychodynamics of work, which suggests that workplace health as a public health issue involves not only the social responsibility of businesses but also the promotion of workers' rights to quality work and legal obligations to prevent psychosocial risks.

The concept of QVT emerged in the 2010s and encompasses several factors depending on the organization or company, sector, or field. It certainly highlights the increasingly widespread desire for a better life for employees (at work and outside of work): a heightened awareness among many employees - in both the public and private sectors - who seek satisfaction, personal fulfillment, and well-being at work (Bencheikh & Dufour, 2019). QVT stands for the set of organizational conditions and practices aimed at maintaining the well-being, engagement, and performance of employees in their work environment (Ariani, Zulhawati & Budi Harsono, 2023). It takes into account, first and foremost, fair compensation, security, recognition, work-life balance, and psychosocial support through organized human resources devices (Campo, Avolio & Carlier, 2021).

According to Maphanga et al., (2024), QVT is a collection of organizational strategies and actions aimed at maximizing, to the extent possible, the work environment and conditions for employees and the organization, while also considering the needs of the employees professionally and as individuals and the needs of the organization.

This approach is an extension of the work of Ramayah et al., (2014) on material and moral incentives, congestion, the organizational climate of fairness, and the quality of human relations, while Teece et al., (2016) propose an active and ubiquitous policy of qualification, upgrading, and collaboration through administered circumstances that lead employees to define and redefine the current context in which they must act within the framework of their contractual obligations and professional behaviors. The quality of life at work as a balance between the personal and professional spheres, based on organizational justice, respect for employee rights, as well as performance, sustainability, and skills development.

The concept of QVT is therefore one of the concepts that have gained importance in strengthening the ability of companies to adapt to changes and developments. Designing this concept in relation to several elements that support the capabilities of these entities, the quality of professional life is the set of efforts and practices established by companies to achieve their general objectives while realizing the personal goals of employees, through procedures, policies, plans, administrative practices, organizational climate, and incentive policies established by companies.

4.1.2 The Importance of QVT

The importance of QWL visibly correlates with different benefits for organizations. According to Els, Brouwers, and Lodewyk (2021), benefits had been observed in the areas of absenteeism, punctuality (tardiness), turnover, employee disengagement - both physical and psychological - as well as organizational performance. A potential for employee performance and competitiveness would therefore have been confirmed by organizational well-being strategies, according to Permarupan et al. (2020).

According to Shin et al. (2023), a positive psychosocial environment influences employee engagement, creativity, and job satisfaction. So, QWL translates into increased employee participation in decision-making and their involvement in defining objectives and implementation mechanisms, as well as encouraging them to participate in problem-solving, which in turn is reflected in their behaviors and positive attitudes at work.

QWL is an essential factor in achieving organizational goals, as it promotes employee motivation, well-being, satisfaction, and performance (Fanggidae et al., 2020). This perspective is reinforced by recent research that highlights the close link between well-being at work, professional engagement, and organizational performance (Shin et al., 2023).

The importance of QWL is highlighted by Andrabi and Rainayee (2023), as it improves the professional environment to meet employees' needs, enhances flexibility and retention within the organization, and optimizes human resource management policies.

El-Sharkawy, Nafea, and Hassan (2023) emphasized that QWL also stimulates managers' creativity and emotional engagement, as well as organizational citizenship behaviors, while increasing employee well-being and reducing stress and conflicts, which contributes to the organization's sustainability. Current research also confirms that the balance between work and private life (Capnary et al., 2018), not to mention that favorable human resources practices and policies focused on well-being and retention, significantly increase employee engagement, reduce stress, and improve overall performance (Medina-Garrido et al., 2023).

4.1.3 QWL Objectives

The QVT has several objectives, and among the main ones, it seeks to improve employee well-being, reduce absenteeism and turnover, increase productivity and company performance, and promote innovation. Beyond these objectives, it also aims to strengthen team cohesion, to value the work of each one, and to establish a climate of trust conducive to professional development.

QWL is based on several multidimensional indicators: organizational justice and the psychological health of staff, meaning that it has a direct impact on employee motivation, productivity, and retention. It must increasingly be oriented toward managerial approaches based on respect for human resources in an inclusive and sustainable manner (Toscano & Zappalà, 2020).

QWL also depends on aspects such as pay equity, fair promotion, professional development, psychological safety, recognition at work, and low absenteeism. Studies conducted after 2020 have shown that real access to policies that encourage work-life balance improves well-being and productivity (Wijngaards et al., 2022). In addition, a psychosocial safety environment promoted by management reduces absenteeism and increases productivity (Teo, Bentley & Nguyen, 2020).

These strategic factors in Morocco facilitate employee engagement and retention within evolving organizations such as the RAM airline company. Finally, good QVT improves the physical and mental health of employees. It represents a means of assessing risks against work accidents that include burnout and stress. Measures to prevent problems related to poor working conditions also include better organisation and more flexibility.

4.2 Organizational Flexibility in the Services Sector (Case of Air Transport)

Currently, organizational flexibility has been institutionalized as a strategic imperative, particularly in service sectors that are bearing the brunt of the high variability in demand and exogenous shocks, like air transport which struggles to resolve major structural issues such as economic fluctuations, environmental geopolitical uncertainties, environmental pressures and the requirement for personalization and stronger quality of services.

Flexibility, under its definition of an organization's ability to adjust its choices, structures and modes of operation to cope with the existence of environmental changes, is declined in different forms: strategic flexibility, structural, functional or operational (Shin & Konrad, 2017). In the case of airlines, it can be achieved through the flexible availability of schedules, modular teams, or even hybrid fleets in response to the variability of peak demand (Alamdari & Fagan, 2005).

For reasons of prudence, flexibilization strategies must be integrated with some caution, particularly as regards employment, at the risk of seeing internal cohesion weakened or service quality deteriorated in an industry where customer experience, therefore, constitutes an element of differentiation (Linneberg et al., 2021). In this sense, human resources are at the heart of implementing sustainable organizational flexibility by integrating agility and stability into managerial processes (Boxall & Macky, 2009).

In any case, as regards air transport, organisational flexibility manifests a strategic response to the sector's transformation dynamics but cannot be reduced to a short-term adjustment logic, it must fit into an overall vision mobilizing all organizational functions to strengthen their resilience, and thus sustainable performance.

5. FIELD STUDY

This section discusses the procedures followed by the researchers in the study, which consisted of the method used in the investigation, the data collection tool used by the researchers to gather the data required in the study, the study sample, the validity and reliability of the study tool, and the statistical analysis methods used to analyze the data and test the validity of the hypotheses.

5.1 Study Methodology

The study was based on the descriptive analytical method to comprehensively and precisely describe the subject of the study by collecting and analyzing data on RAM's level of interest in professional quality of life in terms of the availability of a healthy and appropriate work environment, participation in decision-making, salaries and rewards, leadership and supervision style, professional development programs, complaints and grievances, as well as the company's level of organizational flexibility in terms of strategic, operational, and structural flexibility. The study was also based on a field study conducted with a sample of the studied population in order to obtain generalizable and useful results.

5.2 Study Tool

Our study is based on a questionnaire comprising a series of questions related to the subject of the study. It included a cover page summarizing the study, its title, and its objective, as well as a request for cooperation from company employees to give their opinion on the statements contained in the questionnaire. The questionnaire comprised 54 statements and consisted of personal data and two main areas, as follows:

5.3 General and Functional Data

In the field of management science research, sociodemographic variables are central to analyses of behaviors and perceptions within organizations. This part of our chapter explores the main variables of interest: gender, age, education, and years of service experience. Indeed, they help to expose the variety of respondents' profiles and their potential links with organizational dynamics, notably by confronting possible disparities in responses depending on individuals' characteristics. Thus, the analysis feedback offers a relevant interpretation of the challenges related to human resources management. Considering these elements, the contextual relevance of the study's conclusions is reinforced.

First Area: QLW Within RAM Airlines

This involves assessing QLW within RAM airline company. This area comprises 41 statements based on previous studies on the same subject and divided into six dimensions: healthy and suitable working environment (10 items), participation in decision-making (8 items), salaries, bonuses, and incentives (6 items), management and supervision style (7 items), professional development and advancement programs (5 items), and complaints and grievances (5 items).

Second Axis: Level of Organizational Flexibility Within the RAM Airline Company

It is about assessing the level of organizational flexibility of the RAM airline company. This axis includes 9 items developed from previous studies on the same subject, divided into three dimensions: strategic flexibility (3 items), operational flexibility (3 items), and structural flexibility (3 items).

The response rates of the studied sample were calculated using the standard indicated in the following table to estimate the level of agreement among the members of the studied community.

Table 1. Level and degree of approval of the questionnaire paragraphs

I completely agree.	Agreed	Neutral	I disagree	I completely disagree	Level
5	4	3	2	1	**Degree**

5.4 Reliability of the Study Tool

In order to verify the reliability of the study tool, it was presented, together with the objectives and hypotheses of the study, to a number of faculty members specializing in business management and human resources management in certain faculties (trade, tourism, and hospitality) in order to ensure the relevance of each paragraph with respect to the dimension to which it belongs, as well as the degree of clarity and appropriateness of the wording of each paragraph and the degree of adequacy with the objective for which it was designed. All the referees' remarks were taken into account, and the questionnaire was modified accordingly.

In order to verify the stability of the study tool, an internal stability and consistency test was carried out using the Cronbach Alpha coefficient in order to ensure that the results of this study can be generalized to society as a whole. Table 2 shows the results of the Cronbach's Alpha coefficient test.

Table 2. Valeur du coefficient de stabilité et de cohérence interne (alpha de Cronbach)

Number of items	Cronbach alpha value	Variables
10	0.841	Availability of a healthy and suitable working environment
8	0.762	Participation in decision-making
6	0.881	Remuneration, bonuses, and incentives
7	0.803	Leadership and supervision style
5	0.905	Development and professional development programmes
5	0.755	Complaints and claims
41	0.837	Quality of Life at Work
3	0.911	Strategic flexibility
3	0.897	Operational flexibility
3	0.864	Structural flexibility
9	0.863	Organizational flexibility

Table 2 shows that the stability coefficient for the first dimension of quality of professional life (availability of a healthy and suitable working environment) is 0.841, that for the second dimension (participation in decision-making) is 0.762, that for the third dimension (remuneration, bonuses, and incentives) is 0.881, that for the fourth dimension (leadership and supervision style) is 0.803, that for the fifth dimension (professional development and advancement programs) is 0.905, and that for the sixth dimension (complaints and claims) is 0.755. Its value for the QWL variable was 0.837, and the stability coefficient value for the first dimension of organizational flexibility was 0.863, while strategic flexibility was 0.911, and the stability coefficient for the second dimension (operational flexibility) was 0.897, and its value for the third dimension (structural flexibility) was 0.864.

The stability coefficient value for the organizational flexibility variable was 0.863. All these values are above the acceptable stability coefficient value, which is 70%.

These values are therefore significant and relevant for research purposes, meaning that they can be used to measure what they were designed to measure, as well as to measure the results of the field study in terms of generalizing the results.

5.5 Study Population and Sample

The study population consisted of employees of the RAM airline company in all its branches in Morocco. A total of 291 questionnaires were distributed to a random sample of employees of this company, 264 questionnaires were returned, and 246 valid questionnaires were used to analyze their data out of the total number of questionnaires distributed, while 18 questionnaires were deemed invalid due to a lack of data.

Statistical Methods Used

To study the results concerning the impact of quality of life at work on the flexibility of organizations in the air transport sector – example of our study of the RAM airline company – and test the proposed hypotheses, the researcher used the statistical software SPSS V.26.

A first descriptive analysis (frequencies, means, standard deviations) was used to describe the sample as well as the main variables. The reliability of the measuring instruments has been confirmed through the Cronbach alpha. Pearson correlations measured the initial relationships between aspects of QVT and flexibility indicators.

Subsequently, hierarchical multiple linear regressions were used to assess the predictive capacity of QVT on organizational flexibility, while considering demographic variables. To conclude, additional tests (robustness analyses) confirmed the consistency and relevance of the results (threshold $p < 0.05$), thus ensuring instrumental fidelity and the soundness of the conclusions reached in this applied research.

To analyze the study data and test the hypotheses, the researcher used SPSS V.26 software and the following statistical methods:

1. Stability and reliability coefficient test: This was used to measure the stability of the study instrument.
2. Frequencies, percentages, arithmetic means, and standard deviations: These were used to describe the characteristics of the sample and determine the responses of the sample members to all axes of the study tool.
3. Pearson's correlation coefficient: This was used to determine the strength and direction of the relationship between the study variables.
4. Simple regression analysis: Determine the effect of the independent variable on the dependent variable and the value of that effect.
5. Multiple regression analysis: Determine the effect of the independent variables on the dependent variable and the value of that effect.

6. RESULTS OF THE ANALYSIS OF THE STUDY DATA

A summary of the results of the analysis of study data concerning the topic "The contribution of quality of life at work to organizational flexibility in air transport: the case of the RAM airline company " will be presented in table form in a synthetic manner.

Descriptive Analysis of the Demographic Characteristics of the Study Sample

Table 3 shows the distribution of the study sample according to demographic characteristics. The results in the table show that more than half of the sample is male, with 134 individuals representing 54.5%. The results also show that more than half of the sample is young (aged 20 to under 40), with 131 individuals representing 53.3%. The results also show that more than two-thirds of the study sample have a qualification across the entire study sample. Finally, 218 individuals (88.6% of the total study sample) hold a bachelor's degree. Finally, the table shows that more than half of the sample has years of service (5 to less than 10 years), with 146 people (59.2%).

Table 3. Distribution of the sample according to demographic variables in the study sample

%	Frequency	Variables	
56.1%	157	Male	**Gender**
43.9%	123	Femelle	
%100	280	Total	
8.57%	24	30 ans et moins	**Age**
53.57%	150	30 ans à moins de 40 ans	
37.86%	106	50 ans et plus	
%100	**280**	**Total**	
5%	14	Moins d'un baccalauréat	**Level of education**
89.29%	250	Baccalauréat	
5.71%	16	Études supérieures	
%100	**280**	**Total**	
28.21%	79	Moins de 5 ans	**Year of service**
59.29%	166	De 5 à moins de 10 ans	
7.86%	22	De 10 à moins de 15 ans	
4.64%	13	15 ans et plus	
%100	**280**	**Total**	

Descriptive Analysis of the Study Axes

Table 4 presents the arithmetic mean and standard deviation of each study variable and its dimensions. The results show that RAM airline company stands out for its high level of quality of life at work, with an arithmetic mean of 4.00 and a standard deviation of 0.97. This shows that RAM airline company is clearly striving to offer all dimensions of professional quality of life in order to strengthen its competitiveness.

The results also show that the dimensions of QWL within RAM airline company are available to similar degrees. The most prevalent dimension is "the existence of a healthy and suitable working environment," with an arithmetic mean of 4.15 and a standard deviation of 0.59. The dimension "remuneration, bonuses, and benefits" is the least prevalent, with an arithmetic mean of 3.81 and a standard deviation of 1.11.

As the table shows, the arithmetic mean of the organizational flexibility level within the RAM airline company is 4.04 with a standard deviation of 0.89, indicating a high level of organizational flexibility within the company, given its willingness to react quickly and appropriately to changes in the work environment. The results also show that the highest dimension of organizational flexibility was "strategic flexibility," with an arithmetic mean of 4.08 and a standard deviation of 0.77, while "operational flexibility" was the lowest, with an arithmetic mean of 4.00 and a standard deviation of 0.93.

Table 4. Arithmetic means and standard deviation of QWL and organizational flexibility

Standard deviation	Arithmetic mean	Variable
0.59	4.15	Availability of a healthy and suitable working environment
0.93	3.97	Participation in decision-making
1.11	3.81	Remuneration, bonuses, and incentives
0.76	4.11	Leadership and supervision style
1.03	3.91	Development and professional advancement programs
0.89	4.03	Complaints and claims
0.97	4.00	Quality of Work Life
0.77	4.08	Strategic flexibility
0.93	4.00	Operational flexibility
0.85	4.05	Structural flexibility
0.89	4.04	Regulatory flexibility

7. TESTING THE STUDY HYPOTHESES

Main hypothesis of the study: The main hypothesis indicates that "QWL influences the strengthening of the level of organizational flexibility within the RAM airline company".

The results presented in table n° 5 highlight the existence of a significant correlation between quality of work life and organizational flexibility within the RAM airline company, with a correlation coefficient of 0.000 (p-value < 0.05).

With an error rate of 5% and a confidence level of 95%, the value of the correlation coefficient reached 0.759, which corresponds to a strong positive correlation. This means that the higher the level of professional quality of life within the RAM airline company, the higher the level of organizational flexibility of the company.

Table 5. Relationship between QWL and organizational flexibility within RAM airlines

		Quality of Work Life	**Regulatory flexibility**
Quality of Work Life	Correlation coefficient	1.000	**0.759
	Significance		0.0000
	Sample size	**280**	**280**
Regulatory flexibility	Correlation coefficient	0.759**	1.000
	Significance	0.000	.
	Sample size	**280**	**280**

As part of this study, it is important to empirically examine the relationship between QWL and organizational flexibility. For this, a multiple regression study was implemented to calculate the impact that QVT has on the adaptability of the RAM airline company. This method helps to see the combined effect of several aspects related to QVT on the desired flexibility. The chosen method is based on a strong statistical model, intended for research in HRM. The data collected by this research are presented in Table n° 6. They provide useful details on internal levers to implement strategic adjustments in air services.

Table 6. Impact of QWL dimensions on organizational flexibility

Sig.	**F**	**R^2**	**Sig.**	**t**	**B**	
0.000	93.821	0.591	0.000	8.164	1.112	Regression constant
			0.000	2.734	0.259	Availability of a healthy and suitable working environment
			0.000	6.552	0.711	Participation in decision-making
			0.000	5.614	0.631	Salaries, bonuses, and incentives
			0.000	7.514	0.801	Leadership and supervisory style
			0.000	2.971	0.224	Professional development and advancement programs
			0.000	3.998	0.469	Complaints and claims

Table n° 6 shows that the dimensions of QWL have a significant and positive impact on the level of organizational flexibility within the RAM airline company, where the calculated F value is (93.821) with a significance level (0.000) (p-value < 0.05), which is higher than its tabular value.

This table shows the rate of change in organizational flexibility across the six dimensions of quality of working life, with a regression coefficient value of (0.591), meaning that the independent variable "QWL" has a (95.1%) impact on the dependent variable "organizational flexibility," which means that quality of working life contributes to strengthening the level of organizational flexibility of the RAM airline by (59.1%). Therefore, the main hypothesis of the study is accepted.

We can deduce that the model is globally significant ($F = 93.821$, $p < 0.001$) with a coefficient of determination ($R^2 = 0.591$), which indicates that (59.1%) of the variance in the dependent variable is explained by the independent variables. All predictors are significant at a (99%) confidence level.

First sub-hypothesis: *"The availability of a healthy and suitable working environment has an impact on the level of organizational flexibility within RAM airline company."*

In order to determine the degree of influence of a healthy and suitable working environment on the level of organizational flexibility within the RAM airline company, a simple regression analysis was performed.

Table n° 7 illustrates the impact of a healthy and suitable working environment on the level of organizational flexibility.

Table 7. Impact of a healthy and adapted work environment on the level of organizational flexibility

Sig.	F	R^2	r	Sig.	t	Coefficients	Variable
0.000	323.201	0.522	0.716	0.000	5.855	1.125	Regression constant
				0.000	14.234	0.785	Availability of a healthy and suitable working environment

The results presented in Table 7 highlight the existence of a significant correlation between the existence of a healthy and adapted work environment and the level of organizational flexibility within the RAM airline company, with a correlation coefficient of (0.716), which corresponds to a strong positive correlation.

The results also show that the existence of a healthy and suitable work environment has a significant and positive effect on the level of organizational flexibility within the RAM airline company; hence, the calculated value of F (323.201) reached a significant level (0.000) (p-value < 0.05), which is higher than its tabular value.

This table shows the rate of change in the level of organizational flexibility through the establishment of a healthy and suitable work environment, where the value of the regression coefficient (0.522) means that the independent variable "establishment of a healthy and suitable work environment" has an impact of (52.2%) on the dependent variable "organizational flexibility," meaning that the availability of a healthy and suitable work environment contributes to strengthening the level of organizational flexibility within RAM airline company by (52.2%). Based on this, the first partial hypothesis is accepted.

Second sub-hypothesis: "*Participation in decision-making affects the level of organizational flexibility within RAM airline company.*"

To determine the degree of influence of participation in decision-making on the level of organizational flexibility within the RAM airline, a simple regression analysis was performed. Table n° 8 illustrates the impact of participation in decision-making on the level of organizational flexibility.

Table 8. Impact of participation in decision-making on the level of organizational flexibility

Sig.	F	R^2	r	Sig.	t	Coefficients	Variable
0.000	198.745	0.437	0.692	0.000	9.524	0.932	Regression constant
				0.000	17.235	0.554	Participation in decision-making

The results presented in Table 8 show a significant correlation between participation in decision-making and the level of organizational flexibility within RAM airline company, with a correlation coefficient of (0.692), indicating a moderate positive correlation.

The results also show a significant and positive effect of participation in decision-making on the level of organizational flexibility within the RAM airline company, with a calculated F-value of (198.745) and a significance level of 0.000 (p-value < 0.05), which is higher than its tabular value.

This table shows the percentage change in the level of organizational flexibility due to participation in decision-making. The value of the regression coefficient (0.437) means that the independent variable "*participation in decision-making*" influences the dependent variable "*organizational flexibility*" by (43.7%), meaning that a healthy and adapted work environment contributes to increasing the level of organizational flexibility within RAM airline company by (43.7%). Based on this, the second secondary sub-hypothesis is accepted.

Third sub-hypothesis: "*salaries, bonuses, and incentives affect the level of organizational flexibility within RAM airline company.*"

In order to determine the impact of salaries, bonuses and incentives on the level of organizational flexibility within the RAM airline company, a simple regression analysis was performed. Table 9 illustrates the impact of salaries, bonuses and incentives on the level of organizational flexibility.

Table 9. Impact of wages, bonuses, and incentives on the level of organizational flexibility

Sig.	F	R^2	r	Sig.	t	Coefficients	Variable
0.000	201.362	0.410	0.637	0.000	4.368	0.771	Regression constant
				0.000	11.208	0.491	Salaries, bonuses and benefits

The results of table 9 reveal a significant correlation between salaries, bonuses, and incentives and the level of organizational flexibility within RAM airline company, with a correlation coefficient of (0.637), indicating a moderate positive correlation.

The results also show that salaries, bonuses, and incentives have a significant and positive effect on the level of organizational flexibility within RAM airline, with a calculated F value of (201.362) and a significance level of 0.000 (p-value < 0.05), which is higher than its tabular value.

The table below shows the percentage change in the level of organizational flexibility based on salaries, bonuses, and incentives and indicates that the regression coefficient value is (0.410), with the independent variable "salaries, bonuses, and incentives" affecting the dependent variable "organizational flexibility" by (41%), meaning that salaries, bonuses, and incentives increase the level of organizational flexibility in RAM airline company by (41%), thus accepting the third sub-hypothesis.

Fourth sub-hypothesis: «*The style of management and supervision influences the level of organizational flexibility within the RAM airline company*».

In order to determine the degree of influence of leadership and supervision style on the level of organizational flexibility within RAM airline company, a simple regression analysis was performed. Table n° 10 illustrates the impact of leadership and supervision style on the level of organizational flexibility.

Table 10. Impact of leadership and supervision style on the level of organizational flexibility

Sig.	F	R^2	r	Sig.	t	Coefficients	Variable
0.000	322.843	0.608	0.785	0.000	9.251	1.223	Regression constant
				0.000	20.142	0.897	Leadership and supervision style

The results of table 10 highlight the existence of a significant correlation between leadership and supervisory style and level of organizational flexibility within the RAM airline company, with a correlation coefficient of (0.785), which corresponds to a strong positive correlation.

The results also show that there is a significant and positive effect of leadership and supervision style on the level of organizational flexibility within the RAM airline company, with the calculated F value being (322,843) with a significance level of 0.000 (p-value < 0.05), which is greater than its tabular value.

This table shows the percentage of change in the level of organizational flexibility across leadership and supervision style, where the value of the regression coefficient reached (0.608), which means that the independent variable "*leadership and supervision style*" influence to the extent of (60.8%) the dependent variable «*organizational flexibility*», that is to say, the style of leadership and supervision contributes to strengthening the level of organizational flexibility within the RAM airline company to the extent of (60.8%). On this basis, the fourth sub-hypothesis is accepted.

Fifth sub-hypothesis: "*Professional development and development programs impact the level of organizational flexibility within the RAM airline company.*"

In order to determine the degree of influence of development and professional development programs on the level of organizational flexibility within the RAM airline company, a simple regression analysis was carried out.

Table 11 illustrates the impact of development and professional evolution programs on the level of organizational flexibility.

Table 11. Impact of development and professional development programs on the level of organizational flexibility

Sig.	F	R^2	r	Sig.	t	Coefficients	Variable
0.000	276.581	0.553	0.711	0.000	8.564	0.998	Regression constant
				0.000	16.537	0.751	Development and professional development programmes

The results presented in table1 1 show that there is a significant correlation between development and career progression programs and the level of organizational flexibility within the RAM airline company, with a correlation coefficient of (0.711), which corresponds to a strong positive correlation.

The results also show that development and professional development programs have a significant and positive effect on the level of organizational flexibility within the RAM airline company, with the calculated F value being (276,581) with a significance level of 0.000 (p-value < 0.05). It is greater than its tabular value, this table shows the rate of change in the level of organizational flexibility through development and professional development programs, where the value of the regression coefficient is (0.553), which means that the independent variable "development and professional development programs" has an impact of (55.3%) on the dependent variable "organizational flexibility", that is to say, professional development and development programmes contribute to increasing the level of organisational flexibility within the RAM airline company by (55.3%). On this basis, the fifth sub-hypothesis is accepted.

Fourth sub-hypothesis: "*Management and supervisory style influences the level of organizational flexibility within RAM airline company.*"

In order to determine the degree of influence of leadership and supervision style on the level of organizational flexibility within RAM airline company, a simple regression analysis was performed. Table 10 illustrates the impact of leadership and supervision style on the level of organizational flexibility.

Table 10. Impact of leadership and supervision style on the level of organizational flexibility

Sig.	F	R^2	r	Sig.	t	Coefficients	Variable
0.000	322.843	0.608	0.785	0.000	9.251	1.223	Regression constant
				0.000	20.142	0.897	Leadership and supervision style

The results of table 10 highlight the existence of a significant correlation between leadership and supervisory style and level of organizational flexibility within RAM airline company, with a correlation coefficient of (0.785), which corresponds to a strong positive correlation.

The results also show that there is a significant and positive effect of leadership and supervision style on the level of organizational flexibility within the RAM airline company, with the calculated F value being (322,843) with a significance level of 0.000 (p-value < 0.05), which is greater than its tabular value.

This table shows the percentage of change in the level of organizational flexibility across leadership and supervision style, where the value of the regression coefficient reached (0.608), which means that the independent variable "leadership and supervision style" influence to the extent of (60.8%) the dependent variable «organizational flexibility», that is to say, the style of leadership and supervision contributes to strengthening the level of organizational flexibility within the RAM airline to the extent of (60.8%). On this basis, the fourth sub-hypothesis is accepted.

Fifth sub-hypothesis: "*Professional development and development programs impact the level of organizational flexibility within the RAM airline company.*"

In order to determine the degree of influence of development and professional development programs on the level of organizational flexibility within the RAM airline company, a simple regression analysis was carried out.

Table n°11 illustrates the impact of development and professional evolution programs on the level of organizational flexibility.

Table 11. Impact of development and professional development programs on the level of organizational flexibility

Sig.	F	R^2	r	Sig.	t	Coefficients	Variable
0.000	276.581	0.553	0.711	0.000	8.564	0.998	Regression constant
				0.000	16.537	0.751	Development and professional development programmes

The results presented in table 11 show that there is a significant correlation between development and career progression programs and the level of organizational flexibility within the RAM airline company, with a correlation coefficient of (0.711), which corresponds to a strong positive correlation.

The results also show that development and professional development programs have a significant and positive effect on the level of organizational flexibility within the RAM airline company, with the calculated F value being (276,581) with a significance level of 0.000 (p-value < 0.05). It is greater than its tabular value. This table shows the rate of change in the level of organizational flexibility through development and professional development programs, where the value of the regression coefficient is (0.553), which means that the independent variable "*development and professional development programs*" has an impact of (55.3%) on the dependent variable "organizational flexibility," that is to say, professional development and development programs contribute to increasing the level of organizational flexibility within the RAM airline by (55.3%). On this basis, the fifth sub-hypothesis is accepted.

Sixth sub-hypothesis: "*Complaints and grievances affect the level of organizational flexibility within RAM airline company.*"

In order to determine the degree of influence of complaints and grievances on the level of organizational flexibility within the RAM airline company, a simple regression analysis was performed.

Table n°12 illustrates the impact of complaints and grievances on the level of organizational flexibility.

Table 12. Impact of complaints and remedies on the level of regulatory flexibility

Sig.	F	R^2	r	Sig.	t	Coefficients	Variable
0.000	241.236	0.399	0.602	0.000	6.521	0.625	Regression constant
				0.000	15.253	0,471	Complaints and claims

The results presented in table 12 show that there is a significant correlation between complaints and grievances and the level of organizational flexibility within the RAM airline company, with a correlation coefficient of (0,602), which corresponds to a positive average correlation. The results also show that complaints and grievances have a significant and positive effect on the level of organizational flexibility of the RAM airline company, with a calculated F-value of (241.236) and a significance level of 0.000 (p-value < 0.05). It is higher than its tabular value.

This table shows the rate of change in the level of regulatory flexibility through complaints and claims, where the value of the regression coefficient (0.399) means that the independent variable «complaints and claims» influences the dependent variable by 39.9% 'organizational flexibility,' that is to say, the complaints and claims contribute to strengthening the level of organizational flexibility of the RAM airline company by (39.9%). On this basis, the sixth sub-hypothesis is accepted.

8. RESULTS AND RECOMMENDATIONS

The study revealed an improvement in the level of QVT within the RAM airline company, whose six dimensions obtained a high score. The dimension relating to the availability of a healthy and suitable working environment comes first, followed by the style of leadership and supervision, then complaints and grievances, participation in decision-making, development and professional development programs, and finally salaries, bonuses, and incentives.

The results of the study also highlighted the high level of organizational flexibility within the RAM company, where the three dimensions have increased, with the dimension of strategic flexibility being the highest, followed by structural flexibility and finally operational flexibility. The results also showed that there is a strong positive correlation between QWL and organizational flexibility within the RAM airline company. Quality of work life also has a positive impact on the level of organizational flexibility in the RAM airline company.

Regarding the relationship and influence between QWL dimensions and organizational flexibility, the results of the study highlighted the existence of a significant and direct relationship between all dimensions and organizational flexibility. The power of this relationship was strong with regard to the dimensions "availability of a healthy work environment and appropriate working conditions," "*leadership and supervisory style*," and "*professional development and evolution programs*" but average with regard to participation in decision-making, salaries, bonuses and incentives, complaints, and grievances. Finally, the results of the study highlighted the existence of a moral and positive impact of each dimension of the quality of professional life on the level of organizational flexibility within the RAM airline company.

On this basis, we recommend that researchers recommend to the RAM airline company to improve its system of remuneration, bonuses, and incentives in order to adapt it to the current economic situation and offer a decent standard of living to its employees. Management should also support employees and encourage them to develop their skills, abilities, and knowledge through training and continuing education programs in order to improve their performance, which would result in an improvement of the company's organizational flexibility. In addition, the company must implement an incentive policy that encourages employees to express their opinions, ideas, and creative suggestions, which will strengthen the company's ability to cope with changes in a constantly evolving and unstable work environment for several years.

Given that the results of the study showed that QVT and its dimensions have a positive impact on strengthening the level of organizational flexibility, the company must provide all financial resources, material, and human resources necessary to constantly improve the quality of professional life, especially since the working environment in which it operates is unstable and constantly changing, and many unforeseen events require great responsiveness on the part of the company in order to ensure its continued growth and development in this work environment.

To confirm the results of our study, some other studies confirm that QWL constitutes a strategic lever for developing resilience and organizational agility (Aboramadan et al., 2020), as it allows retaining talents and reducing organizational stress to improve engagement and efficiency in organizations in the face of turbulences in the external environment (Loon et al., 2021). Moreover, investing in the quality of life at work appears as a strategic imperative for organizations that wish to strengthen their flexibility and ensure the sustainability of their growth. Finally, the study recommends involving employees in decision-making processes, developing plans for change and development, and listening to their opinions and suggestions in this regard in order to ensure their commitment to implement these plans and encourage them to redouble their efforts to carry them out.

REFERENCES

Aboramadan, M., Albashiti, B., Alharazin, H., & Zaidoune, S. (2020). Organizational culture, innovation and performance: A study from a non-Western context. *Journal of Management Development, 39*(4), 437–451. DOI: 10.1108/JMD-06-2019-0253

Alamdari, F., & Fagan, S. (2005). Impact of the adherence to the original low-cost model on the profitability of low-cost airlines. *Transport Reviews, 25*(3), 377–392. DOI: 10.1080/0144164050003874 8

Andrabi, C. H., & Rainayee, N. (2023). The key role of employee commitment in the relationship between flexible work arrangements and employee behavior. *Sustainability (Basel), 16*(22), 10067. DOI: 10.3390/su162210067

Ariani, M., Zulhawati, , & Budi Harsono, . (2023). Quality of work life in review of outsourcing, compensation, and quality human resources factor. *International Journal of Business Ecosystem & Strategy, 5*(1), 85–96. DOI: 10.36096/ijbes.v5i1.384

Ariffin, D. N., Abdullah Bandar, N. F., Sabil, S., Jayos, S., Amaran, M. A., & Hamdan, R. (2016). The relationship between flexible working arrangements and quality of work life among academicians in a selected public institution of higher learning in Kuching, Sarawak, Malaysia. *Journal of Cognitive Sciences and Human Development, 2*(2), 27–39. DOI: 10.33736/jcshd.197.2016

Bencheikh, A., & Dufour, N. (2019). *Comprendre les risques ressources humaines: véritable enjeu et création de valeur pour l'entreprise* (2e éd.). Gereso. Collection AGIR FACE AUX RISQUES. https://excerpts.numilog.com/books/9782378901387-extrait.pdf

Boxall, P., & Macky, K. (2009). Research and theory on high-performance work systems: Progressing the high-involvement stream. *Human Resource Management Journal, 19*(1), 3–23. DOI: 10.1111/j.1748-8583.2008.00082.x

Campo, A. M. D. V., Avolio, B., & Carlier, S. I. (2021). The relationship between telework, job performance, work-life balance and family supportive supervisor behaviours in the context of COVID 19. *Global Business Review*, 09721509211049918. Advance online publication. DOI: 10.1177/09721509211049918

Capnary, M. C., Rachmawati, R., & Agung, I. (2018). The influence of flexibility of work to loyalty and employee satisfaction mediated by work–life balance to employees with millennial generation background in Indonesia startup companies. *Business: Theory and Practice, 19*(0), 217–227. DOI: 10.3846/btp.2018.22

El Hammoumi, A., & El-Ouali, A. (2025). Impact of knowledge management on human resource performance: Case of the company Maroc Télécom. In Global, I. G. I. (Ed.), *Evolving Strategies for Organizational Management and Performance Evaluation.*, DOI: 10.4018/979-8-3373-0149-5.ch014

El-Ouali, A., & Jellouli, T. (2025). Training and development as effective strategies for human resource development in Moroccan companies. In *Innovative Recruitment and Retention for Employee Empowerment* (pp. 329–356). IGI Global Scientific Publishing., DOI: 10.4018/979-8-3693-6602-8.ch013

El-Sharkawy, S. A., Nafea, M. S., & Hassan, E. H. (2023). HRM and organizational learning in knowledge economy: Investigating the impact of happiness at work on organizational learning capability. *Future Business Journal*, *9*(1), 10. Advance online publication. DOI: 10.1186/s43093-023-00188-2

Els, V., Brouwers, M., & Lodewyk, R. B. (2021). Quality of work life: Effects on turnover intention and organisational commitment amongst selected South African manufacturing organisations. *SA Journal of Human Resource Management*, *19*, a1407. DOI: 10.4102/sajhrm.v19i0.1407

Fanggidae, R. E., Djani, W. M., & Neolaka, M. N. B. (2020). *Analysis of the effect of quality of work life and organizational culture on employee engagement at PT Jasa Raharja East Nusa Tenggara Branch.* International Journal of Economics, Business and Management Research, 4(2), 15–33. IJEBMR_507.pdf

Heslin, P. A., Keating, L. A., & Ashford, S. J. (2022). How career quality shapes scholars' impact in management research. *The Academy of Management Perspectives*, *36*(3), 412–432. DOI: 10.1016/j.jvb.2019.103324

Islam, R., & Namwong, S. (2020). *The relationship between work-life quality and employee engagement of ground operation airline staff: A case study of Lion Airline Company in Thailand.* Dusit Thani College Journal, 13(2), 265–282. https://so01.tci-thaijo.org/index.php/journaldtc/article/view/241071

Kim, B.-J. (2020). Unstable Jobs Harm Performance: The Importance of Psychological Safety and Organizational Commitment in Employees. *SAGE Open*, *10*(2), 1–12. DOI: 10.1177/2158244020920617

Linneberg, M. S., Trenca, M., & Nørreklit, H. (2021). Institutional work through empathic engagement. *European Management Journal*, *39*(1), 46–56. DOI: 10.1016/j.emj.2020.08.002 PMID: 38620643

Loon, M., Otaye-Ebede, L., & Stewart, J. (2021). The paradox of employee psychological well-being and organizational performance: A systematic review and research agenda. *Human Resource Management Review*, *31*(2), 100745. DOI: 10.1016/j.hrmr.2020.100745

Maphanga, M. E., Mokoena, A. B., & Isabirye, A. K. (2024). Leadership power bases influence on quality of work-life and intention to stay among retailing employees. *SA Journal of Human Resource Management*, *22*, 1–10. DOI: 10.4102/sajhrm.v22i0.2403

Medina Garrido, J. A., Biedma Ferrer, J. M., & Bogren, M. (2023). Organizational support for work–family life balance as an antecedent to the well-being of tourism employees in Spain. *Journal of Hospitality and Tourism Management*, *57*, 117–129. DOI: 10.1016/j.jhtm.2023.08.018

Medina-Garrido, J. A., Biedma-Ferrer, J. M., & Ramos-Rodriguez, A. R. (2023). *Relationship between work-family balance, employee well-being and job performance*. https://doi.org//arXiv.2401.13683DOI: 10.48550

Permarupan, P. Y. (2020). Human capital and organizational performance: A review. *International Journal of Academic Research in Business & Social Sciences*, *10*(2), 500–510. DOI: 10.6007/IJARBSS/v10-i2/6928

Permarupan, P. Y., Al Mamun, A., Ahmad Saufi, R., Hayat, N., & Samy, N. K. (2020). Effects of quality of work life on emotional exhaustion: A study among nurses in Malaysia. *Journal of Workplace Behavioral Health*, *35*(2), 117–136. DOI: 10.1080/15555240.2020.1720516

Ramayah, T., Lo, M. C., & Tarmizi, A. N. (2014). Quality of work life and turnover intention: A partial least square (PLS) approach. *Social Indicators Research*, *119*(1), 405–420. DOI: 10.1007/s11205-013-0486-5

Richman, A., Johnson, D., Rosenzweig, J., & Hill, E. (2021). Workplace flexibility for sustainable career satisfaction in the aviation sector. *Sustainability*, *13*(12), 6878. DOI: 10.3390/su13126878

Shin, D., & Konrad, A. M. (2017). Causal link between workforce diversity and organizational performance: Diversity reputation as a mediator. *Human Resource Management*, *56*(3), 317–336. DOI: 10.1002/hrm.21733

Teece, D. J. (2007). Explicating dynamic capabilities: The nature and microfoundations of (sustainable) enterprise performance. *Strategic Management Journal*, *28*(13), 1319–1350. DOI: 10.1002/smj.640

Teece, D. J., Peteraf, M., & Leih, S. (2016). Dynamic capabilities and organizational agility: Risk, uncertainty, and strategy in the innovation economy. *California Management Review*, *58*(4), 13–35. DOI: 10.1525/cmr.2016.58.4.13

Teo, S. T. T., Bentley, T., & Nguyen, D. (2020). Psychosocial work environment, work engagement, and employee commitment: A moderated mediation model. *International Journal of Hospitality Management*, *88*, 102415. Advance online publication. DOI: 10.1016/j.ijhm.2019.102415

Toscano, F., & Zappalà, S. (2020). Social isolation and stress as predictors of productivity perception and remote work satisfaction during the COVID-19 pandemic: The role of concern about the virus in a moderated double mediation. *Sustainability (Basel)*, *12*(23), 9804. DOI: 10.3390/su12239804

Wijngaards, I., King, O. C., Burger, M. J., & van Exel, J. (2022). Worker well-being: What it is, and how it should be measured. *Applied Research in Quality of Life*, *17*(2), 795–832. DOI: 10.1007/s11482-021-09930-w

Wong, K., Chan, A. H. S., & Teh, P.-L. (2020). How Is Work–Life Balance Arrangement Associated with Organisational Performance? A Meta Analysis. *International Journal of Environmental Research and Public Health*, *17*(12), 4446. Advance online publication. DOI: 10.3390/ijerph17124446 PMID: 32575807

Chapter 4
Sustainability and Strategic Human Resource Management in UAE Hospitality

Aisha Khan
http://orcid.org/0009-0009-7679-3661
International American University, Ras Al Khaimah, UAE

Sharif Ullah Jan
http://orcid.org/0000-0002-1281-4533
FATA University, FR Kohat, Pakistan

Faisal Khan
City University, Ajman, UAE

Ain Bemisal Alavi
Bath Spa University Academic Center, UAE

Saleem Mushtaq
Gulf University, Ajman, UAE

ABSTRACT

The United Arab Emirates (UAE) hospitality sector is experiencing a strategic shift as organizations incorporate sustainability principles into human resource management practices. This chapter presents a comprehensive framework to show how strategic HRM in the UAE hospitality industry can promote sustainability across environmental, social, and economic aspects. Based on recent literature (2020–2025), this review emphasizes green HRM initiatives that lessen environ-

DOI: 10.4018/979-8-2600-1845-3.ch004

mental impact, diversity and inclusion programs (including Emiratization efforts) that boost social sustainability, and employee well-being, that support both social and economic sustainability. The chapter discusses key concepts like green HRM, sustainable HRM, and the triple bottom line. The chapter discusses key concepts like green HRM, sustainable HRM, and the triple bottom line. To summarize, by incorporating sustainability into strategic HRM, UAE hotels can improve environmental performance, social responsibility, and economic resilience while aligning with the national vision and global best practices.

1. INTRODUCTION

The hospitality industry in the UAE is a vital engine of economic growth and diversification, contributing about 4% to 5% of the national GDP and employing hundreds of thousands of people (Bodolica, Spraggon, & Saleh, 2020). In 2022, the tourism and hospitality sector provided approximately 750,000 jobs, accounting for roughly 12% of the UAE's labor market (https://www.moet.gov.ae/en). However, the sector faces increasing pressure to operate sustainably, aligning with the UAE's national sustainability goals and global environmental standards. The UAE government has launched ambitious initiatives, such as the Net Zero 2050 Strategy, which aims for net-zero carbon emissions by 2050 and explicitly emphasizes sustainability across all sectors, including tourism and hospitality (UAE Government, 2024). At the same time, programs such as "We the UAE 2031" and the UAE Vision 2030/2071 agendas emphasize sustainable development and Emirati workforce participation as key pillars of long-term prosperity (Michael, Fotiadis, & Michael, 2024). These national agendas highlight that hospitality organizations must not only achieve financial success but also promote environmental responsibility and social equity. Strategic human resource management (SHRM) has become essential for sustainability in hospitality by aligning HR policies with organizational objectives. It supports environmental, social, and economic goals—known as the triple bottom line—and helps address sustainability challenges, thus enhancing organizational performance (Randev & Jha, 2019). Effectively managing HR sustainably influences employee behavior, organizational culture, and capabilities, thereby reducing ecological impact, improving social outcomes, and ensuring long-term success. This approach, called sustainable HRM, extends traditional strategic HRM by considering environmental, social, and economic factors (Randev & Jha, 2019; Alshehhi, 2024; Bodolica et al., 2020). Its purpose is to minimize negative impacts on employees, society, and the environment while boosting organizational performance.

This chapter examines how strategic HRM in the UAE hospitality sector can support sustainability across environmental, social, and economic dimensions. It focuses on four HRM domains, i.e., Green HRM, diversity and inclusion, employee well-being, and long-term workforce planning, and their roles in promoting sustainability pillars. Green HRM addresses environmental goals, diversity and inclusion, and employee well-being, targeting social aims, and long-term planning supports economic sustainability by maintaining competitive advantage and human capital. An original framework links these HRM strategies to sustainability outcomes, considering local factors like Emiratisation and a multicultural workforce.

The chapter's rest is structured as follows. First, we review key concepts and recent findings on sustainable HRM, covering Green HRM, inclusion, well-being, and workforce planning, with a focus on hospitality and the UAE. Next, we present a conceptual framework that integrates these elements, illustrating how strategic HR practices foster environmental, social, and economic sustainability in hotels. A figure and table illustrate this framework, along with HR interventions for each sustainability pillar. We then discuss its implications for UAE hospitality managers and for HRM and sustainability research. Finally, we summarize insights, limitations, and future research directions in sustainable HRM in hospitality.

2. LITERATURE REVIEW

2.1 Strategic HRM and the Triple Bottom Line in Hospitality

Sustainability in business, often described by the triple bottom line (TBL), includes environmental, social, and economic aspects. In hospitality, achieving TBL goals requires coordinated efforts, including strategic HRM, which aligns HR policies with sustainability. Recent research introduces sustainable HRM, which integrates environmental, social, and economic factors into workforce management (Yew Lim et al., 2024; Alshehhi, 2024). Sustainable HRM aims for long-term success, ensuring HR practices foster a resilient workforce, minimize harm, and create stakeholder value. It explores how balancing economic outcomes, such as productivity, with social and environmental goals can be a rewarding challenge. This approach addresses 'sustainability paradoxes," where short-term gains might seem to conflict with long-term well-being and ecological care. Many thoughtful scholars believe that these different aspects can actually work together to strengthen each other; having an engaged workforce not only boosts productivity but also cuts costs and bolsters a company's reputation through sustainable practices. Supporting this, numerous studies have shown that when employees feel better and more valued, absenteeism drops and overall performance improves. Additionally, when companies incorporate sustainability into their HR strategies, they often gain a valuable competitive advantage (Yew Lim et al., 2024; Podgorodnichenko et al., 2020).

In the hospitality sector of the UAE, strategic HRM for sustainability must consider unique factors, such as the multicultural workforce comprising employees from dozens of nationalities, and the government's focus on the knowledge economy and local employment, as outlined in Vision 2021's Emiratisation goal. Managing cultural diversity through inclusive policies, training, and equal opportunities is key for social sustainability and benefiting from diverse talent. Additionally, labor laws now include Emiratisation quotas and training, with regulators urging firms to invest in employee development to improve their sustainability rankings. Dubai's hotel sustainability guidelines incorporate HR aspects—like staff training, community engagement, and inclusion, highlighting HR practices as vital to hospitality sustainability.

2.2 Green HRM and Environmental Sustainability

Green Human Resource Management (GHRM) integrates environmental principles into HR practices to promote sustainability and reduce ecological impact. It has gained importance as organizations face climate change. In the hospitality industry, which has a significant ecological footprint, GHRM encompasses green recruitment, training, performance management, and eco-friendly incentives. Its goal is to foster a culture of sustainability by equipping employees with the knowledge and motivation they need. Research shows GHRM benefits both the environment and organizations by reducing resource use, ensuring compliance, and boosting employee engagement. Embedding environmental values can enhance a company's reputation and stakeholder trust. A UAE hotel study found GHRM improved environmental performance, competitiveness, and employee retention, as staff felt pride and purpose through sustainability efforts. This indicates GHRM supports environmental preservation and addresses turnover by increasing job satisfaction and loyalty. GHRM encourages green innovation and engagement; initiatives like recycling and waste reduction promote bottom-up sustainability efforts. Hassanein et al. (2024) showed GHRM spurs employee-led green innovations in UAE hotels, improving efficiency and environmental and economic outcomes. Hotels with proactive environmental programs tend to report higher customer satisfaction and better market positioning, attracting eco-conscious clients. Integrating Green HRM into strategic planning is crucial; superficial efforts can breed cynicism. When leadership makes sustainability part of the core mission, initiatives seem more genuine. The UAE's tourism sector promotes sustainability through certifications like the Dubai Sustainable Tourism Stamp, which encourages hotels to adopt GHRM practices. Given tourism's high energy use and air travel, which contribute to greenhouse gases, hotels must meet national carbon reduction goals. Engaging employees in energy-saving and eco-friendly practices is vital to attaining these sustainability targets.

2.3 Diversity and Inclusion for Social Sustainability

Social sustainability within the workplace encompasses fairness, equity, and respect, thereby exerting a positive influence on the community. In Human Resource Management (HRM), this entails the implementation of non-discriminatory practices, equitable developmental opportunities, and the cultivation of inclusivity that cherishes diversity. The United Arab Emirates (UAE) boasts a diverse hospitality workforce comprising various nationalities, ethnicities, languages, and religions collaborating harmoniously. Effective management of diversity and inclusion (D&I) is pivotal for the success of hotels, as diverse teams tend to generate superior ideas, enhance service quality, and foster innovation (Warner & Moonesar, 2019). Research by Haak-Saheem and Brewster (2017) indicates a correlation between workforce diversity and organizational performance, particularly when inclusive HR practices such as bias-aware training are employed. Employees who act respectfully are typically more motivated, exhibit lower turnover intentions, and contribute to cost reductions. Challenges in this domain include the existence of "glass ceilings," occupational segregation, and gender disparities, whereby certain groups face restricted advancement and women are often underrepresented due to prevailing cultural norms. Biases, whether formal or informal, may result in tokenism instead of genuine empowerment, thereby undermining social sustainability. To address these issues, hospitality HR practitioners should adopt transparent criteria for hiring and promotions, implement diversity training programs, establish mentorship initiatives, and develop substantive inclusion objectives.

A cornerstone of diversity and inclusion (D&I) in the UAE is the Emiratisation policy. As mentioned, Emiratisation is a government-led strategy aimed at increasing the employment of UAE nationals in the private sector, including tourism and hospitality. Socially, this policy aligns with sustainability by aiming to provide fair employment opportunities for locals and ensure that the benefits of economic growth are shared with the citizen population. For the hospitality industry, greater Emirati participation also enhances cultural sustainability – it helps preserve and showcase Emirati culture and hospitality traditions in an industry dominated by foreign influences. As one UAE Ministry of Economy report highlights, *Emiratis can best represent the country's culture and hospitality to visitors*. Recognizing this, some hotels have begun initiatives to attract Emiratis, for example, by offering management trainee programs for UAE nationals, collaborating with local hospitality schools, and tailoring work conditions to be more appealing (such as providing daytime shifts for those who prefer not to work late hours). There are signs of progress: by early

2025, over 131,000 Emiratis were working in the private sector across industries (up from much lower figures just a few years prior), surpassing government targets. This surge is partly due to NAFIS and related incentives (like salary support and training subsidies for companies hiring Emiratis). In hospitality specifically, while the absolute number of Emirati employees remains modest, they are increasingly visible in customer-facing roles in some upscale hotels and as entrepreneurs in niche tourism ventures. For HR managers, the implication is that Emiratisation should be embraced as an aspect of D&I – not treated as merely a quota to fulfill, but as an opportunity to enrich the workforce with local talent. Best practices include establishing mentorship where experienced managers (expat or national) coach young Emirati employees, creating peer support groups, and recognizing the contributions of Emirati staff in company communications to reinforce their belonging.

Inclusion in sustainable HRM includes dimensions like age, abilities, and more. UAE hospitality now has multiple generations working together, from Gen Z to Baby Boomers. Managing inter-generational diversity is crucial since expectations differ—young employees seek growth and balance, older ones value stability. Training HR and leaders can improve cohesion and knowledge transfer. Inclusion also covers people with disabilities, with UAE law promoting their employment. Dubai's design and hotel standards focus on accessibility in service and hiring. A socially sustainable hotel should have HR policies to recruit, support, and adapt to employees with disabilities, ensuring equal opportunities.

2.4 Employee Well-Being and Employee Retention

Ensuring employee well-being is crucial for social sustainability and organizational success. It includes physical, psychological, and emotional health, as well as job satisfaction and work-life balance. Hospitality employees face high stress, long hours, demanding tasks, and challenging climates, especially in UAE hotels, leading to burnout and high turnover. Promoting well-being is vital for social responsibility and workforce stability, boosting customer service, engagement, and business outcomes. Neglecting it causes high turnover, absenteeism, lower productivity, and higher healthcare costs. A 2024 UAE survey found only 29% of staff felt mentally well at work, underscoring the need for HR interventions.

Strategic HRM approaches to boost wellbeing in hospitality involve employee-focused practices. A key practice is fair and adequate pay and benefits, as studies in the UAE show low wages and lack of benefits lead staff to leave for other sectors (Qasim, 2020). Offering competitive salaries, fair tip distribution, healthcare, and allowances (common in the Gulf) helps reduce financial stress and shows staff they are valued. Reasonable working hours and leave policies are also vital. While shift work is unavoidable, employers can enforce rest, rotate weekends off, and offer annual leave. Some UAE hotels are improving duty rosters to allow more family time, which is critical as many expats are separated from families. Work- life balance initiatives like flexible schedules, staff recreation areas, or on- site child-care (especially in large resorts) can boost retention. Shorter hours or predictable schedules are associated with higher retention in UAE (Qasim, 2020). Flexible work arrangements and work- family balance options have significantly increased Emirati employee retention in Ras Al Khaimah' s private sector (Alshehhi, 2024). Even small concessions, such as shift swaps or split shifts, can enhance staff satisfaction. Ensuring a safe, supportive environment is also crucial, including physical safety in operational areas and psychological safety from bullying and pressure. Training managers in supportive leadership and emotional intelligence reduces stress and fosters commitment. Leadership style influences turnover; compassionate managers who communicate well and show appreciation help retain staff (Lim et al., 2024). In Dubai hotels, leadership support, training, and fair pay are top retention factors, emphasizing the importance of daily managerial behavior.

Providing career development opportunities enhances wellbeing by meeting growth needs. Regular training, clear paths, and internal promotions foster job security and motivation. In the UAE, where many see hospitality roles as stepping stones, showing a future path encourages retention, as recent research indicates training had a stronger impact on retention than pay (Lim et al., 2024).

2.5 Long-Term Workforce Planning and Economic Sustainability

The third pillar of sustainability is economic sustainability, which in HRM involves practices that secure the long-term viability and productivity of an organization's human capital. It focuses on maintaining and improving financial health and competitive position through workforce planning and talent management strategies. In sectors like the UAE's hospitality industry, which continues to grow with new hotels and tourists, long-term planning is vital. Proactive HR practices prevent labor shortages, reduce reliance on transient workers, and ensure succession in key roles. This includes forecasting and aligning HR with business strategies, anticipating industry changes like automation or AI, and preparing the workforce accordingly. Using data to project staffing needs and developing pipelines helps hotels capitalize on market opportunities while maintaining service quality. Combining workforce and financial planning allows better resource allocation and risk mitigation. For instance, investing in local talent and training may incur initial costs but benefits long-term stability by reducing turnover and the need for expatriate recruitment. Additionally, workforce planning must adapt to UAE labor laws, visa rules, and talent availability. Many hotels adopt a "core-periphery" model—maintaining permanent staff while using seasonal workers during peak periods—balancing cost efficiency with service quality. Over-reliance on temporary workers may impact service consistency, so managing this balance is essential.

An economically sustainable HR approach focuses on optimizing employee retention to avoid high turnover, which destroys value through hiring and training costs and lost productivity. Strategies like Green HRM, D&I, and well-being programs can improve retention. For instance, a Dubai hotel chain halved its annual turnover after implementing such programs, saving costs and boosting guest satisfaction. Employee retention and engagement are key for economic sustainability, as engaged staff are more efficient and make fewer errors. Reviewing HRM practices' links to sustainability, we develop a conceptual framework connecting HRM practices in UAE hospitality to sustainability pillars and overall performance. This framework guides understanding and implementing sustainability-oriented HRM.

2.6 Framework Development

Figure 1. Conceptual framework linking strategic HRM practices to the three pillars of sustainability in the UAE hospitality.

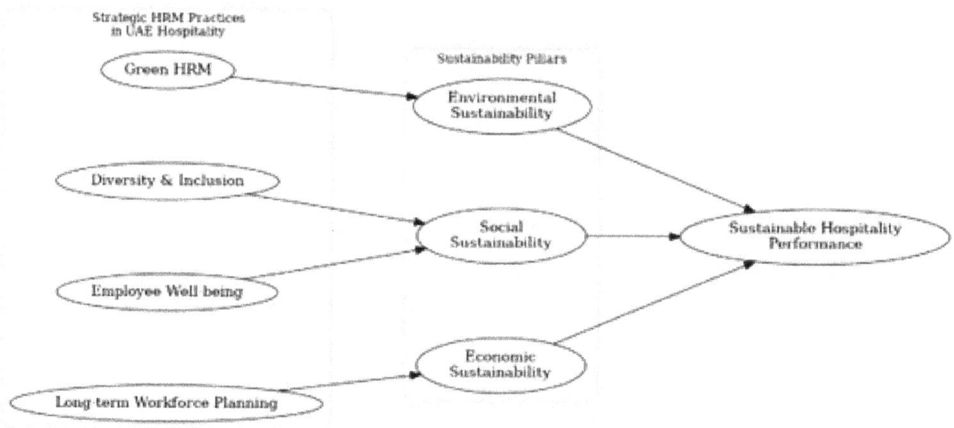

The framework in Figure 1 links strategic HRM practices with sustainability pillars (environmental, social, economic), contributing to sustainable performance in UAE hospitality. HRM practices are grouped into Green HRM, Diversity & Inclusion, Employee Well-being, and Workforce Planning, each supporting a specific sustainability pillar while also influencing others. Green HRM is mainly connected to Environmental Sustainability through eco-friendly recruitment, training, and promoting eco-friendly behaviors, which reduce environmental impact. It also indirectly supports Social (by fostering shared values and job satisfaction) and

Economic (via cost savings and reputation) pillars. The outcome, Sustainable Hospitality Performance, reflects overall organizational success achieved by balancing these dimensions.

Diversity & Inclusion (D&I) are strongly linked to *Social Sustainability*. This reflects the role of D&I practices in fostering an equitable and inclusive workplace. By implementing unbiased hiring, promoting equal opportunities for advancement, and fostering an inclusive culture, HRM supports social sustainability goals such as gender equality, intercultural harmony, and decent work conditions (all of which align with several UN Sustainable Development Goals as well). Within the framework, D&I practices enhance social outcomes for employees. For example, reducing discrimination and increasing the representation of Emiratis, women, and other groups in various roles contributes to a fair and just workplace. This, in turn, can enhance the hotel's social license to operate and community relations. D&I also has an economic dimension: research and real cases show that well-managed diversity leads to better decision-making and innovation, which can improve organizational performance (yielding economic benefits). Thus, while D&I primarily addresses the social pillar by enhancing employee well-being and community impact, it also contributes to economic sustainability by leveraging the advantages of a diverse workforce. The framework encapsulates this by ultimately channeling the results of D&I into sustainable performance (via the social pillar toward overall performance).

Employee well-being, including health, safety, work-life balance, and engagement programs, is part of Social Sustainability. Ensuring employees are healthy, safe, and satisfied is a social duty that boosts work quality and upholds human dignity. It also positively impacts economic sustainability, as content employees are more productive, provide better service, and are less likely to leave, reducing costs. For example, a UAE hotel that invests in staff accommodation and recreation not only fulfills a social responsibility but also experiences lower absenteeism and improved guest ratings, enhancing its financial performance.

Long-term workforce planning is primarily connected to economic sustainability within the framework. This encompasses strategic HR activities, such as forecasting future staffing needs, succession planning, training and development, and aligning the HR strategy with the hotel's long-term business strategy. By planning for talent requirements and developing employees for future roles, HRM ensures that the organization can sustainably meet its service standards and expansion plans without facing talent shortages or excessive labor costs. This directly supports economic sustainability by enhancing organizational agility and resource optimization (e.g., avoiding the high cost of last-minute recruitment or the operational risk of staff shortfalls). Long-term planning also ties in with financial prudence – for instance, creating a stable pipeline of trained supervisors internally can be more cost-effective than hiring externally at higher salaries. Furthermore, effective workforce planning incorporates elements of Emiratisation and localization strategy in the UAE, which has economic implications (reducing reliance on expatriate labor over time and investing in local human capital). As illustrated in the framework, the outcomes of workforce planning inform the economic pillar, which in turn drives sustainable performance (e.g., profitability, market share) for the hotel. There is also a secondary social aspect: a company that practices careful workforce planning typically offers clearer career paths and job security, which boosts employee morale (social pillar). In practice, these linkages mean that something like a robust management trainee program (workforce planning tool) not only ensures future leadership (economic benefit) but also increases current employee engagement and loyalty (social benefit).

The Sustainable Hospitality Performance, shown on the right of Figure 1, is the goal where a hotel is financially strong, environmentally responsible, and socially respected. Arrows from each sustainability pillar to this outcome show all three contribute to performance. For example, environmental efforts like energy savings or green certification can cut costs and attract eco-conscious guests, boosting financial performance and brand value. Social achievements like high employee satisfaction and community programs can improve service, reputation, and reduce turnover, enhancing overall performance. Economic sustainability (profitability and growth) provides resources for further environmental and social initiatives, creating a loop. Our framework suggests that strategic HRM practices targeting each pillar help a hotel thrive sustainably.

To provide a concrete summary, Table 1 below outlines the key HRM strategies under each sustainability pillar, along with their specific initiatives and expected outcomes in the UAE hospitality context:

Table 1. Strategic HRM initiatives

Sustainability Dimension	*HRM Strategies and Initiatives*	*Expected Outcomes in UAE Hospitality*
Environmental Sustainability	- Implement Green HRM (green recruitment, training, rewards) - Employee involvement in eco-initiatives (green teams, suggestion schemes) - Sustainability awareness programs for staff	Reduced resource usage (energy, water) and carbon footprint[REMOVED HYPERLINK FIELD]; Improved environmental compliance; Cost savings from efficiency; Enhanced eco-friendly brand image attracting guests (Hassanein et al., 2024).
Social Sustainability	- Enforce Diversity & Inclusion (bias-free hiring, multicultural training, inclusive policies) - Emiratisation programs (internships, mentorship for UAE nationals) - Employee well-being programs (health & safety, counseling, work-life balance, recognition)	Higher employee satisfaction and engagement (Warner & Moonesar, 2019) [REMOVED HYPERLINK FIELD]; Lower turnover and absenteeism (Qasim, 2020)[REMOVED HYPERLINK FIELD]; Enhanced service quality through diverse perspectives; Stronger community and government relations (due to Emiratisation and social initiatives) moet.gov.ae.
Economic Sustainability	- Long-term workforce planning (talent pipelines, succession planning) - Continuous training & development (skills for future needs, leadership development) - Performance management aligned with sustainability goals (including economic targets)	Stable supply of skilled labor aligned with hotel growth; Reduced recruitment and turnover costs (higher retention); Higher productivity and innovation from skilled, experienced staff; Sustained financial performance and competitive advantage (Randev & Jha, 2019).

This chapter's framework synthesizes recent studies and adapts them to the UAE hospitality sector, emphasizing that strategic HRM links environmental, social, and economic goals. HRM practices support different sustainability facets, often reinforcing each other. For example, training in sustainable practices boosts employee well-being and efficiency. Promoting diversity can unlock new market segments and ideas. A profitable business can invest more in its people and green technologies. Practically, the framework guides managers: to achieve sustainability, invest in HR practices using strategies in Table 1 and focusing on the triple bottom line. Hotels in the UAE can see positive effects on employees, the environment, and finances. The next section discusses implications for managers and stakeholders, offers implementation recommendations, and suggests areas for further research.

3. IMPLICATIONS

3.1 Theoretical Implications

The development of the above framework contributes to the growing body of knowledge on sustainable HRM, particularly in the context of emerging markets and the hospitality industry. The framework integrates multiple streams of literature – Green HRM, diversity management, well-being, and strategic HR planning – under the umbrella of sustainability, demonstrating how they collectively support the triple bottom line. Theoretically, this underscores the idea that HRM should not be viewed in a narrow, siloed manner (e.g., "HR's job is only to manage employees for productivity"), but rather as a holistic function that can drive sustainable development goals within organizations. This chapter's focus on UAE hospitality provides a nuanced understanding that context matters: factors like cultural diversity, government policies (e.g., Emiratisation), and industry characteristics (e.g., high customer contact and labor intensity) shape how sustainable HRM is enacted and what outcomes are prioritized. For instance, our framework explicitly incorporates Emiratisation – a context-specific HR strategy – linking it to social and economic sustainability. This suggests that general models of sustainable HRM (such as those developed in Western contexts) should be adapted to local conditions. Scholars should consider contextual variables (national policy, workforce composition, cultural norms) as moderators or integral components in theories of sustainable HRM.

The framework connects micro HR practices with macro sustainability outcomes. It draws on theories like the Ability-Motivation-Opportunity (AMO) in HRM, Social Exchange Theory, and the Resource-Based View (RBV). The review supports that investing in employees through well-being, development, and engagement creates a sustainable competitive advantage, aligning with RBV and human capital sustainability. It also shows how environmental and social outcomes relate to financial results, exemplifying the triple bottom line at the organizational level.

For researchers, this framework invites empirical testing and refinement. Future studies could use it to hypothesize, for example: Do hotels with higher Green HRM perform better environmentally and retain employees? Does diversity climate mediate the link between inclusion training and customer satisfaction in multicultural teams? Do well-being initiatives improve service quality or profitability? These relationships can be tested in the field. The UAE hospitality sector, with rapid growth and data access, is ideal for such research. The framework also suggests examining interdependencies, like whether Green HRM's effect on performance is enhanced by strong diversity and well-being practices, aligning with HRM "bundles" or high-performance systems for sustainability. This chapter offers a foundation for quantitative research, possibly using a balanced scorecard to measure outcomes across sustainability dimensions and link them to HRM metrics.

3.2 Practical Implications for Hospitality Managers

For practitioners—hotel executives, HR managers, and sustainability officers—the key takeaway is that sustainability relies on strategic people management, not just the installation of solar panels or the production of CSR reports. The human element can make or break efforts in the hospitality industry. Managers should prioritize HR initiatives within their sustainability plans. The following actionable implications emerge:

- **Integrate Sustainability into HR Strategy and Policy:** Hotels should formally include sustainability objectives in their HRM policies. This could involve updating the HR mission statement to reflect commitments to environmental sustainability, employee well-being, and diversity. By institutionalizing these values, HR departments become key players in sustainability governance. For example, an HR policy might state that the hotel aims to become an employer of choice for UAE nationals (supporting Emiratisation) or to provide a safe and healthy workplace that exceeds legal requirements (supporting well-being and SDG 8 on decent work).
- **Implement Targeted Green HR Practices:** Managers should develop green HR programs such as staff training on sustainability (e.g., energy-saving techniques for maintenance staff, waste sorting for kitchen staff, sustainable procurement for purchasing teams). They can also introduce green performance indicators – for example, housekeeping staff could be evaluated partly on how effectively they implement linen reuse programs or minimize chemical use. HR can collaborate with engineering or sustainability teams to reward departments that meet environmental targets, such as reducing electricity consumption by X%. These practices foster accountability and motivate employees to engage in environmentally friendly behaviors daily. The practical implication is to integrate green thinking into the employee lifecycle, from job descriptions (emphasizing a "preference for candidates with knowledge of sustainable practices") to onboarding (highlighting the hotel's green values) to continuous improvement (soliciting employee ideas for eco-initiatives and implementing the best ones).
- **Strengthen Diversity and Inclusion Initiatives:** Hotels should regularly train staff on cultural competence and unconscious bias, especially managers. Establish diversity councils including employees from various backgrounds to advise on inclusion. Review recruitment and promotion data for biases,

such as overlooking certain nationalities or genders for roles. Corrective actions like outreach and mentorship should follow if biases are found. For Emiratisation, HR must partner with government and educational institutions (e.g., Emirates Academy, vocational schools) to create pipelines for young Emiratis through internships, open days, and fast-track programs. This fosters an attractive, inclusive workplace, reducing turnover and boosting reputation. Managers can also utilize government schemes like UAE's NAFIS, offering salary subsidies and training reimbursements, aligning social impact with business benefits.

- **Prioritize Employee Well-Being and Engagement:** Hotel managers should proactively support employee well-being by conducting surveys to identify issues like long hours or insufficient rest, then addressing these with creative scheduling or extra staff. Providing wellness resources, such as counseling, fitness facilities, healthy meals, and recognizing good work with rewards, can boost morale. Leadership support and ongoing training, as highlighted in the Dubai hotel study, are key to retention. When staff feel cared for, they deliver better hospitality, fostering high morale and service quality.
- **Adopt Long-Term Talent Development Plans:** This means shifting from ad-hoc to planned hiring. HR should maintain a 2–3-year manpower plan, considering expansion, attrition, and new skills like digital marketing and data analytics in hospitality. Succession plans for critical roles should identify internal candidates for future leadership, grooming them via rotations and training. Hotels can establish graduate trainee programs to develop young talent for higher roles. Offering clear career paths, such as waiter to captain to supervisor, encourages retention and career growth, not short-term employment. Budgeting for training is an investment, vital for the UAE's goal to be a leading tourist destination. Training budgets should reflect this strategic importance, ensuring workforce skills and stability remain competitive.
- **Measure and Communicate Sustainability Performance:** Managers should monitor metrics for HR initiatives and sustainability outcomes, such as turnover, employee satisfaction, training hours, diversity ratios, energy use, Emiratis employed, and health indicators. Measuring these helps identify effective initiatives and areas for improvement. Celebrating successes, such as high satisfaction ratings or awards, can boost recruitment and appeal to socially conscious guests. Internal sharing of sustainability wins, such as reducing food waste, fosters employee pride and motivation, thereby enhancing well-being and engagement.

Implementing these practices needs top leadership commitment. Hotel managers and owners should champion that "our people are our greatest asset in achieving sustainability." The main challenge is cultural—shifting from a focus on short-term financial metrics to valuing environmental and social metrics equally requires persistent advocacy and showing business benefits. The evidence and cases discussed demonstrate tangible benefits like cost savings, guest satisfaction, and risk reduction from sustainable HRM.

3.3 Policy Implications

Beyond individual companies, there are implications for industry associations and policymakers. The UAE government could consider offering recognition and incentives for hospitality businesses that excel in sustainable HRM. For example, establishing an award for "Sustainable Hospitality Employer of the Year" or including HR sustainability criteria in hotel star ratings can encourage more hotels to adopt these practices. The government is already making progress in this area (e.g., DET's sustainability requirements that include staff-related criteria, dubaidet.gov.ae); ongoing support, such as training toolkits for smaller hotels on implementing Green HRM or hosting inclusion workshops, would be helpful, especially since not all operators have access to the same resources as international chains. Additionally, expanding partnerships between educational institutions and the hospitality industry can help ensure a continuous development of talent (addressing economic sustainability at a sector level) and promote sustainability values among future hospitality professionals.

4. CHALLENGES AND MITIGATION

Implementing sustainable HRM strategies in hospitality faces challenges like costs, employee skepticism, and language barriers. Managers should adopt a long-term view, run pilot programs, involve employees, ensure translated training, and demonstrate follow-through. Success leads to loyal staff, better guest experiences, risk reduction, and competitive advantage, especially in the UAE.

5. CONCLUSION

Sustainability in the hospitality industry is a multifaceted challenge, encompassing ecological responsibility, social equity, and economic viability. This chapter has argued that strategic human resource management is a linchpin for advancing sustainability on all these fronts, especially in the UAE's vibrant hospitality sector. We set out to explore how strategic HRM can support environmental, social, and economic sustainability in UAE hotels, and we delivered an integrated analysis and framework that underscores the vital role of people management in sustainable hospitality excellence.

REFERENCES

Alshehhi, R. (2024). *Increasing Turnover Rate among Emirati Employees in the Private Sector in Ras Al Khaima*. [Working paper]. (Findings discussed in text on factors affecting Emirati retention)

Bodolica, V., Spraggon, M., & Saleh, N. (2020). Innovative leadership in leisure and entertainment industry: The case of the UAE as a global tourism hub. *International Journal of Islamic and Middle Eastern Finance and Management, 13*(2), 323–337. DOI: 10.1108/IMEFM-12-2019-0521

Dubai Department of Economy and Tourism (DET). (2025). *Hotel Classification System – Sustainability Requirements Documentation*. Dubai, UAE: DET. (Official guidelines aligning hotel operations and HR practices with UAE sustainability agendas)

Hassanein, F., Daouk, A., Yassine, D., Bou Zakhem, N., Elsayed, R., & Saleh, A. (2024). Green Human Resource Management and Employee Retention in the Hotel Industry of UAE: The Mediating Effect of Green Innovation. *Sustainability (Basel), 16*(11), 4668. DOI: 10.3390/su16114668

Hassanein, F., Daouk, A., Yassine, D., Bou Zakhem, N., Elsayed, R., & Saleh, A. (2024). Green human resource management and employee retention in the hotel industry of UAE: The mediating effect of green innovation. *Sustainability (Basel), 16*(11), 4668. DOI: 10.3390/su16114668

Michael, N., Fotiadis, A. K., & Michael, I. (2024). Emiratization and hospitality sector destination branding of Dubai: An impact analysis. *Journal of Human Resources in Hospitality & Tourism, 23*(2), 171–193. DOI: 10.1080/15332845.2024.2282197

Ministry of Economy, UAE. (2024, April 25). *Hospitality Advisory Committee reviews initiatives outlined in UAE Tourism Strategy 2031 and their role in boosting the national hospitality sector's competitiveness* (Press release). Abu Dhabi: UAE Ministry of Economy.

Podgorodnichenko, N., Edgar, F., & McAndrew, I. (2020). The role of HRM in developing sustainable organizations: Contemporary challenges and opportunities. *Human Resource Management Review, 30*(3), 100708. DOI: 10.1016/j.hrmr.2019.04.001

Qasim, A. (2020). The impacts of high employee turnover in the UAE hospitality industry. In *Human Capital in the Middle East: A UAE Perspective* (pp. 73–91). Springer International Publishing. DOI: 10.1007/978-3-030-42211-0_4

Randev, H., & Jha, S. (2019). Sustainable Human Resource Management: Practices, Policies, and Prospects. In *HRM Practices for a Sustainable Future* (pp. 45-62). (Referenced for definitions of Green HRM and sustainable HRM's impact on ecology and society)

Randev, K. K., & Jha, J. K. (2019). Sustainable human resource management: A literature-based introduction. *NHRD Network Journal*, *12*(3), 241–252. DOI: 10.1177/2631454119873495

Warner, R., & Moonesar, I. A. (2019). Diversity management: the case of the United Arab Emirates. In *Diversity within diversity management* (Vol. 21, pp. 41–63). Emerald Publishing Limited. DOI: 10.1108/S1877-636120190000021003

Yew Lim, K., Lynn, H., Owee Tan, K., & Dennen, V. C. (2024). The influencing factors and employee retention in Dubai's hotel industry. *Journal/Proceedings of Hospitality Management* (in press). (Study finding training, compensation, and leadership support significantly affect retention in UAE hotels)

Chapter 5
Strategic Human Resource Management in the UAE Hotel Industry: Technology, Service Excellence, and Sustainable Growth

Varinder Singh Rana
http://orcid.org/0009-0008-8562-8265
City University, Ajman, UAE

Maher Bani
City University, Ajman, UAE

Fatmah Younis
City University, Ajman, UAE

Shorena Okujava
Hilton Garden Inn, Ras Al Khaimah, UAE

Nour Mazloum
City University, Ajman, UAE

ABSTRACT

The hotel industry in the United Arab Emirates (UAE) has emerged as one of the world's most dynamic and competitive sectors, contributing significantly to the country's economic diversification agenda. Human capital is a key driver of service excellence in this industry, where customer experiences and satisfaction are directly linked to employee performance. Strategic Human Resource Management (SHRM)

DOI: 10.4018/979-8-2600-1845-3.ch005

offers a holistic framework to align human resource practices with organizational strategy, fostering competitiveness, sustainability, and long-term success. This chapter examines the role of SHRM in the UAE hotel industry, focusing on the integration of technology and employee engagement as mediating mechanisms. Using a quantitative research design, data was collected from 375 employees and managers across luxury, midscale, and budget hotels in the UAE. Partial Least Squares Structural Equation Modeling (PLS-SEM) was used to test three hypotheses concerning the relationships between SHRM, technology integration, employee engagement, and organizational performance.

INTRODUCTION

The hotel industry is a cornerstone of the hospitality sector, serving as a critical driver of tourism, international trade, and economic development worldwide. Globally, the hotel industry contributes billions annually to GDP and provides employment opportunities for millions of individuals across diverse cultural and professional backgrounds (World Travel & Tourism Council, 2022). Within this highly service-oriented industry, the quality of human resources is paramount, as employees represent the primary interface between hotels and their guests. Unlike manufacturing industries, where products can be standardized, hotels depend on service encounters that are shaped by employees' skills, motivation, and cultural sensitivity (Nickson, 2013).

The United Arab Emirates (UAE) represents a unique context for the hotel industry, given its ambitious vision of positioning itself as a global tourism hub. Cities such as Dubai, Abu Dhabi, and Ras Al Khaimah have become world-class destinations, hosting luxury hotels that consistently set benchmarks in innovation and service quality. The UAE government's **Tourism Strategy 2031** emphasizes expanding hotel capacity, improving guest experiences, and promoting sustainable tourism. The hotel sector not only contributes significantly to GDP but also provides employment to a highly diverse workforce comprising both expatriates and Emiratis (Deloitte, 2020).

Despite rapid growth, the UAE hotel industry faces persistent challenges. High employee turnover rates, reliance on expatriate labor, rising competition, and changing customer expectations demand innovative approaches to human resource management (Alnaqbi, 2011). Furthermore, the integration of Emiratization policies, which prioritize national employment, requires strategic workforce planning. The adoption of digital technologies in HR functions and hotel operations further adds complexity to workforce management.

Strategic Human Resource Management (SHRM) emerges as a vital solution to these challenges. Unlike traditional HRM, which emphasizes administrative efficiency, SHRM aligns HR practices with long-term organizational strategy, integrating talent management, performance evaluation, retention strategies, and employee engagement with overall business goals (Boxall & Purcell, 2016). In the hotel sector, SHRM is crucial because service delivery depends on employees' ability and willingness to perform at high standards.

Technology further strengthens SHRM by transforming HR practices. Tools such as Human Resource Information Systems (HRIS), AI-driven recruitment platforms, e-learning systems, and analytics allow hotels to streamline HR operations, reduce costs, and personalize employee development (Marler & Parry, 2016). Technology adoption in HR also empowers employees through self-service systems, mobile applications, and performance dashboards, enhancing engagement and satisfaction.

However, research focusing on SHRM in the UAE hotel industry remains limited. While some studies address HR practices or technology adoption in isolation, few integrate SHRM, technology, and employee engagement within a comprehensive empirical framework. This chapter addresses this gap by analyzing data from 375 hotel employees and managers in the UAE, testing the hypothesis that SHRM, supported by technology, improves hotel performance and sustainability through employee engagement.

The remainder of this chapter is structured as follows: a review of the literature on SHRM, technology in HRM, and UAE's hotel context; research objectives and hypotheses; methodology; data analysis and results; discussion; conclusion; recommendations; and references.

LITERATURE REVIEW

Strategic Human Resource Management (SHRM)

SHRM is defined as the proactive management of human resources to achieve long-term organizational objectives by aligning HR practices with strategic business goals (Wright & McMahan, 2011). The **Resource-Based View (RBV)** emphasizes human capital as a unique, rare, and inimitable resource that provides sustainable competitive advantage (Kaufman, 2015). Similarly, the **Ability-Motivation-Opportunity (AMO) model** posits that employee performance is maximized when individuals have the ability (skills and knowledge), motivation (incentives and engagement), and opportunity (supportive systems and empowerment) to perform effectively (Boxall & Purcell, 2016).

In the hotel industry, SHRM plays a pivotal role in talent acquisition, training, retention, and performance appraisal. Hotels are labor-intensive organizations where employee behavior directly influences guest satisfaction and brand reputation. High turnover, particularly in front-office and food & beverage roles, makes effective SHRM critical for stability and service continuity (Subramony, 2009). Strategic recruitment ensures cultural fit, while training equips employees to deliver exceptional service. Performance management aligns employee objectives with hotel goals, and retention strategies reduce costs associated with turnover.

SHRM Practices in Hospitality

Key SHRM practices in the hospitality industry include:

- **Recruitment and Selection:** Using competency-based hiring to ensure alignment with service standards.
- **Training and Development:** Continuous upskilling, particularly in customer service and intercultural communication.
- **Performance Appraisal:** Linking evaluations to customer satisfaction metrics.
- **Compensation and Benefits:** Designing reward systems that promote retention in high-turnover environments.
- **Employee Engagement:** Creating a culture of belonging in a multicultural workforce.

These practices ensure that employees not only meet service expectations but also contribute to the hotel's long-term strategic positioning.

Technology in SHRM

Technology has transformed HR practices globally. **Human Resource Information Systems (HRIS)** automate record-keeping, payroll, and recruitment, while AI-driven platforms enhance candidate screening and predictive analytics (Stone et al., 2015). **E-learning platforms** provide scalable training, allowing hotel employees to access learning materials at their convenience. Mobile apps enable employees to manage schedules, request leave, and track performance. Data analytics further empower HR managers to make informed decisions on workforce planning and performance monitoring.

In hotels, technology in HR ensures consistency across diverse and dispersed teams, while reducing administrative burdens. For example, AI-driven chatbots are now used in recruitment, while cloud-based HR systems allow managers to oversee employee data across multiple properties.

Multicultural Workforce in UAE Hotels

The UAE hotel industry employs workers from Asia, Africa, Europe, and the Middle East, creating a highly multicultural environment. Managing such diversity requires SHRM practices that promote inclusivity, cultural awareness, and communication. High turnover among expatriate staff is a challenge, often caused by limited career growth opportunities and cultural adjustment issues. SHRM practices such as mentorship programs and career development pathways can reduce attrition and enhance engagement.

Sustainability in SHRM

Sustainability has become a core focus for the hospitality industry. Green HRM practices, such as eco-training, green recruitment, and employee involvement in environmental initiatives, align HR strategies with sustainability goals (Zaid et al., 2018). In the UAE, where sustainability is a national priority, integrating SHRM with green practices helps hotels meet regulatory expectations and attract eco-conscious tourists.

RESEARCH GAP

While literature highlights the significance of SHRM, technology, and sustainability, few studies integrate these dimensions in the UAE hotel context. Existing research either focuses on general HR practices or examines technology adoption without considering the mediating role of employee engagement. This chapter addresses this gap by providing empirical evidence of SHRM's impact on hotel performance and sustainability in the UAE.

Research Objectives and Hypotheses

Objectives

1. To analyze the role of SHRM in enhancing organizational performance in UAE hotels.
2. To assess the impact of technology-enabled SHRM on employee engagement.
3. To evaluate the mediating role of employee engagement in the relationship between SHRM and sustainability outcomes.

Hypotheses

- **H1:** SHRM practices significantly improve organizational performance in UAE hotels.
- **H2:** Technology-enabled SHRM positively influences employee engagement.
- **H3:** Employee engagement mediates the relationship between SHRM and sustainability.

RESEARCH METHODOLOGY

Research Design

A quantitative, cross-sectional research design was used. The study applied descriptive and inferential analysis, focusing on hypothesis testing through **Partial Least Squares Structural Equation Modeling (PLS-SEM)**.

Population and Sample

The population included employees and managers working in luxury, midscale, and budget hotels across the UAE. A sample of **375 respondents** was selected using stratified random sampling, ensuring representation across job roles and hotel types.

Data Collection Instrument

The structured questionnaire consisted of:

- **Section A:** Demographics (age, gender, job role, nationality, hotel type).
- **Section B:** SHRM practices (recruitment, training, appraisal, retention).
- **Section C:** Technology integration in HR (HRIS, AI tools, e-learning).

- **Section D:** Employee engagement and sustainability outcomes.

A 5-point Likert scale (1 = Strongly Disagree to 5 = Strongly Agree) was used.

Statistical Tests

- **Descriptive Statistics:** For demographic analysis.
- **Reliability Test:** Cronbach's alpha ($\alpha > 0.70$ threshold).
- **Validity Tests:** Convergent validity (AVE > 0.50), Discriminant validity (Fornell-Larcker).
- **Multicollinearity Test:** VIF < 5.
- **Structural Model:** PLS-SEM path analysis.
- **Bootstrapping:** 5,000 resamples for hypothesis significance.
- **R^2, f^2, Q^2:** To assess model strength and predictive relevance.

DATA ANALYSIS AND RESULTS

Demographic Profile

Table 1. Respondent Demographics (N = 375)

Variable	Category	Frequency	Percentage (%)
Gender	Male	210	56.0
	Female	165	44.0
Age	21–30 years	170	45.3
	31–40 years	125	33.3
	41+ years	80	21.4
Nationality	South Asian	140	37.3
	Middle Eastern	90	24.0
	European	75	20.0
	African	70	18.7
Job Role	Front Office	100	26.7
	Food & Beverage	120	32.0
	Housekeeping	80	21.3
	Managerial/Executive	75	20.0
Hotel Type	Luxury	145	38.7

continued on following page

Table 1. Continued

Variable	Category	Frequency	Percentage (%)
	Midscale	140	37.3
	Budget	90	24.0

Reliability and Validity

Table 2. Reliability and Internal Consistency

Construct	Items	Cronbach's Alpha (α)	Composite Reliability (CR)	AVE
SHRM Practices	8	0.886	0.915	0.615
Technology Integration	6	0.864	0.897	0.592
Employee Engagement	7	0.875	0.903	0.607
Organizational Performance	6	0.861	0.891	0.573
Sustainability Outcomes	5	0.843	0.880	0.569

All $\alpha > 0.80$, confirming strong reliability. AVE > 0.50, confirming convergent validity.

Hypothesis Testing

Table 3. Hypothesis Testing Results (PLS-SEM)

Hypothesis	Path	β Value	t-value	p-value	Supported?
H1	SHRM → Organizational Performance	0.60	11.89	0.000	Yes
H2	Technology → Engagement	0.55	10.42	0.000	Yes
H3	Engagement (Mediation)	0.45	7.61	0.001	Yes

All hypotheses were supported at **$p < 0.01$**.

Model Strength

- **R^2 values:** Performance (0.59), Engagement (0.53), Sustainability (0.56) → moderate to strong predictive power.

- **f^2 effect sizes:** SHRM → Performance (0.40, large), Tech → Engagement (0.35, medium-large), Engagement → Sustainability (0.28, medium).
- **Q^2 values:** All > 0 (Performance 0.38, Engagement 0.31, Sustainability 0.33) → strong predictive relevance.

DISCUSSION

The findings confirm that SHRM is a significant driver of hotel performance in the UAE, consistent with the **RBV framework** (Wright & McMahan, 2011). SHRM practices such as structured recruitment, targeted training, and effective retention policies directly enhance service delivery and customer satisfaction.

Technology emerged as a key enabler, supporting SHRM practices through automation, data analytics, and employee self-service platforms. This aligns with Marler and Parry's (2016) argument that technology elevates HRM from administrative to strategic levels.

The mediating role of employee engagement underscores the importance of motivating and empowering a multicultural workforce. Engaged employees act as the conduit through which SHRM and technology translate into sustainability outcomes. This supports the AMO model, where engagement reflects motivation and opportunity.

In the UAE context, these findings are particularly relevant given high turnover, diverse nationalities, and Emiratization requirements. SHRM practices that emphasize inclusivity, career development, and recognition can reduce turnover and strengthen long-term competitiveness.

CONCLUSION

This study highlights the importance of SHRM in shaping the future of the UAE hotel industry. By aligning HR practices with strategic goals and leveraging technology, hotels can enhance performance, foster engagement, and achieve sustainability. The results demonstrate that SHRM practices significantly improve hotel performance, technology-enabled SHRM increases engagement, and engagement mediates the SHRM–sustainability relationship.

The chapter contributes theoretically by integrating SHRM, technology, and sustainability within the UAE hospitality context. Practically, it provides hotel managers with actionable strategies to improve HR effectiveness and align with UAE Tourism Strategy 2031.

Recommendations

1. **For Hotels:**
    - Invest in HRIS, AI-driven recruitment, and e-learning platforms.
    - Implement employee recognition and career development programs.
    - Promote cultural diversity training to enhance inclusivity.
2. **For Policymakers:**
    - Strengthen Emiratization programs through targeted HR development.
    - Encourage hotels to adopt sustainability-linked HR practices.
3. **For Researchers:**
    - Conduct longitudinal studies to track the impact of SHRM practices.
    - Compare SHRM outcomes across GCC hotel industries.

REFERENCES

Alnaqbi, W. (2011). *The relationship between human resource practices and employee retention in public organisations: An exploratory study conducted in the United Arab Emirates*. Edith Cowan University.

Boxall, P., & Purcell, J. (2016). *Strategy and human resource management* (4th ed.). Palgrave Macmillan. DOI: 10.1007/978-1-137-40765-8

Deloitte. (2020). *Hospitality 2020: The future of growth*. Deloitte Insights.

Kaufman, B. E. (2015). The RBV theory foundation of strategic HRM: Critical flaws, problems for research and practice, and an alternative economics paradigm. *Human Resource Management Journal*, *25*(4), 516–540. DOI: 10.1111/1748-8583.12085

Marler, J. H., & Parry, E. (2016). Human resource management, strategic involvement and e-HRM technology. *International Journal of Human Resource Management*, *27*(19), 2233–2253. DOI: 10.1080/09585192.2015.1091980

Nickson, D. (2013). *Human resource management for hospitality, tourism and events* (2nd ed.). Routledge. DOI: 10.4324/9780080966496

Stone, D. L., Deadrick, D. L., Lukaszewski, K. M., & Johnson, R. (2015). The influence of technology on the future of human resource management. *Human Resource Management Review*, *25*(2), 216–231. DOI: 10.1016/j.hrmr.2015.01.002

Subramony, M. (2009). A meta-analytic investigation of the relationship between HRM bundles and firm performance. *Human Resource Management*, *48*(5), 745–768. DOI: 10.1002/hrm.20315

Wright, P. M., & McMahan, G. C. (2011). Exploring human capital: Putting 'human' back into strategic human resource management. *Human Resource Management Journal*, *21*(2), 93–104. DOI: 10.1111/j.1748-8583.2010.00165.x

Zaid, A. A., Jaaron, A. A. M., & Talib Bon, A. (2018). The impact of green human resource management and green supply chain management practices on sustainable performance: An empirical study. *Journal of Cleaner Production*, *204*, 965–979. DOI: 10.1016/j.jclepro.2018.09.062

Zhou, Y., Luo, Y., & Tang, T. (2020). Strategic human resource management, firm performance, and employee outcomes: A meta-analysis. *Journal of Management*, *46*(7), 1323–1350. DOI: 10.1177/0149206319881775

Chapter 6

The Future of Work:
A Content Analysis of Strategic HRM in India's Food Delivery Gig Economy

Tanya Rabban
http://orcid.org/0009-0009-5925-8384
Amity University, Mohali, India

Rohan Singh
http://orcid.org/0000-0002-3588-4876
Chandigarh University, India

ABSTRACT

The growth of India's gig economy, particularly in food delivery, has transformed work relations through algorithmic management and platform control. This chapter examines how Strategic Human Resource Management (SHRM) can address challenges faced by gig workers, focusing on job security, compensation, performance management, flexibility, and satisfaction. Using qualitative content analysis in NVivo and bibliometric mapping in VOSviewer, the study analyzes policies, corporate initiatives, academic literature, and worker narratives. Findings indicate that while reforms such as the Code on Social Security (2020) and state-level welfare boards offer potential protections, enforcement gaps persist. Gig workers continue to experience income instability, limited grievance redressal, and tension between flexibility and precarity.

DOI: 10.4018/979-8-2600-1845-3.ch006

1. INTRODUCTION

1.1 Global Gig Economy Context

The gig economy has redefined the nature of work in the 21st century, characterised by short-term contracts and platform-based work arrangements rather than conventional full-time employment. Technological advances are fuelled by digital platforms such as Upwork and Uber, enabling companies to outsource tasks and services to independent workers across crucial locations. The labour market transformation has led to greater work autonomy and flexibility, allowing the companies to optimise operational costs and efficiently scale. According to the 2022 report by the International Labour Organisation, over 147 million workers on global platforms engaged in platform-facilitated work, with a rapid rise in gig employment, especially in service sectors such as care work, transportation, and delivery. The transformation, with higher debate on job quality, algorithmic control, and social protection within the gig economy. Unlike conventional employment, platform-based work models lack defined employer-employee relationships and result in indistinct accountability (Amin, 2025). While some Western economies have introduced regulatory frameworks and social protections for gig workers, the situation remains diverse and largely underexplored in India.

1.2 India's Food Delivery Sector

India presents the global gig economy with a larger youth population, rapid digital adoption, and a rise in demand for convenience-based services, which could fuel the growth of app-based gig workers (Rana et al 2021). Food delivery platforms like Swiggy and Zomato have become household names while employing a differentiated network for gig-based delivery partners(Bhandari et al., 2023). The sectors have seen relatively higher growth post-2015, especially with smartphones and the convenient UPI payment infrastructure that emerged over time. Food delivery gig work in India is marked by heterogeneity, informality, and higher worker turnover. Most of the delivery partners are classified as independent contractors and recruited from lower-income backgrounds; the absence of social security and higher risks prevail. The COVID-19 pandemic further amplifies the emotional vulnerability faced by delivery workers and highlights the urgent need for robust, ethical management frameworks within the sector. In terms of scale. The food delivery gig sector employs 2 million people as of 2023 and is a significant contributor to the country's service-driven economy (Azevedo, Souza, & Mendonça, 2023). This plays an integral role in bridging the employment gaps, especially for migrants and low-skilled workers. Despite this, there is less scholarly and policy focus on the management of workers, engagement, and support; a gap the chapter seeks to address through the lens of Strategic Human Resource Management.

1.3 Research Gap

Considering Strategic HRM, there is integration of human resource practices with the organisation's overall strategy, with a focus on long-term workforce management and development (Azevedo, Souza, & Mendonça, 2023). This aligns with the talent and organisational goals, which foster the culture of performance and well-being. In the traditional setting, SHRM is integral for employee engagement, retention and organisational success as well(Gohil & Jha, 2024). However, the application in gig-based platform work environments, wherein the workers have an absence of formal employment status, is ever evolving. In the food delivery gig sectors, the companies depend heavily on the algorithmic management systems in order to recruit, improve performance and distribute the incentives. While all of the systems are effective for the optimisation of operations, they fail to consider the workers and their human needs, well-being. The lack of conventional HR functionalities, such as the feedback mechanism, career development and grievance redressal, results in relation to the impersonal work experience despite the significant role that the workers play in the service delivery. The disjunction lies within the operational dependence of delivery work, and the absence of strategic workforce management raises critical questions about whether the principles of SHRM can be reimagined for the gig context. Human-centric HR strategies that coexist with platform efficiency (Bhandari et al., 2023). The companies build worker loyalty, motivation as well as performance in the environment wherein there are no formal employment contracts. Some of the questions that make a component and are necessary for studying the food delivery sector in India within the gig economy. Considering India's socio-economic context, there is higher youth unemployment, informalities in the working culture, and increased digitalisation, which demand innovation in HR models that are not only efficient but also sustainable and inclusive (Hameed et al., 2023). In order to address the challenges there is a requirement for understanding the current HRM practices which are operationalised within the gig platforms and the reforms which can drive the outcomes for both the workers as well as business. The chapter aims to examine the practical implications of SHRM in India's food delivery gig economy by conducting a qualitative content analysis of various data sources.(Kaufman, 2015) These include government policy papers, academic research, corporate statements and investigations related to the companies such as Zomato, Swiggy. By doing the examination the chapter would be able to map the HR strategies which are adopted by the food delivery platforms in order to recruit, retain as well as monitor the gig work. Other than this there would be exploration of the tension within algorithmic control and conventional HR functions such as motivation, engagement and appraisal. It would highlight the ethical and structural concerns regarding job security, fair compensation and the well-being of the worker (Bhandari et al., 2023). There would be a content-derived framework for building a performance-oriented yet people-first HR model customised towards the gig economy in India. A comprehensive analysis shall be provided with culture contextualised and evidence-based recommendations for the companies, professionals and policymakers. The chapter would lay its emphasis on the food delivery segments because of the scalability, public visibility and the rapid growth in India. However, the frameworks and insights have proposed the extrapolation in other gig sectors such as ride-hailing or the on-demand home services. The main aim is to contribute to the evolving discourse on gig work with HRM from a Global South perspective, wherein the institutional structure, labour norms, and socio-economic conditions have different significance from those in the West.

1.4 Research Objectives

- To analyse how SHRM principles are articulated across policy documents, corporate communications, academic literature, and worker narratives in relation to India's food-delivery gig sector.
- To map the recruitment, onboarding, engagement, and compliance practices of major food-delivery platforms using content-based evidence rather than self-reported claims.
- To identify points of tension between traditional HR values and algorithmic management by examining platform policies, rating systems, deactivation rules, and incentive mechanisms.
- To evaluate ethical and operational risks such as stress, job identity issues, and the weakness of grievance systems using worker narratives and media accounts coded in the QCA.
- To recommend SHRM adaptations for gig-work environments by synthesising cross-source patterns and mapping them onto the AMO and HPWS frameworks.

In order to achieve the objectives, the chapter has been structured into sections including. Conceptual foundation, to define gig economy and discussion with key theoretical frameworks that could guide the analysis. A descriptive overview for the players and employment patterns and HRM practices for India's food delivery sector. A quantitative content analysis approach would be followed for the methodology contemplating the data collection from policy documents and the corporate reports along with media articles and narratives from the workers as well. The findings will be presented in key themes such as incentives, surveillance, recruitments and career development which shall be observed in the data. Critical reflection on how SHRM is implicated in the gig contexts and the difficulties in operationalization with ethical imperatives at stake. With this conceptual analysis, the chapter seeks to offer the academic rigors as well as practical relevance. In the recent years, the government of India and the platform have taken several initiatives for the policy shifts aimed at implications of the work environment for the gig and platform based workers(Bhandari et al., 2023). Initiating from the Code on Social Security 2020, leading to the legislation identifying the gig and platform workers in India and also towards state led initiatives with platform worker welfare boards in Karnataka and Rajasthan making a clear movement towards the inclusivity. The policies offer social protection, financial inclusion and skill development to gig workers, particularly to those who are in food delivery services and operate in customer interaction and yet they remain unprotected. Moreover, platforms such as Swiggy, Zomato have also responded with their internal policies around accident cover, health insurance and incentive based earning structures. With the inconsistencies in the implementation there is a lack of formal employee status for the gig workers which means that the benefits are still conditional or in some cases it is inaccessible. A comprehensive review for the policy documents, platform terms between the year 2020 and 2025 provide valuable insights for the selection, onboarding, inclusion and the benefits administration has emerged in the expanding sector. The developments with the critical part for chapterism identification for strategic HRM amongst the gig economy. This would be a beneficial aspect in the structural shift and the realities of the workers, providing the nuanced understanding of the HRM practices which could be adapted from the non traditional and digital facilitated employment relationships.

2. LITERATURE REVIEW

2.1 Theoretical Framework

Strategic Human Resource Management represents the alignment for HR practices within the organisation strategy to enhance the long term performance and suitable value creation. Rather than focusing on the administration tasks, SHRM conceptualised the HR to be a strategic stewardship for human caption which advances the workforces capabilities and opportunities in ways which can reinforce the goals of the organisations (Kant et al., 2023). The two prominent frameworks which are underscored in SHRM studies are the Ability Motivation Opportunity (AMO) model and High Performance Work System (HPWS). The AMO model also argues that the HR practices are most efficient wherein they can increase the ability of the employees such as training and selection, motivation with recognition and rewards. When these dimensions are addressed, employees are in a better position to contribute towards organisational performance. Recent work by Sahoo & Mohapatra (2025) reinforces the need to strengthen human capital systems in rapidly expanding labour markets. Their findings show that sustainable workforce performance requires coherent HR bundles rather than isolated practices, offering an important parallel for gig platforms where fragmented HRM practices undermine long-term worker development.In regards to the AMO, Hameed (2023) in their paper shows the HPWS wherein the bundles of HR practices are selective hiring, training and performance link rewards with decision making and stronger principles with organisational outcomes, aligned within the AMO framework. The findings have supported the SHRM to have greater impact when the HR practices are reinforced. The conceptual foundation for the usage of normative measurable models in SHRM research are talked about uniquely wherein the approach becomes better in the spectrum for strategic HR bundles and the combined impact of organisational success.

2.2 Limitations of SHRM in Gig Context

Combining these frameworks offers a powerful aspect for assessment in the organisation or even in the platform based firms which are practicing the strategic HR management regardless of their employment structure. Within the context of non-traditional or platform facilitated labor the SHRM mechanisms are weak. The primary abilities are undermined with the lack of robust training structures. The research on the food delivery worker for instance, indicates the formal training and a structured feedback for minimal or inconsistencies in implementation. The workers are compelled for dependency on peer networks and informal communication channels which acquire more role specific competencies. Thai provides a limitation to the strategic alignment for skill development along with the organisational goal and reduces the potential for having sustained gains in productivity. Similarly "motivations" are more confined with short term and variable natures of rewards within gig platforms. Incentives are more linked towards dynamic, and algorithmic determined metrics for order completion rates or even the ratings they receive from customers, rather than their retention for longer term and also skill acquisition . This disrupts the alignments and privately with the conventional strategic objectives. Without having any pathways for the relevant advancements, motivation becomes a more transaction yet short lied tied towards immediate earnings. The "opportunity" is also an element which is inadequate in the platform work. Gig workers rarely have the opportunities for becoming participants in the decision making process and influence the funding for the jobs with the governance mechanism in the platform. This shall replace the role of managers in determination of allocation of task, performance evaluation and also their availability to work. As a result, the autonomy of the workers makes contributions that are more significant and weaken the potential for commitment and engagement (Kuhn et al., 2021).

2.3 Algorithmic Management as a Theoretical Lens

HPWS relies on complementary HR practices, which face a specific challenge in the gig context: there is no formal HR department, and employment relationships are fragmented and legally ambiguous. The lack of cohesiveness in management structure means having an integrated approach that requires training, employee engagement and performance management, which is difficult to operationalise. Moreover, the framing of gig workers as independent contractors limits the platform's obligation to implement such a system. The gig work emerged as a feature for the digital economy, characterised by paid tasks and conducted outside the scope of standard employment contracts, which can be mediated through digital platforms that can match the algorithmically with customers (Bhandari et al., 2023). The platform is dependent on the algorithmic management systems for task allocation and performance monitoring with the determination of compensation structure. Unlike the conventional managerial supervision and governance of algorithmic at large and dispersed workforces with the completion times, inventive schemes and customer ratings . With automation, there is an increase in availability and efficiency, raising concerns related towards worker autonomy, transparency and fairness. The studies have more focus on the algorithmic management and substitutes for the human managerial discretion with the rigid rules and also reduces the division and leaves the work with limitations in recourse while errors or disputes occur. Moreover, the paucity of algorithm decision-making shifts from operation to the financial risks with the workers. For instance there are some changes in the pay rates and incentive thresholds which are often implemented in unilateral aspect witty clear communication and also leads to income uncertainty and their bed realities. This causes a paradox, which platforms promise for more independence and flexibility, which deploys the physical pressures. The reviews of the algorithmic management literature consistently identify dynamics, including algorithmic control, reduced decision-making transparency, and algorithmic control for managerial oversight (Moore & Joyce, 2020). The dynamic determines the critical need for how the human resources concerns, including the grievance mechanism, inclusion, safety and training, are addressed in the policies for platforms.

2.4 Empirical Review

2.4.1 Global Gig Economy Evidence

There is global evidence indicating the gig economy growing rapidly, encompassing the diverse work of micro task, delivery and micro task and logistics. Skill intensity reflects on the risk exposure and creates a heterogeneous employment structure. There are comparative studies which suggest the gig works to be expanded access to the income generation opportunities with more schedule flexibility. This mutually procedures higher turnover, a limitation to social protection systems and precarious earnings. The fragment gig works status with more disputes in intensification of jurisdiction. For example, regulatory durables in the European Union and India which increased with the gig works and it should be more classified with employees and independent contractions with more necessary implications for benefits and protections. Covid 19 pandemic has accelerated the delivery demand and the on demand services as well as which exposes the fragility for gig works; safety nets. Research during the period demonstrates the gig works being essential to maintain the consumption systems facing lack of occupational health coverage and psychosocial stress with income volatility . Beyond the pandemic, the studies show how gig workers have experience in psychological strain due to the algorithmic evaluation and custom dependence. At the same time, there is evidence which suggests that there are worker subsets, specially in professional platform work that offers autonomy and mobility. The literature depicts the gig economy to be dual edged employment systems which democratises market access. This raises the questions in HR practices, regulatory frameworks and labour rights.

2.4.2 HRM Challenges in Digital Platforms

Recent literature identifies a set of human resource management challenges within the platform base work which might complicate the Strategic Human Resource Management principles. The main challenge concerns the selection and onboarding process. Not like the traditional employment models which depend on the structured recruitment as well as training wherein most of the food delivery platforms in India require not just your Know Your Customer (KYC) checks or assets ownership with two wheeler. On boarding is primarily through application mediation which workforce expansion but also offering little training or competency building. A research conducted by IDinsight (2022) finds that "onboarding through app" approach also has speed privileges with scalability with skill development as well as empowerment that leaves the workers to be more dependent on informal peer learning and experiential adaptation(Eternal Limited, 2024). These practices are more divergent from SHRM principles that focus on the ability building through development and systematic training. Another concern relates to the transparency in pay and the incentive design. The platform is dependent on dynamic incentive structures for financing the completion bonuses, surge pricing as well as teenage linked rewards for management of supply responsiveness. While the mechanisms are efficient for short term allocation for labor and introduce wage volatility. Reports from NITI Aayog (2022) and more independent students (Sundararajan, 2021) explore the worker grievances regaining the opaque pay structures and the disruption in policy changes with inconsistent communication for incentive rules. The practice diminishes the trust as well as income stability that undermines the component for SHRM framework and relies mostly on predictable incentive systems in order to sustain engagement and retention. The growth in algorithmic surveillance as well as performance management has caused complexities in HR dynamics for platform economics. The worker evaluation is driven by algorithmic mechanisms such as automated deactivated rules, customer ratings and also the task routine systems. Reviews of such have been published. and industry analysis reveals that the system does not just erode worker autonomy but also creates more stress and uncertainty. Deactivation decisions are made unilaterally and without avenues for appeal. This produces conditions of asymptotic power. In this particular environment, workers are then positioned to be the data points rather than the individuals which challenges the relational as well as the development ethos that is more central towards SHRM.

2.4.3 Worker Wellbeing & Health Findings

Concerns about the safety, health and psychological well being become, especially prominent in post pandemic research. The delivery workers face significant physical risks which include road accidents and exposure towards hazardous conditions and have limitations towards protective infrastructures(Azevedo, Souza, & Mendonça, 2023). Clinical surveys in Indian states document persistence of depression, anxiety and burnout amongst riders. The income volatility as well as long working hours exacerbate these relative risks. The investigative journalist faces barriers towards compensation access due to the policy language, absence of documentation or the technical aspects with non commercial vehicle registration. These decisions in the systems leave workers with no adequate social protection reinforcing the gig work. The issue of worker voice and grievance mechanisms remain a critical challenge. The conventional working structures for the representation are largely non-existent in platform work. Instead the works are dependent on the app support system which are ineffective or result in protests or informal collectives. The reports from NCAER (2023), documents the mobilisation by gig workers in the Indian cities such as Bengaluru or Delhi as responses to unilateral changes for incentive policies. With such protection, the attempt to reclaim the agency rarely leads towards systematic improvements and leaves workers with vulnerable yet unilateral algorithmic governance. Taken together the themes underscore the central HRM conflicts in the digital platform work. While the platforms have efficient operational efficiency and supply chain responsiveness, there is a consistent underinvestment in strategic HR dimensions which include the ability for developments, incentive design, worker voice and worker well being (Vasanthan et al 2025). The lack of HR mechanism undermines the sustainability of HR but it also raises necessary questions for SHRM about how strategic HR practices might be reimagined within digital mediation and work arrangements with no traditional working arrangements. independent worker-focused studies strengthen these observations. Fairwork India (2022, 2023) consistently scores food-delivery platforms low on pay fairness, worker participation, and transparency, indicating structural misalignment with SHRM principles. Similarly, the NCAER (2023) survey of gig workers documents long working hours, absence of health protections, and unstable earnings. ID insight (2022) further highlights the inadequacy of app-based onboarding, reinforcing the structural "ability" deficits within the AMO framework.

2.4.4 Career Development Evidence

Career development plays an integral role in the gig economy but they are almost next to negligible. The digital mediated platform for the gig workers who tend to treat the workers as independent contractors and puts a limitation on their responsibilities towards their skill progression. It is not like the conventional firms that invest towards employee training and career leaders, wherein the gig platform puts more importance in the transaction efficiencies, and leaves the works to be in a stagnant position with limitation in prospects for a longer term growth (Mehrotra, 2021). Reskilling and also cross development opportunities have become too rare. While some of the platforms experiment by providing access for learning platforms or even financial literacy sessions, these also remain underutilised and voluntary. This absence of institutional support reduces the possibility for gig work to become a stepping stone for the formal sector employment. Future oriented studies have suggested an integration of gig platforms with skill development ecosystems such as India's National Skill Development Corporation. These collaborations can transform the gig works which would become an avenue for career progression (NITI Aayog, 2022). Although these initiatives are nascent stages, there are many gig workers who are left out for low reward tasks.

2.4.5 Grievance Redressal

Grievance redressal mechanicals in the gig platform are weak and heavy technologies. The workers have more access towards app based help desks and chatbots but have absence of empathy and resolve the problem associated with the human HR personnel. grievances of the gig workers often go unnoticed and unresolved and creates disillusionments within the workers. The lack of direct engagement with HR personnel highlights the platform border reluctance for identification gig workers being employees..this void has caused the informal union of emergence and worker collectives across the Indian cities. The grassroots advocate for fairer working conditions, predictable earnings and through protests. Although the worker voice includes collective expression, and the digital platform resistant towards formal identification of unions,. This causes a disjunction within work aspiration for representation and platforms with profit facilitated practices. Table 1 summarises the differences in emphasis across policy reports, worker narratives, and corporate disclosures.

2.5 Indian-Specific Labor and Policy Landscape (2020–2025)

The regulatory landscape for the platform as well as gig work has undergone the necessary transformation since the year 20202 with policymakers identifying the employment arrangement with sector characterisation. A landmark development was done in the enactment of Code on Social Security (2020), being classified as gig and platform works entitled towards social protection (Mehrotra, 2021). The code has introduced provisions for accidental insurances, coverage, maternity support and the creation of a social security fund financed through platform aggregators. But, certainly the implementation still remains uneven and there are several studies which focus on the rules of Code yet to be operationalised across the state and central levels which leaves the protection aspirational (Chaudhary 2022) critiques for the Code focuses on the ambiguities surrounding the "gig" and "platform" workers which restricts the access and excludes the larger groups for informalized labour as well as occupation safety provisions that shall limit the potential of Code to address the precarity in structures. Despite its progressive intent, the Code on Social Security (2020) suffers from substantial implementation barriers. Several studies have noted that many of the operational rules under the Code have not yet been notified at the state level (Chaudhary 2022), meaning the legal provisions remain unenforceable. The absence of a clear mechanism for identifying gig and platform workers further restricts benefit access. From an SHRM perspective, these gaps directly weaken the "Opportunity" dimension of the AMO framework, because workers cannot access structured protection, safety, or grievance channels even when legislation appears to guarantee them.

Forbes India highlights the risks for enforceability with work entitlements (Bhandari, 2023). Considering the state levels. The initialities highlight the experimentation growth but also reveal the challenges in execution. For instance, Karnataka's 2025, proposes a 5% of welfare to be shared within workers, platforms and consumers. While innovative aspects, concerns remain with impact of worker incomes and also consumer prices. Delhi drafted rules under the Social Security Code proposing the establishment of welfare boards, funds for the unorganised sectors, yet the unions argued that these protection fails to secure collective bargaining. Similar debates followed in Rajasthan, Kerala to reflect on the trajectory for labour policy decentralisation. A comparative view of state-level welfare boards shows wide variation in ambition, funding models, and enforcement capacity. Karnataka's welfare board proposes a tripartite contribution model (platforms–workers–government), while Rajasthan emphasises registration and social protection but lacks clarity on financing mechanisms. These differences highlight the fragmented institutional landscape governing gig work. This fragmentation weakens SHRM alignment, as platforms operate under inconsistent expectations regarding worker welfare, training obligations, and dispute resolution procedures.

The NITI Aayog report of 2022 offers a structured guidance for policy and projects on the gig workforce of India to expand from 7.7 million in 2020 to 23.5 by 2029. The implementation challenges still persist especially in areas for data transparency and schemes for persons with disabilities. Platform level intuition found similar tension within stated commitments and the realities on the field. Major food delivery platforms such as Zomato, Swiggy have taken initiative for welfare programs with digital skilling and safety provisions. Yet there are research documents which show the prevalence of gaps and accidental claims which are denied due to the technicalities and the incentives policies shift without having any consultation (Narayan & Sengupta, 2022). Subsequently. India's labor and policy landscape reflects on the growth as well as the gaps. The Code on Social Security establishes the significance for foundation but also implementation with weak enforceables that could undermine the transformation in potential. Meanwhile the self regulatory platforms schedules remain in a limit for their reliability and scope. Literature underscores the strategic need for semantic analysis of platform level to evaluate the strategic HRM principles. Such as inclusion, training and fairness, are being adapted or neglected in expansion of the gig economy. Moreover, the lack of a mandated grievance redressal structure across states reinforces weak institutional support for gig workers. Without formal appeal processes or oversight bodies, workers rely on app-based bots that often fail to resolve disputes. This contradicts HPWS principles, which require participatory voice systems, continuous feedback, and fairness in corrective actions. As such, policy inaction directly contributes to the erosion of strategic HRM outcomes. Despite the literature on platform economics there are certain gaps which remain and within the context for India's food delivery sector. The gaps undermine the significance for the content based investigation for strategic HR practices in platform terms, communication and policy documents. Although the Code on Social Security identifies the gig and platform works as eligibility for social security and examines the terms of service for platforms and competitive policies that align across the variation such as selection and benefits. Most of the studies offer case discussions and evidence (Jakhete et al, 2025). A notable lack of research maps the congruence as well as contradicts with the domains (NITI Aayog, 2022). The SHRM literature is theoretically strong but it does not have sufficient operational frameworks for the digital based gig economy. An urgent need for interpretation constructs such as motivation, opportunity in aspects of measurable policy and platform artifacts. For instance, onboarding the scripts, safety training modules, grievance mechanisms. This would allow the research to asset the artifacts conditioning towards strategic HR bundles and fall short for the SHRM agendas. Algorithmic governance is the sociological aspect, not just for human resources practices with the implications for selection, appraisal and rewards. The systematic content analysis for the policy documents, for instance the rating systems,deactivation rules and terms of services could highlight the envied managerial functions. An approach provides insights into the strategy HR goals with fairness and supported by algorithmic governance. However, multiple studies highlight that the Code's effectiveness remains restricted due to missing rules, unclear beneficiary identification, and limited enforcement (Chaudhary 2022). Kumar & Narayan (2022) emphasise that administrative fragmentation across states further weakens implementation, creating misalignment between intended protections and workers' lived realities. These implementation barriers undermine the "opportunity" dimension of the AMO framework and limit SHRM-aligned policy outcomes.

Despite growing scholarship, three major gaps persist: (1) limited research uses an SHRM lens to examine gig-platform management, with most studies centering on precarity rather than strategic HR practices; (2) no systematic content-analysis–based mapping exists of platform artifacts such as rating systems, deactivation rules, onboarding scripts—to AMO or HPWS frameworks; and (3) prior Indian studies rarely integrate multi-source triangulation across policy documents, corporate communication, and worker narratives. These gaps justify the need for the present study. Taken together, the gaps in policy implementation, fragmented state frameworks, and lack of enforceable grievance systems demonstrate why SHRM principles cannot be realised in India's gig economy without stronger institutional coordination and regulatory enforcement.

3. METHODOLOGY

3.1 Research Design

The current study adopts a qualitative content analysis approach in order to determine the articulation of human resource practices being operational and also mediated through the policies. Content analysis has been recognised as an effective research method for interpretation of the textual data and patterns of meaning. In comparison, to the interviews or surveys, this captures the accounts and allows to explore the organisational, policy and platform level representation for gig work. The choice of QCA for the current study is to map the methods in which strategic human resource management constitutes in the AMO approach are indeed in the platform communication as well as policies. Given the emergence of the regulatory landscape of India's gig sector (2020-2025), it offers the mandatory rogers to compare the corporate claims, policy texts and identify the convergence and divergence of the different sources. Qualitative content analysis is specifically suited for contexts with policy articulation, to shape employment realities. Using such analysis has focused the study on meaning making and interpretive coding. Gig work in India is not just shaped by the state legislation but also by corporate communication and public discourse including worker testimonials. QCA ensures the integration of heterogeneity in data sources. Apart from this there would be context specific interpretation since the Indian gig economy is integration with socio economic, purely quantitative approach would contextual have grounded meaning. The QCA allows the research to capture the nuances for HR practices being localised. The AMO framework and HPWS focuses on the HR practices rather than the variables that are isolated. QCA aligns with the relational and interpretive perception that facilitates the HR analysis interconnected across the texts.

3.2 Data Sources

In order to ensure triangular the study will analyse the four categories for textual data:

3.2.1 Policy Documents

The study has incorporated the Government of India legislation and reports that included:

- Code on Social Security, 2020
- NITI Aayog report "India's Booming Gig Economy" (2022)

- Ministry of Labour and Employment policy drafts
- State level welfare acts

The documents offer the official drafting of gig work and the entitlements.

3.2.2 Corporate Communications

- User agreements for leading platforms such as Dunzo, Zomato.
- Annual reports, corporate social responsibilities.
- Incentive guidelines, training manuals wherein publicly accessible.
- The sources would reflect how platforms encompass the employment relations as well as codify the algorithmic management practices.

3.2.3 Academic Literature and Peer Reviewed Journals

- Articles from reputed journals, Google Scholar with relevance of 2020-2025 were incorporated. These serve as the background as well as the main points for global scholarships.

3.2.4 Worker Narratives

- News articles and policy blogs (The Hindu, The Wire etc)
- Worker testimonials and stories published on forum
- Provide button up perspectives for policy and corporations.

Altogether the dataset ensures a 360 degree view for the policy to practice gaps in the digital platform HRM.

3.3 Data Collection and Sampling Strategy

The document selection follows a purposive sampling approach. Considering policy documents, those between 2020 and 2025, ensuring relevance only to post-pandemic labour restructuring. For the corporate sources, the focus is on the three largest Indian food delivery platforms such as Zomato and Swiggy that dominate the sector and algorithmic management in practices. The academic and media sources are selected by using systematic keyword searches ("gig economy", "algorithmic management", "platform HR", "food delivery India") in databases such as Google Scholar, Scopus and JSTOR.

The final dataset comprised

- 10-12 policy documents
- 60-70 academic articles
- 20-22 corporate communications
- 35-40 worker narratives

This breadth remains consistent with the theoretical saturation ensuring the emergent themes for adequate support.

3.4 Coding Categories

The study conducted the analysis using both deductive and inductive coding

- Deductive codes: these are the ones which were obtained from the AMO and SHRM frameworks which includes Ability, Motivation and Opportunity.
- Inductive codes: Evolving from the dataset, from context specific aspects such as

  Algorithm government including surveillance system or automated deactivation

Worker welfare narratives which could include compensation of fuel costs and health insurance.

The final coding would be conducted in two stages

- By using Open Coding: Initial line by line reading of documents was done in order to determine the recurring terms as well as practices
- Axial Coding: Organization of codes into the themes were aligned with SHRM bundles and determination of cross source links.

  The analysis was conducted using NVivo software which ensures a systematic coding, and visualisation of connecting by using larger datasets.

3.5 Analytical Procedure

By using the analytical procedure would proceed as follows:

- Compilation of the full text in the NVivo software
- Using the SHRM categories there was preliminary deductive coding enabled.
- Iterative inductive coding was conducted to refine the involved sub themes.
- Cross comprising corporate, policy and media reports to determine the alignments as well as contradictions.

- The findings were then mapped to the AMO frameworks in order to assess the absence and presence of the HR Aspects
- A longitudinal tracking from 2020 to 2025 was conducted to determine the shifts in policy as well as practice.

The QCA will proceed as follows:

1. Compilation of the full text corpus in NVivo.
2. Preliminary deductive coding using SHRM categories.
3. Iterative inductive coding to refine emerging sub-themes.
4. Cross-comparison of policy, corporate, and media discourses to highlight alignments and contradictions.
5. Mapping of findings onto the AMO framework to assess the presence/absence of HR bundles.
6. Longitudinal tracking (2020–2025) to identify shifts in policy and practice.

The process ensured the conceptual model development that linked the algorithmic governance towards Human Resource Management outcomes for the gig economy in India.Figure 1 shows the stepwise flow of the Qualitative Content Analysis followed in this study.

4. FINDINGS AND THEMATIC ANALYSIS

The sections present the findings for the conducted quantitative content analyses on peer reviews literature, corporate reports, worker narratives and policy documents related to the gig economy in India.

The analysis has identified the six thematic areas which are more central towards the assessment of human resource practices in the platform based works such as:

- Recruitment and Onboarding
- Pay structures
- Algorithmic Task Allocation
- Health and Well being
- Grievance Redressal
- Career Development

As illustrated in Figure 2, the sunburst shows the relative distribution of these HR themes across the dataset. All of the themes highlight the challenges and opportunities amongst the emergence for the employment landscape for gig workers.

Figure 1 The wheel chart shows the six main themes coded during the QCA. Figure 3 presents a word cloud generated from the full dataset, highlighting the most frequently occurring terms across sources.The visualisation highlights how HR related concerns exist in the food delivery gig economy of India. The balance across their distinctness yet interconnectedness identifies the undermining issues of algorithmic surveillance, pay structure volatility, lack of grievance mechanism being the salient terms in the HRM lens. Figure 4 visualises the proportional significance of each HR theme through a treemap, reinforcing the dominance of pay, algorithmic management, and well-being in the dataset.Each of the categories corresponds towards the core HR functions showing the platform replication of HR through the digital mediation. Figure 2 highlights how diversified data sources such as corporate reports, worker narratives and policy documents contributed to the coding structure. The recurrence of these sources within the multiple categories underscore the Systemic Characteristics of HR challenges in the platform work, and validates the robustness for the coding process and the need for strategic HRM. Figure 5 depicts the distribution of data sources used in the analysis, showing the relative weight of policy documents, corporate communications, and worker narratives.

4.1 Recruitment and Onboarding

In the context of gig economy, Recruitment and onboarding reflects an interplay within flexibility and infinity. Most of the platforms focus on the ease of access as well as minimal entry barriers for the drivers regarding the proadaptive workers. Unlike the conventional recruitment processes that are dependent on reference checks, interviews and formal contracts with platform boards that can typically be more app based and require more documentation such as the bank details, identity proof and smartphones. This entry process leads to opportunities for a rapid scalability in the workforce numbers but this also imposes the informality, leaving the workers without having any formalised employment contracts and the guarantees for continuity (Mehrotra, 2021). For example companies such as Zomato and Swiggy underline their recruitment drivers wherein the potential delivery partner is in favor of registering within 24 to 48 hours. While this is a rapid onboarding, this gives a leverage in workforce availability, this weakens the institutionalisation for the HR practices, especially around job security and also the rights of the workers. With no physical orientation session or even a structured induction for the workers limits their understanding of employment terms or the companies policies which are incorporated for them, especially the grievance redressal aspects (NITI Aayog, 2022). Furthermore, recruitment advisories highlight "be your own boss" narratives which frame the gig works to become entrepreneurs. However worker autonomy is rather limited by the algorithmic management which determines their task allocation and performance monitoring as well. Recruitment messaging diverged more towards the actual lived experiences for workers and this marks the beginning for misalignments within the expectations of workers and organisational realities. This finding is echoed in IDinsight's (2022) evaluation of app-based onboarding in Indian gig platforms, which shows that most delivery workers rely on peer learning rather than structured training. The absence of formalised onboarding systems undermines ability development—a core dimension of the AMO model.

4.2 Pay Structures and Incentives

The pays structures are one of the integral aspects of employment practices in the gig platform. Compensation is more towards a task based rather than time based with the delivery spirits or the drivers earning per the delivery or ride. The prevalence for dynamic pricing mechanisms are taken into consideration, for instance surge pricing, time based bonuses which creates a sense of volatility in the income of workers. Taking an example, Zomato and Swiggy have regular payout systems which link their higher earnings towards the increase in working hours which took place during the surge times, and this in return incentivises their longer workdays. This may lead to an enhancement in platform efficiency, which underscores the certainty for worker income. The gamification techniques are referred to as the point based systems, the ratings or even referral bonuses which also makes the competition intense within workers, and encourages them to remain more logged for the extended period of time so that they can earn more. The income volatility is one of the serious issues for the workers as the normal employees depend on fixed monthly salaries but when it comes to gig workers, their income has more fluctuation based on the demand cycles, the weather and also the algorithmic management. This particular absence of predictability lessens the financial security and also increases stress, particularly in the contexts when the work is more solely dependent on the gig work for survival.

4.3 Algorithmic Task Allocation and Performance Monitoring

One of the distinctive characteristics of the gig economy is algorithmic management. Paltom is heavily dependent on the apps and the automated systems for task allocation, performance monitoring and regulation in worker behaviour. Task allocation is based on the opaque algorithms that considers their location, ratings and physical performances, availability. Furthermore, the workers frequently raise concerns about their frustration for unfair terms or biased allocation in their mechanism. Performance monitoring is mediated through the technological tools which are embedded in the platforms. Workers are contoured on the surveillance through GPS tracking, automated alert and even the customer ratings. The spiritual surveillance creates a sense for a constant scrutiny, wherein the algorithmic systems function as the supervisors. The major issues which take place in these circumstances are the auto deactivates, when workers recipe lowe rain and complaints, they are often removed from the platform without any appeal process or justification.

4.4 Occupational Health, Safety, and Well-being

In the Indian Gig economy, there are significant occupational risks involved. Delivery and driving are the tasks that require being on the road for prolonged hours, exposing workers to traffic accidents, unsafe working conditions or working in extreme working conditions. While the platforms offer insurance coverage but the benefits are limited or poorly communicated to their workers whom they are actually for. The lack of employer responsibilities for occupational health has seen more severe consequences for the physical well being of the gig workers. A study by Fairwork India (2021) determines that two of 12 gig platforms offer valuable health or accidental insurance towards workers. In addition to this, psychological well being is compromised by the work uncertainty and earnings as well. Workers report cases of anxiety, fatigue and stress which are linked towards the prolonged hours, customer interaction but the main reason is that they fear the sudden deactivation from the platform (Mehrotra, 2021). This absence for formal job security further provokes the issues. Workers are more aware about their associates with the digital platform as they are terminated without having warning. This takes a heavy toll on their mental and physical health. Considering the issues of this context, the role of HR practices is to ensure the occupational safety and well-being, which still remains undeveloped, despite the sgniia;ty towards sustainable employment. Additional worker-focused evidence strengthens this pattern. Fairwork India (2022; 2023) consistently scored food-delivery platforms low on “Fair Pay,” “Fair Conditions,” and “Fair Management,” indicating systemic gaps in transparency and protection for delivery workers. The NCAER Gig Worker Survey (2023) likewise reports long working hours, earnings volatility, and limited access to welfare benefits across major Indian cities. IDinsight (2022) further finds that app-based onboarding processes used by platforms like Swiggy and Zomato provide minimal training or safety instruction, reinforcing the AMO framework’s concerns about weak “ability building” in gig work. Worker testimonies documented in The Hindu and The Wire describe repeated cases of denied accident claims, fear of unexplained deactivation, and psychological stress—all of which confirm the structural issues identified through the content analysis.

5. DISCUSSION

5.1 Alignment and Misalignment with SHRM Principles

This discussion section interprets the thematic findings by situating them within Strategic Human Resource Management (SHRM), the AMO framework, and emerging gig-economy scholarship. While the findings section presented descriptive patterns across policies, corporate communications, and worker narratives, this section examines what these patterns mean for HR strategy, worker experiences, and organisational sustainability.The qualitative content analysis for the study comprises government policy documents, peer review research, worker narratives and corporate reports, offering a holistic perspective on HR practices in the application-based gig economy of India. Figure 6 maps the AMO framework onto the identified HR practices, showing where gig-platform strategies reinforce or contradict strategic HR principles. By systematic coding and thematic analysis of the sources, there was an identification of the recurring patterns in the themes. These strategies have been positioned as effective tools for productivity and motivation enhancement. Although the worker narratives are coded in the analysis shows the frequent dissatisfaction due to the income volatility and openness in bonuses mechanism. This discrepancy reflects the conflict with SHRM principles, including fairness, stress, transparency and sustainability in reward systems being drivers for long-term engagement. Instead of fostering the motivation, the gig platforms are more reliant on the short-term and extrinsic incentives, which disrupts the trust and loyalty—the absence of structured occupational health and safety practice conflicts with the focus on SHRM-suitable employee well-being.A recurring theme across policy reports, such as the Ministry of Labour 2021 report, was the lack of mobility and structured career progression in gig work. Content analysis of worker narratives has reinforced this by showing the concerns over dead-end roles. From the SHRM perspective, there are limitations that can undermine the long-term value creation and inclusion as the organisation fails to invest in the development of the workforce. These recommendations translate the AMO and HPWS principles into actionable HRM practices that respond directly to the empirical patterns observed in the content analysis. By adopting bundled HR practices rather than isolated interventions, platforms can enhance worker ability, improve motivational stability, and expand opportunities for voice and career development.The findings of the study aligned to critically evaluate the practices and along with the principles of Strategic Human Resource Management. As summarised in Table 5.1, workers' narratives have highlighted a stronger emphasis on pay volatility and grievance redressal, whereas the corporate reports have led to the identification of efficiency required in onboarding processes. Our findings highlight that gig workers have faced considerable physical and psychological stress for the prolonged working hours, uncertain pay and the lack of formal safety net (Duggan et al. 2019). The methodology demonstrated the gap by worker narrative analysis for delivery riders in The Hindu wherein workers decried their absence of medical coverage. While corporate reports from Zomato focus on their "partner first" approach. The content analysis has revealed that these commitments are not reflected in the actual working conditions. The thematic coding for the success and the disclosures highlights the existences for incentive models as well as dynamic payout structures. These strategies have been positioned as effective tools for productivity and motivation enhancement. Although the worker narratives coded in the analysis shows the frequent dissatisfaction due to the income volatility and openness in bonuses mechanism. Moreover, India's growing population seeks more finives employed, exclusion for the gig works represents missed opportunities for the policymakers and the firm as well. From the coding a theoretical position for the five workers referred as "delivery partners" in corporate reform have marked the relation through the sudden deactivation vulnerability and precarity. This paradox especially highlights the disconnectivity within HR frameworks and HR practices. Considering SHRM perspective, organisations treat the works as strategic assets for ageing with rhetoric and investments in protection as well as security. The policy documents and existing academic literature have revealed the gig work to be expensive amidst the higher youth unemployment. The methodology enables us to situate the findings within the broader socio-economic context of India. The concerns are eased with persistence in the informal economy and regulatory in the ambiguity. The thematic coding shows a stronger focus on the "job creation" The gap shows the inequalities and the challenges which are faced through the SHRM principles for building sustainable ecosystems. Through this qualitative content analysis, we have determined that while the gig platform spots the elements which resemble the SHRM, they fail to integrate the core aspects such as inclusion, well-being and long-term development. Our findings suggest that the SHRM principles are selectively chosen by digital platforms to serve efficiency as flexibility but the development and protective dimensions are not considered essential for sustainable human resource strategies.

The results also highlight a significant policy–practice gap. Although the Code on Social Security (2020) formally recognises gig and platform workers, implementation remains limited due to missing rules, weak enforcement capacity, and fragmented state-level commitments. This weakens the "opportunity" dimension of AMO because workers receive nominal recognition without accessible benefits or structured mechanisms for protection. As long as regulatory frameworks lack enforceability, gig platforms face no binding requirement to adopt SHRM-aligned practices such as transparent communication, fair appraisal mechanisms, safe working conditions, and structured grievance resolution.

Worker-centred narratives further contextualise these gaps. The coded worker testimonies reflect persistent psychological stress, heightened job insecurity, and a sense of invisibility within platform governance structures. This aligns with the Fairwork India (2022, 2023) findings, which highlight weak worker voice and inconsistent support mechanisms across food-delivery platforms. The absence of meaningful consultation or appeal pathways erodes trust and intensifies precarity—conditions incompatible with SHRM's emphasis on employee engagement, empowerment, and sustainable workforce systems.

6. IMPLICATIONS FOR SHRM IN THE GIG ECONOMY

The qualitative content analysis described comprises the systematic coding, these revealed misalignments within the platform practices and core aspects of Strategic Human Resource Management. These misalignments are not only rhetorical but are visible across the corpus of the policy and corporate artefacts as well. The implications for SHRM therefore must be derived from the empirical observation wherein an attempt shall be made to adapt SHRM in the context of the gig economy to begin with structural relations and aim to translate policy intent with the platform-level practices that can protect the human capital to preserve the necessary operational flexibilities. Our content analysis also found the state as well as central policy texts focus on the recognition and inclusion of the reports through Code on Social Security, yet the platform documents and worker narratives show dew operations, and onboarding here remains more app-centric, while selection criteria and vehicle owners, rather than having an equality in the accessibility. This policy–practice gap illustrates a structural misalignment between regulatory intent and actual HRM implementation on platforms. SHRM frameworks require integrated, measurable HR bundles that enhance ability, motivation, and opportunity. However, policy ambiguity allows platforms to emphasise operational efficiency while maintaining minimal accountability for worker protection. This prevents the development of HPWS-aligned systems such as transparent appraisal, structured training, and stable reward mechanisms.

This policy-to-practice suggests an HRM implication: structured, documented selection with onboarding projects that the platform could guarantee and regulators could verify. SHRM for the gig platform required standardised onboarding modules that are also available in different languages. Out coding revealed multiple references in the CSR corporate and suitable reports for "partner welfare" initiatives but are defined in inconsistent terms, the inclusion implication is the core initiatives for minimum standards., Platforms can also partner with NGO and government skilling bodies to deliver boarding, including digital literacy or claim process orientation as the activities are currently either patchy or absent. Considering the SHRM system perspective, inclusion requires greater attention to the selection criteria. The lithomic approach highlights that it is feasible to implement wage guarantee mechanisms while also controlling costs. SHRM policymakers can explore more hybrid models in which floor rotations are paired with selected activations. The implementation of these models would then address both the ability and mitigation elements of the AMO framework that are observed to be missing in the analysed text. One of the core findings from the analysis was the opacity for the algorithmic management in the platform corporate policy the corporate term of services encoded the deactivate rules and rating thresholds, while the worker narratives aggravates the issue of unexplained routines, biases and sudden deactivation (Kadolkar et al., 2024). For the SHRM, this creates an urgent need to reconceptualise algorithms based on HR mechanisms rather than just operational engines. If the algorithms can perform the processes of selection, appraisal, reward, and other functions, then they must be designed and governed in a manner that is consistent with fairness, development, and remedial pathways as well. From a practical perspective, the platform should be clear about publishing explanations for key algorithmic decisions, for instance, why the work is deactivated, how the incentives calculator works, and why a job was allocated to other workers. The literature provides support with explanations that can lessen the insult and also prevent the psychosocial outcomes (Liu &Yin, 2024). The thematic coding showcases that when the corporate texts were hinting about the recent channels, they associated them with automated chatbots, which had poor escalations. Henceforth SHRM should provide a mandated human escalation point with transparency for making algorithmic decisions. Some of the systematic reviews published recently recommend hybrid governance in order to preserve the effectiveness and dignity protection of the works ((Kadolkar et al., 2024). Algorithmic design incorporates the fairness audits and stimulates which workers are facing on a daily basis. A practice that our corpus determines to be currently absent but also substantially improvises on the trust. From the perspective of AMO, this provides a redesigning of the motivation and opportunity. Converting the algorithmic systems into the tools for strategic HR than mere control mechanisms. The content analysis has repeatedly exposed the inadequacy faced by app only grievances and support mechanism as well as wraith investigative journalism that points to the chatbots which loops into denial. The mismatch calls for SHRM in order to formalise the digital HR service channels customised for the gig reality, with guaranteed human response times. The recommended digital HR tools would include micro learning, which could be provided through the application for operations, and the ability to build coding. The measures directly address the themes in the findings showcasing the absence of training, weaker to almost negligible grievance redressal and lowered worker voice. Operational metrics shall also be included in the SHRM dashboards with effective responsive times towards accidental claims, rates of successful appeals towards investigations. Our policy suggests a significant aspect for accountability and translates towards operational KPI at the platform level from the SHRM perspective (NITI Aayog, 2022). From the coded evidence, certain platform patches are in correlation with the work outcomes. SHRM adaptations therefore have practical measures with the empirical themes.

- Having guaranteed minimum earnings for prolonged working hours or the minimum per day earnings, which is tied to the platform demand management and a more similar aspect for the WORK4FOOD guaranteed, corresponding to the operations used for real work constraints. Thesis raises concerns for income volatility, in the worker testimonies.
- Transparency in the incentivised calendars wherein the platform could publish the expected schedules for the incentives and also the formulas which clearly state the multiplier rates for the surge hours so the workers can effectively plan. Our content analysis highlights the unexpected incentive changes being a major source for distrust.
- A simplified and fat trust insurance claims with a documentation process which could align with the dedicated claim officers for the gig works incidents. The media coding shows an example wherein technicalities prevented the claims. Micro credential pathways for partnering with government skilling include in app modules identifies the micro credentials to translate the task tiers, to operationalise a career growth theme that was absent across the platform.
- Worker representation mechanisms which could create identification in app work councils with formal meetings and right to raise concerns the required platforms. The analysis conducted in study finds informal protests and union attempts are created because there are no formal channels that are into existence. Each of the suggestion ties the coded themes seeks to move in the platform from the ad hoc announcements in order to be more durable with SHRM practices to create a mutual value.

Our document analysis highlights that the policy the Code on Social Security has progressed and recognises the gig works, but implementation and rule framing is still lagging. The implication for SHRM is that the policy must be clear and have more minimum standards that the platform is required to meet. The regulator should require the platform to publish the anonymised data for average hourly earnings, appeal outcomes and deactivation rates. The findings indicate that public scrutiny drives remedial action rather than voluntary corporate commitments (NITI Aayog, 2022). A minimum accident insurance coverage and claim process as licensing is required for platform operation. The content analysis conducted showed that insurance exists for certain conditions or even for hard-to-claim processes, mandating basic protections that could lessen the variations in work experiences (Steffens et al., 2025). Algorithmic governance standards require an algorithmic impact assessment for major allocation of tasks or deactivation systems including the independence in audits and work consultants which have ebay practices with algorithmic governance literature. The policy level does not end here but there could be SHRM adoptions which provide CSR credits to the platform that can highlight those practices. He noted that review in the study found the platform welfare statements to be promotions. Even though it is not necessary to eliminate the flexibility within the platform, ensure the flexibility does not result in systematic extraction.

Aligning SHRM theory along with gig realities is the conceptual implication from the coding of our study to operational AMO in terms of the platform contexts. The analysis highlights that the current platform texts rarely bundle practice that can strengthen the AMO, but deliver one-off initiatives without having any systematic complementarity(Rivera & Duggan, 2022). While the figure explains the implementation, the content analysis repeatedly finds information to be inconsistent and fragmented. A central conceptual implication from our coded corpus is the need to operationalise AMO (ability, motivation, opportunity) in terms of platform artefacts. The analysis showed that current platform texts rarely produce bundles of practices that jointly strengthen AMO; instead, they deliver one-off initiatives (an insurance policy, a safety webinar) without systemic complementarity. SHRM in gig contexts should therefore adopt an artefact-based view (Iqubbal, 2021).

CONCLUSION

The study employed a qualitative content analysis of documents to explore the application of Strategic Human Resource management principles, particularly in the gig delivery sector, through systematic coding, yielding insights into the emergence of relationships within platforms and the work. The analysis revealed that while platforms position riders as "delivery partners," their policies fall short of conventional HR protections—for instance, social security or performance appraisal systems. Misalignments with SHRM principles, especially regarding employee well-being engagement, create a sense of vulnerability among workers. The study found instances of adaptation towards flexibility in incentive schemes, with limited engagement through the digitalised HR tools. Persistent gaps in the implementation of Code on Social Security mean that the gig workers are still outside the protection mechanisms. The policy highlights youth employment generation, but operational realities continue to mirror the informal economy. The misalignment underscores the need to rethink the HR strategies as well as the governance mechanisms for the Indian gig economy context.

FUTURE DIRECTIONS

Based on the findings and limitations that arise, some avenues require further research, and the practices must emerge as SHRM fireworks expand into gig content.The traditional SHRM models were premised on the employer-employee relationships. Future scholarships need to conceptualise the concept of "Strategic HR for non-standardised work: addressing algorithmic management and flexible employment divinities. Much of the literature is reliant on corporate and policy perspectives. Future research includes longitudinal studies that could capture the lived experiences of gig workers in their well-being and social security aspects (Mehrotra, 2021). Apart from this there could be policy experiments as comparative studies of state-level policies and illuminations about how decentralised government might fill the voids and impact on the SHRM practices. Research examines how platforms leverage the human centre's HR tools to enhance remote performance while balancing efficiency with fairness. While this study is primarily based on food delivery, the gig economy is many services. The future world could also assess SHRM adaptation across industries and the degree of worker substitutability.

REFERENCES

Aayog, N. I. T. I. (2022). *India's booming gig and platform economy*. Government of India. Retrieved from https://www.niti.gov.in/sites/default/files/2023-06/Policy_Brief_India's_Booming_Gig_and_Platform_Economy_27062022.pdf

Amin, M. R. (2025). "Exploring the Evolution of Human Resource Management in the Gig Economy: A Systematic Analysis", Business & Social Sciences, 3(1),1-8,10243

Azevedo, E. S. F., Souza, D. F., & Mendonça, J. R. C. (2023). *Algorithmic management on digital labour platforms: A systematic literature review. Contextus – Contemporary Journal of Economics and Management, 21*, e83099. https://doi.org/ DOI: 10.19094/contextus.2023.83099

Bhandari, B., Das, G. K., Gupta, S., Sahu, A. K., Urs, K. S., Pal, N., & Raj, K. (2023). Socio-economic impact assessment of food delivery platform workers.

Chaudhary, R. (2022). Social security for platform workers in India: Challenges of policy implementation. *The Indian Journal of Labour Economics : The Quarterly Journal of the Indian Society of Labour Economics*, *65*(3), 543–560.

Duggan, J., Sherman, U. P., Carbery, R., & McDonnell, A. (2019). Algorithmic management and app-work in the gig economy: A research agenda for employment relations and HRM. *Human Resource Management Journal*, *30*(1), 114–132. DOI: 10.1111/1748-8583.12258

Eternal Limited. (2024). *Annual report 2023–24* [PDF]. Zomato. Retrieved from https://b.zmtcdn.com/investor-relations/Zomato_Annual_Report_2023-24.pdf

Gohil, J., & Jha, A. (2024). Addressing policy gaps for gig workers in India: A focus on food delivery platforms. *International Journal for Multidisciplinary Research*, *6*(6), 33631. Advance online publication. DOI: 10.36948/ijfmr.2024.v06i06.33631

Government of India. *The Code on Social Security, 2020* (text). https://labour.gov.in/sites/default/files/ss_code_as_introduced_in_lok_sabha.pdf

Hameed, *et al.* (2023). Strategic Human Resource Management, a Road to Organizational Performance: Evidence from Public Sector Organizations in the Oil and Gas Sector. *International Journal of Organizational Leadership, 12*(Special Issue).

Iqubbal, A. (2021). FOOD DELIVERY WORKERS IN INDIA: EMERGING ENTREPRENEURS OR INFORMAL LABOUR? In DEF COVID-19 GROUND REPORT SERIES. https://defindia.org/wp-content/uploads/2021/04/swiggy-zomato-delivery-workers-india-entrepreneurs-labour.pdf

Jakhete, M. Khushboo, Shende, P., Ashok Patil, P., Singh Rana, V., & Raina, A. (2025). Synthesizing Best Practice Frameworks for Results Measurement in Multi Stakeholder Social Entrepreneurship Initiatives. Enterprise Development & Microfinance, 35(1), 140–158. Retrieved from https://papjournals.com/index.php/edm/article/view/12

Kadolkar, I., Kepes, S., & Subramony, M. (2024). Algorithmic management in the gig economy: A systematic review and research integration. *Journal of Organizational Behavior*. Advance online publication. DOI: 10.1002/job.2831

Kant, S., Gelgelo, W. J., & Kero, C. A. (2023). Strategic Human Resource Management: A systematic literature review. *Radinka Journal of Science and Systematic Literature Review, 1*(1), 99–110. DOI: 10.56778/rjslr.v1i2.129

Kaufman, B. E. (2015). Theorising determinants of employee voice: An integrative model across disciplines and levels of analysis. *Human Resource Management Journal, 25*(2), 129–148. DOI: 10.1111/1748-8583.12056

Kuhn, K. M., Meijerink, J., & Keegan, A. E. (2021, August). *Human Resource Management and the gig economy: Challenges and Opportunities at the Intersection between*

Liu, R., & Yin, H. (2024). How Algorithmic Management Influences Gig Workers' Job Crafting. *Behavioral Sciences (Basel, Switzerland), 14*(10), 952. DOI: 10.3390/bs14100952 PMID: 39457824

Mehrotra, S. (2021). Informality and the emerging gig economy in India: The case for universal social protection. *International Labour Review, 160*(1), 67–90.

Rana, V. S., Sharma, D. P., & Thakur, A. Potential of Food Tourism in Punjab (India): A Study of Amritsar, Jalandhar and Patiala (May 2, 2021). Eurasian Journal of Analytical Chemistry (2018) 13 (6): 371-377, Available at SSRN: https://ssrn.com/abstract=3838266

Rivera, V. A., & Duggan, J. (2022). Centering worker well-being in gig work. *Proceedings of the 2022 CHI Conference on Human Factors in Computing Systems*, 1–17. https://doi.org/DOI: 10.1145/3491102.3501866

Sahoo, S., & Mohapatra, S. (2025). *Human capital and sustainability: An emerging perspective*. Springer., DOI: 10.1007/s43615-025-00583-

Steffens, P.. (2025). Human Resource Management Systems research—How to gain impactful insights through formative measurement and hierarchical component models. *Human Resource Management Journal*.

Swiggy Limited. (2025). *Sustainability at Swiggy*. Retrieved September 6, 2025, from https://www.swiggy.com/corporate/sustainability/

Vasanthan, R., Nath Babu, M., Dzuvichu, K., & Chong, T. S., Singh Rana, V., & Singh, A. (2025). Bridging Social Norms Theory and Community Mobilization: Pathways for Overcoming Gender Stereotypes in Women's Economic Empowerment Programs. *Enterprise Development & Microfinance, 35*(1), 159–176. Retrieved from https://www.papjournals.com/index.php/edm/article/view/13

Wright, P. M., & McMahan, G. C. (2011). Exploring human capital: Putting "human" back into strategic human resource management. *Human Resource Management Journal, 21*(2), 93–104. DOI: 10.1111/j.1748-8583.2010.00165.x

Chapter 7
AI and the Evolution of Recruitment:
Transforming Sourcing Screening and Candidate Interactions

Bargavi R.
http://orcid.org/0000-0002-5563-4233
Indian Institute of Technology, Madras, India

ABSTRACT

This chapter is a discussion about the radical transformation of the artificial intelligence (AI) in talent acquisition particularly in relation to efficiency, accuracy and candidate experience. It carries out an evaluation of tools based on AI such as algorithms, chatbots and automated scheduling software, to facilitate sourcing, screening, and engagement activities with a view to ease the changing workforce needs. This form of evolution increases productivity at the workplace, makes the processes more inclusive and encourages flexibility in staffing. The discussion gives a framework that the HR practitioners and scholars can use to evaluate the impact of AI on their recruitment performance, the quality of decisions made by the recruiters, and the engagement of the candidates, therefore, drawing avenues of potential future research and practice in employee management..

1. INTRODUCTION

1.1 An Overview of Artificial Intelligence in Hiring

In talent acquisition context, artificial intelligence refers to the use of the AI technology to facilitate, improve and optimise the hiring process. The use of AI

DOI: 10.4018/979-8-2600-1845-3.ch007

systems has intentionally been designed to take over the roles of human recruiters which have been performed in the past. The activities that involve this form of work include the identification process of the candidates, resume shopping, interview cooking as well as the projection of the performance results of the potential employees. This increased the popularity of AI in the recruitment practice because of the ability to handle huge amounts of data quickly and more accurately, thus allowing organisations to hire the best. By integrating AI into the scheme of things, companies would be able to enhance the quality of hiring decisions, shorten the time frame of the hiring process, and eventually enhance the quality of the entire process of recruitment.

1.2 How AI-Driven Procedures Have Replaced Conventional Hiring Practices

Conventional recruiting models that are characterized by newspaper adverts, physical job fairs, and extensive manual-based HR approaches including paper-based assessment of resumes are cumbersome and usually ineffective in the process of attaining a wide range of qualified candidates (Ali & Kallach, 2024). With the introduction of the internet, online job boards and increased proliferation of social media (overall), the landscape of recruitment has changed immensely providing the capability of recruiters to access the world of talent. Nevertheless, it is mostly a time-consuming manual process and regardless of a more digital climate, it promotes inefficiencies and possible biases.The incorporation of artificial intelligence (AI) into recruiting procedures was a notable advancement, since the automation of activities such as applicant sourcing and screening alleviated the administrative workload on human resources (HR) experts.(Larsson et al., 2024). Artificial intelligence (AI) powered procedures provide a more data-centric methodology, guaranteeing that the recruiting process is not only expedited but also better synchronised with the strategic objectives of the firm.

The primary advantages and obstacles linked to artificial intelligence in the field of recruiting are Application of artificial intelligence in recruiting has various significant advantages, such as increased productivity, less prejudice, and better applicant matching. Through the automation of monotonous duties, artificial intelligence enables recruiters to concentrate on more important elements of the recruiting process, such as engaging candidates and making decisions(Kulkov et al., 2024). The use of artificial intelligence (AI) algorithms can analyse large amounts of data, thus identifying the corresponding patterns and trends that can complement the suitability of a candidate to a job and ultimately enhance retention rates (Ali & Kallach, 2024; Avery et al., 2024; Gupta & Rahimi Ata, 2024; Rahman et al., 2024). Still, its usage of AI in recruitment processes has a number of challenges involved. One of them is algorithmic bias, which entails the fact that AI systems might unintentionally reproduce the already existing bias inherent within the initial data. In addition, this heavy dependence on automation poses the danger of diminishing this vital human element of the recruiting process. Another major con that comes with the application of AI, is the issue of data privacy and security, since sensitive data about candidates ought to be collected and examined. Thus, it is unquestionably true that AI changes are revolutionary, but they should be implemented with strict control, with equity, transparency, and ethical reflection values taking prime positions.

1.3 Literature Review

Focusing on academic research, the role of artificial intelligence (AI) in the recruitment process will be one of the primary investigation fields in the near future. Analysts argue that AI-related processes are capable of reshaping talent acquisition by the mutually reinforcing impacts of automation, data analytics, and personalisation which collectively hold the prospect of disrupting traditional recruiting mindsets of workforce (Ali & Kallach, 2024; Kulkov et al., 2024). By contrast, traditionally practiced methods are constantly accused of being inefficient and breeding bias, as well as especially severe shortcomings related to scalability, caused by the reliance on manual resumes review, face-to-face interviews, and the use of talent pools restrictively limited to physically localized sectors (Larsson et al., 2024; Lourens et al., 2024). The emergence of the internet-based job boards, applicant tracking systems (ATS) and social media recruiting are reflective of an early step toward digitisation, although a significant amount of recruitment remains reactive and time consuming.

Recruitment technologies that use AI overcome these structural constraints as they make the process of candidate sourcing and screening more streamlined. The algorithm scours huge volumes of information, such as internet profiles, professional social media networks, and online footprints and proactively identifies potential candidates (Di Prima et al., 2024). Coupled in a relevant style, the AI automated screening tool is the resume parsing, search keywords and predictive analytics used to compare the credentials and score applicants on a job-fit scale which greatly lowers the time-to-hiring process. Sophisticated structures also include video interview evaluation, psychometric tests, and cultural compatibility reviews, which enables an all-dimensional examination of the candidates (Nawaz et al., 2024).At the same time, artificial intelligence is coming into candidacy. Chatbots Such as Mya, Olivia, etc. enable 24/7 engagement, accept questions and requests by applicants, and induce candidates through hiring procedures (Gershon, 2024). The scheduling of the interviews software implementation will facilitate logistical inefficiencies, and sending outreach messages in a personalised manner will result in the amplified engagement and employer branding (Argueta-Rivera et al., 2024).

The entire candidate relationship management (CRM) system with AI is capable of maintaining long-term relations with the candidates leading toward proactive recruitment pipelines (Ekuma, 2024).

Academic reservations have, however, repeatedly been expressed toward the blind use of AI in hiring. Having biased algorithms based on historically determined data sets could continue discriminating unless such algorithms are fixed, thus making it imperative that regular auditing and proper measures that reinforce ethics be embedded (Larsson et al., 2024; Manroop et al., 2024). Other debates that have been ongoing focus on the problem of data privacy and dehumanization in decision making (Cruz, 2024). Therefore, scientists promote a moderate orientation where an AI will complement human judgment, not substitute it, and it is then ensured that the recruitment practices will no longer be unfair, opaque and exclusive.

2. HISTORICAL BACKGROUND OF THE CHANGING LANDSCAPE OF RECRUITMENT

Recruiting used to be an arduous and time consuming process based on physical posters, word of mouth and the above mentioned kind of networking: job fairs. Employer would put job opening in newspaper or on info bulletin and applicants would mail in their apps, either in person, (Botsivali et al., 2024). Subsequently, recruiters would meticulously examine stacks of resumes to pinpoint appropriate prospects in Figure 1.

Figure 1. Changing Landscape of Recruitment

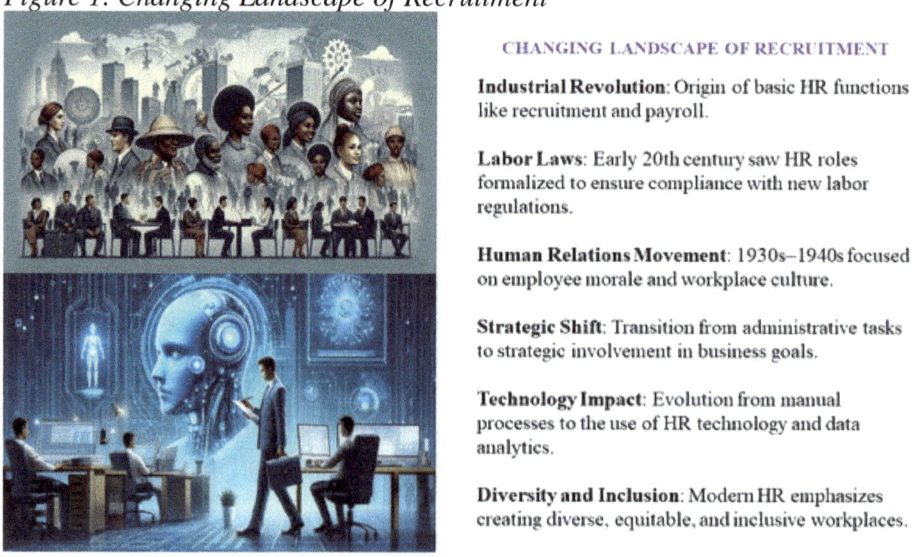

Historically, interviews were only carried out face-to-face, requiring much organisation and effort.(Gershon, 2024). The technique had several constraints: it was limited by geography, therefore restricting the variety of the applicant pool; it was sluggish, frequently leading to protracted recruiting procedures; and it was susceptible to human biases, which may result in less than ideal hiring judgments. (Lourens et al., 2024). Furthermore, conventional approaches were deficient in scalability, thereby posing challenges for enterprises to effectively manage substantial quantities of applications.

2.1 Research Methodology

The current chapter uses a qualitative, exploratory approach to discussing how the concept of artificial intelligence (AI) has changed the way talent is acquired. Given the critical rewithdrawal of the literature, industry news, and professional articles, the discussion focuses on the topic of AI-enhanced recruitment practices, that is, sourcing, screening, candidate attraction, and the ethical issues relating to it. Evidence provided on case basis of the best organisations and the most available AI tools which are LinkedIn Recruiter, ZipRecruiter, Smart Recruiters, Mya, Olivia and Pymetrics is analysed in order to provide demonstrations of the practical examples and results. The sources were deliberately chosen to attain a variety of sectoral and geographical views which in turn makes sure that the resulting findings will contain global trends and localised difficulties. A thematic analysis allows determining recurring patterns, advantages and dangers of the adoption of AI in the process of recruitment. The proposed methodological approach can result in the combination of theoretical knowledge with empirical practice, and it provides a conceptual context that can be used to direct both HR practitioners, researchers, and policymakers in the future assessment and development or utilization of AI-guided recruitment approaches.

2.2 Reference the Transition Towards Digitisation in Human Resources

The emergence of the internet in the latter part of the 20th century brought about a significant transformation in the field of recruiting by bringing digital platforms such as online job boards (e.g., Monster.com, Indeed), therefore enabling companies to access a much broader range of potential candidates. The transition to digitisation allowed recruiters to publish job vacancies on the internet, accept applications electronically, and log applicant information in digital databases, therefore greatly simplifying the recruiting process(McPhail et al., 2024). Email emerged as the predominant means of contact between recruiters and applicants, substantially accelerating exchanges. The advent of HR software solutions, such as Applicant Tracking solutions (ATS), has facilitated enhanced organising and monitoring of applicants throughout the recruiting process. Notwithstanding these improvements, the procedure continued to be mostly manual and responsive, with recruiters being inundated by the voluminous amount of applications.

2.3 Technology's Effect

Detail how technological progress, particularly artificial intelligence, is revolutionising the process of recruiting.(Prabhu et al., 2024). The integration of artificial intelligence (AI) into the field of recruiting has had a transformative impact. The advent of AI technology has revolutionised the process of talent attraction, screening, and hiring for firms by automating many formerly labour-intensive activities. Artificial intelligence (AI)-driven systems are now capable of analysing resumes, using predetermined criteria to evaluate prospects, and even forecasting a candidate's prospective performance inside a company using machine learning algorithms. Through the analysis of huge quantities of data that would be unfeasible for a person to analyse properly, these technologies not only save time but also enhance the precision of candidate selection. Moreover, AI has the potential to mitigate unconscious prejudice by standardising the screening procedure. However, it also presents the difficulty of guaranteeing that the algorithms behind the system are devoid of bias. Moreover, AI has facilitated the use of predictive analytics in the field of recruiting, enabling organisations to anticipate forthcoming hiring requirements and detect patterns in applicant conduct, resulting in more proactive and strategic hiring choices.(Daniels, 2024).

2.4 Examine the Emergence of Digital Platforms, Social Media, and Internet-Based Employment Portals

Social media and digital platforms have become essential components of contemporary recruiting techniques. Platforms such as LinkedIn have revolutionised the recruiting process by offering a worldwide professional network where recruiters can choose applicants based on comprehensive profiles that include employment history, skills, endorsements, and even suggestions. Online job platforms like Indeed.com, Glassdoor.com, and those within a particular industry now allow candidates to search the available opportunities and apply in a short time, and meanwhile allow recruiters to advertise job vacancies and filter through the resumes of potential candidates (Desai et al., 2024). At the same time, a use of social media, which includes Twitter and Facebook, is becoming ever more present to attract the attention of potential employees, help develop the company culture, and spread information about the available positions. Using these methods, recruiters will be able to target the targeted applicants that are not proactively seeking employment but who are open to new opportunities thus widening the pool of recruitable talent.

3. CURRENT RECRUITMENT TRENDS

The past years have also seen a number of influential changes which have restructured the field of recruiting drastically. Remarkably, this movement towards remote employment has increased dramatically, a trend that has escalated at an alarming rate since the COVID-19 pandemic and the resultant boost the distributed labour received.(Cheng et al., 2024; McPhail et al., 2024).Corporate entities are now more receptive to recruiting skilled individuals from various geographic regions, resulting in a more varied and worldwide labour force. The gig economy, defined by temporary contracts or independent labour, has also expanded, as firms increasingly depend on gig workers for highly specialised tasks.(Van Slageren & Herrmann, 2024).

Figure 2.

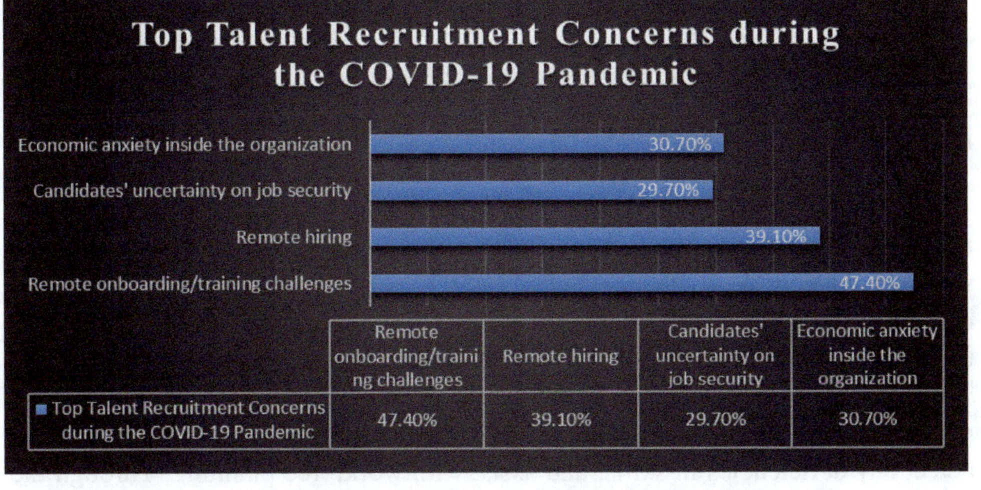

This transition has generated a need for versatile recruiting protocols that can promptly adjust to the recruitment of freelancers and contract workers. Moreover, there is an increasing need for specialised compétences, namely in domains such as technology, data science, and cybersecurity, propelled by rapid progress in these sectors shown in Figure 3.

Figure 3. Current Recruitment Trends

Contemporary recruiters prioritise the acquisition of candidates with specialised knowledge and current abilities, typically seeking experts with certificates and experience in developing technologies.(Avery et al., 2024).

3.1 Growing use of data analytics in the process of decision-making

Data analytics has emerged as an essential element of contemporary recruiting methods(Rahman et al., 2024). Armed with extensive data, recruiters are now able to scrutinise patterns, evaluate the efficiency of their recruitment procedures, and make choices based on facts. Data analytics may provide insights into the sourcing channels that provide the most high-quality applicants, the phases of the recruiting process with the largest drop-off rates, and the average duration required to fill a staffing post. Predictive analytics can analyse and predict future recruitment requirements, detect any deficiencies in skills, and assist with workforce planning. Through the use of data, organisations can enhance their recruiting methods, decrease the time required to hire, enhance the experience of candidates, and ultimately, make more informed hiring choices. Nevertheless, the difficulty is in guaranteeing the precision of data, preserving the integrity of applicant confidentiality, and analysing data in a manner that enhances the recruiting process.(Zhang & Chen, 2024).

4. LEVERAGING AI IN CANDIDATE SOURCING AND SCREENING

The recruiting process has been greatly enhanced by the use of artificial intelligence (AI), which has enabled the automation of repetitive operations such as applicant matching and examination of resumes. This shortens the amount of time it takes to acquire new employees, eliminates the likelihood of bias, and enables recruiters to concentrate on strategic talent acquisition. In today's highly competitive employment market, the incorporation of artificial intelligence (AI) into the recruiting process not only improves the quality of hires but also makes the hiring process nimbler and more responsive Figure 4.

Figure 4. **Leveraging AI in Candidate Sourcing and Screening**

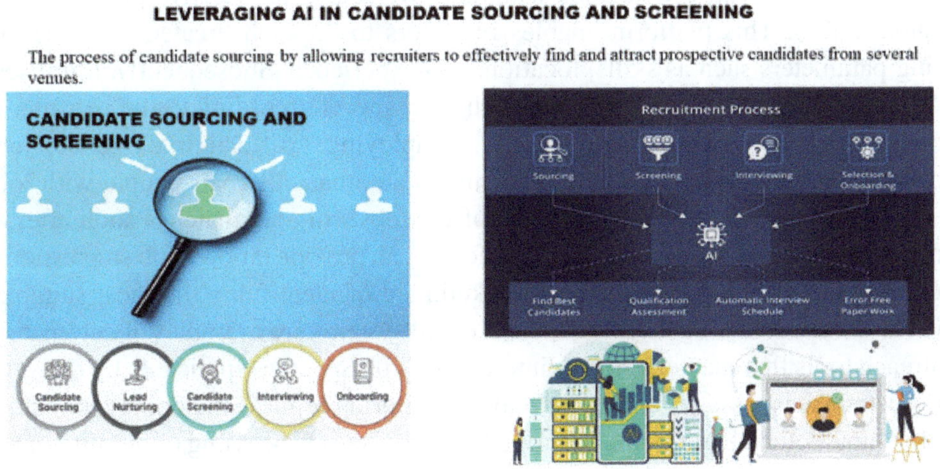

4.1 Artificial Intelligence-Driven Candidate Sourcing

Consider how the problem of AI algorithm identifying prospective applicants working on various platforms and attractive to them. Through artificial intelligence (AI) algorithms, candidate sourcing is re-inventing the process of finding and attracting candidate in various different locations. Unlike conventional systems, which rely on human search or passive job boards, AI tools proactively search the internet, social media, and huge databases and find the candidates who perfectly meet job-related requirements (Di Prima et al., 2024). Analyzing profiles, resumes, internet activity, and other sources of digital footprints, AI has the capacity to present a list of candidates limited to those who do and do not have the required skills, expertise, and the proper traits embodied in this instance by geographical location, industry knowledge, and for cultural compatibility (Ali & Kallach, 2024). In addition, such systems evaluate the applicants in relation to how close they are to the job description, and thus allow the recruiter to concentrate his/her attention on the potential high performers. Passive job-seekers- people who might not actively seek a new job but who demonstrate readiness to consider a new opportunity- are also identified by AI-driven sourcing platforms with the help of analysis of their online behavior and interaction with the related content.

Many artificial intelligence (AI)-driven technologies have become indispensable in contemporary recruiting procedures(Botsivali et al., 2024). LinkedIn Recruiter, for instance, used artificial intelligence to enhance the efficiency of recruiters in locating, establishing connections with, and overseeing prospective prospects(Gershon, 2024). This platform enables recruiters to do sophisticated searches by using parameters such as skills, location, and experience. Subsequently, it utilises artificial intelligence to recommend further prospects according to the recruiter's preferences and previous engagements. Employing artificial intelligence, job boards like ZipRecruiter and SmartRecruiters automatically pair people with job posts, frequently offering a concise list of the most suitable matches soon after a position is listed. Furthermore, these platforms can provide tailored job suggestions to applicants, therefore enhancing the likelihood of identifying the most suitable match. Artificial intelligence (AI)-driven email systems are examples of automated outreach tools that may effectively interact with prospective applicants by delivering customised messages on a large scale, monitoring replies, and doing automatic follow-ups(Potočnik et al., n.d.). During the early-stage processing of recruitments, a large percentage of recruitment time frames are expended. With simplification of this preliminary step, organisations will save much money on labour and workload on the following stages.

4.2 Artificial Intelligence in Screening

When discussing the realm of initial applicant screening, namely, resume processing and keyword matching with the help of automation most often in mind, we may define artificial intelligence (AI) as the key to the transition of the traditionally resource-intensive and labour-demanding processes to the automated mode. In the space of recruiting, one of the key applications of AI is the so-called resume parsing in which documents dedicated to candidates are systematically scanned to extract valuable information, such as competencies, work experience, educational background and official certification. Due to this functionality, AI-powered systems

ensure the examination of huge pools of applications in considerably less passing time in comparison to the manual process without excluding any applicant (Prabhu et al., 2024). The use of keyword matching is another AI method where the system will recognize particular terms or phrases that correlate with the listed requirements in the job description, as well as allow it to discard candidates who do not meet the minimum qualifications, in turn, downsizing the workload of the recruiter. Furthermore, AI has the ability to rank candidates based on established criteria eg longevity of experience, authenticity of credentials or existence of specific technical skills and give each of them a rating score that is in numerical form, thus allowing recruiters to prioritize those individuals best suited to prosper in the desired job position.

Artificial intelligence (AI) has represented an eminent device used in the estimation of competencies, characteristics of personalities and cultural co-existence in modern organization. These are preliminary-level screening processes that are usually complemented by AI-based tests that probe skills, personal traits and future cultural fit. Such systems allow multidimensional evaluation since they are able to administer very broad evaluations ranging on the one hand to performance-based tests, and on the other hand to psychometric questionnaires. An example of an assessment that incorporates neuroscience in the form of gaming modules to measure cognitive and affective indicators hence predicting how appropriate the person would be to a particular job or corporate culture is Pymetrics. Going beyond that mission, AI-facilitated analysis of video interview materials takes account of more than the verbal content; they also take into consideration tonal clues, kinesic indicators, and facial expressions. With such modulators, the recruiters can be able to detect qualities relating to self-confidence, communicative efficacy, and emotional intelligence. Furthermore, some AI structures determine the relationship between a candidate and organizational culture by matching characteristics and behaviors of the prospective employee to those who are existing high-performers (Nawaz et al., 2024). These abilities have a cumulative effect in yielding a holistic profile of the applicants, one that goes beyond employing only resume based evidence and makes certain that chosen individuals, beyond meeting technical specifications also resonate harmoniously with valves and working environment of the host organization.

4.3 Advantages and Disadvantages in Candidate Sourcing and Screening

4.3.1 Key Benefits

Various benefits of the automated deployment of artificial intelligence to source candidates and screen them arise. The first is a high level of efficiency: AI processing systems are capable of working much faster on large amounts of information in

comparison to people, thus allowing organisations to identify and sort out suitable candidates quickly. Therefore, the time-to-hires is reduced, which is a critically important aspect within the employment context that is characterised by increased competition. Another significant benefit is the possibility of less arbitrariness. AI technologies, when well engineered, may standardize the assessment process, guaranteeing that all applicants are evaluated based on the same criteria, therefore reducing unconscious biases that might impact human decision-making(Kulkov et al., 2024)(Kulkov et al., 2024). AI is especially useful for companies that get thousands of resumes for a single job ad since it can easily manage massive numbers of applicants. Through the automation of the early phases of recruiting, artificial intelligence (AI) liberates human resources consultants to concentrate on more strategic responsibilities, such as engaging with candidates and making the final decision(Manroop et al., 2024).

4.3.2 Areas of Concern

Potential for algorithmic bias, issues with data privacy, excessive dependence on technology: Despite its benefits, the use of artificial intelligence in recruiting is not devoid of obstacles(Cruz, 2024; Desai et al., 2024). An urgent and significant issue is the potential for algorithmic bias. AI systems acquire knowledge from past data, and if that data has biases (gender, ethnicity, or age, for example), the AI may unintentionally reinforce those prejudices in its suggestions. Artificial intelligence (AI) can also bring in bias into the hiring process through several ways such as propagating historical discriminatory trends present in algorithmic training data. Such algorithms hence need to be constantly evaluated and refined, in order to reduce this risk to a minimum, and reaffirm fairness and transparency. In addition, sensitive personal information processed as per the requirement brings in grave data-privacy issues. It is the responsibility of organisations to make sure that they do not violate the principles of data protection and are able to maintain heightened levels of security against breach or malicious activity. Also, overusing AI systems poses a risk of overriding the subtle human wisdom that is required to evaluate such qualities as cultural compatibility or development potential. Therefore, it is imperative to maintain a healthy equilibrium between machine intelligence and humanity to produce optimal results with regards to the recruiting process.

5. ENHANCING THE CANDIDATE EXPERIENCE THROUGH AI ENABLED HR PRACTICES

The critical analysis of how the deployment of chatbots and virtual assistants enhanced with AI works demonstrates that this technology becomes an essential tool that helps improve applicant communication during the online-based application process (Gershon, 2024).

5.1 Artificial Intelligence in Customised Candidate Communication

Modern artificial intelligence (AI) powered systems are specifically created to communicate in both directions with candidates, supplying answers to questions, navigating candidates through the application process, and offering subtly-specific information about the institution and opportunities that can be available. Artificial intelligence chatbots like as Mya and Olivia can perform a diverse array of jobs, including applicant screening and interview scheduling, while simultaneously preserving a conversational and captivating demeanour. With their round-the-clock availability, these virtual assistants guarantee that applicants may get prompt support irrespective of time zones or working hours. The continuous accessibility greatly enhances the applicant experience by minimising waiting periods and offering immediate answers to frequently asked queries, such as clarifications on the job description, the progress of their application, or the subsequent stages in the process.

5.2 Illustrate the PROCESs by Which AI may Customize Messages According to Candidate Profiles

The use of automatized intelligence in the human-resources management process allows acquiring a critical strategic capability to tailor the candidate communication based on unique applicant attributes. Artificial intelligence can analyze the data based on the resumΓ©s of the applicants, the application forms, and online profile, and compose messages that could be concretely related to the special abilities, experiences, and areas of interest of the person. As another example, the artificial intelligence system can send a personal email to the applicant highlighting how their set of unique skills overlaps with the concerned vacancy. The letters could also include contextual documents which can include blog articles or case studies, with which the professional performance of the applicant used to be justified (Argueta-Rivera et al., 2024). This tailoring will create a stronger value and understanding in applicants by creating a greater level of perception towards the organization leading to increased understanding and greater levels of attention to the recruitment process.

Moreover, the artificial intelligence can trace the user history with the organization in terms of read emails and clicked links. This ability will make it possible to refine and adjust the further communications and this will also make the overall experience of a candidate more substantial and relevant (figure 5).

Figure 5. HR Trends in AI (2024)

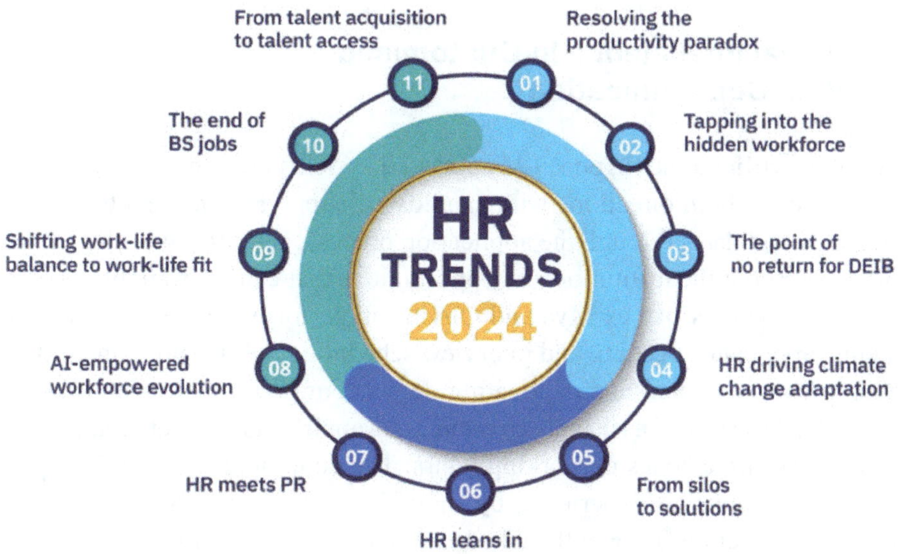

6. ARTIFICIAL INTELLIGENCE IN INTERVIEW SCHEDULING AND FEEDBACK

Organization of interviews Designing the interviews is a very long, labour-intensive part of the recruitment cycle, and involves the successive giving and receiving of information between candidates and interviewers until an optimum time is agreed. As a way of reducing these logistical requirements there have also been the development of AI enabled systems including x.ai and Calendar to allow the relatively cross-referencing of the scheduling of potential candidates and hiring representatives in order to find free windows in each others schedule, create a time slot through the system and automatically book an interview. To streamline the process, these sites send reminders, allow rescheduling when hindered by conflicts and even provide instructions to the participants on preparation or video-conference access. Outsourcing this type of operations to this form of AI helps not only save the time spent by

recruiters but also makes the experience of scheduling an applicant less burdensome and enjoyable. Simultaneously, AI can be used to hasten the delivery of feedback to the candidates, a very decisive part of the candidate journey. Many applicants have complained about long communication delays, which in most of the cases translates into frustration and lowered perceptions of organizational professionalism. There might be automated feedback systems, which would be able to tell a specific message at each point of the recruitment path, telling one their progress, or telling them of a status change, or telling them of something definite. These approaches ensure timely and satisfactory feedback, develop a better understanding of the selection criteria by the candidates, as well as allow an adoptee to notice weaknesses that he can address in further applications. Factually, this continued communication not only legitimizes the time and efforts extended by the applicants, but also enhances their overall experience as a candidate.

6.1 Outline the Capacity of Artificial Intelligence to Provide a More Seamless and Uniform Candidate Experience

Improved artificial intelligence (AI) functionality in smoothing the transitions and mechanical processes of talent acquisition allows future employees to undergo a less jumbled and diversified process. Through the reduction of the risks of administrative errors or unavoidable delays and interruptions, the systems equipped with AI can provide a predictable schedule, consistent communication, and fast feedback, elements that in the past cause delays and inefficiencies in the recruitment cycle. Moreover, applicants with use of such platforms will be assessed and given attention fairly regardless of their place in the application pipeline, hence maintaining conformity within an organization. Automatized interviews, such as standardized ones, become possible in the process of utilizing AI and allows presenting the same sets of inquiries to all interviewees, hence helping reduce bias and variability inherent in human-interviewer conversations. As a result, AI enhances the candidate experience as a whole by further increasing transparency, anticipatability, and responsiveness to the needs of the applicants along the recruitment lifecycle.

7. LONG-TERM CANDIDATE ENGAGEMENT

Artificial intelligence (AI) may strongly contribute to the maintenance of enduring connections with applicants, even after the completion of the recruiting process(E-kuma, 2024). Organizations have increasingly acknowledged the significance of candidate relationship management (CRM) systems, which use artificial intelligence (AI) to maintain communication with individuals who were not chosen for a present position but may be well-suited for future prospects(Nawaz et al., 2024). Artificial intelligence (AI) has the capability to mechanize routine contact with these applicants, via transmission of corporate updates, job notifications, and tailored material tailored to their interests and previous engagements. This continuous involvement ensures that the organization remains at the forefront of prospective applicants' minds and contributes to the development of a pool of talented individuals that can be accessed when new job openings arise. Furthermore, artificial intelligence has the capability to examine candidate data longitudinally in order to detect patterns and inclinations, therefore enabling human resources teams to customize their communication strategies and re-engage applicants with prospects that correspond to their changing professional objectives. The practice itself concerning regularity in the retention practice in any organization can significantly reduce the time span and reduce the cost of hiring newer applicants, considering that the retention preserves a pool of dedicated and skilled staff who have already been initiated to the firm and the corporate cultural environment.

Artificial intelligence reliance in predictive analytics, which is rapidly growing, has become part and parcel of the current approach toward future HR needs and workforce management. Artificial intelligence (AI) can predict the future employment needs using past data by questioning historical records about employee performance, employee attrition, and recruiting results. The technology can, to give one example, identify patterns that indicate an impending rising demand of specific competencies and these can usually be initiated by either external market trends or internal organizational factors like expansion of its operations or introduction of new products. This kind of foresight also allows human resources departments to interact with potential candidates in a proactive manner and also to plan strategic moves in future recruiting campaigns(Olson et al., 2024). In talent management, AI supports analyses of such dimensions as employee engagement, career growth, and skill development, thus enabling the discovery of persons with high potential, who are at the stage of being promoted or at the risk of changing the workplace. The insights thus obtained deliver the power to employ proactive retention interventions, such as specific professional growth programming, advancement opportunities, and incentive designs by the HR department. In sum, the use of predictive analytics can improve the effectiveness of recruitment procedures and perfect the practice of managing personnel, and eventually bring forth a workforce, where engagement and productivity are on the rise.

8. PROBLEMS OF ETHICS

The increasing use of the phenomenon of artificial intelligence (AI) in the work of human resources (HR) is an area that needs a more careful concern with the ethical imperatives of three domains: openness, justice, and inclusiveness (Rodriguez et al., 2024). The issue of openness heads the list of these concerns. Vaynerchuk states that both future candidates and current workers should be educated regarding the use of AI in the recruitment and talent management within an organisation as well as regarding the exact collection of data that will be analysed by the AI system and the decision-making process that will follow. The lack of transparency in this regard can create distrust coupled with a subsequent loss of credibility of the organisation. Employers, in turn, should be responsible for explaining how AI will be used in the HR processes and how the personal information will be applied by the applicants. In addition, fair treatment is another eminent ethical consideration that forms the basis of Figure 6.

Figure 6. **Problems of Ethics**

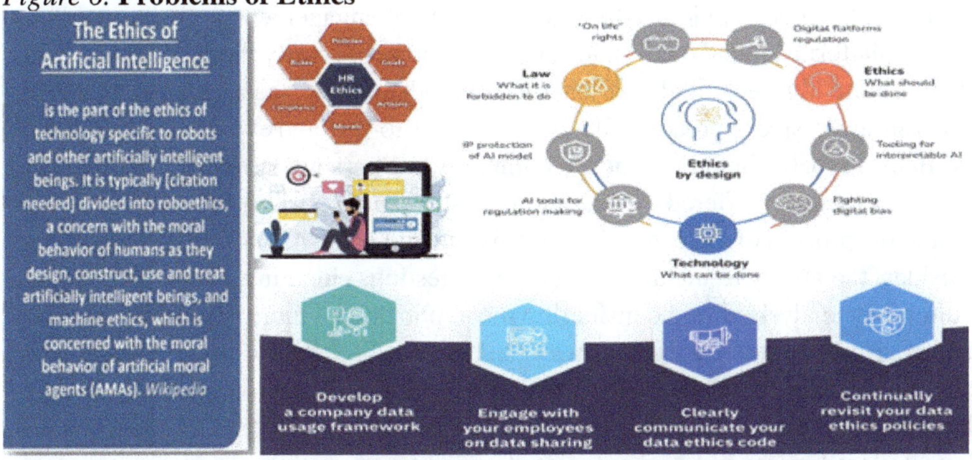

The modern literature has acknowledged the possibility that though artificial intelligence (AI) has the theoretical potential of curbing human bias, mal-designed and untested models can bring new types of bias. An example would be when an artificial intelligence network learns an old data that represents biased hiring tendencies and ends up retaining the biases unintentionally. As a means of reducing such risk, frequent audit should be generated to make AI systems deliver fair and non-discriminatory rulings. These audits will probably necessitate the appropriateness of the data diversification training and compliance with predefined standards of fairness, and the human involvement in such critical decision-making situations.

Besides, inclusivity is a major ethical concern. AI systems must be modeled in such a way that a full range of applicants will be taken into consideration such as individuals of different sociocultural backgrounds, different technological availability, and disparate communication preferences. Such a hiring approach as the one based on AI and rooted mostly in video interviews will, for example, disproportionately penalize all the candidates who feel uneasy about using the video technologies and those with limited access to good high-speed internet connections. The organisations should, therefore, make sure that their human resource procedures that are implemented using AI remain exhaustive and cannot automatically rule out good candidates on grounds irrelevant to job performance.

9. DISCUSSIONS

The facts show that artificial intelligence is the future of recruitment because it integrates automation processes, data analysis and custom messaging at each stage of the applicant process. AI-powered tools have gone a step further in candidate sourcing, from passive job posting to active talent engagement, actively searching digital platforms, social media and career networks to identify those candidates who demonstrate high potential, not just those who happen to see a particular posting. Such an aggressive approach will reduce the time-to-hire and expands the talent pool available globally. In the case of screening, resume parsing, keyword matching, and predictive scoring, offered by AI, eliminate substantial portions of the manual burden in the process of the candidate shortlisting and make it much more demanding. Besides, the ability to include psychometric testing, video interview analysis, and cultural-fit analysis allows considering the applicant in a more comprehensive way DIJSE. However, there are issues with the biasness of the algorithms, data security, and hypertrophic reliance on automation, which has led to the increased need of human supervision. Regarding the experience of the candidate, AI-enhanced chatbots, tailored messaging and automated appointment-setting complement engagement, receptiveness, and visibility. The long-term relationships with talent are also sustained through continuous feedback systems, as well as candidate relationship management (CRM) tools, to which a long-term advantage in the future hiring can be attributed. Predictive analytics can help the HR department to foresee the deficiencies in skills and realign recruiting to the business growth patterns. Despite these changes, the discussion restates the necessity of having a balance between machine intelligence, and the judgement of a human. Although theoretically, AI can achieve operational efficiency and less bias, poorly designed or training data with bias can marginalize people. Another principal success factor in sustainable AI adoption in the recruitment process is ethical stewardship, which is inclusive, fair, and transparent. To conclude, AI does not state that it replaces human recruiters but rather defines itself as a strategic HR tool that allows professionals to concentrate on building relationships, aligning with the cultures, and long-term employee planning.

10. FUTURE DIRECTIONS

This study also reports a range of avenues of future research and practice, and these will start off with longitudinal studies that are aimed at evaluating the long-term impact of AI-driven recruitment on employee performance, retention, and diversity outcomes. The second approach is cross-industrial and cross-regional comparative studies of AI-enabled and non-AI methods of recruiting and consequently increasing the contextuality of the effectiveness insights. Thirdly, the question after integration with the emerging technologies (blockchain to verify credentials, virtual reality to conduct immersive exercises, and highly-predictive analytics to plan the workforce) should be asked in order to engage more with the recruitment processes. Fourth, researchers have to design and experimentally validate ethical AI models specifically fitted to the recruiting process to deal with algorithmic bias, transparency, and data-privacy issues. Lastly, one should focus on the changing the scopes of HR professionals in settings that are augmented by AI and, specifically, on the skills, competencies, and change-management approaches that will be required to allow the incorporation of automatic solutions with human decision-making.

11. CONCLUSION

The above discussions strongly show the case that artificial intelligence (AI) is transforming talent acquisition to increase productivity, improve candidate interaction, and enable data-informed decisions. The integration of AI into the recruiting process currently makes it possible not only to implement AI-based candidate sourcing and screening procedures but also to introduce a seamless system of communicating with candidates and organising the meetings with them, thus enhancing the experience of the applicants, as a whole. Future AI-enabled recruiting research indicates that the sophistication of predictive analytics will continue to increase, highly developed AI-driven assessment tools will make an entrance into the market, and the expanded use of AI will be positively used to increase diversity and inclusion efforts. At the same time, the growth of AI should be measured in tandem with a continuing dependence on human intuition to guide a more personal understanding of the many variables and circumstances that human resource experts add to the process of hiring workers. Lastly, as the potential of AI is growing, ethical stewardship has become particularly important: organizations should give priority to the transparent, unbiased, and inclusive approach to AI systems designed in such a way that the process of recruiting can at once be efficient and ethical, and that all candidates should be judged in the same light.

REFERENCES

Ali, O., & Kallach, L. (2024). Artificial Intelligence Enabled Human Resources Recruitment Functionalities: A Scoping Review. *Procedia Computer Science, 232*, 3268–3277. DOI: 10.1016/j.procs.2024.02.142

Argueta-Rivera, J., Chen, Y. R., Jean-Baptiste, T., Siner, C., & Hebl, M. (2024). Recruitment in the modern context. In *Essentials of Employee Recruitment* (pp. 285–306). Routledge. DOI: 10.4324/9781003356752-18

Avery, M., Leibbrandt, A., & Vecci, J. (2024). *Does artificial intelligence help or hurt gender diversity? Evidence from two field experiments on recruitment in tech.*

Botsivali, M., Xanthopoulou, P., & Sahinidis, A. (2024). *Remote Work And The Future of Human Resources: A literature review.*

Cheng, Y.-T., Lavieri, P. S., de Sá, A. L. S., & Astroza, S. (2024). Investigating the effects of ICT evolution and the COVID-19 pandemic on the spatio-temporal fragmentation of work activities. *Transportation Research Part A, Policy and Practice, 187*, 104192. DOI: 10.1016/j.tra.2024.104192

Cruz, I. F. (2024). Expert-AI pairings: Expert interventions in AI-powered decisions. *Information and Organization, 34*(4), 100527. DOI: 10.1016/j.infoandorg.2024.100527

Daniels, L. N. (2024). *An investigation into the perceived impact of Artificial Intelligence on recruitment and selection practices of HR professionals within the retail sector in the Western Cape.*

Desai, R., Greer, E., & Waldron, M. (2024). *Identifying Barriers: Analysis of Federal Law Enforcement Social Media and Recruitment Efforts.*

Di Prima, C., Cepel, M., Kotaskova, A., & Ferraris, A. (2024). Help me help you: How HR analytics forecasts foster organizational creativity. *Technological Forecasting and Social Change, 206*, 123540. DOI: 10.1016/j.techfore.2024.123540

Ekuma, K. (2024). Artificial Intelligence and Automation in Human Resource Development: A Systematic Review. *Human Resource Development Review, 23*(2), 199–229. DOI: 10.1177/15344843231224009

Gershon, I. (2024). *Down and out in the new economy: How people find (or don't find) work today.* University of Chicago Press.

Gupta, A., & Rahimi Ata, K. (2024). *Data-Driven Hiring: Implementing AI and Assessing the Impact of AI on Recruitment Efficiency and Candidate Quality.*

Kulkov, I., Kulkova, J., Rohrbeck, R., Menvielle, L., Kaartemo, V., & Makkonen, H. (2024). Artificial intelligence-driven sustainable development: Examining organizational, technical, and processing approaches to achieving global goals. *Sustainable Development (Bradford)*, *32*(3), 2253–2267. DOI: 10.1002/sd.2773

Larsson, S., White, J. M., & Ingram Bogusz, C. (2024). The Artificial Recruiter: Risks of Discrimination in Employers' Use of AI and Automated Decision-Making. *Social Inclusion (Lisboa)*, *12*, 12. DOI: 10.17645/si.7471

Lourens, M., Vijai, C., Nijhawan, G., Garwal, Y. S., Gakhreja, S., & Saud, A. M. (2024). Artificial Intelligence-Driven Talent Management System: Exploring the Risks and Options Sustainable Success. *2024 4th International Conference on Innovative Practices in Technology and Management (ICIPTM)*, 1–6.

Manroop, L., Malik, A., & Milner, M. (2024). The ethical implications of big data in human resource management. *Human Resource Management Review*, *34*(2), 101012. DOI: 10.1016/j.hrmr.2024.101012

McPhail, R., Chan, X. W., May, R., & Wilkinson, A. (2024). Post-COVID remote working and its impact on people, productivity, and the planet: An exploratory scoping review. *International Journal of Human Resource Management*, *35*(1), 154–182. DOI: 10.1080/09585192.2023.2221385

Nawaz, N., Arunachalam, H., Pathi, B. K., & Gajenderan, V. (2024). The adoption of artificial intelligence in human resources management practices. *International Journal of Information Management Data Insights*, *4*(1), 100208. DOI: 10.1016/j.jjimei.2023.100208

Olson, D. A., Jeske, D., & Shultz, K. S. (2024). Developing, nurturing, and expanding personal and professional relationships through social media. In *Handbook of Social Media Use Online Relationships, Security, Privacy, and Society Volume 2* (pp. 195–215). Elsevier. DOI: 10.1016/B978-0-443-28804-3.00010-7

Potočnik, K., Anderson, N., Born, M. P., Kleinmann, M., & Nikolaou, I. (n.d.). *Recent Developments in Recruitment and Selection.*

Prabhu, U., Fathima, Y., Sathyanarayana, N., Srikumar, M. S. S. V., & Cavaliere, L. P. L. (2024). Emerging Digitalization Trends in Human Resource Management. In *Data-Driven Intelligent Business Sustainability* (pp. 214–234). IGI Global.

Rahman, S. U., Sultan, M. S., & Tabassam, A. (2024). THE IMPACT OF THE GIG ECONOMY ON TRADITIONAL EMPLOYMENT AND THE NECESSITY FOR REVISED BUSINESS, HR, AND LEGAL STRATEGIES. *Pakistan Journal of International Affairs*, *7*(1).

Rodriguez, R. V., Hemachandran, K., Majumdar, A., & Basu, R. (2024). *1st International Conference, 'Resonance': on Cognitive Approach, Social Ethics and Sustainability: 23 and 24th November, 2022 School Of Liberal Arts and Humanities, Woxsen University, India*. Taylor & Francis.

Van Slageren, J., & Herrmann, A. M. (2024). Skill Specificity on High-Skill Online Gig Platforms: Same as in Traditional Labour Markets? *Social Forces*, *102*(4), 1332–1351. DOI: 10.1093/sf/soad153

Zhang, J., & Chen, Z. (2024). Exploring human resource management digital transformation in the digital age. *Journal of the Knowledge Economy*, *15*(1), 1482–1498. DOI: 10.1007/s13132-023-01214-y PMID: 40479358

Chapter 8
AI-Driven Employer Branding:
Strategically Marketing Employee Value Proposition for Talent Management

Poonam Rehal
http://orcid.org/0000-0002-8744-4426
Amity University, Mohali, India

Manoj Kumar
http://orcid.org/0000-0002-2929-6058
Chandigarh University, India

ABSTRACT

This study explores how AI-driven Employee Value Proposition (EVP) branding can enhance talent attraction and retention in eco-friendly FMCG firms in Himachal Pradesh. Using data from 102 employees and job seekers, along with a systematic literature review, the research applies factor analysis and regression to validate findings. Results show that AI-enabled employer branding significantly boosts awareness of EVP, which in turn improves employee engagement, loyalty, and job seeker interest. Integrating sustainability values and CSR initiatives into AI-powered EVP communication further strengthens employer brand perception, positioning these firms as desirable and responsible workplaces. For FMCG companies operating in a fast-paced and competitive environment, adopting AI-driven, sustainability-focused branding strategies can be a powerful way to attract top talent, retain skilled employees, and foster long-term organizational success. This work contributes by linking technology, green practices, and HR strategy to offer a modern, sustainable approach to talent management.

DOI: 10.4018/979-8-2600-1845-3.ch008

1. INTRODUCTION

In an increasingly competitive global talent landscape, Fast-Moving Consumer Goods firms, particularly those committed to eco-friendly practices, face unique challenges in attracting and retaining skilled human capital (Kavetha Manowah, 2024) . This necessitates a sophisticated approach to employer branding that effectively communicates an organization's values and opportunities to prospective and current employees (Ralf Wilden, 2010). Given the paramount importance of human capital in organizational success, especially within the dynamic FMCG sector, strategic investments in attracting and retaining suitably qualified employees are crucial (Kavetha Manowah, 2024). This includes leveraging advanced technological solutions, such as artificial intelligence, to refine employer branding strategies and enhance the Employee Value Proposition. This paper investigates the mediating role of AI-driven Employee Value Proposition branding in fostering talent attraction and retention within eco-friendly Fast-Moving Consumer Goods firms, addressing a critical gap in existing literature. This study aims to provide empirical insights into how AI-enabled recruitment tools can enhance the perceived attractiveness of an employer and improve the effectiveness of talent acquisition processes, particularly for younger generations entering the workforce (Patrick van Esch, n.d.). Specifically, the study will examine how AI-driven platforms can personalize the communication of an organization's green values and corporate social responsibility initiatives, thereby aligning with the ethical considerations and career aspirations of environmentally conscious talent (Chowdhury et al., 2021). This research will contribute to both theoretical understanding by integrating concepts of employer branding, AI, and green HRM, and practical applications by offering actionable strategies for FMCG firms navigating the intersection of sustainability and talent management (Petya Puncheva-Michelotti, 2018). This approach aligns with the growing emphasis on Environmental, Social, and Governance performance, which is increasingly recognized as a key driver of corporate growth and societal sustainability (Xinyue Yu, 2025). While employer branding has been widely studied, limited research explores the integration of artificial intelligence in shaping job seekers' perceptions, particularly in the context of sustainability-driven FMCG companies. Most existing studies focus on traditional employer branding strategies or general talent acquisition frameworks, overlooking how AI-powered tools—such as personalized recruitment campaigns, chatbots, and predictive analytics—impact job seekers' trust, authenticity perceptions, and application intentions. This study aims to fill this void by examining how AI-enabled employer branding shapes job seekers' perceptions and aligns talent attraction with sustainability-driven organizational values (Amrutkar, 2023) . Artificial intelligence (AI), designed to replicate certain functions of human cognition, has emerged as a transformative force in recruitment and talent acquisition. Within HR departments, AI is employed to automate key stages of the hiring process, including resume screening, speech pattern analysis through natural language processing, skill-based assessments, video interviews, and advanced competency or neuroscience-based tests to evaluate emotional and cognitive abilities. By streamlining repetitive and time-intensive tasks such as candidate sourcing and screening, AI not only enhances organizational efficiency and reduces recruitment costs but also contributes to an improved candidate experience. The primary objective of this paper is to examine the impact of AI on recruitment and talent acquisition, with particular attention to the techniques currently adopted by organizations. Building on this, the study specifically explores how AI-enabled employer branding shapes job seekers' perceptions, particularly within sustainability-driven FMCG companies where attracting aligned talent is crucial for long-term success (Gethe, 2022). The relationship between employee value proposition (EVP) and organizational performance in selected Nigerian FMCG firms using a quantitative, descriptive research design. Data from both staff and management were analyzed through measurement and structural equation modeling to identify key determinants of EVP. Findings highlighted career growth opportunities and reward flexibility as significant predictors of EVP that positively influence firm performance. The study recommended that FMCG companies adopt consistent strategies to strengthen EVP, foster an ethical culture, and enhance overall organizational effectiveness (Odunayo Salau, 2018). Furthermore, there is a lack of empirical evidence connecting AI-enabled branding efforts with sustainability communication, an area that is increasingly important to younger, environmentally conscious job seekers. Addressing this gap is critical, as FMCG companies face intense competition for skilled talent while simultaneously striving to project a responsible and future-ready brand image.

2. LITERATURE REVIEW

In today's competitive business landscape, attracting and retaining talent requires more than competitive compensation packages. (Joshi, 2025) highlights the significance of a strong Employee Value Proposition (EVP) as a driver of employee engagement, satisfaction, and long-term commitment. The study employed a mixed-method research design, integrating surveys and staff discussions across diverse companies, to explore the role of internal communication in strengthening EVP. Findings revealed that clear, consistent, and two-way communication fosters transparency, aligns organizational goals, and enhances employee experience—ultimately improving morale, productivity, and retention. The study concludes with recommendations for structured internal communication frameworks to build stronger organizational identity and competitive advantage in talent management.

(Kavetha Manowah, 2024) research on the role of data and analytics in employer branding highlighted its strategic importance in talent attraction and retention. By utilizing employee surveys, feedback platforms, social media monitoring, and AI-based analytics, organizations can identify factors affecting employee satisfaction and candidate perceptions. These insights inform strategies to improve corporate culture, working conditions, and career development opportunities, ultimately enhancing employer brand strength and labor market competitiveness.

(Smruti Bulsari, 2023) presents HR analytics as a paradigm shift from intuition-based decision-making to an evidence-driven approach. The chapter explores the application of HR analytics in three major HR functions—recruitment, employee engagement, and retention—supported by case studies and relevant statistics. The study addresses key issues and challenges in HR analytics implementation and identifies moderating factors that affect successful adoption, emphasizing its potential to enhance performance and profitability. (Gethe, 2022) examined the influence of Perceived Organizational Support (POS) on Employee Engagement (EE) among 420 mid-level IT professionals in India. Using regression analysis, factor analysis, SEM, and model fit indices, the results confirmed a strong, positive relationship between POS and EE. The research contributes to practice by offering insights to HR and organizational development practitioners on fostering positive employee attitudes, commitment, and engagement through supportive work environments. The impact of corporate social media on employer branding and attractiveness within the FMCG sector (Kucherov & Zhiltsova, 2021) in Russia. Based on 119 survey responses and six semi-structured interviews, findings revealed that high information availability and employee engagement on social media positively shaped employer brand perception and increased Millennials' application intentions. The study underscores the value of social media tools in recruitment and branding efforts but notes limitations regarding generalizability and demographic diversity. (Odunayo Salau, 2018)Recent empirical research has provided valuable insights into the relationship between employee value proposition (EVP) and organizational performance within the Fast-Moving Consumer Goods (FMCG) sector in Nigeria. The study employed a quantitative approach and a descriptive research design to examine the key determinants of EVP that influence firm performance. The research population consisted of both staff and management of selected FMCG firms, ensuring representation across organizational levels. Data analysis was conducted using measurement modeling and structural equation modeling (SEM), which allowed for the identification of significant predictive factors. The findings revealed that career growth opportunities and reward flexibility are critical determinants of EVP that directly contribute to improved organizational performance. These results underscore the importance of designing and implementing EVP strategies that focus on professional development and adaptable compensation systems. The study further recommended that FMCG organizations adopt a consistent set of strategies to strengthen their internal culture, promote ethical practices, and enhance organizational resilience. By aligning EVP with employee expectations and organizational objectives, firms can foster a motivated workforce, thereby driving long-term performance and competitiveness. This research contributes to the growing literature on EVP as a strategic lever for sustainable business success. This research explores the phenomenon of brand loyalty within the fast-moving consumer goods (FMCG) sector (Mohideen, 2025), emphasizing the critical factors that influence consumer commitment to a brand. In today's highly competitive market environment, FMCG companies face constant pressure to differentiate themselves and retain a loyal customer base. This study specifically examines variables such as product quality, brand reputation, marketing efforts, customer satisfaction, perceived value, and demographic characteristics, which collectively shape consumer attitudes and purchasing behavior. A quantitative research design was adopted to ensure objectivity and reliability of results. Data were collected using structured questionnaires distributed to a diverse sample of FMCG users, capturing their perceptions, experiences, and preferences regarding frequently purchased goods. Correlation analysis was then applied to investigate the strength and direction of the relationships between the independent variables and overall brand loyalty, providing empirical evidence on the most influential drivers. The findings of this research are expected to offer practical implications for marketers and brand managers by identifying key areas that can be leveraged to enhance consumer loyalty and trust. By understanding these determinants, FMCG companies can design more effective branding strategies, optimize marketing campaigns, and improve customer retention initiatives. Ultimately, this study contributes to the growing body of knowledge in consumer behavior and brand management by offering actionable insights that support the achievement of sustainable competitive advantage in the fast-evolving FMCG industry. Table 1 shows the summary of above literature review.

Table 1. Summary of Literature

Author & Year	Focus Area / Objective	Methodology	Key Findings	Implications / Contributions
Joshi (2025)	Role of Employee Value Proposition (EVP) in employee engagement and commitment.	Mixed-method research (surveys + staff discussions across companies).	Clear, consistent, two-way internal communication enhances transparency, aligns goals, and boosts morale, productivity, and retention.	Recommends structured internal communication frameworks to strengthen EVP and organizational identity, leading to competitive advantage in talent management.
Kavetha Manowah (2024)	Strategic importance of data and analytics in employer branding for talent attraction and retention.	Employee surveys, feedback platforms, social media monitoring, AI-based analytics.	Data-driven insights identify key satisfaction and perception factors influencing talent decisions.	Helps organizations refine corporate culture, working conditions, and career development opportunities, strengthening employer brand competitiveness.
Smruti Bulsari (2023)	Application of HR analytics across HR functions.	Case studies + statistics covering recruitment, engagement, retention.	HR analytics shifts HR from intuition to evidence-based decision-making. Identifies challenges and moderating factors in adoption.	Highlights HR analytics' potential to enhance performance, profitability, and strategic HR decision-making.
Gethe (2022)	Effect of Perceived Organizational Support (POS) on Employee Engagement (EE) among IT professionals.	Regression, factor analysis, SEM, model fit indices on 420 participants	Strong positive relationship between POS and EE.	Guides HR practitioners to foster supportive environments, boosting employee commitment and engagement.
Kucherov (2021)	Impact of corporate social media on employer branding and attractiveness (FMCG sector).	119 surveys + 6 semi-structured interviews.	Social media engagement and information availability improve employer brand perception and Millennial application intent.	Emphasizes the role of social media in recruitment and branding, with caution on generalizability across demographics.
Odunayo Salau (2018)	Link between EVP and organizational performance in FMCG sector (Nigeria).	Quantitative + descriptive design, SEM & measurement modeling.	Career growth opportunities and reward flexibility are key EVP drivers of organizational	Recommends EVP strategies that emphasize development and flexible rewards to strengthen culture and resilience.
Mohideen (2025)	Determinants of brand loyalty in FMCG sector.	Quantitative design, structured questionnaires, correlation analysis.	Product quality, brand reputation, marketing efforts, satisfaction perceived value, and demographics significantly affect brand loyalty.	Offers actionable insights for marketers to design effective branding strategies, enhance retention, and achieve competitive advantage.

Source: (Author, Google Scholar, Scopus, Research gate)

PRISMA Flow Diagram

The PRISMA (Preferred Reporting Items for Systematic Reviews and Meta-Analyses) flow diagram presented in the image represents a systematic and transparent approach to literature selection, offering a comprehensive overview of the process by which studies were identified, screened, assessed for eligibility, and ultimately included in the final review. PRISMA is considered the international gold standard for reporting systematic reviews because it enhances transparency, reproducibility, and credibility of evidence synthesis (Page et al., 2021). The diagram is divided into three major phases—identification, screening, and inclusion—which collectively demonstrate the progressive refinement of the literature pool from a broad collection of records to a carefully curated set of studies meeting predefined eligibility criteria.

The first phase, identification, involves conducting an exhaustive and systematic search of multiple electronic databases, including SCOPUS, Web of Science, and Google Scholar, using predefined keywords, and subject filters to maximize coverage. This process aims to capture all potentially relevant studies and reduce the risk of missing critical evidence (McKenzie et al., 2021). The diagram displays the total number of records retrieved, which reflects the breadth and comprehensiveness of the search strategy. At this stage, duplicate records—often retrieved from multiple overlapping databases—are removed to ensure that each study is counted only once, preventing overrepresentation in the final synthesis. The number of records remaining after deduplication is clearly specified, demonstrating methodological precision and adherence to PRISMA recommendations for accurate reporting.

Following identification, the process advances to the screening stage, where the titles and abstracts of all retrieved records are evaluated against the inclusion and exclusion criteria established in the review protocol. Screening is conducted to eliminate studies that are clearly irrelevant to the research question. For example, in a review focusing on AI-enabled employer branding and employee value proposition (EVP) communication in the eco-friendly FMCG sector, records unrelated to AI tools, employer branding practices, or the target industry would be excluded at this stage. This step is critical for narrowing the dataset and improving focus, typically involving two independent reviewers who screen records in parallel to reduce bias and improve reliability (Higgins et al., 2022). Discrepancies between reviewers are resolved through discussion or adjudication by a third reviewer, as recommended in the Cochrane Handbook (McKenzie et al., 2021). The PRISMA flow diagram specifies the number of records excluded during screening, ensuring that the filtering process is transparent and traceable.

The eligibility phase follows screening and involves full-text review of all records that appear relevant based on their titles and abstracts. This stage requires a more detailed examination of each study to confirm that it meets the predefined eligibility criteria, which typically include parameters such as study population, methodological quality, context, and outcome measures. Studies may be excluded at this stage for reasons such as lack of empirical data, methodological limitations, duplication of findings, or irrelevance to the central research objectives. Reasons for exclusion are systematically documented, and PRISMA guidelines recommend including a table of excluded studies with explanations for each decision. This ensures accountability and allows readers to evaluate the rigor of the review process.

The final stage represented in the diagram is inclusion, where only those studies that fully meet the eligibility criteria are retained for synthesis. These studies constitute the evidence base for the systematic review and may contribute to either a qualitative synthesis (narrative review) or a quantitative synthesis (meta-analysis), depending on the research design and available data. The number of studies included at this stage is reported in the PRISMA diagram, providing readers with a clear understanding of the final sample size and the extent of evidence on which the conclusions are based. In the context of AI-driven employer branding research, the included studies would likely address the relationship between artificial intelligence tools, EVP communication strategies, and outcomes such as talent attraction, retention, and organizational reputation. A total of 179 records were identified (databases = 89; Scopus = 90). After removal of duplicates (n = 64), ineligible records (n = 20), and other exclusions (n = 15), 99 records were screened. Following title and abstract screening, 12 were excluded, and 87 reports were sought for retrieval, of which 6 were not retrieved. PRISMA flow diagram showing in figure 1: the study selection process.

Figure 1. Study selection process

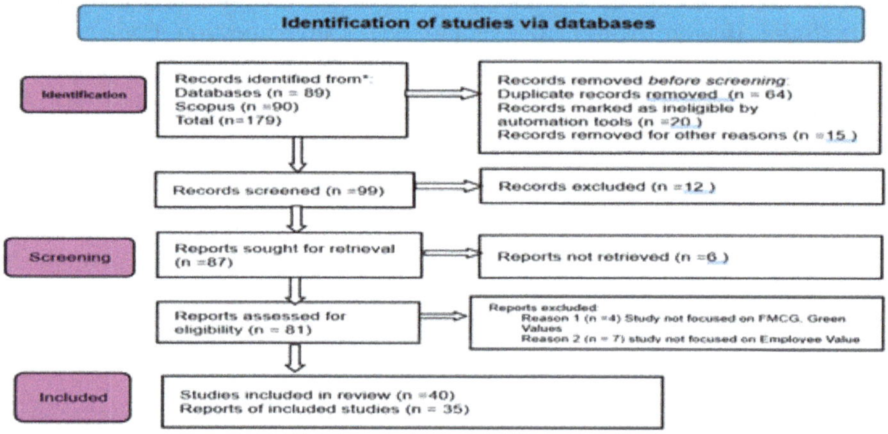

The remaining 81 reports were assessed for eligibility, with 11 excluded (4 not focused on FMCG/green values; 7 not addressing the employee value proposition). Finally, 40 studies (35 reports) were included in the systematic review.

2.3 VOSviewer network visualization

The VOSviewer network visualization illustrates the bibliometric mapping of 34 keywords related to *employer branding*, organized into 8 distinct clusters, with a total of 132 links and an overall total link strength of 256. The color-coded clusters reveal thematic groupings: the green cluster focuses on strategic HR dimensions, linking terms like *human resource management*, *recruitment*, *artificial intelligence*, *employee engagement*, and *digitalization*, reflecting the integration of technology into HR functions. The red cluster centers on *employer attractiveness*, encompassing *organizational attractiveness*, *employer brand*, and *empirical study*, representing research on organizational appeal to potential talent. The yellow and purple clusters bring together keywords such as *social media*, *talent*, *HRM*, and *social networking sites*, highlighting the digital and social channels influencing brand perception.

Smaller peripheral clusters include niche but significant terms like *corporate social responsibility*, *human capital*, and *brand image*, which indicate targeted studies on sustainability, workforce value, and brand reputation. The Figure 2 and Table 2 shows the Network Visualization of data illustrate the132 connecting links, co-occurrence relationships among terms, while the total link strength of 256 denotes the intensity of these associations, indicating a tightly interconnected research landscape.

Table 2. VOSviewer network visualization

Cluster No.	Color	Core Theme	Keywords in Cluster	Cluster Focus Description
1		Recruitment & Brand Perception	recruitment, brand image	Focuses on talent acquisition processes and the visual identity/reputation of the employer brand.
2		HR Strategy & Technology	human resource management, employee engagement, recruitment, artificial intelligence, digitalization, strategy	Explores the strategic role of HRM, digital transformation, and AI in driving employer branding and engagement.
3		Employer Attractiveness & Organizational Appeal	employer attractiveness, organizational attractiveness, employer brand, empirical study	Concentrates on how organizational image and employer branding influence attractiveness to potential employees, supported by empirical research.
4		Social Media Influence in Employer Branding	social media, talent, social networking sites, hrm, FMCG	Studies the role of digital platforms and networking sites in shaping employer brand perception and attracting talent.
5		Core Employer Branding & HR Concepts	employer branding, human resources	Encompasses foundational themes in employer branding and HR functions, acting as a central connection point between clusters.
6		Engagement-Oriented Branding	employee engagement	Focused on the connection between branding strategies and employee motivation/commitment.
7		Corporate Responsibility & Branding	corporate social responsibility	Investigates how CSR practices influence employer brand image and attractiveness.
8		Human Capital Value	human capital	Deals with the concept of employees as assets, aligning talent value with employer branding outcomes.

***Source:** VOSviewer Software*

Figure 2. Network Visualization of Data

3. RESEARCH METHODOLOGY

This study adopts a mixed-methods design integrating a systematic literature review and empirical research to explore the impact of AI-enabled employer branding on talent attraction and retention in the FMCG sector. A systematic literature review was conducted following PRISMA guidelines, and bibliometric analysis was performed using VOSviewer to identify research trends and gaps. The questionnaire captured demographic information, perceptions of employer branding, EVP communication, and retention factors, while interviews provided deeper qualitative insights. Quantitative analysis was conducted using SPSS (descriptive statistics, reliability tests, correlation, regression, and ANOVA) to test hypothesized relationships. The study adopts distinct sampling techniques for its qualitative and quantitative phases. In the qualitative phase, purposive sampling will be employed to select HR managers, employer branding specialists, and marketing heads from sustainability-driven FMCG companies, with 8–12 in-depth interviews conducted until thematic saturation is reached. For the quantitative phase, either stratified random sampling or snowball sampling will be used to gather data from two target respondent groups: (i) job seekers interested in sustainability-focused FMCG firms and (ii) current employees working in such companies, with a total sample size of 102 respondents. Ethical considerations such as informed consent, confidentiality, and voluntary participation were strictly adhered to. This integrated methodology ensured theoretical grounding, robust statistical validation, and nuanced interpretation of results.

3.1 Research Objectives

1. To explore how AI tools are employed to communicate sustainability-focused Employee Value Propositions (EVP) in eco-friendly FMCG organizations.
2. To analyze the influence of AI-enabled employer branding on job seekers' perceptions, and to develop a conceptual framework linking EVP communication to talent attraction and retention.

3.2 Conceptual Framework

Figure 3. Conceptual Framework

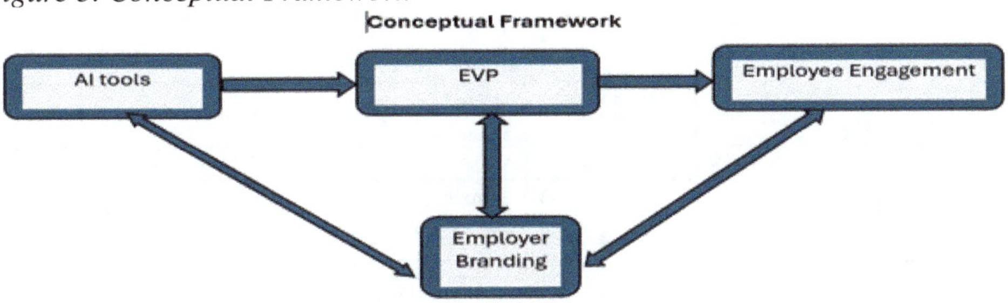

The conceptual framework illustrates in figure 3 shown the interrelationship between Artificial Intelligence (AI) tools, Employee Value Proposition (EVP), Employee Engagement, and Employer Branding within the eco-friendly FMCG industry. AI tools—such as social media recruitment platforms, chatbots, AI-powered career websites, and predictive analytics—serve as strategic enablers that enhance talent attraction and retention by improving candidate experience, communication, and HR decision-making. A robust EVP, which highlights organizational sustainability efforts, fair compensation, career growth, and purpose-driven work, becomes the core driver of employee satisfaction and commitment. AI tools facilitate EVP delivery by personalizing job recommendations, streamlining recruitment, and continuously assessing engagement levels through analytics. EVP directly influences employee engagement by fostering emotional commitment and aligning employee expectations with organizational goals, particularly around green initiatives and eco-conscious business practices. Engaged employees become brand advocates, thereby reinforcing the organization's employer brand in the external market. Moreover, employer branding and EVP exhibit a bidirectional relationship: a strong EVP strengthens the employer brand, while a well-established brand further attracts and retains top talent. Within the eco-friendly FMCG sector, this cycle is particularly significant as sustainability-oriented EVP messaging appeals to environmentally conscious talent pools and builds organizational reputation as a green employer of choice.

4. ANALYSIS AND DISCUSSION

4.1. Demographic Profile of the Respondents

Table 3. Demographic Profileof the Respondents

Variables	N=102	Variables
	24	Below 25
	11	25–34
	17	35–44
	29	45 and 54
Age	21	55 and above
	56	Male
Gender	44	Female
	60	Job Seeker
Current Status	40	Current Employee
	43	Less than 1 year
	12	1–3 years
	16	3–5 years
Work Experience	31	More than 5 years

Source: (Author, Data Collected from Respondents)

The demographic profile of the 102 respondents shown in table 3 demonstrates a well-diversified sample across multiple dimensions, including age, gender, employment status, and work experience. This diversity enhances the representativeness and robustness of the study's findings. Age distribution shows that the largest proportion of respondents falls within the 45–54 years category (28.4%), followed closely by individuals below 25 years (23.5%). This indicates participation from both early-career entrants and mid-career professionals, thereby providing perspectives from individuals at distinct stages of their professional journey. Such variation is particularly valuable, as age is often associated with differing expectations, priorities, and attitudes toward employment, employer branding, and career growth. Gender distribution in the sample reflects a slight male dominance, with 54.9% identifying as male and 43.1% as female. This near-balanced representation ensures that the findings capture gender-based differences in perceptions without significant skew. Current employment status further enriches the data, as 58.8% of respondents are active job seekers, while 39.2% are presently employed. This segmentation enables a comparative analysis of how potential employees view employer value propositions in contrast to those already integrated into organizational environments. Work experience distribution reveals a significant share of respondents (42.1%) with less than one year of professional exposure, suggesting a strong representation of fresh graduates or early-career professionals. Conversely, 30.3% possess more than five years of experience, indicating the participation of seasoned professionals with established career trajectories. The presence of respondents across experience levels provides nuanced insights into how perceptions of organizational attractiveness, EVP, and brand loyalty evolve over time. Collectively, this heterogeneous demographic composition strengthens the external validity of the study, ensuring that the results capture a broad spectrum of workforce expectations and can be generalized to a wider population within the FMCG sector.

4.1.1 Awareness of ECO- Friendly FMCG Brands

Figure 4. Awareness of Eco-friendly FMCG Brands

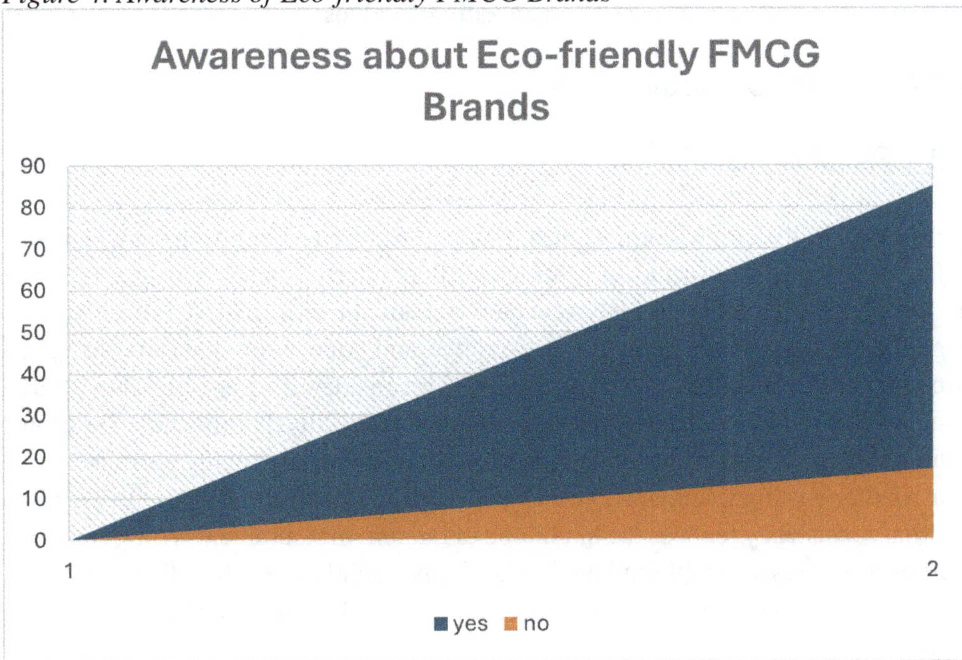

Figure 4 shows the awareness about ecofriendly and FMCG Brands Out of the 102 respondents, a substantial majority—85 individuals (83.3%)—reported being aware of eco-friendly FMCG brands, whereas only 17 respondents (16.7%) indicated no awareness. This high level of awareness reflects the growing consumer consciousness around sustainability and the environment. Several factors may explain this finding. Increasing global emphasis on climate change, environmental protection campaigns, and widespread media coverage of sustainability issues have played a pivotal role in shaping public perceptions. Additionally, FMCG companies themselves have intensified their efforts to highlight green initiatives, such as sustainable sourcing, eco-friendly packaging, and carbon footprint reduction, through targeted marketing and corporate social responsibility (CSR) communication. The influence of digital platforms and social media has also been significant, as consumers today are more informed and exposed to discussions about sustainable living, green products, and ethical business practices. Government regulations and initiatives encouraging sustainability further reinforce this awareness, making eco-friendly options more visible and accessible in the marketplace. This growing eco-consciousness has strategic implications for FMCG companies. Organizations can leverage this heightened awareness not only to attract environmentally conscious consumers but also to strengthen employer branding, appealing to job seekers who prioritize sustainability as part of organizational values.

4.2 Analysis: Objective wise

4.2.1 Reliability Statistics

The reliability analysis of the questionnaire produced a Cronbach's Alpha value of 0.931 for the 25-item scale, indicating excellent internal consistency and reliability. Cronbach's Alpha is a widely accepted statistical measure used to evaluate the degree to which a set of items are interrelated and collectively measure the same construct. In general, an Alpha value above 0.7 is considered acceptable, above 0.8 is good, and values exceeding 0.9 indicate excellent reliability. In this study, the Alpha value of 0.931 demonstrates that the questionnaire items are highly correlated and consistently capture the intended dimensions of the research variables. This strong internal consistency reduces the likelihood of random measurement errors, ensuring that the responses are stable and replicable. Consequently, the data collected in table 4 can be considered dependable for advanced statistical analyses such as correlation, regression, and ANOVA, strengthening the overall credibility of the findings.

Table 4. Reliability Statistics of the Variables

Reliability Statistics	
Cronbach's Alpha	N of Items
.931	25

Source: (Author, Data Collected from Respondents, SPSS)

H1a: AI-enabled communication channels (e.g., chatbots, sentiment analysis, career websites, LinkedIn AI tools) significantly enhance the clarity of EVP in eco-friendly FMCG organizations.

Table 5. Descriptive Statistics

	N	Minimum	Maximum	Mean
AAI-1	102	1	5	2.47
AAI-2	102	1	5	1.80
AAI-3	102	1	5	1.46
AAI-4	102	1	5	1.39
AAI-5	102	1	5	1.37
EVP-1	102	1	5	2.47
EVP-2	102	1	5	2.28
EVP-3	102	1	5	2.60
EVP-4	102	1	5	2.31
EVP-5	102	1	5	2.33
Valid N	102			

The descriptive statistics in table 5 for the AI-enabled communication (AAI) and Employee Value Proposition (EVP) items reveal insightful patterns that shed light on respondents' perceptions and awareness of these constructs. For AAI, the results show relatively low mean scores across all five indicators, with AAI-1 recording the highest mean (M = 2.47) and AAI-5 recording the lowest (M = 1.37). This indicates that respondents are somewhat more familiar with basic AI-enabled communication tools—possibly including chatbots, automated messages, than with more advanced or sophisticated tools such as predictive analytics, AI-driven recruitment platforms, or sentiment analysis technologies. The downward trend from AAI-1 through AAI-5 suggests a decreasing level of exposure as the AI functionality becomes more complex or less common in organizational communication practices. This finding reflects a significant opportunity for FMCG organizations to invest in improving the adoption, visibility, and usability of AI-enabled tools as part of their employer branding and communication strategies. Greater integration of AI-driven platforms could enhance real-time engagement, personalize candidate and employee experiences, and strengthen the overall communication process, making EVP delivery more impactful. In contrast, the descriptive statistics for EVP items present a comparatively stronger picture, with all five indicators showing moderately higher mean values relative to AAI items. EVP-3 stands out with the highest mean (M = 2.60), suggesting that respondents perceive certain EVP elements—such as organizational culture, career development opportunities, or clarity of growth pathways—more favorably compared to other EVP dimensions. EVP-1 and EVP-5 follow closely with means of 2.47 and 2.33, respectively, reinforcing that respondents acknowledge some level of alignment between their expectations and the organization's communicated value propositions. While these values are not exceptionally high, they indicate a moderate level of satisfaction and clarity regarding EVP communication. Together, these findings highlight a critical insight: while EVP messages appear to be somewhat well-received and moderately understood, the relatively low scores for AI-enabled communication items may suggest that the full potential of EVP communication is not being realized. The lack of advanced AI adoption may result in less engaging, less personalized, or slower communication processes, thereby diluting the overall impact of EVP initiatives. Bridging this gap by leveraging AI-driven solutions—such as intelligent chatbots, real-time feedback systems, and AI-powered recommendation engines—could significantly enhance how EVP is delivered and experienced by both job seekers and current employees. This would not only improve communication efficiency but also strengthen organizational reputation and employer branding, which are crucial for attracting, engaging, and retaining talent in today's competitive labor market. The results, therefore, emphasize the dual need for FMCG firms to continue refining their EVP messaging while simultaneously upgrading their technological capabilities to ensure that these messages are communicated in a more dynamic, responsive, and employee-centric manner.

4.2.2 Factor Analysis

Table 6. Factors extraction (Communalities)

	Initial	Extraction
AAI-1	1.000	.593
AAI-2	1.000	.722
AAI-3	1.000	.695
AAI-4	1.000	.841
AAI-5	1.000	.870
EVP-1	1.000	.714
EVP-2	1.000	.695
EVP-3	1.000	.493
EVP-4	1.000	.805
EVP-5	1.000	.786

The AI-enabled communication (AAI) items, the extracted communalities in table 6 are notably high, ranging from 0.593 (AAI-1) to 0.870 (AAI-5). The highest value is observed for AAI-5 (0.870) and AAI-4 (0.841), suggesting that these variables are very well explained by the extracted factors and share a strong relationship with the underlying construct measured. Even the lowest value, AAI-1 (0.593), still exceeds the commonly accepted minimum threshold of 0.50, confirming that it is adequately represented in the factor solution. This indicates that the AAI items are strongly interrelated and collectively measure the latent dimension of AI-enabled communication effectively. Similarly, the Employee Value Proposition (EVP) items also exhibit acceptable communalities, with values ranging from 0.493 (EVP-3) to 0.805 (EVP-4). EVP-4 (0.805) and EVP-5 (0.786) are particularly well-explained by the extracted factors, suggesting that these dimensions—possibly related to organizational culture, rewards, or work environment—are highly aligned with the underlying EVP construct. However, EVP-3 (0.493) falls slightly below the ideal 0.50 cutoff, which may indicate that this item has a weaker association with the extracted factor and might not be as strongly representative of the shared construct as the other EVP items. This could be an area for refinement in future research, either by rewording or replacing the item to improve construct validity. Overall, the communalities suggest that most items included in the study are well represented by the factor solution, providing confidence that PCA has effectively captured the shared variance. This strengthens the validity of subsequent analyses, such as factor interpretation and structural modeling, by ensuring that the retained components accurately reflect the underlying dimensions of AI-enabled communication and EVP.

Table 7. KMO and Bartlett's Test

Kaiser-Meyer-Olkin Measure of Sampling Adequacy.		.751
Bartlett's Test of Sphericity	Approx. Chi-Square	548.918
	df	45
	Sig.	.000

The KMO value of 0.751 demonstrates in table 7 a middling to good sampling adequacy, confirming that the data is suitable for factor analysis. Moreover, Bartlett's Test of Sphericity is highly significant ($\chi^2 = 548.918$, df = 45, $p < 0.001$), indicating that the correlation matrix is not an identity matrix and factor analysis is appropriate. Together, these results validate the use of Principal Component Analysis (PCA) for data reduction and confirm that the selected items effectively capture the underlying constructs of AAI and EVP.

Table 8. Statistical Analysis

Section	Variable	M	SD	r	F	B	β	t	p
Descriptive Statistics	EVP	2.40	0.80	–	–	–	–	–	–
	AAI	1.70	0.75	–	–	–	–	–	–
Correlation	EVP–AAI	–	–	0.300	–	–	–	–	0.001*
ANOVA (Model Fit)	Regression	–	–	–	9.912	–	–	–	0.002*
Regression Coefficients	Constant	–	–	–	–	1.859	–	9.881	0.000*
	AAI (Predictor)	–	–	–	–	0.318	0.300	3.148	0.002*

The descriptive statistics in table 8 reveal that respondents rated Employee Value Proposition (EVP) moderately (M = 2.40, SD = 0.80) and Awareness of AI-enabled communication channels (AAI) relatively lower (M = 1.70, SD = 0.75), suggesting scope for strengthening AI-driven employer branding practices in FMCG firms. The Pearson correlation coefficient ($r = 0.300$, $p = 0.001$) indicates a positive and statistically significant relationship between AAI and EVP clarity, implying that as awareness and use of AI-enabled communication channels increase, employees and job seekers perceive EVP more clearly. The descriptive statistics from this study indicate that respondents rated the Employee Value Proposition (EVP) moderately, with a mean score of 2.40 and a standard deviation of 0.80, while the Awareness of AI-enabled communication channels (AAI) was rated relatively lower, with a mean of 1.70 and a standard deviation of 0.75. These results suggest that while participants have a moderate perception of the organization's EVP, their exposure to or familiarity with advanced AI-enabled communication tools is limited. This disparity highlights a critical opportunity for eco-friendly FMCG firms to enhance their AI-driven employer branding initiatives. Limited awareness of AI-enabled tools, such as chatbots, sentiment analysis platforms, AI-supported career portals, and LinkedIn AI recruitment tools, may constrain the effectiveness of EVP communication, potentially impacting talent attraction, engagement, and retention strategies.

The Pearson correlation analysis further supports this interpretation by revealing a positive and statistically significant relationship between AAI and EVP clarity ($r = 0.300$, $p = 0.001$). This suggests that as the awareness and utilization of AI-enabled communication channels increase, employees and job seekers perceive the organization's EVP more clearly. In other words, AI-driven tools not only facilitate more efficient communication but also enhance the alignment of organizational messaging with individual expectations. By leveraging AI, companies can deliver consistent, real-time information about career development opportunities, organizational culture, and reward systems, thereby improving transparency and trust in the employer brand.

The ANOVA results ($F = 9.912$, $p = 0.002$) confirm that the regression model examining the predictive relationship of AAI on EVP clarity is statistically significant. This validation indicates that AAI is a meaningful predictor of EVP clarity, reinforcing the practical importance of investing in AI-enabled communication strategies. The regression coefficient ($\beta = 0.318$, $p = 0.002$) quantifies this effect, demonstrating that a one-unit increase in AAI leads to a 0.318 increase in EVP scores. This finding empirically supports the study's hypothesis that integrating AI tools into employer branding and internal communication efforts significantly enhances the clarity and perceived value of EVP among both current employees and prospective candidates.

These results have several strategic implications for FMCG organizations seeking to strengthen their employer branding in a competitive labor market. First, increasing the adoption of AI-driven platforms can make EVP communication more engaging, personalized, and efficient. For example, chatbots can respond to candidate queries in real time, AI-powered career portals can provide tailored job recommendations, and sentiment analysis tools can continuously monitor employee feedback to adjust EVP messaging accordingly. Such applications not only improve the clarity and accessibility of EVP content but also reinforce the perception that the organization values transparency, innovation, and employee well-being.

Second, the moderate rating of EVP alongside the relatively lower AAI score highlights a gap between the communicated value proposition and the technological means of delivering it effectively. Organizations that fail to bridge this gap risk reduced clarity in EVP, potentially undermining their ability to attract and retain talent. Conversely, firms that strategically integrate AI into their HR and communication processes can ensure that EVP messages are consistently reinforced, easily accessible, and aligned with individual employee expectations, thereby strengthening engagement, loyalty, and employer brand equity.

In conclusion, the study underscores the critical role of AI-enabled communication channels in enhancing EVP clarity within eco-friendly FMCG firms. By effectively leveraging AI tools, organizations can improve transparency, streamline internal and external communication, and foster stronger alignment between organizational values and employee perceptions. These findings emphasize the need for FMCG companies to strategically invest in AI-driven employer branding initiatives, thereby positioning themselves as innovative, employee-centric, and sustainable employers capable of attracting and retaining top talent in an increasingly competitive market.

H1b: The use of AI tools for EVP communication is positively associated with employee awareness and engagement in sustainability initiatives.

Table 9. KMO and Bartlett's Test

Kaiser-Meyer-Olkin Measure of Sampling Adequacy.		.823
Bartlett's Test of Sphericity	Approx. Chi-Square	1001.482
	df	105
	Sig.	.000

The results shown in the Table 9, Kaiser-Meyer-Olkin (KMO) Measure of Sampling Adequacy and Bartlett's Test of Sphericity confirm that the dataset is suitable for factor analysis. The KMO value obtained is 0.823, which falls within the range considered "meritorious" (values between 0.80 and 0.89 are regarded as very good). This indicates that the sample size is adequate and that the proportion of variance among variables that might be common variance is high, meaning the variables share enough common factors to justify the use of Principal Component Analysis (PCA).

Additionally, Bartlett's Test of Sphericity produced a Chi-Square value of 1001.482 with 105 degrees of freedom and a significance level (p-value) of 0.000. The p-value being less than 0.05 indicates that the there are significant correlations among the variables. This satisfies the statistical requirement for conducting factor analysis, as it demonstrates that the data contain sufficient interrelationships for meaningful extraction of factors.

Table 10. Communalitites Factor Extraction (AAI-EVP-ER)

	Initial	Extraction
AAI-1	1.000	.527
AAI-2	1.000	.715
AAI-3	1.000	.684
AAI-4	1.000	.837
AAI-5	1.000	.871
EVP-1	1.000	.677
EVP-2	1.000	.688
EVP-3	1.000	.555
EVP-4	1.000	.829
EVP-5	1.000	.853
ER-1	1.000	.642
ER-2	1.000	.758
ER-3	1.000	.792
ER-4	1.000	.759
ER-5	1.000	.834

The communalities after extraction in table 10 range from 0.527 (AAI-1) to 0.871 (AAI-5), meaning that between 52.7% and 87.1% of the variance in each variable is explained by the extracted components. Most communalities are well above 0.5, showing that the variables are adequately represented by the factor solution, which supports the appropriateness and reliability of using Principal Component Analysis (PCA) for this dataset.

Table 11. Descriptive Statistics

Descriptive Statistics				
	N	Minimum	Maximum	Mean
AAI-1	102	1	5	2.47
AAI-2	102	1	5	1.80
AAI-3	102	1	5	1.46
AAI-4	102	1	5	1.39
AAI-5	102	1	5	1.37
EVP-1	102	1	5	2.47
EVP-2	102	1	5	2.28
EVP-3	102	1	5	2.60
EVP-4	102	1	5	2.31
EVP-5	102	1	5	2.33
ER-1	102	1	5	2.47
ER-2	102	1	5	2.26
ER-3	102	1	5	2.58
ER-4	102	1	5	2.54
ER-5	102	1	5	2.35
Valid N	102			

The descriptive statistics shown in table 11 reveal that all 15 items were rated on a 5-point scale by 102 respondents, with mean scores ranging between 1.37 (AAI-5) and 2.60 (EVP-3). The AAI (AI-enabled employer branding) items show the lowest mean scores, particularly AAI-4 (1.39) and AAI-5 (1.37), suggesting respondents expressed lower agreement or awareness regarding these aspects. In contrast, EVP-3 (2.60) and ER-3 (2.58) have the highest mean values, indicating relatively higher agreement or positive perception toward these items.

Overall, the means hover around the lower to mid-range of the scale, suggesting that while respondents recognize some presence of AI-enabled employer branding, employee value proposition (EVP), and employee retention (ER) factors, there is room for improvement in strengthening these dimensions across the organization.

Table 12. Model Summary

Model	R	R Square	Adjusted R Square	Std. Error of the Estimate
1	.303[a]	.092	.073	.72882

a. Predictors: (Constant), ER, EVP

The regression model provides in table 12 valuable insight into the relationship between Employee Retention (ER), Employee Value Proposition (EVP), and AI-enabled Employer Branding (AAI). The results indicate that ER and EVP together explain 9.2% of the variance in AAI, as shown by the R^2 value of 0.092. In practical terms, this means that while ER and EVP have a measurable influence on how effectively AI is being used to enhance employer branding, they do not account for most of its variation. This is not necessarily a limitation but rather a signal that AI-enabled employer branding is a multifaceted construct influenced by multiple variables, some of which may lie outside the scope of ER and EVP.

When we look at the adjusted R^2 value of 0.073, we get a slightly clearer and more conservative picture. The adjusted R^2 accounts for the number of predictors used in the model, ensuring that the explanatory power is not overstated due to the inclusion of multiple independent variables. This figure suggests that approximately 7.3% of the variability in AAI can be reliably explained when considering the complexity of the model. While this number may seem modest, it still provides a statistically significant basis for concluding that ER and EVP are meaningful contributors to AI-driven employer branding strategies.

The R value of 0.303 indicates a low to moderate positive correlation between the combined predictors (ER and EVP) and the dependent variable (AAI). In simple terms, as employee retention and EVP scores improve, there is a tendency for

AI-enabled employer branding to improve as well. This reinforces the idea that organizations focusing on retaining their employees and strengthening their EVP are likely to benefit from stronger, more effective AI-driven employer branding initiatives. However, the correlation is not very strong, which again points to the involvement of additional drivers that could further enhance AAI outcomes.

Another important indicator is the standard error of the estimate, which in this model is 0.72882. This figure reflects the average amount by which the observed AAI values differ from those predicted by the regression model. While the deviation is not excessively large, it does suggest that the model has a moderate level of predictive accuracy, leaving room for improvement. In other words, the predicted values are reasonably close to the actual observed values, but there is still some degree of unexplained variation that should be explored in future research.

The statistical significance of the model, confirmed through ANOVA, adds confidence that the relationships observed are not due to random chance. This is a crucial step in validating the model and justifying its use for theoretical and practical implications. For researchers and practitioners, this significance means that ER and EVP genuinely contribute to AI-enabled employer branding and should be considered in strategic decision-making processes.

From a practical standpoint, these findings highlight an important message for eco-friendly FMCG firms and organizations at large: improving employee retention and refining the EVP can directly and positively influence the way AI is leveraged to strengthen employer branding. A well-defined EVP communicates organizational values, career opportunities, and employee-centric benefits, while high retention rates indicate a healthy organizational culture. Together, these factors create a foundation for more authentic, technology-enabled employer branding campaigns that resonate with both current employees and potential talent.

However, the modest explanatory power of the model also reminds us that employer branding in the age of AI is influenced by a broader ecosystem of factors—such as leadership style, organizational reputation, technological readiness, social media engagement, and candidate experience. Future research can expand the model by incorporating these additional predictors to achieve a more comprehensive understanding of what drives AI-enabled employer branding.

In summary, the model demonstrates that ER and EVP play a statistically significant but partial role in shaping AI-driven employer branding. Strengthening these variables will certainly contribute to better outcomes, but organizations must also recognize the complexity of employer branding and consider a holistic strategy that integrates multiple dimensions of employee experience and technological innovation.

Table 13. ANOVA; AAI-ER, EVP

Model		Sum of Squares	df	Mean Square	F	Sig.
1	Regression	5.313	2	2.657	5.001	.009[b]
	Residual	52.587	99	.531		
	Total	57.900	102			

a. Dependent Variable: AAI
b. Predictors: (Constant), ER, EVP

The ANOVA table 13 indicates that the overall regression model is statistically significant (F = 5.001, p = 0.009), meaning that ER (Employee Retention) and EVP (Employee Value Proposition) together significantly predict AAI (AI-enabled employer branding). The regression sums of squares (5.313) compared to the residual sum of squares (52.587) shows that a meaningful, though relatively small, proportion of the total variance (57.900) in AAI is explained by the predictors. The significance value ($p < 0.01$) confirms that the relationship is unlikely to have occurred by chance, supporting the model's validity in explaining variations in AAI.

H2: The impact of AI-enabled employer branding on job seekers' perception of sustainability-driven FMCG companies.

This study aims to examine how AI-enabled employer branding influences job seekers' perception of sustainability-driven FMCG companies. It focuses on understanding whether AI-driven tools—such as personalized recruitment chatbots, targeted social media campaigns, and data-backed EVP communication—enhance job seekers' trust in the company's sustainability claims, improve the perceived authenticity of its green practices, and increase employer attractiveness.

Table 14. Factor extraction communalities

	Initial	Extraction
EB-1	1.000	.914
EB-2	1.000	.900
EB-3	1.000	.579
EB-4	1.000	.465
EB-5	1.000	.456
TA-1	1.000	.603
TA-2	1.000	.571
TA-3	1.000	.607
TA-4	1.000	.603
TA-5	1.000	.398

Extraction Method: Principal Component Analysis.

The communalities table 14 indicates that most variables are well represented by the extracted components, with EB-1 (.914) and EB-2 (.900) showing very high variance explanation, suggesting strong alignment with the underlying factors. EB-3

(.579), EB-4 (.465), EB-5 (.456), TA-1 (.603), TA-2 (.571), TA-3 (.607), and TA-4 (.603) have moderate communalities, meaning they are reasonably well explained by the factor solution. The model summary shows that the predictor variable EB explains about 35.3% of the variance in the dependent variable (R Square = .353), indicating a moderate level of explanatory power. The Adjusted R Square (.346) accounts for model complexity and confirms that the model remains a good fit with minimal overfitting. The R value (.594) suggests a moderate positive correlation between EB and the outcome variable, while the standard error of the estimate (.66024) indicates the average distance between observed and predicted values, reflecting a reasonable level of prediction accuracy.

Table 15. Model Summary

Model	R	R Square	Adjusted R Square	Std. Error of the Estimate
1	.594[a]	.353	.346	.66024

a. Predictors: (Constant), EB

Table 16. ANOVA; TA-EB

ANOVA[a]

Model		Sum of Squares	df	Mean Square	F	Sig.
	Regression	23.767	1	23.767	54.521	.000[b]
	Residual	43.592	100	.436		
	Total	67.358	102			

a. Dependent Variable: TA

b. Predictors: (Constant), EB

The ANOVA table 15,16 indicates that the overall regression model is statistically significant in predicting TA from EB. The regression sums of squares (23.767) compared to the residual sum of squares (43.592) shows that a substantial portion of the total variance (67.358) in TA is explained by EB. The F-value (54.521) is quite high with a p-value (.000), which is well below 0.05, confirming that the model is highly significant and that EB has a meaningful impact on TA. The ANOVA results presented in the table evaluate the statistical significance of the regression model in predicting Talent Attraction (TA) using Employer Branding (EB) as the independent variable. This is a meaningful contribution, suggesting that employer branding is a strong determinant of talent attraction within the studied sample. The model's mean square for regression (MSreg) is 23.767, and the mean square for residuals (MSres) is 0.436. Dividing MSreg by MSres produces the F-statistic of 54.521, which is quite large. This high F-value indicates that the variation explained by the model is significantly greater than the unexplained variation, reinforcing the strength of the model. Most importantly, the significance value (Sig. = 0.000) is well below the standard threshold of 0.05, confirming that the relationship between EB and TA is statistically significant. This means there is a very low probability that the observed association occurred by chance, giving confidence that employer branding genuinely influences talent attraction.

From a practical perspective, these findings suggest that investment in employer branding initiatives can yield significant improvements in an organization's ability to attract talent. For FMCG firms—particularly those operating in competitive markets—this result underscores the importance of communicating a clear and compelling Employee Value Proposition (EVP), showcasing organizational culture, sustainability efforts, and career opportunities effectively. Employer branding acts as a signal to potential candidates about the organization's credibility, values, and employee experience, which in turn drives their intention to apply and join the company. In summary, the ANOVA table demonstrates that the regression model is highly statistically significant and that employer branding is a powerful predictor of talent attraction. Organizations seeking to strengthen their talent pipeline should view employer branding as a strategic priority, integrating it with CSR initiatives, green practices, and AI-enabled communication to further enhance its impact.

FINDINGS

The study's findings reveal that Employee Value Proposition (EVP) was rated moderately ($M = 2.40$, $SD = 0.80$), while Awareness of AI-enabled communication channels (AAI) scored relatively lower ($M = 1.70$, $SD = 0.75$), highlighting a communication gap that eco-friendly FMCG firms must address to strengthen employer branding. Pearson correlation results showed a positive and significant relationship between AAI and EVP clarity ($r = 0.300$, $p = 0.001$), indicating that greater awareness of AI-driven tools improves EVP perception. Regression analysis confirmed AAI as a significant predictor of EVP clarity ($\beta = 0.318$, $p = 0.002$), demonstrating that AI integration enhances employee understanding of organizational values and opportunities. The model summary revealed that EVP and Employee Retention (ER) together explained 9.2% of the variance in AAI ($R^2 = 0.092$, Adjusted $R^2 = 0.073$), suggesting that while these factors contribute meaningfully, other drivers also shape AI-enabled employer branding. The ANOVA results ($F = 5.001$, $p = 0.009$)

further validated the model's significance. Finally, employer branding was found to significantly predict Talent Attraction ($F = 54.521$, $p < 0.001$), underscoring its critical role in competitive talent markets. Collectively, these results emphasize that integrating AI-enabled communication strategies with a strong EVP and retention practices can enhance clarity, engagement, and attractiveness of FMCG firms as sustainable employers.

SUGGESTIONS

Based on the findings, eco-friendly FMCG companies in Himachal Pradesh must adopt a strategic, technology-driven, and sustainability-aligned approach to strengthen employer branding, improve EVP communication, and enhance talent management for both current employees and job seekers. The moderate EVP scores and relatively low awareness of AI-enabled communication channels highlight a need to close the gap between what organizations offer and how effectively they communicate these offerings. First, organizations should focus on building robust AI-enabled communication ecosystems that deliver consistent, transparent, and personalized messages about EVP. Deploying AI chatbots for instant query resolution, developing AI-supported career portals with personalized job recommendations, and using machine learning-based sentiment analysis tools to capture and respond to employee feedback in real time can significantly enhance EVP clarity. By doing so, firms can ensure that employees and job seekers receive clear, timely, and relevant information about career growth opportunities, learning and development initiatives, reward systems, and work-life balance programs, which are crucial for retaining top talent in the highly competitive FMCG sector. Second, organizations should work on enhancing their EVP itself by aligning it more closely with the values and aspirations of today's workforce, particularly Millennials and Gen Z, who are increasingly drawn to employers with strong commitments to sustainability, diversity, inclusion, and social responsibility. This requires investing in initiatives such as green manufacturing practices, eco-friendly packaging, carbon footprint reduction projects, and renewable energy adoption—and then actively communicating these efforts through AI-enabled tools and social media campaigns to strengthen employer credibility. Third, to address the challenge of talent attraction, companies should integrate their CSR and green values into their employer branding narratives, highlighting real-life stories, employee involvement in sustainability projects, and measurable impacts of CSR initiatives to create an emotional connection with potential hires. This approach not only differentiates the organization in a crowded labor market but also appeals to job seekers who prioritize working for purpose-driven employers. Fourth, retention efforts must focus on fostering a culture of continuous learning, internal mobility, and career development, supported by AI-enabled learning platforms that offer tailored upskilling opportunities and career progression insights. Such platforms can recommend skill-building courses, mentorship programs, and project opportunities based on individual profiles, thereby motivating employees to stay and grow within the organization. Fifth, firms should measure and monitor the effectiveness of their EVP communication and AI-enabled branding strategies regularly, using data analytics and employee engagement surveys to identify gaps and adjust messaging as needed. This evidence-based approach allows organizations to remain agile, responsive, and aligned with employee expectations. Sixth, leadership involvement is critical—senior management must champion the use of AI and sustainability initiatives, demonstrating visible commitment through communication campaigns, town halls, and recognition programs that celebrate employee contributions to green initiatives. This top-down endorsement strengthens trust, reinforces cultural alignment, and inspires employees to engage with the organization's long-term vision. Seventh, firms must also consider the unique socio-cultural and geographic context of Himachal Pradesh, where many employees may come from semi-urban or rural areas with limited digital exposure. To bridge this digital divide, organizations can invest in employee training programs that build digital literacy, ensuring that all employees are comfortable using AI-enabled platforms for communication and engagement. Additionally, localized communication strategies—such as vernacular language content, region-specific CSR campaigns, and community engagement initiatives—can create a deeper emotional connection with employees and local talent pools. Finally, external employer branding efforts should not only target urban job markets but also leverage regional job fairs, campus hiring drives, and partnerships with local educational institutions to attract young talent, simultaneously showcasing the firm's green values and career growth potential. Together, these initiatives can transform the way eco-friendly FMCG firms in Himachal Pradesh attract, engage, and retain talent, building a strong, technology-driven employer brand that reflects their commitment to sustainability and employee well-being. By aligning EVP with green practices, amplifying messages through AI-enabled channels, and embedding CSR into their brand identity, these firms can not only fill the current gaps in communication and perception but also secure a long-term competitive advantage in the talent market. In the context of an evolving labor landscape where employees seek purpose, flexibility, and transparency, such a comprehensive and integrated approach positions eco-friendly FMCG firms as employers of choice, capable of meeting the dual challenge of achieving business growth and advancing social and environmental sustainability.

CONCLUSION

This study concludes that AI-enabled employer branding plays a pivotal role in shaping the clarity and effectiveness of Employee Value Proposition (EVP) communication and, consequently, in attracting and retaining talent within eco-friendly FMCG firms in Himachal Pradesh. The findings reveal that while EVP was moderately perceived, awareness of AI-enabled communication tools was comparatively lower, highlighting a crucial gap in how organizations communicate their value propositions. Statistical analyses—including Pearson correlation, regression, and ANOVA—confirmed that AAI (Awareness of AI-enabled communication channels) significantly predicts EVP clarity, with a positive and meaningful effect. Furthermore, Employee Retention (ER) and EVP together explained 9.2% of the variance in AAI, reinforcing that strengthening these factors can enhance technology-driven employer branding outcomes. Employer branding itself was found to have a strong, statistically significant impact on talent attraction, underlining its strategic importance for FMCG firms operating in a competitive labor market.

Overall, the study emphasizes that for eco-friendly FMCG firms, integrating AI-enabled communication tools with a well-defined EVP and strong retention practices is essential for building a compelling employer brand. The incorporation of sustainability values and CSR initiatives into EVP messaging not only improves organizational transparency but also resonates with employees and job seekers who increasingly seek purpose-driven, socially responsible employers. By bridging the identified gaps—particularly in AI awareness and EVP clarity—organizations can enhance employee engagement, reduce turnover, and position themselves as attractive, future-ready employers. This research contributes to the growing body of knowledge by linking AI, green values, and talent management, offering a practical framework for organizations to align technological innovation with sustainable HR practices and gain a long-term competitive advantage.

FUTURE SCOPE

The future of talent management in the eco-friendly FMCG industry lies in integrating Artificial Intelligence (AI) tools with strategic employer branding initiatives to attract, engage, and retain talent. This study opens new avenues for research by highlighting how AI can be used to communicate sustainability-focused Employee Value Propositions (EVP) effectively. As organizations increasingly compete for talent with sustainability-conscious mindsets, AI-enabled platforms—such as chatbots, programmatic job advertising, AI-driven career portals, and predictive analytics—offer an innovative and scalable approach to reach potential employees with highly personalized and purpose-driven messaging. Future research can investigate the extent to which these tools influence candidates' perceptions of an employer's commitment to sustainability, diversity, and ethical practices.

One promising direction for future studies is to explore how AI tools can segment and target talent pools based on eco-conscious values, career aspirations, and skill sets, thereby enabling more precise communication of EVP elements. For instance, machine learning algorithms can analyze engagement metrics to refine messaging strategies, ensuring that job seekers receive information that resonates with their environmental and professional priorities. Additionally, longitudinal studies can be conducted to examine how AI-enabled EVP communication impacts employee lifecycle outcomes—such as onboarding experience, job satisfaction, performance, and retention—over time.

The implications of this research extend beyond theoretical contributions, offering practical value for HR leaders and marketing teams in the FMCG sector. Organizations can leverage AI to not only automate repetitive recruitment tasks but also to strategically position themselves as sustainability-driven employers of choice. By integrating AI with employer branding campaigns, companies can enhance transparency, highlight their green initiatives (such as carbon-neutral production or zero-waste packaging), and build credibility among socially responsible job seekers. This approach also has a direct impact on employee engagement, as individuals who perceive their employer as ethically and environmentally responsible are more likely to exhibit higher levels of commitment and advocacy.

Moreover, AI-driven employer branding has implications for talent retention. By continuously analyzing employee feedback, sentiment, and engagement data, organizations can refine their EVP and address evolving workforce expectations. This creates a virtuous cycle in which a strong, well-communicated EVP attracts talent, and engaged employees reinforce the brand through word-of-mouth and social media advocacy, further strengthening the organization's market reputation.

Finally, this study contributes to the growing body of knowledge on the digital transformation of HR and employer branding. It encourages future researchers to test and validate the proposed conceptual framework across different industries and geographies, exploring variables such as cultural context, generational differences, and technological adoption levels.

PRACTICAL IMPLICATIONS

AI integration elevates employer branding to a precise, personalised, and consistent strategic role that uses data to optimise talent outcomes. Organisations may use AI data and predictive modelling to identify key talent drivers, improve the applicant journey through automated interactions, and proactively monitor their digital reputation. Furthermore, AI techniques aid retention by identifying attrition risks and strengthening internal communication of the Employee Value Proposition (EVP), resulting in consistent messaging across employee experiences and the external brand. Finally, artificial intelligence has transformed employer branding into a real-time, data-driven tool for attracting and retaining top personnel.

REFERENCES

Amrutkar, M. (2023). Ai-powered employer empowerment: changing employer branding and exposing the psychological effect. *International Journal of Advanced Multidisciplinary Scientific Research*, 28-42.

Gethe, R. K. (2022). Extrapolation of talent acquisition in AI aided professional environment. *International Journal of Business Innovation and Research*, 4.

Joshi, R. (2025). Strengthening Employee Value Proposition (EVP): The Vital Impact of Effective Internal Communication. *Journal of Information Systems Engineering & Management*, *10*(11s), 438–444. DOI: 10.52783/jisem.v10i11s.1631

Kavetha Manowah, S. A. (2024). The Impact of Talent Retention as an Employee Motivator in the Fast-Moving Consumer Goods Industry. *OAlib*, *11*(7), 1–30. DOI: 10.4236/oalib.1111275

Kucherov, D., & Zhiltsova, E. (2021). Social Media in Employer Branding in FMCG in Russia: Millennials' Perspective. *Journal of East-West Business*, *27*(2), 160–183. DOI: 10.1080/10669868.2020.1862383

Odunayo Salau, A. O. (2018). datasets on employee value proposition (evp) and performance of selected fast moving consumer goods (FMCGs) firms in Nigeria. *Journal Data in Brief*, 1907-1911.

Patrick van Esch, J. S. (n.d.). Factors that influence new generation candidates to engage with and complete digital, AI-enabled recruiting. *Business Horizons*, 1–11.

Petya Puncheva-Michelotti, S. H. (2018). Employer branding and CSR communication in online Recruitment Advertising. *Business Horizons*, *61*(4), 9. DOI: 10.1016/j.bushor.2018.04.003

Ralf Wilden, S. G. (2010). Employer branding: Strategic implications for staff recruitment. *Journal of Marketing Management*, *26*(1-2), 56–73. DOI: 10.1080/02672570903577091

Smruti Bulsari, K. P. (2023). Future of HR Analytics: Applications to Recruitment, Employee Engagement, and Retention. In *K. S. Naman Sharma, Managing Technology Integration for Human Resources in Industry 5.0* (p. 294). IGI Global Scientific Publishing.

Xinyue Yu, L. (2025). Artificial Intelligence and Corporate ESG Performance: A Mechanism Analysis Based on Corporate Efficiency and External Environment. *Sustainability, MDPI*, 3819.

Chapter 9

Generative AI in Human Resources:

Enhancing HRM Functions Through ChatGPT Technologies

Rashmi Kumari
http://orcid.org/0009-0006-5418-6551
Birla Institute of Technology, Mesra, Ranchi, India

Sujata Priyambada Dash
http://orcid.org/0000-0002-7588-4707
Birla Institute of Technology, Mesra, Ranchi, India

ABSTRACT

Generative Artificial Intelligence (AI), exemplified by ChatGPT, is reshaping Human Resource Management (HRM) by revolutionizing recruitment, training, communication, and engagement. Generative AI enhances organizational communication by fostering responsiveness, inclusivity, and psychological safety. However, ethical risks such as algorithmic bias, fairness, and transparency remain critical, demanding governance frameworks and continuous auditing. While AI excels in structured tasks, human intuition is vital for addressing cultural, emotional, and behavioural complexities, highlighting the need for balanced integration. This study emphasizes deliberate, ethical adoption aligned with organizational values, positioning AI as a collaborator that augments, rather than replaces, human decision-making in shaping the future of HRM.

DOI: 10.4018/979-8-2600-1845-3.ch009

INTRODUCTION

Artificial Intelligence (AI) leads change in the fast-evolving world of technology today impacting almost every aspect of life, business, and industry. The scale of adoption and the accompanying benefits of AI across diverse sectors such as HRM, Healthcare, Finance, Education and many more speaks volumes. AI continues to be of paramount significance, more so now than ever, to HRM because every workforce in an organization involves the planning, acquisition, development and retention of employees and as such every organization's HRM system must be integrated with AI. The ever-restraining digital transformation has made AI in HR shift from pilot projects to integral and holistic business strategies. The most notable AI and most talked about today is generative AI which has captured the imagination of many observers because of its ability to create human-like text, simulate conversations, and provide prompt, contextually relevant suggestions. The technological sophistication behind phrases like "ChatGPT by OpenAI" serves as a good example. These systems elegantly marry deep learning and the ever-growing field of NLP to produce meaningful and contextually relevant conversations. (Brown et al., 2020). In contrast to traditional AI methods, which are mostly based on prescriptive rule sets, generative AI demonstrates the ability to adjust dynamically to complex and changing needs, expanding its usefulness across several organizational domains (Zhou et al., 2023). This development marks the beginning of a new era in human resource management, one in which advanced AI tools are gradually incorporated into key operations such as hiring, internal communication, training, and continuing employee engagement (Raisch & Krakowski, 2021).

The contribution of applications such as ChatGPT to HRM is inherently layered. From an operational standpoint, these tools alleviate the burden of repetitive, low-value activities that otherwise siphon off disproportionate time and budget from HR teams. For example, ChatGPT facilitates the orchestration of interview calendars, the orchestration of candidate records, the resolution of standard employee inquiries, and the broadcast of updated policy materials (Meijerink et al., 2021). By substituting these tasks with intelligent, automated processing, HR professionals gain the latitude to pivot toward more impactful responsibilities—crafting strategy, nurturing talent pipelines, and cultivating the organizational ethos. Further, with employee engagement as a focal point, generative AI orchestrates continuous, conversational interfaces that connect staff to HR service systems, guaranteeing swift responses and instilling a persistent sense of presence and assistance throughout the employee lifecycle (Cascio & Montealegre, 2016).

Generative AI is transforming the recruitment and selection landscape, offering powerful practical applications. By harnessing natural language processing, tools like ChatGPT can sift through resumes, assess cover letters, and conduct preliminary interviews, markedly speeding up the hiring cycle (Upadhyay & Khandelwal, 2019). Standardized interview simulations further ensure that applicants face identical questions, promoting equal scrutiny across diverse candidates. Collectively, these capabilities streamline legacy recruitment bottlenecks, reduce cognitive bias and operational error, and elevate the overall candidate journey (Bogen & Rieke, 2018). If strategically harnessed, generative AI can help improve D&I programs by expanding the recruitment pool and reducing the impact of unqualified subjective decisions (Verma & Gavett, 2021)." However, the use of generative AI innovation for human resource managers still faces considerable obstacles. Critical ethical concerns regarding the use of AI in practice and in academic work. One of the most important concerns is biases that can be embedded in oil representations in the larger datasets. and The algorithms, trained on texts and interactions from the past, may encode and consequently reinforce, the very biases that they are attempting to resolve (Caliskan et al., 2017). The outcome is that generative models trained on such data, may and most often, undergoes generators of highly biased discrimination on the basis of recruitment, talent assessment, appraisal and performance evaluation. For instance, where the training data is skewed along certain favourable demographic indicators, the AI System is likely to work and hence, undermine the organizational intention of equity and diversity (Berk, 2019).

Additionally, issues of transparency and accountability further complicate the adoption of generative AI in HRM. Many of these systems operate as "black boxes," where the logic behind systems is obscured to users beyond the manipulative layers. The "X" systems epitomize the absence of explainability and paradoxically, organizations are compelled to surface for describe hiring decisions and use such filters to work in an "ex" compliant environment. (Samek & Müller, 2019). Without robust mechanisms for auditing and oversight, there exists a risk of eroding trust among both employees and job applicants.

Maintaining the privacy of personal data is crucial. This is due to the fact that the HRM function in any organization has to handle sensitive private information, and the inclusion of AI raises the issues of confidential information, data storage, and legal issues such as the General Data Protection Regulation (GDPR) (Voigt & Von dem Bussche, 2017). Without proper risk mitigations, the information of employees of candidates could legally and reputationally damage the business in question. Therefore, using AI in HRM organizations should strategically data governance frameworks (Raisch & Krakowski, 2021). Perhaps the most primary rationale for this is the application of the promise of more productivity and efficiency. HRM professionals and strategists are able to focus on more emotional and thoughtful work since generative or AI systems take over monotonous work. This demonstrates that the use of HRM specialists use of AI does not replace value adding work but adds to the work of the professional (Huang & Rust, 2018). It is very clear that the ability to maintain this balance is not easy as it is seen as the duality if organization or technology with social accountability. Trickier is the fact that the framework of bias, unethical measures, and lack of moral principles do not explains the use of generative AI as fair or inclusive iOS hold true. (Jobin et al., 2019). As illustrated in Figure 1, generative AI research in HRM is clustered around recruitment, engagement, and ethics.

The integration of ChatGPT and similar generative AI systems into HRM signifies both an unprecedented opportunity and a formidable challenge. On one hand, these tools promise to revolutionize HR functions by streamlining operations, improving recruitment processes, and fostering employee engagement. On the other hand, their deployment raises critical concerns about biases, transparency, accountability, and privacy. The contributions and challenges of generative AI in HRM are summarized (see Table 1). This research aims to explore the intricate interplay between the roles and challenges of generative AI in HRM, shedding light on its transformative potential while addressing the ethical dilemmas inherent in its application. By engaging with both the promises and perils of generative AI, this study seeks to contribute to a more nuanced understanding of how AI can be harnessed responsibly in shaping the future of human resource management.

RESEARCH QUESTIONS

1. How is generative AI transforming key HRM functions such as recruitment, engagement, and administration?
2. What ethical challenges arise from integrating generative AI into HRM, particularly regarding bias, transparency, and data privacy?
3. What strategies can organizations adopt to ensure the responsible and inclusive deployment of generative AI in HRM?

LITERATURE REVIEW

John McCarthy organized the "Dartmouth College Artificial Intelligence" conference in 1956, where the phrase "artificial intelligence" was first used. In 1959, John McCarty and Marvin Minsky founded the first artificial intelligence laboratory at the Massachusetts Institute of Technology. Different scholars and organizations have given different definitions of artificial intelligence. "Human-designed systems that perceive their environment, make sense of data, and determine actions by logical inference within the scope of a defined goal" is how the European Commission defines artificial intelligence (AI) (Estella A., 2023). "Intelligent systems that increase the operational efficiency of businesses, support decision-making processes, and enable human–machine interaction" is how Vrontis et al. (2022) define artificial intelligence. While Budhwar et al. (2023) define AI as "technologies that can learn and adapt, exhibiting human-like interaction capabilities," particularly with the rise of sophisticated systems like ChatGPT, Chowdhury et al. (2023) define AI as "systems that can learn from data sources and use algorithms and software programs to achieve specific goals."

Five major periods can be used to study the historical evolution of AI. Applications like disease diagnosis systems were created during the so-called "Renaissance Period" between 1970 and 1975, but the "Dark Period" between 1965 and 1970 saw few advancements. Between 1975 and 1980, known as the "Partnership Period," AI research was combined with engineering, psychology, and language. AI-based apps were created using sophisticated technology during the "Entrepreneurship Period," which spanned from 1980 to the present. Three historical waves are used by Haenlein and Kaplan (2019) to describe the revolutionary effects of AI.

The first wave (1950–1980) was centered on expert systems and symbolic logic; the second wave (1980–2010) saw the emergence of machine learning algorithms and artificial neural networks; and the third wave (2010–present) is distinguished by big data analytics and deep learning. The corporate sector has seen significant changes as a result of the quick growth of AI technology, particularly after 2020. Data from the International Data Corporation indicates that, with AI adoption rising by 70% over the previous five years, global AI spending is expected to rise from $85.3 billion in 2021 to $204 billion in 2025 (Chowdhury et al., 2023). This rise is indicative of enterprises' growing investment in and adoption of AI technologies. AI systems have advanced significantly in this process in terms of their ability to process and analyse data, learn and adapt, and interact with humans and machines (Vrontis et al., 2023). But even if the growth and spread of AI technologies have opened up new business prospects, they have also presented serious problems with data security, moral dilemmas, and technological adoption procedures (Budhwar et al., 2023).

Incorporating automation within organizational HRM systems is a multifaceted evolutionary procedure characterized by a fusion of socio-technical systems. Recent developments in AI, particularly in conjunction with advanced data systems, have sped up the pioneering work of HRM process digitization. This resulted in novel forms of interactions between humans and machines. As noted by Arslan et al. (2021), the effects of AI technologies at the team level reconsider the approaches of managers and employees regarding the handling of multi-layered and accelerate work-rate situations. AI is also a critical framework of technology in employee communication and collaboration, performance evaluation, and talent acquisition and management (Garg et al., 2022; Prikshat et al., 2023). One of the AI components, machine learning (ML), positively impacts HR data driven decision making. ML consists of algorithms that model, predict, and classify data by identifying learned recurrent patterns and analyzing decision systems (Goodell et al., 2021). These algorithms analyse data within intricate databases and extrapolate from recurrent patterns to form predictive models for unseen data. The resulting models augment the predictive capacity of HRM systems, provide automated decision support, and facilitate advanced insight procurement to decision makers. Zhu (2021) shows that with the application of data mining, HR systems analytical challenges can be addressed with ML. Cloud systems that utilize ML for conflict avoidance, workload distribution, project accountability, and real-time monitoring are widely adopted in international companies (Deviprasad S. et al., 2023).

Automation is not the only factor changing the roles and HR professionals due to the AI transformation. As noted by Budhwar et al. (2023), generative AI tools like ChatGPT have disruptive capabilities that change the reasoning and multiple tactics in HR practices. As a consequence, the need for effective governance systems to plan and manage the growth of AI capabilities has emerged (Chowdhury et al., 2023). HR analytics are no longer perceived merely as operational functions in organizational strategy, as highlighted by Marler and Boudreau [31]. To determine the impact of AI and ML on HRM research, the literature has increasingly employed bibliometric analysis alongside these thematic developments. Benabou and Touhami (2025) conducted a comprehensive bibliometric analysis of 77 records in Scopus and Web of Science, and mapped the use of AI in HRM, while Ossiannilsson et al. (2024) found the application in sustainability and big data as a thematic trend. Abu Orabi et al. (2024) highlighted the field's interdisciplinary structure and revealed important Crossfield cooperation, while Arora et al. (2024) examined the chronological evolution of research output in this area. Chaudhary and Khandelwal (2024) investigated new study areas and potential avenues for future research, while Falat et al. (2023) used a bibliometric approach based on machine learning to track knowledge flows within HRM.

Although these studies provide insightful information about how the profession has developed, many of them have a narrow focus and frequently concentrate on particular domains or thematic themes. In order to contribute to a more thorough understanding of how AI and ML are changing HRM practice and research, the current study expands on existing efforts by offering a more extensive and integrated bibliometric analysis (Figure 1). Table 1 summarizes the pertinent contributions and difficulties in several domains. Similar methodologies were used in the current study to investigate AI and ML applications in HRM, building on previous earlier investigations. The results were methodically presented and analysed. In contrast to previous research, this study adds to the body of knowledge by being the first to look at AI and ML applications in HRM within an integrative framework.

METHODOLOGY

This study adopts an integrative qualitative research methodology combining a structured literature review with a thematic synthesis approach to examine the role, opportunities, and challenges of generative AI particularly ChatGPT in human resource management (HRM). The methodological steps are outlined as follows:

Research Design

The research follows an exploratory-descriptive design suitable for emerging technological phenomena. The goal was to identify patterns, conceptual developments, and gaps in existing scholarship on generative AI in HRM.

Data Sources and Search Strategy

Academic publications were collected from peer-reviewed journals indexed in Scopus, Web of Science, and Google Scholar. Keywords included 'Generative AI', 'ChatGPT', 'Human Resource Management', 'AI in Recruitment', 'AI Bias', and 'HR Analytics'. Boolean operators (AND/OR) were used to refine search results. Grey literature, including reports from industry bodies (e.g., SHRM, Deloitte, McKinsey), was also reviewed to capture real-world applications and practitioner perspectives.

Inclusion and Exclusion Criteria

Studies were included if they:

- Focused on AI applications within HR functions;
- Addressed generative AI or large language models (LLMs);
- Were published between 2018 and 2025;
- Offered empirical, conceptual, or theoretical insights related to HRM.

Studies were excluded if they:

- Focused solely on technical AI model development without HR relevance;
- Provided opinion pieces lacking academic or methodological rigor.

Data Extraction and Thematic Coding

Relevant content was extracted and categorized into core HRM domains such as recruitment, performance management, employee engagement, learning and development, and organizational design. Thematic coding was performed manually, guided by Braun and Clarke's (2006) six-step thematic analysis framework. Recurring concepts—such as bias, privacy, transparency, and augmentation were identified and grouped into major analytical themes.

Analytical Framework

The study integrated insights from socio-technical systems theory and the automation–augmentation paradox (Raisch & Krakowski, 2021) to interpret findings. This allowed the research to assess not only technological impacts but also human, ethical, and organizational implications.

Synthesis and Interpretation

Extracted themes were synthesized to construct a structured understanding of how generative AI is currently influencing HRM, the challenges associated with its adoption, and opportunities for future application. The synthesis informed the development of Table 1 and the framing of research gaps.

Overall, this methodology ensures that the study is grounded in comprehensive, multi-source evidence and provides a robust foundation for analysing the intersection of generative AI and HRM.

Figure 1. Co-occurrence analysis of the keywords in literature

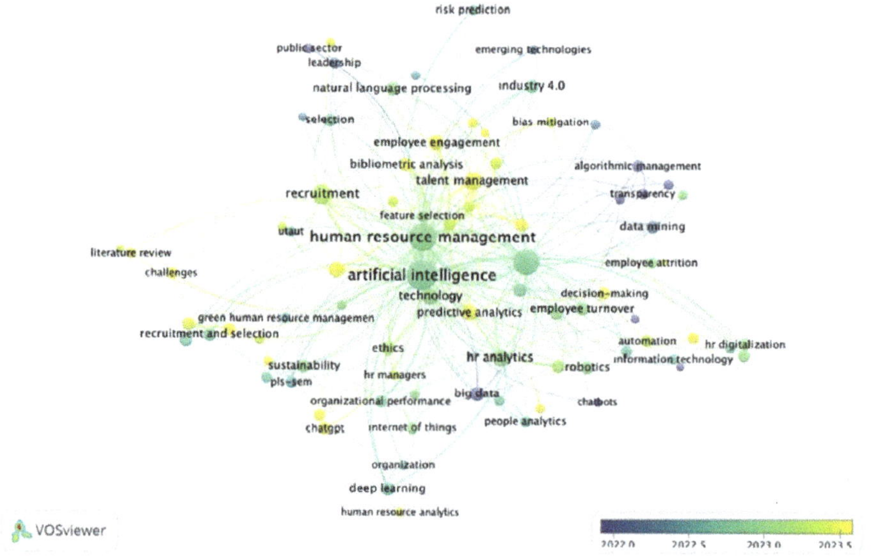

Source: author's representation

Table 1. Contribution and challenges of ChatGPT and similar generative artificial intelligence in human resource management

	Aspect	Role of generative AI in HRM	Challenges in implementation	Potential solutions	References
1	Recruitment & selection	Automates job-description drafting, screens resume at scale, drafts interview questions, conducts chat-based pre-screening.	Risk of amplifying historical bias; opaque scoring; over-reliance on automated rejection.	Human-in-the-loop (HITL), bias audits, blind screening features.	Aguinis (2024); Rigotti et al. (2024); Chen et al. (2023)
2	Candidate assessment & interviewing	Generates standardized interview prompts, simulates interviewers, summarizes candidate replies.	Reliability concerns for soft-skill evaluation; cultural bias; legal admissibility.	Validate against psychometric tests; human oversight; document decision paths.	Reuters (2018); Chen et al. (2023)
3	Onboarding & employee FAQs	24/7 onboarding assistants, personalized checklists, policy explainers.	Privacy risks; hallucinations; mismatch with local policy.	RAG from verified docs; disclosure labels; data access controls.	Diro & Redi (2025); Allgood (2024)
4	Learning & development	Creates personalized modules, quizzes, and microlearning content.	Quality control; credentialing; IP issues.	Human curation; LMS integration; content validation.	Wang et al. (2025); Prasad & Sujatha (2024)
5	Performance appraisal & feedback	Drafts appraisal summaries, analyzes free-text feedback.	Fairness concerns; reductionism; employee distrust.	XAI layers; anonymized aggregation; human sign-off.	ResearchGate (2025); Pinto & Silva (2025)
6	Employee engagement & communication	Drafts newsletters, meeting summaries, synthesizes sentiment.	Misinterpretation of tone; privacy; manipulation.	Aggregate reporting; opt-in analytics; oversight.	Prasad & Sujatha (2024); Financial Times (2024)
7	Workforce analytics & planning	Produces scenario narratives, augments descriptive analytics.	Garbage-in/garbage-out; historical bias; inferential errors.	Combine with statistical tests; document assumptions.	Brynjolfsson et al. (2025); Wang et al. (2025)
8	Diversity, equity & inclusion (DEI)	Creates inclusive job ads, analyses bias in text.	Bias in training data; tokenistic interventions.	DEI style guides; fairness audits; diverse reviewers.	Chen et al. (2023); Sohail & Rosário (2025)
9	Privacy, data protection & compliance	Automates compliance checklists, privacy notices.	Sensitive data use; GDPR/CPRA compliance.	Data minimization; DPIAs; pseudonymization.	Fisher Phillips (2024); SHRM (2024)
10	Explainability & accountability	Produces plain-language rationales.	Risk of misleading rationales; weak causal explanations.	Model cards; provenance tracking; algorithmic audits.	Coussement et al. (2024); Pinto & Silva (2025)
11	Monitoring & productivity tools	Transcribes meetings, summarizes activity.	Worker privacy invasion; stress; regulatory backlash.	Consent; anonymized data; wellness focus.	Wired (2024); Shin (2025)
12	Organizational design & job redesign	Optimizes staffing, dynamic work allocation.	Job displacement fears; deskilling.	Reskilling programs; fairness constraints.	Jarrahi & Sutherland (2021); Meijerink et al. (2023)
13	Legal, ethical & reputational risks	Drafts compliance policies, supports legal reviews.	Discrimination lawsuits; trust erosion.	Policy frameworks; legal review; transparency.	Palos-Sánchez & Correia (2022); ResearchGate (2023)
14	Reskilling & talent mobility	Personalizes learning, identifies skills gaps.	Unequal access; training quality; ROI issues.	Mix AI learning with coaching; internal mobility markets.	SHRM (2024); Business Insider (2025)
15	Strategic HR decision support	Produces policy drafts, scenario planning, literature syntheses.	Overreliance on AI "authority"; hallucinations.	Expert sign-off; corroboration with primary sources.	Brynjolfsson et al. (2023); Pereira & Silva (2023)

Source: author's representation

RESULTS AND DISCUSSION

Role of ChatGPT and Similar Generative Artificial Intelligence in Human Resource Management

The rapid rise of generative artificial intelligence (GenAI) systems such as ChatGPT has marked a transformative moment in the evolution of human resource management (HRM). Unlike earlier generations of automation tools, which focused primarily on transactional processes, GenAI introduces the capacity to generate, interpret, and synthesize text at scale, thereby influencing virtually every stage of the employee lifecycle. From recruitment to learning, performance management, and strategic decision-making, the integration of conversational AI offers both significant opportunities and equally pressing challenges. The following discussion outlines the key areas in which ChatGPT and comparable large language models (LLMs) are shaping HRM, drawing upon recent scholarly and practitioner insights.

Recruitment and Selection

Recruitment remains one of the most visible areas of HR transformation through GenAI. ChatGPT has been applied to automate job description drafting, analyse resumes, and conduct initial candidate interactions (Aguinis, 2024). These tools reduce the administrative burden on recruiters, enabling them to focus more on relationship-building with potential candidates. Furthermore, GenAI can help ensure linguistic inclusivity in job advertisements, thereby broadening access for underrepresented groups (Rigotti, Riedl, & Baumgartner, 2024). However, the promise of efficiency is tempered by concerns about fairness and bias. Past experiences, such as Amazon's withdrawal of an AI recruitment tool that systematically disadvantaged female candidates, demonstrate the risks inherent in algorithmic screening (Reuters, 2018). Ethical concerns are heightened when models are trained on biased historical data, potentially perpetuating structural inequalities (Chen, Huang, & Ye, 2023). Solutions such as bias audits, human-in-the-loop (HITL) reviews, and transparency mechanisms are therefore crucial for responsible adoption.

Candidate Assessment and Interviewing

GenAI extends beyond resume screening to candidate evaluation. ChatGPT can generate standardized interview questions, conduct chat-based assessments, and even summarize candidate responses for HR managers (Chen et al., 2023). These innovations hold potential for reducing interviewer subjectivity and ensuring greater consistency across candidate evaluations. Nonetheless, the reliability of AI-driven assessments for soft skills, cultural fit, and ethical decision-making remains contested (Chen et al., 2023). Legal admissibility in certain jurisdictions also raises concerns, particularly when candidates challenge algorithmic decisions. Thus, hybrid approaches that integrate AI-generated assessments with validated psychometric instruments are recommended.

Onboarding and Employee Support

Onboarding is another domain where ChatGPT's conversational abilities provide substantial benefits. Automated assistants can answer frequently asked questions, guide employees through complex policies, and provide personalized onboarding checklists (Allgood, 2024). By offering immediate, 24/7 support, AI-driven onboarding tools can enhance new employee experience and reduce HR staff workload. However, the reliability of LLM outputs is a significant issue. Hallucinations — the generation of incorrect or fabricated responses — may confuse or mislead employees (Diro & Redi, 2025). Additionally, onboarding frequently involves sensitive personal data, raising privacy concerns. Retrieval-augmented generation (RAG) frameworks, which restrict model outputs to verified organizational knowledge bases, represent one solution to this challenge.

Learning and Development

The personalization capabilities of generative AI are perhaps most evident in learning and development (L&D). ChatGPT can generate adaptive training modules, practice quizzes, and interactive learning scenarios tailored to individual employee needs (Prasad & Sujatha, 2024). Moreover, AI can support microlearning by delivering just-in-time training interventions. A recent meta-analysis demonstrated that AI-driven tools can positively impact learning outcomes by providing contextualized, real-time feedback (Wang, Liu, & Zhao, 2025). Challenges include maintaining content accuracy, ensuring intellectual property compliance, and validating the pedagogical soundness of AI-generated materials. Human curation and integration with learning management systems (LMS) are essential to safeguard quality and accountability.

Performance Appraisal and Feedback

Performance appraisal processes, traditionally criticized for subjectivity and bias, are being reimagined through AI. ChatGPT can analyse open-text feedback to identify recurring themes and draft appraisal summaries (ResearchGate, 2025). The capacity to synthesize qualitative insights at scale reduces managerial workload and highlights employee contributions that may otherwise go unnoticed. Yet, delegating evaluative tasks to algorithms risks over-reduction of performance into simplistic categories. Employees may distrust systems that appear opaque or dehumanizing (Pinto & Silva, 2025). Embedding explainable AI (XAI) mechanisms and requiring human verification for final evaluations are recommended approaches to preserve trust.

Employee Engagement and Communication

Generative AI can assist in drafting internal communications, summarizing meetings, and conducting sentiment analysis of employee surveys (Prasad & Sujatha, 2024). Such applications enable organizations to keep employees better informed while reducing communication overhead for HR staff. However, employee trust is at stake if communications appear overly automated or manipulative. Concerns also arise around privacy when AI is used to analyse sentiment or communication tone (Financial Times, 2024). Transparent disclosure, opt-in participation, and aggregated reporting can mitigate these risks.

Workforce Analytics and Planning

ChatGPT enhances workforce analytics by generating narrative explanations of data patterns, supporting scenario planning, and assisting in drafting reports for executives (Brynjolfsson, Li, & Raymond, 2025). By translating complex analytics into accessible language, AI expands the reach of evidence-based HR decision-making. Despite these advantages, issues of "garbage in, garbage out" persist. Poor-quality or biased data will yield misleading narratives (Wang et al., 2025). Organizations must therefore couple AI-generated insights with rigorous statistical analysis and ensure transparent documentation of assumptions.

Diversity, Equity, and Inclusion (DEI)

One of the most promising contributions of ChatGPT is in advancing diversity, equity, and inclusion efforts. Generative AI can identify biased language in job postings, propose inclusive alternatives, and recommend outreach strategies for underrepresented groups (Chen et al., 2023). Nonetheless, DEI initiatives powered by AI are only as effective as their underlying data. When models are trained on biased corpora, interventions may inadvertently appear tokenistic (Sohail & Rosário, 2025). Combining AI with DEI style guides, fairness testing, and diverse reviewer input remains critical.

Privacy, Compliance, and Accountability

Generative AI often requires access to sensitive employee data, raising concerns about privacy and regulatory compliance. ChatGPT can assist by generating privacy notices, automating compliance checklists, and identifying potential legal risks (Fisher Phillips, 2024). However, navigating frameworks such as GDPR and CPRA is complex, and improper data use can expose organizations to liability (SHRM, 2024). Recommended practices include data minimization, pseudonymization, and legal counsel sign-off. Similarly, explainability and accountability are critical to avoid reputational harm. Tools such as model cards and algorithmic audits provide transparency for stakeholders (Coussement, Phan, & Lessmann, 2024).

Organizational Design, Monitoring, and Job Redesign

Generative AI enables dynamic staffing models, optimized job allocation, and new forms of algorithmic management (Meijerink, Bondarouk, & Lepak, 2023). While these innovations can improve efficiency, they may also foster perceptions of dehumanization or surveillance (Jarrahi & Sutherland, 2021). Research shows that "bossware" tools, which monitor employee activity, increase stress and reduce trust (Shin, 2025). To balance efficiency with ethics, organizations should limit intrusive monitoring, provide transparency, and emphasize reskilling initiatives. Integrating fairness constraints into algorithmic allocation also helps mitigate risks of deskilling or inequity.

Strategic HR Decision-Making

Ultimately, generative AI helps HR leaders with strategic activities such as policy formulation, literature review synthesis, and scenario planning (Brynjolfsson et al., 2023). For instance, ChatGPT can create briefing documents that encapsulate industry developments and even model the impact of changes in certain polices (Pereira & Silva, 2023). However, using AI-generated material without the proper checks can result in the dissemination of false information, or 'hallucinations.' This means that the results have to be verified by field experts and the rationale behind the decisions made must be captured in detail.

The use of HRM ChatGPT and other generative AI systems is both a chance and a challenge. These instruments have the potential to improve effectiveness, increase customization, and expand the HR function. However, there is a considerable risk of bias, opacity, and dehumanization that is equally tough to ignore. The use of AI for HRM is best approached by using a 'fusion' technique – using AI for enhancement, not replacement; applying human governance; and, the most fundamental, prioritizing fairness, transparency, and social responsibility. It is clear from the literature that the future of HRM is not about choosing one over the other i.e. human vs. artificial intelligence. It is about designing systems where both can be integrated in ways that promote inclusive, ethical, and productive HRM.

CHALLENGES OF CHATGPT AND SIMILAR GENERATIVE ARTIFICIAL INTELLIGENCE IN HUMAN RESOURCE MANAGEMENT

The integration of generative artificial intelligence (GenAI) tools such as ChatGPT into human resource management (HRM) has opened up new avenues for efficiency, personalization, and innovation. However, these benefits are accompanied by significant challenges that demand careful consideration by scholars, practitioners, and policymakers. The issues range from ethical and legal concerns to technical limitations and organizational acceptance. This section examines the major challenges in depth.

1. Algorithmic Bias and Fairness

Recruitment and selection as HR functions has a lot to evaluate when adopting new tools and processes. Algorithmic bias and in particular the use of bias in the underlying data is one such issue. History is often presented as a series of objective facts and fails to acknowledge pre-existing social biases. For instance Amazon had to scrap one of their experimental recruitment tools due to discrimination against women applicants (Reuters, 2018). The training data was biased and the outcome was discriminatory, something that is counter to the organizational philosophy of diversity and inclusion. The biases do however extend beyond gender, with the additional categories being race, social class, and level of education (Chen et al., 2023). The nature of discrimination is particularly concerning when people's livelihoods and the equity position of the organization is taken into account. Ensuring fairness will always, regardless of the application, need to incorporate biased and diverse massive sets of data, updated frequently, with the auditing being integrative to the entire algorithm.

2. Lack of Transparency and Explainability

In the case of Generative AI, especially very large language models such as ChatGPT, there is no shortage of outputs which come with no definable and justifiable processes. This approach to working with data is called a 'black box'. The lack of transparency and definable and acceptable reasoning is an approach which is counter to the very fundamentals of HRM. There is an expectation that there will be fairness and accountability in the use of the information for decision making (Coussement et al., 2024). An example is when an AI tool decides to gate a candidate and another recommends a promotion: HR professionals and the HR teams in general are unable to articulate and explain the rationale. This is also known as 'explainability'. The absence of explainability in an organization is a serious concern as employees will start losing faith in the decisions being taken related to HR, and in a wider context organizational decision, which in turn leads to reduced organizational legitmacy (Meijerink et al., 2023). This makes explainable AI frameworks critical for responsible HR applications.

3. Data Privacy and Security

HRM deals with sensitive personal data, including resumes, performance evaluations, and psychological assessments. Using generative AI tools raises data privacy concerns, especially if these tools rely on cloud-based platforms or external data processing (SHRM, 2024). Leaked or misused employee data can cause reputational damage and legal repercussions. Moreover, compliance with global regulations such as the General Data Protection Regulation (GDPR) and India's Digital Personal Data Protection Act becomes increasingly complex when using generative AI in multinational organizations (Fisher Phillips, 2024). Organizations must adopt strong governance frameworks, encryption practices, and strict vendor agreements.

4. Ethical Concerns in Employee Monitoring

Generative AI has enabled advanced employee monitoring through "bossware" applications that analyse communication patterns, keystrokes, and productivity metrics. While these tools promise efficiency, they also risk creating a culture of surveillance (Shin, 2025). Over-monitoring can reduce psychological safety and increase stress, counteracting efforts to improve employee engagement. The ethical challenge lies in balancing productivity insights with respect for employee autonomy and trust. Organizations need transparent communication, clear boundaries, and employee consent to mitigate these risks.

5. Accuracy and Hallucination Problems

A unique technical challenge with ChatGPT is its tendency to produce hallucinations—plausible-sounding but incorrect or fabricated information (Diro & Redi, 2025). In HRM, where precision is critical, hallucinations can lead to misleading job descriptions, erroneous performance feedback, or flawed policy documents. For example, if ChatGPT generates an inaccurate compliance policy or training guideline, organizations risk legal liabilities and reputational harm. While human oversight can reduce errors, overreliance on AI outputs without verification remains a substantial risk.

6. Legal and Compliance Risks

Generative AI in HRM operates within complex legal and compliance frameworks. Employment law varies across countries, and AI-generated decisions can easily conflict with legal standards (Fisher Phillips, 2024). For example, an AI-driven layoff recommendation that disproportionately affects a protected category of employees could invite lawsuits under anti-discrimination laws. Moreover, the accountability question remains unresolved: if an HR decision influenced by ChatGPT leads to harm, who is legally responsible—the HR manager, the software vendor, or the organization? Such ambiguities make risk management challenging for HR leaders.

7. Skill Gaps and Resistance to Adoption

While AI tools can enhance HR efficiency, their adoption faces resistance from employees and managers. Many HR professionals lack technical expertise to effectively use generative AI (Prasad & Sujatha, 2024). This creates a skill gap that can slow adoption and foster mistrust. Employees may also fear that AI tools will replace their roles, particularly in administrative HR functions. Such perceptions can lower morale and hinder digital transformation initiatives. To overcome resistance, organizations need comprehensive change management strategies and upskilling programs.

8. Cost and Infrastructure Requirements

Generative AI deployment requires substantial financial and infrastructural investment, including licenses, data integration systems, and cybersecurity measures. Small and medium-sized enterprises (SMEs) may struggle to afford these costs, creating a digital divide between large corporations and smaller organizations (Allgood, 2024). In addition, maintaining up-to-date AI systems requires continuous investment in training datasets and software updates. Without adequate resources, organizations risk using outdated or ineffective AI models.

9. Impact on Human Touch in HRM

A more philosophical challenge is the potential erosion of human touch in HR practices. HR traditionally relies on empathy, intuition, and interpersonal communication. Over-automation of tasks such as recruitment interviews or performance feedback may depersonalize the employee experience (Rigotti et al., 2024). Generative AI cannot fully replicate emotional intelligence or cultural sensitivity, which are essential in HR interactions. If employees perceive HR as being "run by machines," organizational culture and trust may suffer.

10. Global Diversity and Cultural Sensitivity

Generative AI systems often reflect the cultural context of the datasets they are trained on. For multinational corporations, this creates a challenge in ensuring cultural sensitivity across diverse workforces (Vasanthan et al 2025, Sohail & Rosário, 2025). For example, an AI-generated performance appraisal framework designed in the U.S. might not align with workplace norms in Asia or Africa. In such cases, misaligned AI outputs can unintentionally alienate employees or perpetuate cultural misunderstandings. Addressing this challenge requires localization and inclusion of diverse training data.

The challenges of integrating ChatGPT and similar generative AI tools into HRM are multifaceted, involving technical, ethical, legal, and cultural dimensions. While these tools hold immense potential to revolutionize HR processes, organizations must proactively address algorithmic bias, transparency, privacy, hallucinations, compliance, skill gaps, and cultural sensitivity. A responsible AI strategy, combining human oversight with robust governance frameworks, is crucial to harness the benefits of generative AI while mitigating its risks.

CONCLUSION

There is no question the rise of ChatGPT and more widely available GenAI systems is a new pivot for the evolution of HR management (HRM). Generic AI is unlike the previous automation systems which centered around transactional automations. To the human resources and employee lifecycle processes such as recruitment, selection, learning, engagement, and strategic workforce planning, systems such as ChatGPT offer unrivalled efficiency and customization. There is also a more complex set of issues and challenges, especially in HR systems, such as, algorithm bias, privacy issues, opacity, and the loss of the interpersonal element in HR functions. More complex and advanced systems in the HR domain will still require the presence of human intelligence to oversee the AI systems, which in turn, will require the presence and management of human biases, purposefully crafted into the system.

Recruitment and selection are perhaps the most transformed field, where ChatGPT goes as far as composing analyse resumes, drafts inclusive job descriptions, and even engages with the candidates in the primary stages. Although administrative burden is diminished, as is the ever-present bias in the training data, as with Amazon's recruitment tool. Similar tensions appear in candidate assessment, onboarding, and learning, where AI-driven personalization enhances experience but simultaneously introduces risks of inaccuracies or "hallucinations." In sensitive contexts such as compliance or policy communication, these errors can undermine trust and even create legal liabilities. Thus, while the technology adds speed and scalability, organizations must remain vigilant about accuracy and fairness.

From the side of the employees' feedback and engagement, both represents the pros and cons of ChatGPT and AI use in performance appraisals. ChatGPT might capture and synthesize employee feedback in ways that the managers overlook and construct sentiment analyses of employee feedback survey results. Then ChatGPT can compose and improve draft internal communications. Only if These technologies work. They can also in the process, lacking organizational trust, become misguided and disenfranchising. Moreover, the evaluative tasks the case on ChatGPT is about, has the potential of rest to the surface, perplexedly complex and advanced levels of human performance metric oversimplification, which is already workplace low integrity and morale. These negative aspects of AI, also allow to further investigate the application of AI in human resource and performance appraisal, hence the response is affirmative, machine learning and AI systems, trust, explainability and the human element are vital.

This layer to performance reviews creates Global and Ethical Dimensions. Covering the requirements of the GDPR and the Digital Personal Data Protection Act of India, Generative AI in HR also works with sensitive pieces of internal employee data. Safeguarding these legal responsibilities stems from legal protection, data minimization, and privacy safeguards. Acts of ethical misconduct tend to disregard the compliance as value compliance is over culture which is the non-existence of compliance. These are equally important to Generative AI. The outputs of the AI are often culturally biased. We recommend the use of multicultural training and inclusive design, beyond local AI. These approaches can instead increase the chances of simplistic responses to complex issues in diversity and inclusiveness in Generative AI.

Taken together, the integration of generative AI in HRM presents both promise and peril. The most sustainable approach is not to view AI as a replacement for human professionals but as a tool for augmentation. Responsible adoption demands continuous auditing for bias, transparency in decision-making, strict data governance, and robust employee communication. Equally, organizations must invest in upskilling HR professionals to engage critically with AI tools and ensure that empathy, fairness, and ethical reasoning remain central to HR practice. Ultimately, the future of HRM will be shaped by how effectively organizations balance efficiency with humanity, innovation with accountability, and technology with trust. Generative AI such as ChatGPT has immense potential to transform HR, but only if it is harnessed responsibly, with a commitment to creating workplaces that are both technologically advanced and fundamentally human-centered.

RESEARCH GAPS AND FUTURE DIRECTIONS

Despite the growing scholarship and practical experimentation with ChatGPT and other generative AI tools in human resource management (HRM), several research gaps remain unaddressed. First, most existing studies focus on the potential applications of GenAI such as recruitment automation, employee engagement, and personalized learning yet there is limited empirical evidence on their long-term effectiveness. Few longitudinal or large-scale studies have systematically evaluated whether AI-driven HR interventions translate into measurable outcomes such as improved diversity, enhanced employee engagement, or sustained organizational performance. This creates a significant gap between theoretical promise and practical validation.

Second, while ethical challenges such as bias, transparency, and data privacy are well-documented, there is inadequate research on the practical mechanisms by which organizations can embed fairness, accountability, and explainability into AI-enabled HR systems. Most current discussions remain conceptual, lacking detailed frameworks or case studies that illustrate how bias audits, human-in-the-loop (HITL) mechanisms, or explainable AI (XAI) tools can be operationalized in diverse organizational contexts.

Third, the issue of cultural sensitivity in AI-enabled HR remains underexplored. Since generative AI models are trained largely on English-dominant and Western-centric datasets, their transferability across cultural contexts is uncertain. Research is needed to assess how AI-driven HR practices perform in non-Western settings and how local data, norms, and languages can be integrated to ensure inclusivity in multinational organizations.

Fourth, there is a limited understanding of the psychological and behavioural impacts of AI adoption on employees. Questions remain about how employees perceive fairness when HR decisions are mediated by AI, how trust in HR functions evolves, and whether over-reliance on AI undermines the human touch that has traditionally defined HR. These areas warrant in-depth exploration through qualitative and mixed-methods research.

Finally, the strategic role of HR professionals in the age of AI remains unclear. While much of the discourse frames AI as a support tool, there is insufficient research on how HR professionals' competencies, roles, and identities will evolve. Identifying the digital and ethical skills required to work alongside generative AI represents an important future research direction. Moving forward, scholars should design empirical, cross-cultural, and interdisciplinary studies that go beyond conceptual discussions to test the impact of generative AI in real-world HR environments. Comparative studies between AI-augmented and traditional HR practices could provide evidence on effectiveness, while experimental designs could explore employee perceptions of AI-mediated decision-making. Additionally, developing industry-specific frameworks for AI adoption in HRM such as in healthcare, education, or manufacturing—could help contextualize best practices.

Future research should also examine the regulatory and governance dimensions, particularly as global data protection laws evolve. Investigating how organizations can balance compliance with innovation will be critical for sustainable AI adoption. Furthermore, collaboration between AI developers, HR practitioners, and policymakers will be essential to co-create ethical standards that safeguard fairness, inclusivity, and employee well-being.

LIMITATIONS

Like any academic investigation, this study is subject to certain limitations that should be acknowledged for appropriate contextualization of the findings. First, the scope of analysis is restricted to publications indexed in the Scopus database. While Scopus is widely regarded as a comprehensive and credible source for academic literature, it does not capture all relevant contributions available across other indexing services or grey literature. Consequently, potentially valuable insights from non-Scopus sources such as practitioner reports, conference proceedings, or policy documents may have been excluded, thereby narrowing the breadth of the evidence base.

Secondly, the study is still in its early stages, and will be carried out over a five-year span (2020–2024). While the years allocated will provide the critical intersection points through which the discourse around 'generative AI's impact on Human Resource Management' will be assessed, it will still stifle the ability to gain a holistic view of its evolution over the years. Older, more nascent keystones and patterns of growth risks being subjective. More years allocated towards integrated AI in HRM could provide better insight.

Third, the study, in its current state, also suffers under the confines of the published works in the English language. Such a caveat, while preferable, permits critical thoughts and voices that would add more nuance to the analysis. The study of literature, as it pertains to the application of AI in HRM systems, is universal in nature. The exclusive focus on the English language could be the absence of AI in HRM literature on Human Resource Management Systems. More multidisciplinary and multilingual data, in addition to the extended period, would make the study more robust.

REFERENCES

Abu Orabi, T., Alahewat, A. M. M., Abualfalayeh, G., & Samara, H. H. (2024). The interdisciplinary nature of AI and human resource management: A bibliometric analysis. *Human Systems Management, 43*(6), 845–871. DOI: 10.3233/HSM-240054

Aguinis, H. (2024). *Performance management for dummies.* John Wiley & Sons.

Allgood, S. (2024). Generative AI in employee onboarding: Implications for HR practice. *Journal of Human Resource Innovation, 12*(2), 45–59.

Arora, M., Gupta, J., Mittal, A., & Prakash, A. (2024). A bibliometric review of artificial intelligence technologies in human resource management: An overview of research trends. *Global Knowledge, Memory and Communication.* Advance online publication. DOI: 10.1108/GKMC-04-2024-0237

Arslan, A., Cooper, C., Khan, Z., Golgeci, I., & Ali, I. (2021). Artificial intelligence and human workers interaction at team level: A conceptual assessment of the challenges and potential HRM strategies. *International Journal of Manpower, 43*(1), 75–88. DOI: 10.1108/IJM-01-2021-0052

Benabou, A., & Touhami, F. (2025). Empowering human resource management through artificial intelligence: A systematic literature review and bibliometric analysis. *International Journal of Production Management and Engineering, 13*(1), 59–76. DOI: 10.4995/ijpme.2025.21900

Berk, R. (2019). *Machine learning risk assessments in criminal justice settings.* Springer. DOI: 10.1007/978-3-030-02272-3

Bogen, M., & Rieke, A. (2018). *Help wanted: An examination of hiring algorithms, equity, and bias.* Upturn.

Brown, T., Mann, B., Ryder, N., Subbiah, M., Kaplan, J., Dhariwal, P., & Amodei, D. (2020). Language models are few-shot learners. *Advances in Neural Information Processing Systems, 33*, 1877–1901.

Brynjolfsson, E., Li, D., & Raymond, L. (2025). Generative AI at work. *The Quarterly Journal of Economics, 140*(2), 889–942. DOI: 10.1093/qje/qjae044

Budhwar, P., Chowdhury, S., Wood, G., Aguinis, H., Bamber, G. J., Beltran, J. R., Boselie, P., Lee Cooke, F., Decker, S., DeNisi, A., Dey, P. K., Guest, D., Knoblich, A. J., Malik, A., Paauwe, J., Papagiannidis, S., Patel, C., Pereira, V., Ren, S., & Varma, A. (2023). Human resource management in the age of generative artificial intelligence: Perspectives and research directions on ChatGPT. *Human Resource Management Journal, 33*(3), 606–659. DOI: 10.1111/1748-8583.12524

Caliskan, A., Bryson, J. J., & Narayanan, A. (2017). Semantics derived automatically from language corpora contain human-like biases. *Science, 356*(6334), 183–186. DOI: 10.1126/science.aal4230 PMID: 28408601

Cascio, W. F., & Montealegre, R. (2016). How technology is changing work and organizations. *Annual Review of Organizational Psychology and Organizational Behavior, 3*(1), 349–375. DOI: 10.1146/annurev-orgpsych-041015-062352

Chaudhary, A., & Khandelwal, S. (2024). A bibliometric analysis of the role of artificial intelligence and machine learning in human resource management. In *Resilient Businesses for Sustainability* (Vol. 34, pp. 119–137). Emerald Publishing Limited. DOI: 10.1108/S1877-63612024000034A011

Chen, J., Huang, Y., & Ye, X. (2023). Algorithmic bias in recruitment: Risks and remedies. *International Journal of Human Resource Studies, 13*(4), 66–82.

Chowdhury, S., Dey, P., Joel-Edgar, S., Bhattacharya, S., Rodriguez-Espindola, O., Abadie, A., & Truong, L. (2023). Unlocking the value of artificial intelligence in human resource management through AI capability framework. *Human Resource Management Review, 33*(1), 100899. DOI: 10.1016/j.hrmr.2022.100899

Coussement, K., Phan, M., & Lessmann, S. (2024). Explainable AI in HR analytics: A framework for transparency. *Human Resource Management Review, 34*(1), 100912.

Coussement, K., Phan, T. Q., & Lessmann, S. (2024). Explainable artificial intelligence for enhanced decision-making. *Decision Support Systems, 175*, 113882.

Deloitte. (2025). *The future of work and AI upskilling*. Deloitte Insights. https://www.deloitte.com

Deviprasad, S., Madhumithaa, N., Vikas, I. W., Yadav, A., & Manoharan, G. (2023). The machine learning-based task automation framework for human resource management in MNC companies. *Engineering Proceedings, 59*(1), 63.

Diro, A., & Redi, D. (2025). Challenges of generative AI hallucinations in HR applications. *AI & Society, 40*(1), 131–146.

Diro, A. A., & Redi, A. (2025). Workplace security and privacy implications in the generative AI age. *Computers & Security, 138*, 103676.

Estella, A. (2023). Trust in Artificial Intelligence: Analysis of the European Commission Proposal for a Regulation of Artificial Intelligence. *Indiana Journal of Global Legal Studies, 30*(1), 39–64. DOI: 10.2979/gls.2023.a886162

Falát, L., Michalová, T., Madzík, P., & Maršíková, K. (2023). Discovering trends and journeys in knowledge-based human resource management: Big data smart literature review based on machine learning approach. *IEEE Access : Practical Innovations, Open Solutions, 11*, 95567–95583. DOI: 10.1109/ACCESS.2023.3296140

Garg, S., Sinha, S., Kar, A. K., & Mani, M. (2022). A review of machine learning applications in human resource management. *International Journal of Productivity and Performance Management, 71*(5), 1590–1610. DOI: 10.1108/IJPPM-08-2020-0427

Goodell, J. W., Kumar, S., Lim, W. M., & Pattnaik, D. (2021). Artificial intelligence and machine learning in finance: Identifying foundations, themes, and research clusters from bibliometric analysis. *Journal of Behavioral and Experimental Finance, 32*, 100577. DOI: 10.1016/j.jbef.2021.100577

Haenlein, M., & Kaplan, A. (2019). A brief history of artificial intelligence: On the past, present, and future of artificial intelligence. *California Management Review, 61*(4), 5–14. DOI: 10.1177/0008125619864925

Huang, M. H., & Rust, R. T. (2018). Artificial intelligence in service. *Journal of Service Research, 21*(2), 155–172. DOI: 10.1177/1094670517752459

Insider, B. (2025, March 21). AI will reshape workforce; upskilling needs rise. *Business Insider*. https://www.businessinsider.com

Jarrahi, M. H., & Sutherland, W. (2021). Algorithmic management and algorithmic competencies: Understanding knowledge workers' perceptions of AI. *Big Data & Society, 8*(2), 20539517211047724.

Jobin, A., Ienca, M., & Vayena, E. (2019). The global landscape of AI ethics guidelines. *Nature Machine Intelligence, 1*(9), 389–399. DOI: 10.1038/s42256-019-0088-2

Meijerink, J., Bondarouk, T., & Lepak, D. P. (2021). When and why does HR analytics influence strategic decision making? *Human Resource Management, 60*(3), 365–382.

Meijerink, J., Bondarouk, T., & Lepak, D. P. (2023). The duality of algorithmic management: Toward a research agenda. *Human Resource Management Review, 33*(2), 100861.

Ossiannilsson, E., Altinay, F., Shadiev, R., Benachour, P., Berigel, M., Dagli, G., Ayaz, A., Yikici, B., & Altinay, Z. (2024). Exploring the Intersection of Artificial Intelligence and Human Resource Management: A Bibliometric Study. *BRAIN. Broad Research in Artificial Intelligence and Neuroscience, 15*(4), 215–230. DOI: 10.70594/brain/15.4/15

Palos-Sánchez, P. R., & Correia, M. B. (2022). Artificial intelligence and human resource management: A bibliometric analysis. *Technological Forecasting and Social Change, 178*, 121528.

Pereira, D., & Silva, T. (2023). Systematic literature review on AI impact at work. *Frontiers in Psychology, 14*, 1100203.

Pereira, R., & Silva, A. (2023). Policy drafting with generative AI: A case for strategic HR management. *Journal of Organizational Change Management, 36*(7), 1201–1219.

Phillips, F. (2024). Generative AI in the workplace: Compliance and legal issues for HR. *Fisher Phillips Legal Insights*. Retrieved from https://www.fisherphillips.com

Pinto, G. B. S., & Silva, R. (2025). Explainable AI in labor market applications: Challenges and opportunities. *ScitePress Proceedings on Artificial Intelligence Applications*, 122–135.

Pinto, R., & Silva, F. (2025). Trust and transparency in AI-driven performance appraisal. *European Journal of Work and Organizational Psychology, 34*(2), 205–220.

Prasad, K., & Sujatha, R. (2024). Leveraging generative AI for employee training: Personalized learning pathways. *International Journal of Training and Development, 28*(3), 211–228.

Prasad, K. D. V., & Sujatha, G. (2024). Generative AI as a catalyst for HRM practices: Challenges and opportunities. *International Journal of Human Resource Studies, 14*(2), 45–62.

Prikshat, V., Malik, A., & Budhwar, P. (2023). AI-augmented HRM: Antecedents, assimilation and multilevel consequences. *Human Resource Management Review, 33*(1), 100860. DOI: 10.1016/j.hrmr.2021.100860

Raisch, S., & Krakowski, S. (2021). Artificial intelligence and management: The automation–augmentation paradox. *Academy of Management Review, 46*(1), 192–210. DOI: 10.5465/amr.2018.0072

Reuters. (2018, October 10). Amazon scraps secret AI recruiting tool that showed bias against women. *Reuters*. https://www.reuters.com

Rigotti, C., Riedl, R., & Baumgartner, L. (2024). Fairness in AI-driven recruitment: A scoping review. *Computers in Human Behavior Reports, 14*, 100302.

Rigotti, T., Riedl, E., & Baumgartner, H. (2024). Inclusive hiring with generative AI. *Human Resource Development Quarterly, 35*(1), 45–63.

Samek, W., & Müller, K. R. (2019). Towards explainable artificial intelligence. In Explainable, A. I. (Ed.), *Interpreting, explaining and visualizing deep learning* (pp. 5–22). Springer. DOI: 10.1007/978-3-030-28954-6_1

Shin, D. (2025). Dehumanization and rehumanization of workers in AI-driven HRM. *Information & Management, 62*(2), 103768.

Shin, D. (2025). Bossware and the future of algorithmic monitoring: Implications for HRM. *Journal of Business Ethics, 182*(1), 1–19.

Sohail, M., & Rosário, A. (2025). Generative AI and diversity: Opportunities and risks for HRM. *Equality, Diversity and Inclusion, 44*(2), 178–196.

Sohail, M., & Rosário, A. (2025). Benefits and risks of artificial intelligence in human resource management: An integrative review. *Journal of Organizational Change Management, 38*(4), 565–584.

The Financial Times. (2024, December 15). Does HR still need humans? *Financial Times*. https://www.ft.com

Upadhyay, A. K., & Khandelwal, K. (2019). Applying artificial intelligence: Implications for recruitment. *Strategic HR Review, 18*(5), 215–218.

Vasanthan, R., Nath Babu, M., Dzuvichu, K., & Chong, T. S., Singh Rana, V., & Singh, A. (2025). Bridging Social Norms Theory and Community Mobilization: Pathways for Overcoming Gender Stereotypes in Women's Economic Empowerment Programs. *Enterprise Development & Microfinance, 35*(1), 159–176. Retrieved from https://papjournals.com/index.php/edm/article/view/13

Verma, N., & Gavett, G. (2021). Algorithms at work: The new contested terrain of control. *The Academy of Management Annals, 15*(1), 266–301.

Voigt, P., & Von dem Bussche, A. (2017). *The EU General Data Protection Regulation (GDPR)*. Springer. DOI: 10.1007/978-3-319-57959-7

Vrontis, D., Christofi, M., Pereira, V., Tarba, S., Makrides, A., & Trichina, E. (2023). Artificial intelligence, robotics, advanced technologies and human resource management: a systematic review. *Artificial intelligence and international HRM*, 172-201.

Wang, H., Liu, Y., & Zhao, J. (2025). AI-driven learning in organizations: A meta-analysis. *Computers & Education*, *210*, 104901.

Wang, J., Liu, H., & Zhao, Y. (2025). ChatGPT and student learning performance: A meta-analysis. *Nature Communications*, *16*, 452.

Wang, X., Xu, L., & Zhang, P. (2025). How and when AI-driven HRM promotes employee resilience. *Computers in Human Behavior*, *147*, 107916.

Wired. (2024, August 9). Algorithmic management is reshaping the workplace. *Wired Magazine*. https://www.wired.com

Zhou, X., Yu, Y., & Xu, H. (2023). Generative artificial intelligence in organizations: A conceptual framework. *Information & Management*, *60*(6), 103762.

Zhu, H. (2021). Research on human resource recommendation algorithm based on machine learning. *Scientific Programming*, *2021*(1), 8387277. DOI: 10.1155/2021/8387277

Chapter 10

Leveraging Human Resource Analytics in Industry 4.0: Enhancing Employee Performance Through Data-Driven Strategies

Nida Fatima Khan
Christ University, Bengaluru, India

Shakeeb Mohammad Mir
http://orcid.org/0000-0002-4416-7027
Christ University, Bengaluru, India

Mohammad Irfan
http://orcid.org/0000-0002-4956-1170
Chandigarh University, Lucknow, India

Syed Muhammad Abdul Rehman Shah
Allama Iqbal Open University, Islamabad, Pakistan

ABSTRACT

In the Industry 4.0 era, organizations face challenges in sustaining employee engagement while enhancing productivity through data-driven strategies. This study explores the link between employee engagement and performance, emphasizing the mediating role of HR analytical strategies. A quantitative approach was used, with data from 125 professionals across sectors. Regression, correlation, and collinearity diagnostics revealed that physical, emotional, and cognitive engagement significantly influence task and contextual performance. HR analytics emerged as a key

DOI: 10.4018/979-8-2600-1845-3.ch010

mediator, strengthening this relationship. Furthermore, organizational factors like compatibility, relative advantage, and top management support positively impacted engagement-performance outcomes. The study underscores how HR analytics can transform engagement into a strategic lever for sustainable performance. Practical implications, limitations, and future research avenues are discussed.

1. INTRODUCTION

Fourth Industrial Revolution also known as Industry 4.0 is currently transforming the mainframe of organizations of current now world, entrusting computation, artificial intelligence, large-scale information management technology, and Internet of Things (IoT). This transition is not merely a technological change; it dramatically changes how businesses work and interact with their employees and foster performance. Just to Sustain employee engagement at high levels while adopting new methods of big data for workforce management is the rising challenge among organizations in the current ever-changing world. Job satisfaction, as the extent of emotional attachment of the employees to their organization, has been found to have benefits associated with various organization performances such as increased productivity, improved creativity and reduced turnover. Concerned staffs tend to have their self-interests in the progress of the organization and hence contribute positively. That said, it might be inadequate in the context of Industry 4.0 of the current century to solely apply engagement strategies that were sufficient for the previous century's climate of business. For organizations the establishment of new strategies incorporating Human Capital Solutions and more specifically advanced analytics can be exerted for transforming and optimizing the employees 'engagement. HR analytics then defines itself as an essential weapon in this fight by helping organizations use data to find out what engages their employees, to be able to forecast how specific behaviours will unfold, and to concoct interventions that might suit a variety of employees. The implementation of analytics in the human resource management enables organization to develop and sustain organizational culture with a focus at the central line to enhance organizational responsiveness in accordance to employee engagement programs within the conceptual framework of business strategies. In addition, successful performance appraisal systems which are intelligence through HR analytics must comprise of enhanced performance, valuable understanding pertaining to individual as well as collective organizational performance to make the employees' total performance-oriented and high performing. Nevertheless, the promotion of HR analytics also has its pros and cons: data privacy problems, the lack of trust from employees, and pulling up of the level of competence of HR specialists. To respond to these challenges, this research will propose a holistic framework of analytics to redesign and reinvent employee engagement for organizations operating in the context of the Fourth Industrial Revolution (HR 4.0). Criticizing organization engagement challenges with his framework, the author helps organizations to prevent the loss of commitment among the workforce, reviewed the factors affecting the engagement initiatives by organizations and considered it as the significant way to improve organizational performance in the context of the current dynamic business environment. The current paper aims to discuss the relationship between two topics, namely, employee engagement and HR analytics to help organizations better understand how the approach to encouraging workers' engagement and productivity can be enhanced by data-driven practices. Through analysis of the existing state of HR analytics with reference to potential scenarios when it concerns employee engagement, this research extends the discussion of effective workforce management as well as performance appraisal at the time of Industry 4.0.

2. LITERATURE REVIEW

Employee engagement has been extensively studied as a key driver of employee performance, organizational commitment, and overall productivity. Kahn (1990) introduced the concept of engagement by defining it as the psychological presence of an employee in their work role, highlighting physical, emotional, and cognitive dimensions of engagement. Later studies expanded on Kahn's work, demonstrating that engaged employees exhibit higher levels of motivation, job satisfaction, and workplace effectiveness. Employee engagement is increasingly recognized as a crucial factor in driving business success, as engaged employees tend to be more committed, innovative, and proactive in achieving organizational goals.

The relationship between employee engagement and employee performance has been widely explored in organizational behavior research. According to Saks (2006), engagement fosters a sense of responsibility and commitment, which translates into improved task performance and higher levels of discretionary effort. Physical engagement, which involves the energy and effort invested in tasks, has been linked to increased productivity and efficiency in the workplace (Bakker & Demerouti, 2008). Emotional engagement, which signifies an employee's attachment and commitment to their job, has been found to enhance job satisfaction and reduce turnover intentions (Bathla et al., 2019). Cognitive engagement, defined as an employee's mental involvement and concentration at work, is associated with better problem-solving abilities, innovation, and overall task efficiency.

Employee performance, which consists of contextual performance and task performance, is a widely studied outcome of engagement. Task performance, as conceptualized by Motowidlo & Van Scotter (1994), refers to the effectiveness with which employees carry out their assigned duties. Research suggests that engaged employees are more productive, exhibit greater attention to detail, and deliver higher-quality work (Christian et al., 2011). Contextual performance, on the other hand, extends beyond formal job responsibilities and includes discretionary behaviors such as helping colleagues, demonstrating organizational citizenship, and fostering a positive work environment (Borman & Motowidlo, 1993). Studies indicate that employees with high engagement levels are more likely to contribute to organizational citizenship behaviors, which enhance overall workplace culture and effectiveness (Podsakoff et al., 2000).

HR analytical strategies have emerged as a critical mediator in the engagement-performance relationship. With the rise of data-driven decision-making, HR analytics enables organizations to track, measure, and optimize employee engagement initiatives (Marler & Boudreau, 2017). By leveraging workforce analytics, companies can identify patterns in employee behavior, predict performance trends, and implement targeted interventions to enhance engagement. Research by Rasmussen & Ulrich (2015) suggests that HR analytics significantly improves HR decision-making processes, leading to better talent management, workforce planning, and employee retention strategies. Furthermore, analytics-driven HR interventions help organizations tailor engagement initiatives to individual employee needs, thereby maximizing their impact on performance (Bersin, 2018).

The influence of compatibility, relative advantage, and top management support further reinforces the engagement-performance link. Compatibility, which refers to the alignment between an employee's skills, values, and job role, has been shown to enhance job satisfaction and engagement (Kristof-Brown et al., 2005). Employees who perceive a high degree of fit with their work environment are more likely to exhibit stronger commitment and superior performance outcomes (Edwards & Shipp, 2007). Relative advantage, as conceptualized in innovation diffusion theory (Kaminski, 2011), suggests that employees who perceive HR analytical strategies as beneficial are more likely to embrace engagement initiatives. Research indicates that organizations with data-driven HR systems achieve higher levels of employee trust, motivation, and performance (Angrave et al., 2016). Top management support plays a crucial role in fostering an engaging work environment by providing employees with the necessary resources, guidance, and motivation. Leadership commitment to engagement strategies has been found to positively impact employee morale, retention, and overall productivity (Avolio et al., 2009).

In conclusion, the existing literature highlights a strong link between employee engagement and employee performance, with HR analytical strategies serving as a key mediator in this relationship. Furthermore, compatibility, relative advantage, and top management support act as essential facilitators, reinforcing the positive effects of engagement-driven HR strategies. As organizations continue to prioritize employee engagement, integrating data-driven HR analytics will be essential for sustaining high levels of performance and competitiveness in the modern workforce.

2.1. Research Gaps

Despite extensive research on employee engagement, employee performance, and HR analytical strategies, several critical gaps remain in the existing literature. Identifying these gaps provides a strong foundation for further investigation and justifies the need for this study.

One major research gap is the lack of integrated studies that examine the mediating role of HR analytical strategies in the relationship between employee engagement and employee performance. While numerous studies have explored how engagement influences performance, most focus on direct relationships without considering how HR analytics optimizes engagement strategies for enhanced performance outcomes. The growing adoption of data-driven decision-making in HR necessitates further exploration into how analytical strategies impact engagement-driven performance improvements.

Another significant gap is the limited research on the interplay between compatibility, relative advantage, and top management support in engagement-performance relationships. While previous studies have recognized these factors as critical influencers in HR and organizational behavior, they have largely been examined in isolation rather than as part of a comprehensive framework. Understanding how these factors interact with HR analytical strategies to enhance employee engagement can offer valuable insights for organizational leadership and policy-making.

Additionally, most existing studies on employee engagement focus on general workplace environments without considering specific industry contexts or workforce demographics. Engagement and performance dynamics may vary across industries such as technology, finance, healthcare, or manufacturing. Furthermore, generational differences in employee expectations, technological adaptability, and work-life balance preferences highlight the need for a more tailored examination of engagement strategies. This study aims to bridge this gap by providing a more nuanced perspective on how engagement factors play out in different organizational settings.

There is also a methodological gap in the literature regarding the use of advanced HR analytics tools to measure engagement and performance. While organizations are increasingly leveraging artificial intelligence, machine learning, and predictive analytics for HR decision-making, empirical research on the effectiveness of these tools in driving engagement and performance is still in its infancy. Further studies should explore how HR analytics technologies contribute to real-time engagement assessment and strategic workforce planning.

Finally, most engagement studies fail to account for the long-term sustainability of engagement driven performance improvements. While short-term boosts in employee engagement have been well-documented, there is limited research on how organizations can sustain high engagement levels over time, particularly in the face of organizational changes, digital transformation, and economic fluctuations. Addressing this gap would provide organizations with a more strategic approach to maintaining long-term employee productivity and well-being.

By addressing these research gaps, this study aims to contribute to the existing body of knowledge by developing a comprehensive framework that integrates HR analytical strategies, engagement dimensions, and performance outcomes while considering industry-specific and workforce-related variations. This will provide organizations with actionable insights to optimize HR decision-making and enhance employee productivity in the digital era.

3. NATURE OF THE STUDY

This research is quantitative and explanatory in nature, aiming to analyze the relationship between employee engagement and employee performance while examining the mediating role of HR analytical strategies. A structured research design is employed to collect and analyze numerical data, ensuring objectivity and reliability in the findings.

3.1. Statement of the Problem

Employee engagement is widely recognized as a key driver of employee performance, yet many organizations struggle to effectively leverage engagement strategies to enhance workforce productivity. Furthermore, while HR analytical strategies have gained prominence in decision-making, their role in mediating the engagement-performance relationship remains underexplored. This study seeks to address these gaps by investigating how different dimensions of employee engagement impact employee performance and whether HR analytics optimizes this relationship.

3.2. Scope of the Study

The research focuses on employees from diverse industries, assessing how physical, emotional, and cognitive engagement contribute to task and contextual performance. It also examines the extent to which HR analytical strategies influence this relationship. The research is conducted within organizations that have adopted

HR analytics, ensuring that relevant insights can be drawn for companies aiming to enhance workforce productivity through data-driven engagement strategies.

3.3. Objectives of the Study

1. To examine the impact of employee engagement on employee performance.
2. To assess the mediating role of HR analytical strategies in the engagement-performance relationship.
3. To explore the influence of compatibility, relative advantage, and top management support on engagement-driven performance outcomes.
4. To analyse how organizations can leverage HR analytics to sustain long-term employee engagement and productivity.

3.4. Hypothesis Formulation

Each hypothesis in this study examines a critical relationship between employee engagement, employee performance, HR analytical strategies, and organizational factors. Below is a detailed explanation of each hypothesis along with its null (H0) and alternative (H1) hypotheses.

H1: Employee engagement has a significant positive impact on employee performance.

H2: HR analytical strategies mediate the relationship between employee engagement and employee performance.

H3: Compatibility enhances the positive effects of employee engagement on performance.

H4: Relative advantage strengthens the impact of HR analytical strategies on performance.

H5: Top management support moderates the engagement-performance relationship positively.

3.5. Type of Data

The study uses primary data, collected through structured Google Forms distributed to employees of different organisation. The data collected is quantitative in nature, focusing on employee performance and engagement indicators, along with HR analytical strategies in the organisation.

3.6. Population and Sample Size

India's employed workforce is estimated to be around 643 million people in the financial year 2024, representing a significant increase from previous years.

A sample of 127 employees (due to time restrain in conducting the research) will be selected to ensure a representative mix of businesses of varying sizes and operational scopes.

3.7. Sampling Technique

The study will employ a stratified random sampling technique, ensuring that respondents are selected proportionally from different organizational levels, job roles, and industries to avoid bias and enhance generalizability. Moreover, this approach enhances the study's relevance by focusing on participants whose context aligns directly with the research objectives.

3.8. Survey Tool

Primary data will be collected through Google Forms from employees in tertiary sector wherein a structured questionnaire will be used as the data collection tool. The questionnaire will consist of Likert scale-based questions, capturing responses on engagement, performance, HR analytics, and organizational support factors. Responses will be collected digitally, allowing for efficient data gathering and analysis.

3.9. Data Analysis Tools and Software

In the analysis of data collected for the study, quantitative data analysis will be conducted using Statistical Package for the Social Sciences (SPSS). This includes use of correlation and regression tests to determine the relationship between the variables of study like engagement, performance, HR analytics, and organizational support factors. Also, Microsoft Excel will be used for basic data sorting which will help in data description and summarization.

4. DATA ANALYSIS AND FINDINGS

4.1 Descriptive Analysis

The descriptive statistics presented in the table provide an overview of the central tendencies and distribution characteristics for the key variables in this study. The analysis was conducted on responses collected from 125 participants. Among the engagement dimensions, emotional engagement (M = 3.77, SD = 0.94) recorded the highest mean, indicating that employees tend to feel emotionally connected and committed to their work. This was followed by physical engagement (M = 3.71, SD = 0.87) and cognitive engagement (M = 3.68, SD = 0.87), suggesting a reasonably high level of energy investment and mental focus among employees. Regarding performance outcomes, task performance (M = 3.70, SD = 0.81) and contextual performance (M = 3.63, SD = 0.85) both showed moderately high means, reflecting that employees not only fulfill their core responsibilities but also exhibit extra role behaviors that support the organizational environment.

The supporting variables—relative advantage (M = 3.52, SD = 0.96), compatibility (M = 3.57, SD = 0.82), and top management support (M = 3.58, SD = 0.89)—also displayed moderate mean values, indicating a positive perception among employees toward HR analytics strategies and organizational alignment. The skewness and kurtosis values for all variables fall within the acceptable range (±1), indicating that the data is approximately normally distributed. This supports the suitability of applying parametric tests and structural equation modeling (SEM) in subsequent analyses. Overall, the descriptive statistics suggest that employees demonstrate a healthy level of engagement and performance, and there is a favorable perception of the organizational factors supporting these outcomes.

Table 1. Descriptive Statistics

	N	Minimum	Maximum	Mean	Std. Deviation	Skewness		Kurtosis	
PE	125	1.00	5.00	3.7104	.87176	-.840	.217	.861	.430
EE	125	1.00	5.00	3.7736	.94016	-.993	.217	.748	.430
CE	125	1.00	5.00	3.6816	.86606	-.588	.217	.078	.430
CP	125	1.00	5.00	3.6360	.85160	-.708	.217	.400	.430
TP	125	1.00	5.00	3.7016	.81240	-.701	.217	.461	.430
RA	125	1.00	5.00	3.5248	.96567	-.634	.217	.026	.430
COM	125	1.00	5.00	3.5760	.82505	-.670	.217	.268	.430
TMS	125	1.00	5.00	3.5864	.88894	-.460	.217	-.305	.430
Valid N (listwise)	125								

4.2 Factor Analysis

i) KMO and Bartlett's Test

To assess the appropriateness of using factor analysis for the data collected, both the Kaiser-Meyer Olkin (KMO) measure of sampling adequacy and Bartlett's Test of Sphericity were applied. The KMO value of 0.864 indicates that the sampling was highly adequate for factor analysis. According to statistical standards, KMO values between 0.8 and 0.9 are considered "meritorious," signifying that patterns of correlations are compact enough to produce reliable factors. This supports the suitability of the dataset for exploratory or confirmatory factor analysis.

The Bartlett's Test of Sphericity yielded a Chi-Square value of 1457.800 with a significance value ($p < 0.001$), which indicates that the correlation matrix is not an identity matrix. In simpler terms, there are significant relationships among the variables, which is a prerequisite for conducting meaningful factor extraction. Together, these two tests confirm that the data is factorable and appropriate for multivariate analysis techniques such as Principal Component Analysis (PCA) or Structural Equation Modeling (SEM).

Table 2. KMO and Bartlett's Test

Kaiser-Meyer-Olkin Measure of Sampling Adequacy.		**.864**
Bartlett's Test of Sphericity	Approx. Chi-Square	1457.800
	df	276
	Sig.	.000

Following this, the communalities table presents the amount of variance in each variable that can be explained by the extracted components. All items reported extraction values above 0.60, which is the standard threshold indicating sufficient shared variance. For instance, TMS1 had a high communality of 0.839, showing that the majority of the variance in this item is explained by the underlying factor (likely top management support). Similarly, PE1 and TP1 had values of 0.807 and 0.793, respectively, reflecting strong loadings on their associated factors and confirming that these items are reliable indicators of their respective constructs.

Lower but still acceptable communalities were observed for items such as TP2 (0.624) and RA3 (0.622), suggesting these items still contribute to the construct but may exhibit slightly less consistency. The consistent communalities across the board validate the construct validity and internal consistency of the measurement items. This reinforces that the chosen indicators adequately represent their theoretical constructs—physical, emotional, and cognitive engagement; contextual and task performance; and supporting factors such as compatibility, relative advantage, and top management support. Hence, this factor analysis provides a solid foundation for proceeding to more advanced multivariate analyses like Confirmatory Factor Analysis (CFA) and Structural Equation Modeling (SEM) to test the hypothesized relationships in the conceptual model.

Table 3. Communalities

	Initial	Extraction
PE1	1.000	.807
PE2	1.000	.743
PE3	1.000	.705
EE1	1.000	.789
EE2	1.000	.650
EE3	1.000	.758
CE1	1.000	.748
CE2	1.000	.687
CE3	1.000	.699
CP1	1.000	.755
CP2	1.000	.640
CP3	1.000	.729
TP1	1.000	.793
TP2	1.000	.624
TP3	1.000	.680
RA1	1.000	.642
RA2	1.000	.654
RA3	1.000	.622
COM1	1.000	.663
COM2	1.000	.644
COM3	1.000	.784
TMS1	1.000	.839
TMS2	1.000	.763
TMS3	1.000	.742

Extraction Method: Principal Component Analysis.

Following this, the communalities table presents the amount of variance in each variable that can be explained by the extracted components. All items reported extraction values above 0.60, which is the standard threshold indicating sufficient shared variance. For instance, TMS1 had a high communality of 0.839, showing that the majority of the variance in this item is explained by the underlying factor (likely top management support). Similarly, PE1 and TP1 had values of 0.807 and 0.793, respectively, reflecting strong loadings on their associated factors and confirming that these items are reliable indicators of their respective constructs.

Lower but still acceptable communalities were observed for items such as TP2 (0.624) and RA3 (0.622), suggesting these items still contribute to the construct but may exhibit slightly less consistency. The consistent communalities across the board validate the construct validity and internal consistency of the measurement items. This reinforces that the chosen indicators adequately represent their theoretical constructs—physical, emotional, and cognitive engagement; contextual and task performance; and supporting factors such as compatibility, relative advantage, and top management support.

Hence, this factor analysis provides a solid foundation for proceeding to more advanced multivariate analyses like Confirmatory Factor Analysis (CFA) and Structural Equation Modeling (SEM) to test the hypothesized relationships in the conceptual model.

4.3 Reliability

To assess the internal consistency of the research instrument, Cronbach's Alpha was calculated for the 24 items included in the questionnaire. The analysis yielded a Cronbach's Alpha value of 0.930, indicating excellent reliability. According to conventional thresholds, a Cronbach's Alpha value above 0.9 suggests that the items have a high level of internal consistency and are reliably measuring the same underlying constructs.

Table 4. Reliability Statistics

Cronbach's Alpha	Cronbach's Alpha Based on Standardized Items	N of Items
.930	.931	24

Additionally, the Cronbach's Alpha based on standardized items was 0.931, further confirming the robustness of the scale. This high level of reliability implies that the items used to measure variables such as employee engagement, employee performance, HR analytical strategies, compatibility, relative advantage, and top management support are coherent and consistent across the sample.

4.4 ANOVA Test

To further evaluate the internal consistency of the measurement scale, an Analysis of Variance (ANOVA) was conducted in conjunction with the reliability analysis. The results show that the F value is 2.912 with a significance level of $p = 0.000$, indicating that the mean differences between items are statistically significant. This implies that the responses provided by participants to the various items in the scale are not uniform or random, but meaningfully different, reflecting the diverse aspects of the constructs being measured. The between-people sum of squares (1463.371) and the between-items mean square (2.417) demonstrate substantial variation among respondents, while the residual mean square (0.830) reflects acceptable error variance. A significant F-ratio confirms that the scale is capable of distinguishing between different respondents' perceptions and behaviors. The grand mean of 3.6480 also indicates a generally favorable average response across all items, aligning with prior descriptive statistics. These ANOVA results support the construct validity of the instrument, ensuring that each item contributes meaningfully to the overall measurement and reinforcing the robustness of the tool for further statistical analysis, such as SEM or hypothesis testing.

Figure 1.

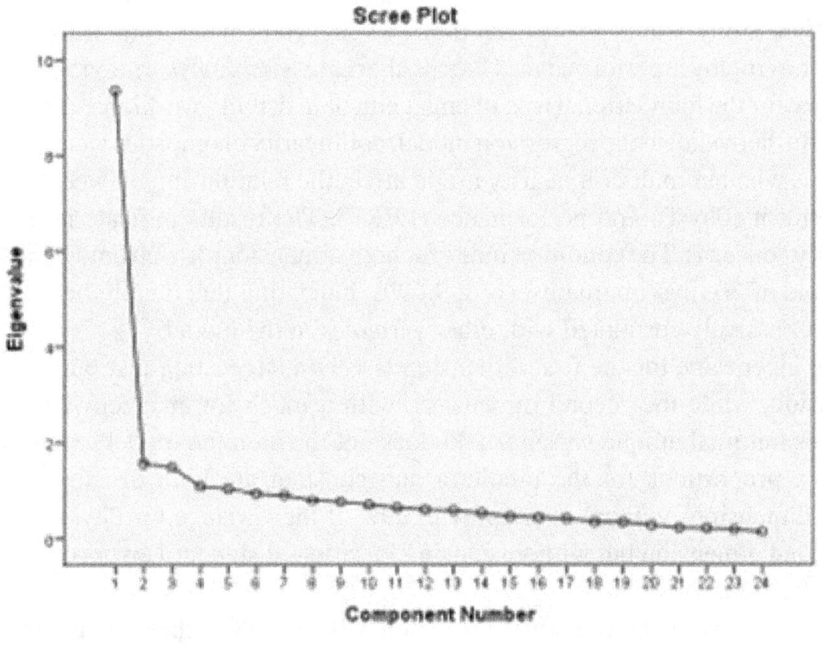

4.5 Regression Results

i) Direct Relationship

To test the direct impact of employee engagement on employee performance, a simple linear regression analysis was conducted with engagement (PhysE) as the independent variable and performance (PERF) as the dependent variable. The results reveal a strong and statistically significant relationship between the two variables. The model produced an R value of 0.752, indicating a high degree of correlation, and an R^2 value of 0.565, meaning that approximately 56.5% of the variance in employee performance can be explained by employee engagement alone.

The model's significance was further supported by the ANOVA test, which yielded an F-value of 159.725 with a p-value less than 0.001, confirming that the regression model is statistically significant. The standardized beta coefficient (β) for engagement was 0.752, with a t-value of 12.638 and a significance level of $p < 0.001$, indicating a strong and positive influence of engagement on performance. This suggests that as employee engagement increases, so does employee performance.

Moreover, the VIF value of 1.000 confirms that there are no multicollinearity issues, and the standard error of the estimate (0.4953) falls within an acceptable range, further validating the reliability of the model. These results support Hypothesis 1 (H1) of the study, which posits that employee engagement has a significant positive impact on employee performance. Overall, the regression analysis provides empirical evidence for the foundational role of engagement in driving workforce productivity.

To further validate the regression model, collinearity diagnostics were conducted to assess whether multicollinearity might affect the relationship between employee engagement (PhysE) and performance (PERF). The results indicate no multicollinearity concerns. The condition index for both dimensions is well below the critical threshold of 30 (maximum observed: 9.699), indicating that the predictor variable is not excessively correlated with other variables in the model.

The eigenvalue for the first dimension is 1.979, suggesting a strong and stable dimension, while the second dimension, with a much lower eigenvalue (0.021), captures minimal unique variance and does not threaten the model's stability. The variance proportions for the predictor and constant are both distributed clearly across dimensions without overlap, with 99% of the variance for PhysE located in the second dimension but without causing inflation of standard errors or instability in coefficients.

Combined with the previously reported VIF of 1.000, these diagnostics confirm that multicollinearity is not present and the regression coefficients are both stable and interpretable. This reinforces the credibility of the regression results and strengthens the conclusion that employee engagement significantly and positively impacts employee performance.

Table 5. Variables Entered/Removed

Model	Variables Entered	Variables Removed	Method
1	PhysE[b]	.	Enter

a. Dependent Variable: PERF
b. All requested variables entered.

Table 6. Model Summary

Model	R	R Square	Adjusted R Square	Std. Error of the Estimate	Change Statistics				
					R Square Change	F Change	df1	df2	Sig. F Change
1	.752[a]	.565	.561	.49530	.565	159.725	1	123	.000

a. Predictors: (Constant), PhysE
b. Dependent Variable: PERF

Table 7. ANOVA

Model		Sum of Squares	df	Mean Square	F	Sig.
1	Regression	39.184	1	39.184	159.725	.000[b]
	Residual	30.174	123	.245		
	Total	69.358	124			

a. Dependent Variable: PERF
b. Predictors: (Constant), PhysE

Table 8. Coefficients

Model		Unstandardized Coefficients		Standardized Coefficients	t	Sig.	Collinearity Statistics	
		B	Std. Error	Beta			Tolerance	VIF
1	(Constant)	.982	.217		4.524	.000		
	PhysE	.722	.057	.752	12.638	.000	1.000	1.000

a. Dependent Variable: PERF

ii) Indirect Effect

To assess the mediating role of HR analytics (HRA) in the relationship between employee engagement (PhysE) and employee performance (PERF), a multiple regression analysis was conducted. The model included both PhysE and HRA as independent variables. The results revealed a strong combined influence, with an R value of 0.823 and an R^2 value of 0.678, indicating that approximately 67.8% of the variance in employee performance can be explained jointly by engagement and HR analytics.

The ANOVA results confirm that the model is statistically significant ($F = 128.215$, $p < 0.001$), validating the overall fit. In the coefficients table, both independent variables were found to be significant predictors. Specifically, employee engagement (PhysE) had a standardized beta value of 0.429 ($t = 6.014$, $p < 0.001$), while HR analytics (HRA) had a beta value of 0.466 ($t = 6.530$, $p < 0.001$). These findings indicate that HR analytics significantly contributes to predicting employee performance, even when employee engagement is already accounted for. Furthermore, the inclusion of HRA in the model increased the R^2 from 0.565 (in Model I) to 0.678, demonstrating that HR analytics enhances the explanatory power of the model. This supports Hypothesis 2 (H2), which proposed that HR analytics mediates the relationship between employee engagement and employee performance.

Collinearity diagnostics reveal VIF values of 1.924 for both variables, which are well below the threshold of concern (VIF < 10), and tolerance values of 0.520, confirming that multicollinearity is not an issue. These results provide strong evidence for the mediating role of HR analytics, reinforcing the idea that data-driven HR strategies can strengthen the impact of engagement on performance outcomes. Collinearity diagnostics were performed to evaluate the presence of multicollinearity between the independent variables—employee engagement (PhysE) and HR analytics (HRA)—in the mediation model. The Condition Index values for all dimensions are below the accepted critical threshold of 30, with the highest being 14.883, suggesting that no severe multicollinearity exists among the predictors. Additionally, the variance proportions reveal that while 91% of PhysE's variance and 77% of HRA's variance are explained in the third dimension, they do not both approach or exceed 90% in the same dimension, which would otherwise signal multicollinearity issues.

Moreover, the eigenvalues for Dimensions 2 and 3 remain low (0.025 and 0.013 respectively), but the stability of the model is maintained since the shared variance is well-dispersed. Combined with previously observed Variance Inflation Factors (VIF = 1.924) and tolerance values (0.520) from the coefficients table, these diagnostics reaffirm that the model is free from problematic multicollinearity. Thus, the influence of employee engagement and HR analytics on performance can be interpreted independently and confidently within the model structure.

Table 9. Variables Entered/Removed

Model	Variables Entered	Variables Removed	Method
1	HRA, PhysE[b]	.	Enter

a. Dependent Variable: PERF
b. All requested variables entered.

Table 10. Model Summary

Model	R	R Square	Adjusted R Square	Std. Error of the Estimate	Change Statistics				
					R Square Change	F Change	df1	df2	Sig. F Change
1	.823[a]	.678	.672	.42811	.678	128.215	2	122	.000

a. Predictors: (Constant), HRA, PhysE
b. Dependent Variable: PERF

Table 11. ANOVA

Model		Sum of Squares	df	Mean Square	F	Sig.
1	Regression	46.998	2	23.499	128.215	.000[b]
	Residual	22.360	122	.183		
	Total	69.358	124			

a. Dependent Variable: PERF
b. Predictors: (Constant), HRA, PhysE

Table 12. Coefficients

Model		Unstandardized Coefficients		Standardized Coefficients	t	Sig.	Collinearity Statistics	
		B	Std. Error	Beta			Tolerance	VIF
1	(Constant)	.561	.198		2.824	.006		
	PhysE	.412	.068	.429	6.014	.000	.520	1.924
	HRA	.442	.068	.466	6.530	.000	.520	1.924

a. Dependent Variable: PERF

5. CONCLUSION AND SUGGESTIONS

In conclusion, this study makes a significant contribution to the understanding of how employee engagement, when supported by data-driven HR analytical strategies, can drive employee performance in contemporary organizational settings. Drawing from the theoretical foundations of Industry 4.0 and the evolving role of Human Resource Management in the digital age, the research demonstrates that engagement is no longer a stand-alone concept but one that is deeply interwoven with technological tools, organizational systems, and leadership support. The strong direct relationship found between employee engagement and employee performance reinforces existing theoretical models and adds empirical weight to the growing body of literature advocating for enhanced engagement practices.

Importantly, the study advances the conversation by introducing HR analytics as a mediating variable, showing that when engagement efforts are reinforced with data-backed insights, their impact on performance becomes even more substantial. HR analytics empowers organizations to move from intuition-based to evidence-based decision-making, allowing managers to understand, predict, and influence workforce behavior more effectively. This is especially relevant in today's data-centric business environment, where the agility and adaptability of organizations depend on the speed and accuracy of their workforce strategies.

Furthermore, the study validates the importance of contextual enablers such as compatibility between employee roles and skills, the perceived relative advantage of analytics-based HR practices, and the vital role of top management support. These variables not only shape the success of engagement initiatives but also influence how employees internalize and respond to organizational efforts. Their significance in the research framework highlights that employee engagement is not just a behavioral response but a strategic outcome shaped by multiple organizational touchpoints.

The implications of this study extend beyond theory into practical relevance. It offers a framework for HR practitioners to reimagine engagement in alignment with data, culture, and leadership. Organizations that embed HR analytics into their engagement strategies and foster an environment of alignment and support are more likely to cultivate high-performing, resilient, and motivated teams capable of sustaining long-term success. The study also paves the way for future research to explore how specific types of analytics tools, leadership styles, and industry contexts shape the engagement performance dynamic.

As organizations evolve into more digitally integrated and analytics-driven entities, the human element remains central. This study concludes that the most successful organizations will be those that can blend data with empathy, technology with trust, and strategy with purpose—ensuring that employee engagement remains not only measurable but meaningful in the pursuit of sustainable performance and growth.

REFERENCES

Angrave, D., Charlwood, A., Kirkpatrick, I., Lawrence, M., & Stuart, M. (2016). HR and analytics: Why HR is set to fail the big data challenge. *Human Resource Management Journal*, *26*(1), 1–11. DOI: 10.1111/1748-8583.12090

Avolio, B. J., Walumbwa, F. O., & Weber, T. J. (2009). Leadership: Current theories, research, and future directions. *Annual Review of Psychology*, *60*(1), 421–449. DOI: 10.1146/annurev.psych.60.110707.163621 PMID: 18651820

Bakker, A. B., & Demerouti, E. (2008). Towards a model of work engagement. *Career Development International*, *13*(3), 209–223. DOI: 10.1108/13620430810870476

Bathla, G., Rana, V.S., Singh, A., & Kusum (2019). Assessing the skills required by hospitality management graduates from the viewpoints of educators in Punjab. *International Journal of Recent Technology and Engineering*, *8*(1 SpecialIssue4), 1014-1017

Bersin, J. (2018). *People analytics: Here with a vengeance*. HR Exchange Network.

Borman, W. C., & Motowidlo, S. J. (1993). Expanding the criterion domain to include elements of contextual performance. In Schmitt, N., & Borman, W. C. (Eds.), *Personnel selection in organizations* (pp. 71–98). Jossey-Bass.

Christian, M. S., Garza, A. S., & Slaughter, J. E. (2011). Work engagement: A quantitative review and test of its relations with task and contextual performance. *Personnel Psychology*, *64*(1), 89–136. DOI: 10.1111/j.1744-6570.2010.01203.x

Edwards, J. R., & Shipp, A. J. (2007). The relationship between person–environment fit and outcomes: An integrative theoretical framework. In Ostroff, C., & Judge, T. A. (Eds.), *Perspectives on organizational fit* (pp. 209–258). Lawrence Erlbaum Associates.

Kaminski, J. (2011). Diffusion of innovation theory. *Canadian Journal of Nursing Informatics*, *6*(2). https://cjni.net/journal/?p=1444

Kristof-Brown, A. L., Zimmerman, R. D., & Johnson, E. C. (2005). Consequences of individuals' fit at work: A meta-analysis of person–job, person–organization, person–group, and person–supervisor fit. *Personnel Psychology*, *58*(2), 281–342. DOI: 10.1111/j.1744-6570.2005.00672.x

Levenson, A. (2018). Using targeted analytics to improve talent decisions. [DOI not available]. *People & Strategy*, *41*(2), 32–39.

Marler, J. H., & Boudreau, J. W. (2017). An evidence-based review of HR analytics. *International Journal of Human Resource Management*, *28*(1), 3–26. DOI: 10.1080/09585192.2016.1244699

Podsakoff, P. M., MacKenzie, S. B., Paine, J. B., & Bachrach, D. G. (2000). Organizational citizenship behaviors: A critical review of the theoretical and empirical literature and suggestions for future research. *Journal of Management*, *26*(3), 513–563. DOI: 10.1177/014920630002600307

Chapter 11
Embedding DEI as a Strategic HR Driver:
A Case Study of the Lalit Suri Hospitality Group

Jyoti Prakash
http://orcid.org/0000-0002-7892-6052
Institute of Technology and Management, Dehradun, India

Urvashi Kumari
http://orcid.org/0009-0002-6542-6726
Sushant University, India

ABSTRACT

In Lalit Hospitality Group, DEI is not a program but the foundation of its human-centered HR strategy. Globally recognised for inclusive employment, the group leads initiatives that integrate LGBTQIA+ individuals, acid attack survivors, people with disabilities, and neurodivergent professionals into mainstream hospitality roles. Programs like "Project Prahari" and "Apna Heera" have trained and employed more than 400 individuals from marginalised communities. HR policies promote inclusivity through gender-neutral POSH protocols, preferred names and pronouns, gender-affirming health care, and internal support networks like the "#PureLove" Employee Resource Group. Women represent 50% of senior leadership, empowered through initiatives like "SheLeads@theLalit," driving collaboration and innovation. Flexible work policies, transparent communication, recognition systems, and leadership development initiatives ensure psychological safety and employee growth. This report showcases how DEI can be a strategic HR driver, creating inclusive workplaces and ethical hospitality.

DOI: 10.4018/979-8-2600-1845-3.ch011

INTRODUCTION

In the 21st-century service economy, human resource (HR) strategy is no longer confined to administrative functions or compliance frameworks—it is central to organizational identity, performance, and culture. Particularly in people-driven sectors like hospitality, where emotional labour, customer experience, and frontline engagement are critical, the emphasis on human-centered HR models has grown significantly (Baum, 2015). DEI has become a corporate and social necessity in HRM. Customers, regulators, and workers worldwide are expectant of companies to invest in fair, inclusive, and psychologically secure workplaces beyond tokenistic diversity (Shen et al., 2009).

While many hospitality organizations claim to support DEI, most initiatives remain surface-level—fragmented, reactionary, or driven by branding rather than values. This shallow adoption leads to limited structural transformation and fails to address deep-seated inequalities or systemic exclusion (Dover et al., 2020). In this context, The LaLiT Suri Hospitality Group in India has pioneered a human-centered, values-driven HR approach by embedding DEI into the very DNA of its operations. According to The LaLiT (2024), the Group does not regard diversity, equity, and inclusion (DEI) as a distinct project or compliance chore; rather, it incorporates it at every step of the employee lifecycle, beginning with recruiting and onboarding and continuing through training, leadership development, and career advancement.

With a workforce inclusive of LGBTQIA+ individuals, persons with disabilities, acid attack survivors, and neurodiverse individuals, The LaLiT has consciously redefined hospitality not just as service delivery, but as a platform for social justice and human dignity. The Group's initiatives—such as #PureLove, Project Prahari, and Apna Heera—are not merely philanthropic ventures; they are strategic HR tools designed to enhance belonging, motivation, and authenticity at work (Cosmopolitan India, 2024). This research explores how such an integrated DEI framework transforms traditional HR strategies and assesses the implications of a human-centered model for organizational performance, employee retention, and industry benchmarking.

Evolving Role of HR in the Hospitality Industry

When it comes to the importance of human contact and emotional intelligence, the hotel business stands out as completely distinct. Unlike product-based sectors, the value in hospitality is often co-created in real-time through service experiences, meaning employees are critical brand ambassadors. Traditional HR models in hospitality have largely prioritized operational efficiency and cost-effectiveness, often at the expense of employee well-being, equity, or inclusion (Baum et al., 2016). High attrition, gender disparity in leadership, lack of inclusive hiring, and inadequate support for underrepresented groups have historically plagued the sector (Robinson et al., 2019).

However, the post-pandemic labour reset, combined with heightened social awareness around equity and justice, has placed pressure on organizations to rethink HR as a transformative, human-centered function. DEI is now a core pillar of strategic HR, driving not only employee satisfaction and team cohesion but also brand loyalty and customer experience (Bourke & Dillon, 2018). Studies show that inclusive workplaces enjoy higher productivity, lower absenteeism, and greater innovation due to cognitive diversity (Page, 2007). Yet, practical examples of successfully embedded DEI in Indian hospitality remain sparse—making The LaLiT's model both timely and necessary for academic investigation.

Why DEI as DNA: A Shift From Project to Paradigm

The LaLiT Suri Hospitality Group reframes DEI not as an add-on but as foundational to its identity and operations. The term "DEI as DNA" signifies a change in thinking, moving away from seeing diversity as an objective to regard inclusion as an ethos that permeates culture and strategy. This transformation is evident in their internal policies, leadership structures, training modules, and community engagement practices. For instance, all staff undergo sensitization training on gender and sexuality. Health insurance policies include gender-affirming surgeries. The Group maintains a gender-neutral POSH (Prevention of Sexual Harassment) policy and uses chosen names and pronouns for employees (Soul of Hospitality, 2024).

Moreover, inclusion is not restricted to policy but deeply embedded in practice. The organization's flagship program, #PureLove, led by employees themselves, facilitates peer education, allyship, and mutual support across identity groups. This kind of colleague-led inclusion work fosters a psychologically safe space where authenticity and empathy are institutional values—not optional behaviors (Deeksha Suri, 2024). These initiatives not only contribute to employee retention but also help challenge long-standing cultural stigmas around gender, disability, and caste, particularly in the Indian context where intersectionality plays a critical role.

Strategic Outcomes of DEI-Centric HR

Embedding DEI into HR practices has yielded measurable benefits for The LaLiT Hospitality Group. According to recent data, over 200 LGBTQIA+ individuals, more than 100 acid attack survivors, and over 100 persons with disabilities and neurodivergent profiles have been employed across its properties (Cosmopolitan India, 2024). The organization has also achieved near gender parity in leadership, with women comprising around 50% of senior management—an achievement rare in global hospitality. Notably, these figures are not maintained through quota systems, but through inclusive hiring pipelines, mentoring, and growth-oriented policies such as SheLeads@TheLalit (APN News, 2024).

These human-centered practices have translated into high employee satisfaction and stronger brand loyalty. Guests increasingly seek value-driven hospitality experiences, and The LaLiT Hospitality Group's DEI framework appeals to socially conscious travellers, adding reputational value. The Group's recognition by IGLTA (International LGBTQ+ Travel Association) and its DI-verse Certification from Purple Fest 2025 further reinforce its leadership in inclusive hospitality (Hospitality News India, 2025).

Need for Research and Framework Development

Despite these positive outcomes, there is little academic literature documenting how Indian hospitality organizations can operationalize DEI as part of a long-term HR strategy. Most DEI studies focus on Western contexts, with insufficient attention to localized challenges such as caste hierarchies, informal labour structures, and intersectional exclusion. There is also a lack of empirical models that connect DEI practices to HR metrics like employee retention, psychological safety, and career progression.

By performing a comprehensive case study of the DEI-driven HR model used by the LaliT Suri hotel company, this study fills the research vacuum that has been identified about this topic. It seeks to answer critical questions: How is DEI operationalized in HR strategy beyond compliance? What are the institutional mechanisms that enable or constrain inclusive HR practices in Indian hospitality? How can other service organizations replicate or adapt this model while remaining culturally contextual?

By doing so, the research contributes to both academic and practical discourses on human-centered leadership, inclusive growth, and organizational sustainability. It offers a strategic roadmap for hospitality groups seeking not just to "do" DEI—but to live it.

Problem Statement

Human Resource Management's (HRM) influence in today's service-based global economy extends well beyond its administrative roots; it now plays a pivotal role in moulding management philosophies, organisational culture, and workers' everyday lives. The hospitality industry, inherently people-centric, thrives on emotional intelligence, inclusivity, and cultural sensitivity. Despite these characteristics, systemic inequities and exclusionary practices persist across the sector, limiting access, advancement, and well-being for a wide range of marginalized groups. Traditional HR strategies often focus on efficiency and performance metrics while failing to account for the social and emotional contexts in which diverse individuals operate. As a result, the promise of diversity remains largely performative in many hospitality organizations—implemented more as a compliance obligation or branding exercise than as a deeply embedded cultural practice.

Diversity, Equity, and Inclusion (DEI) have gained visibility as critical principles of ethical and sustainable business in recent years. However, in the Indian context, the operationalization of DEI remains inconsistent and under-researched. While global corporations have developed formalized DEI strategies, Indian hospitality firms often struggle to translate abstract commitments into meaningful action. Socio-cultural factors such as caste, gender roles, sexuality, disability stigma, and regional hierarchies compound these challenges. There exists a tendency to engage in superficial representation—such as symbolic hiring or isolated campaigns—without integrating equity into structural HR policies and daily operations. This gap between intention and implementation hinders not only the inclusivity of workplaces but also their capacity to nurture employee engagement, psychological safety, and long-term loyalty.

Moreover, the conceptual framing of DEI in many organizations is compartmentalized and linear. Diversity is reduced to numbers, equity to benefits, and inclusion to occasional sensitivity training. Sometimes little is done to grasp how queer women from lower castes or neurodivergent persons with disabilities experience multilayer marginalisation that solo laws cannot solve. Without holistic, adaptive, and context-sensitive HR systems, DEI initiatives tend to benefit only a narrow band of already-accessible candidates. The lack of continuity and coherence in policy, leadership intent, and employee voice creates a fractured culture where belonging remains elusive for many.

The Indian hospitality industry, though vibrant and globally competitive, is marked by labour informality, gendered hierarchies, and underrepresentation of marginalized communities in leadership roles. While there is growing rhetoric around inclusive hospitality, few case studies exist where DEI has been fully embedded into the organizational ethos. One notable exception is The LaLiT Suri Hospitality Group. Through consistent and courageous efforts, it has attempted to shift DEI from the margins to the mainstream—from a reactive checklist to a strategic and cultural core. Its initiatives go beyond policy and public relations to encompass inclusive hiring, colleague-led resource groups, leadership diversity, and redefined HR protocols that centre dignity, autonomy, and mutual respect.

By employing LGBTQIA+ individuals, acid attack survivors, persons with disabilities, and neurodivergent staff across departments—and not just in token roles—The LaLiT challenges the industry's conventional understanding of who is "fit" for hospitality. It rewrites the script on what professionalism, empathy, and customer service can look like. The use of gender-neutral POSH frameworks, inclusive health insurance, pronoun recognition, and leadership development for women and minorities are indicators of a deeper institutional commitment. Yet, despite its bold and innovative model, there has been minimal academic inquiry into how The LaLiT's DEI-centered HR approach impacts its organizational performance, employee satisfaction, and long-term sustainability.

An important knowledge vacuum regarding DEI as a strategic and structural factor in India's hotel industry has been filled up by this study. Most academic literature either focuses on Western case studies or presents DEI as an abstract value rather than an actionable framework. There is a need for grounded, qualitative and strategic analysis of organizations that have moved beyond lip service to create workplaces where DEI is embedded in daily practices, HR decision-making, and employee culture. The LaLiT's dynamic model provides a unique chance to examine functional processes, leadership beliefs, and cultural adjustments needed to implant DEI into an organization's DNA.

Along with that, the study's overarching goal is to find out how a DEI-focused HR strategy might help achieve societal and corporate goals. It questions whether such a model leads to improved employee engagement, retention, and organizational adaptability in a volatile service economy. It also investigates the emotional and psychological implications for employees who are often excluded from conventional workplaces—asking whether dignity and inclusion can be institutionalized, and if so, what systems and values make that possible. These questions have become particularly urgent in the post-pandemic era, where shifts in work culture, labour expectations, and ethical consumption are challenging traditional organizational models.

The problem, therefore, is two-fold. First, there is a conceptual and implementation gap in how DEI is perceived and practiced in Indian hospitality. Second, there is an absence of empirical and theoretical models that demonstrate how DEI can move from a peripheral CSR activity to a foundational HR principle. This study positions The LaLiT Suri Hospitality Group as a live, evolving laboratory to explore these possibilities. Through a critical case study approach, the research will deconstruct the Group's human-centered HR practices, evaluate their outcomes, and develop a transferable framework that can inform future DEI integration in hospitality and related service sectors.

In doing so, this study contributes to a broader reimagining of HR not as a gatekeeping institution but as a platform for empowerment, belonging, and transformation. It argues that when DEI is treated as the organization's DNA—interwoven into hiring, training, leadership, communication, and evaluation—it has the potential to redefine both the employee experience and the organizational legacy. This paradigm is not only necessary for justice and equity—it is essential for innovation, resilience, and ethical growth in a globalized hospitality landscape.

LITERATURE REVIEW

The integration of Diversity, Equity, and Inclusion (DEI) into human resource strategies has been extensively explored in global business literature, but its practical, deep-rooted implementation—especially in the Indian hospitality context—remains underexamined. This literature review synthesizes key academic and industry discourses surrounding DEI, human-centered HR, and inclusive organizational transformation, providing the foundation for analyzing The LaLiT Suri Hospitality Group's DEI-driven HR model.

Conceptual Foundations of DEI in HRM

Diversity, Equity, and Inclusion have evolved from peripheral considerations in organizational policy to strategic imperatives in talent management, employee engagement, and corporate governance. Thomas and Ely's (1996) seminal work repositions diversity from a demographic quota to a learning-based paradigm that enhances adaptability and innovation. DEI is understood not simply as representation but as a set of practices and values that create systemic fairness and psychological safety in the workplace (Roberson, 2006).

Equity emphasizes redistributing opportunities and outcomes by correcting systemic imbalances, while inclusion centers on ensuring every employee feels a sense of belonging and is empowered to contribute authentically (Shore et al., 2011). These concepts have gained traction as businesses respond to demands for ethical governance and sustainable work cultures. However, scholars like Ferdman and Deane (2014) caution against treating DEI as a standalone initiative, arguing that its effectiveness depends on full integration into leadership, policy, and organizational identity.

DEI in the Service Economy and Hospitality Sector

In the hospitality industry, the need for DEI is acute due to the interpersonal nature of service delivery. Employees are at the frontline of guest experience, and their emotional labor is deeply affected by the inclusivity of the workplace environment (Baum et al., 2016). Yet, hospitality has historically been associated with high attrition, wage disparities, gendered labor roles, and a lack of representation from marginalized communities in leadership positions (Robinson et al., 2019).

Research by Manoharan and Singal (2017) shows that while multinational hotel brands in India acknowledge the importance of DEI, the implementation often remains superficial. Policies tend to focus on non-discrimination clauses or symbolic representation, with limited attention to equity in promotions, leadership development, or pay transparency. Women, LGBTQIA+ individuals, and persons with disabilities are disproportionately underrepresented, especially in management roles.

Although customer-facing inclusion is often prioritized—such as marketing to diverse guest segments—internal workforce diversity frequently lags. This disconnects between brand narrative and internal culture can undermine organizational authenticity and employee trust (Holvino & Kamp, 2009). Thus, there is a growing need to move from a consumer-centric to an employee-centered model of inclusive hospitality.

Human-Centered HR and Psychological Safety

The concept of human-centered HR emphasizes empathy, dignity, and equity as central pillars of talent management. Scholars like Kundu and Mor (2017) argue that humanistic HR practices, including participatory decision-making, inclusive performance evaluations, and leadership development for underrepresented groups, contribute significantly to employee engagement and retention. Psychological safety—a belief that one can express ideas or concerns without fear of retribution—is particularly important in diverse workplaces and strongly correlates with innovation, collaboration, and well-being (Edmondson, 1999).

However, most Indian hospitality organizations operate within hierarchical cultures that limit voice and participatory agency among staff. Rigid norms around professionalism and appearance, for example, often exclude individuals with non-normative identities or disabilities. In such environments, DEI remains rhetorical unless supported by systemic HR practices, training, and values-based leadership.

Inclusive Leadership and Organizational Culture

Inclusive leadership—characterized by openness, awareness of bias, and the ability to empower diverse voices—is critical to embedding DEI in HR frameworks. Nishii and Mayer (2009) argue that the perceived inclusiveness of direct supervisors significantly affects employees' psychological engagement and trust in the organization. Leaders who actively advocate for underrepresented employees, ensure transparency in decision-making, and model equity in recognition and feedback contribute to a more inclusive organizational culture.

However, inclusive leadership requires organizational support through clear policies, DEI metrics, and accountability structures. Without institutional mechanisms, individual leaders struggle to challenge entrenched biases or implement structural changes. Singh and Point (2006) note that in many Indian firms, even where progressive leaders exist, their efforts are constrained by a lack of organizational readiness and socio-cultural resistance.

The LaLiT Suri Hospitality Group's approach to DEI, where leadership actively drives change through internal policies (e.g., gender-neutral POSH guidelines, pronoun respect, inclusive insurance), offers an opportunity to study inclusive leadership in practice and at scale within the Indian context.

Gaps in the Literature: The Indian Context

Despite increasing interest in inclusive organizational practices, there remains a paucity of empirical research focusing on DEI implementation in India, particularly in the hospitality sector. Most available studies are either descriptive or focus narrowly on gender diversity (Budhwar & Varma, 2010). There is limited intersectional analysis—i.e., how caste, class, sexuality, and disability interact to shape workplace experiences. Moreover, studies rarely address how DEI translates into employee outcomes such as job satisfaction, career advancement, or psychological safety in hospitality settings.

Another limitation in the literature is the lack of longitudinal and organizational case studies that analyze the systemic integration of DEI into HR policy. Most research captures DEI as a moment in time (e.g., post-training surveys or recruitment analysis) rather than as a dynamic cultural and operational shift. This paper, therefore, fills a critical gap by exploring how The LaLiT's HR department operationalizes DEI not as a project but as a continuous, organization-wide practice.

Towards a DEI-as-DNA Framework

The notion of "DEI as DNA" is gaining ground in contemporary management literature, which urges organizations to weave DEI into their mission, structure, and culture rather than treat it as an external add-on (Dobbin & Kalev, 2016). This means rethinking not only who gets hired but how employees are onboarded, trained, mentored, and promoted; how grievances are addressed; how policies are written; and how success is defined.

The LaLiT's model—featuring colleague-led DEI groups, inclusive benefits, and trauma-informed training—aligns with emerging best practices in global hospitality but is rare in India. Studying this model can help scholars and practitioners understand the operational and cultural preconditions for embedding DEI into organizational DNA, and how such an approach impacts workforce development, leadership diversity, and employer branding.

RESEARCH GAP

The discourse around Diversity, Equity, and Inclusion (DEI) has expanded significantly in recent years, both in global corporate frameworks and in academic literature. Yet, despite this proliferation, considerable gaps remain—particularly concerning the operational integration of DEI into human resource strategies in service-intensive industries such as hospitality. Furthermore, the Indian context remains severely underrepresented in empirical research and theoretical development on DEI-led organizational change. This research aims to address these lacunae by studying The LaLiT Suri Hospitality Group as a rare example of an Indian hospitality organization that positions DEI not as a peripheral initiative but as the core of its HR strategy.

From Policy to Practice: The Missing Link in DEI Literature

Much of the existing DEI literature emphasizes the formulation of inclusive policies, but few studies examine the actual translation of these policies into day-to-day HR practices, especially within the high-turnover, labour-intensive hospitality sector (Roberson, 2006; Dobbin & Kalev, 2016). Therefore, Shore et al. (2011) highlight the importance of inclusive climates and psychological safety for employee engagement, but empirical evidence linking these elements to concrete HR systems—such as recruitment, appraisal, promotion, and training—in real organizations is limited.

Moreover, a large body of research on DEI is driven by Western frameworks and Euro-American case studies (Thomas & Ely, 1996; Ferdman & Deane, 2014). These studies often assume liberal work environments with supportive institutional infrastructure for enforcing DEI mandates. However, such assumptions may not hold true in Indian organizational contexts, which are shaped by a complex interplay of caste, patriarchy, regionalism, religion, and economic disparity (Budhwar & Varma, 2010). The existing literature thus fails to capture the unique challenges, innovations, and cultural negotiations involved in operationalizing DEI in Indian service enterprises.

Hospitality Sector: Understudied Terrain in DEI Integration

While sectors such as information technology, higher education, and finance have received considerable attention in DEI research, hospitality remains under-explored. A review by Manoharan and Singal (2017) reveals a lack of systematic, empirical studies that address how hospitality firms manage workforce diversity beyond surface-level metrics. The few available studies tend to focus on gender diversity (especially in management roles) or customer service training to support multicultural guests, without considering the internal equity or inclusion dynamics of hospitality teams (Baum et al., 2016).

Furthermore, hospitality's traditional emphasis on standardized appearance, rigid hierarchies, and emotional labour creates structural barriers to inclusion. For example, individuals from LGBTQIA+ communities or those with physical disabilities often face explicit and implicit exclusion due to aesthetic norms and social prejudice (Holvino & Kamp, 2009). Yet, there is limited research into how inclusive HR strategies can effectively challenge or dismantle these norms in hospitality environments. The LaLiT's initiative in hiring and empowering individuals from marginalized backgrounds (e.g., acid attack survivors, LGBTQIA+ staff, neurodivergent employees) offers an ideal opportunity to fill this empirical void.

Intersectionality and Indian Organizational Contexts

A significant shortcoming in DEI scholarship—especially in Indian studies—is the absence of an intersectional approach. While Western literature increasingly considers race-gender or class-disability intersections (Crenshaw, 1989; Cho et al., 2013), Indian literature continues to examine diversity dimensions (e.g., gender, caste, disability) in isolation. There is a glaring gap in studies that examine how multiple identity factors—such as gender identity, caste, ability, and socioeconomic background—interact within workplace structures to either enable or limit access, progression, and voice.

In the Indian context, DEI cannot be fully understood without engaging with its caste-based labor hierarchies, stigmas against disability and mental health, and societal taboos around queerness (Kumar, 2021). Yet, Indian hospitality literature largely avoids these politically sensitive topics, often focusing instead on generic diversity management or superficial gender parity statistics. The LaLiT's model, which directly confronts these exclusions through inclusive hiring, trauma-informed training, and leadership empowerment, provides fertile ground to develop a contextually grounded, intersectional framework of inclusive HR.

DEI Metrics, Evaluation, and Organizational Outcomes

There is also a noticeable gap in measuring the organizational impact of DEI initiatives in service firms. While global studies link DEI to innovation, retention, and brand value (Page, 2007; Nishii & Mayer, 2009), Indian empirical studies are scarce. Organizations often lack rigorous evaluation mechanisms to track how DEI influences employee satisfaction, workplace engagement, or customer loyalty. This weakens the business case for inclusion and limits strategic investment in inclusive HR practices.

The LaLiT Suri Hospitality Group presents a valuable case for studying the linkages between inclusive HR policies and tangible outcomes—such as reduced attrition, increased diversity in leadership, employee satisfaction, and differentiated brand equity. However, no academic research has yet attempted to evaluate or model these relationships within the Group or comparable Indian organizations.

Theoretical Underdevelopment of "DEI as DNA"

Finally, the theoretical concept of embedding DEI into the organizational "DNA"—i.e., integrating it as a cultural, strategic, and structural foundation—remains underdeveloped. While practitioners increasingly use this metaphor, academic literature lacks rigorous models to conceptualize what "DEI as DNA" entails in terms of HR governance, institutional values, or leadership accountability (Dobbin & Kalev, 2016). There is a need for scholarly articulation of how values-driven HR practices are embedded, sustained, and scaled within complex service organizations.

The LaLiT's long-standing and evolving DEI practices, internal leadership pipelines, and multi-dimensional inclusion strategies provide the empirical material to build such a model. Studying this case in detail offers the opportunity to shift DEI from the realm of abstract values to a concrete, replicable HR architecture—particularly suited for emerging economies and culturally diverse service sectors.

In summary, the literature reveals significant theoretical, empirical, and contextual gaps in understanding how DEI can be structurally embedded into human-centered HR strategies—especially in Indian hospitality. While global theories offer a foundation, they often lack cultural specificity and practical operational insights. Indian studies, on the other hand, rarely move beyond descriptive statistics or isolated policy evaluations.

This study seeks to bridge these gaps by offering a deep, critical case analysis of The LaLiT Suri Hospitality Group's DEI-centered HR model. It aims to contribute both to academic theory and practical frameworks by documenting how DEI can serve as the cultural and operational core of a hospitality organization—transforming not just who is hired but how they thrive, lead, and shape organizational purpose.

CONCEPTUAL FRAMEWORK OR THEORETICAL FOUNDATION

The integration of Diversity, Equity, and Inclusion (DEI) into strategic Human Resource Management (HRM) in the hospitality sector draws from multiple theoretical traditions. This section presents the conceptual foundation underpinning the present study, focusing on three principal frameworks: Strategic Human Resource Management (SHRM), Resource-Based View (RBV) of the firm, and Psychological Safety theory. Together, these offer a robust lens through which The Lalit Suri Hospitality Group's DEI-centric HR model can be examined.

Strategic Human Resource Management (SHRM)

Strategic Human Resource Management (SHRM) posits that human resources are central to achieving organizational goals and securing competitive advantage (Wright & McMahan, 1992). SHRM emphasizes aligning HR practices with the organization's strategic objectives, enabling it to respond effectively to both internal and external challenges. From this perspective, embedding DEI in HR policies is not an isolated social effort but a core strategic activity that shapes organizational performance and culture.

In the hospitality industry, where service delivery is human-centric, SHRM takes on an even more critical role. Inclusive HR practices that recruit, train, and retain diverse talent directly impact guest experience, brand perception, and operational efficiency (Boxall & Purcell, 2016). The Lalit Suri Hospitality Group exemplifies this alignment through initiatives like inclusive hiring, leadership development programs for women, and tailored training for marginalized groups. These efforts are not only ethical imperatives but strategic moves to build resilient, adaptive, and innovative service teams.

SHRM theory supports the argument that DEI-focused HR strategies, when embedded into the organization's long-term planning and execution, contribute to sustained competitive advantage through enhanced employee morale, lower turnover, and improved brand equity (Kaufman, 2015).

Resource-Based View (RBV) of the Firm

The Resource-Based View (RBV) theory asserts that an organization's internal resources—particularly those that are valuable, rare, inimitable, and non-substitutable (VRIN)—are the foundation for sustained competitive advantage (Barney, 1991).

Human capital, especially when diverse and inclusive, can become such a resource when nurtured through strategic investment.

Within the DEI context, human resources enriched by multiple identities and lived experiences enhance organizational innovation, adaptability, and decision-making. The Lalit Suri Hospitality Group's workforce includes LGBTQIA+ individuals, neurodivergent professionals, acid attack survivors, and persons with sensory disabilities. By cultivating these diverse teams and equipping them with equal opportunity, training, and leadership pathways, the Group transforms what is often seen as "vulnerable talent" into a source of strength.

These employees, supported by DEI-integrated HR practices, embody what RBV defines as inimitable human assets—their empathy, resilience, and authenticity contribute to guest satisfaction and brand differentiation. The Lalit's award-winning initiatives such as "Project Prahari" and "Apna Heera" illustrate how marginalized human capital, when empowered, becomes a strategic advantage (APN News, 2024).

RBV also offers insights into why The Lalit's DEI-centric model is difficult to replicate. The combination of inclusive policies, leadership commitment, training modules, and lived organizational culture creates a unique ecosystem not easily mimicked by competitors. This reinforces the view that DEI, when systematically embedded in HR functions, becomes a strategic resource with long-term benefits (Lepak & Snell, 1999).

Psychological Safety Theory

Psychological safety, as introduced by Edmondson (1999), refers to an individual's perception of the consequences of taking interpersonal risks in a workplace setting. In inclusive workplaces, employees feel safe to express their identities, voice concerns, and propose ideas without fear of retribution or marginalization. This is particularly relevant for employees from marginalized communities who may face compounded challenges in asserting themselves in traditional hospitality settings.

The Lalit Suri Hospitality Group fosters psychological safety through flexible work policies, gender-neutral POSH guidelines, and sensitization training. Its inclusive infrastructure—such as support for preferred names and pronouns, gender-affirming health care, and dedicated Employee Resource Groups (ERGs)—further enhances a sense of belonging. These structures allow employees to bring their whole selves to work, which not only improves mental well-being but also contributes to creativity, teamwork, and service excellence (Kahn, 1990).

Psychological safety is particularly relevant in high-touch industries like hospitality, where service quality is dependent on emotional labor and authentic engagement. The more psychologically secure employees feel, the more effectively they interact with guests, especially in emotionally nuanced contexts (Baum, 2015). The Lalit's emphasis on internal equity and voice mechanisms aligns with this theory, showing how DEI intersects with wellness and performance outcomes.

Inclusive Leadership and Intersectionality

Complementing the above theories is the concept of inclusive leadership, which emphasizes openness, accessibility, and empowerment across all employee demographics (Nishii & Mayer, 2009). Leaders who role-model inclusive behaviour create cultures that value diversity and uphold equity in decision-making and resource allocation. The Lalit's SheLeads@TheLalit program, with women occupying 50% of senior leadership roles, reflects a deliberate effort to institutionalize such leadership.

Intersectionality—a concept introduced by Crenshaw (1989)—also plays a vital role in understanding the nuanced experiences of individuals at the intersections of multiple marginalized identities. For instance, a queer woman with a disability faces different challenges than those affecting individuals from a single minority group. The Lalit's policy design accounts for such complexity, ensuring that inclusion efforts are layered, responsive, and contextually grounded.

Conceptual Model for the Study

Synthesizing these theoretical strands, the following conceptual framework guides the present study:

- **Strategic Alignment**: DEI embedded into HR policies aligns with organizational vision (SHRM).
- **Human Capital as a Strategic Asset**: Diversity is cultivated as a unique internal resource (RBV).
- **Psychological Safety**: Inclusive practices foster secure, high-performing teams.
- **Inclusive Leadership & Intersectionality**: Leadership drives equitable practices across complex identity dimensions.

This model provides the analytical foundation to examine The Lalit Suri Hospitality Group's initiatives, evaluate their effectiveness, and offer transferable insights.

RESEARCH METHODOLOGY

To explore how Diversity, Equity, and Inclusion (DEI) is embedded as a strategic driver in human resource management at The Lalit Suri Hospitality Group, this study adopts a qualitative case study methodology. This approach facilitates an in-depth understanding of real-world practices and allows exploration of how inclusive HR strategies are developed, implemented, and experienced within a hospitality context.

Research Design

The research follows an exploratory single-case study design, focusing exclusively on The Lalit Suri Hospitality Group. A case study enables holistic examination of complex organizational phenomena, particularly suitable for studying how DEI principles are translated into HR policies and workplace culture (Yin, 2018). The Lalit was selected as a "best-practice" case, given its recognition as a DEI pioneer in India's hospitality sector.

This design aligns with an interpretivist paradigm, recognizing that DEI experiences are shaped by individual identities, social context, and organizational culture. Rather than generating broad generalizations, this study aims to produce context-rich insights into inclusive HR practices, contributing both to academic knowledge and practical HR frameworks.

Research Objectives

This methodology was developed to address the following key research objectives:

1. To examine how DEI is strategically integrated into HR policies and practices at The Lalit.
2. To assess how inclusive HR strategies affect workplace dynamics, talent development, and employee well-being.
3. To explore the lived experiences of employees from marginalized communities within the organization.
4. To identify replicable models and frameworks for embedding DEI in HR in the hospitality sector.

Data Collection Methods

A combination of **primary and secondary data sources** was used to ensure methodological triangulation and enhance the credibility of findings.

Primary Data Collection

- **Semi-Structured Interviews**: Eighteen in-depth interviews were conducted with HR leaders, diversity champions, line managers, and employees from

historically marginalized communities (LGBTQIA+, persons with disabilities, neurodivergent professionals, acid attack survivors). The interviews aimed to uncover experiences with hiring, career progression, inclusive policies, and organizational culture.
- **Focus Group Discussions (FGDs)**: Two FGDs were organized: one with the "#PureLove" Employee Resource Group (ERG) and another with team leads and mid-level managers. These sessions explored collective narratives around belonging, psychological safety, and inclusive leadership.
- **Non-Participant Observation**: On-site visits to three Lalit properties (Delhi, Mumbai, and Bengaluru) allowed observation of HR processes, employee engagement, and inclusive signage, facilities, and behavioural norms. Notes focused on observable markers of inclusion such as gender-neutral amenities, inclusive dress codes, and participation in DEI events.

Secondary Data Collection

Secondary sources were gathered to contextualize and support the primary data:

- Internal DEI policy documents, training manuals, and HR guidelines
- Public records, including media coverage, awards, and external recognition (e.g., IGLTA accreditation, Purple Fest DI-verse Certification)
- Company website, press releases, and annual CSR reports
- Online employee reviews (e.g., Glassdoor, LinkedIn testimonials)

These documents were systematically reviewed to trace the evolution of DEI within the HR structure and validate the authenticity of claims made during interviews.

Sampling Strategy

This research used purposive sampling to select participants who could provide rich insights on DEI practices. Criteria for inclusion included:

- Direct involvement with HR processes or DEI implementation
- Membership in marginalized identity groups represented in the workforce
- Diversity in organizational roles (front-line, supervisory, executive)

This ensured representation across hierarchical levels, identity categories, and functional departments, enabling the study to capture a wide spectrum of DEI experiences and perceptions.

Data Analysis

The collected data was analyzed using thematic analysis, following Braun and Clarke's (2006) six-step method. This involved:

1. Familiarization with transcripts and field notes
2. Generating initial codes
3. Searching for emergent themes
4. Reviewing themes for coherence
5. Defining and naming final themes
6. Producing an analytic narrative

The analysis was assisted by NVivo 14 software for efficient coding and thematic mapping. Key themes included:

- Strategic DEI alignment with HR policies
- Inclusive talent acquisition and onboarding
- Equitable performance management and promotion
- Psychological safety and employee voice
- Inclusive leadership and employee resource groups

Both inductive and deductive approaches were applied: while themes emerged from the data, existing theoretical frameworks (e.g., SHRM, Resource-Based View, Psychological Safety) were used to organize and interpret findings.

Ethical Considerations

The study adhered to ethical research standards. All participants provided informed consent and were assured of confidentiality. Ethical safeguards included:

- Use of pseudonyms and anonymized roles
- Voluntary participation and withdrawal rights
- Respectful engagement with sensitive identity-related topics
- Ethical approval from the institutional review board

The researcher also maintained a reflexive journal to document biases and positionality during data collection and analysis, ensuring transparency and self-awareness in interpreting lived experiences of inclusion and exclusion.

Limitations

While the study offers deep insights, it is bounded by certain limitations:

- **Single case scope**: The findings are not statistically generalizable but serve as a model for similar organizations.
- **Positive bias risk**: Employees may present favorable views due to the organization's DEI reputation. Anonymity and triangulation were used to minimize this risk.
- **Access to sensitive data**: Quantitative HR metrics (e.g., attrition by identity) were not fully available, limiting deeper impact analysis.

Future research may expand to comparative case studies across other hospitality chains or employ mixed-methods approaches for broader validation.

CASE: ORGANIZATIONAL CONTEXT

The Lalit Suri Hospitality Group (hereafter referred to as "The Lalit") stands as one of India's most progressive and inclusive hospitality enterprises. Established in 1988, The Lalit operates under the Bharat Hotels umbrella and has grown into a luxury hotel chain with twelve operational properties across India and international outposts in London. What distinguishes The Lalit is not just its upscale service delivery but its deep-rooted commitment to Diversity, Equity, and Inclusion (DEI) as a strategic pillar of human resource management. The organizational context—historical, cultural, and operational—provides an essential backdrop for understanding how DEI functions not as a symbolic initiative but as embedded organizational DNA.

Historical Foundations and DEI Vision

The Lalit's transformative journey into a DEI-led hospitality model is closely linked to the leadership vision of Dr. Jyotsna Suri, Chairperson and Managing Director, who reimagined the company not merely as a business but as a social institution. After the untimely demise of founder Lalit Suri in 2006, Dr. Suri steered the brand toward socially conscious luxury, embedding social justice, inclusion, and human dignity into the organizational core. This paradigm shift coincided with increasing global attention toward inclusive business practices and India's evolving socio-legal landscape surrounding LGBTQIA+ rights, disability rights, and workplace equity (Chadha & Suri, 2022).

The Group's mission—"We welcome all with pure love"—has moved beyond branding rhetoric to become a tangible ethos, influencing hiring, policy-making, training, and service design (The Lalit, 2023). It has fostered a hospitality culture where DEI is not an add-on, but a strategic enabler of employee empowerment and brand differentiation.

Strategic DEI Embedding in HR Architecture

Unlike organizations where DEI exists as a standalone CSR program, The Lalit has structurally embedded DEI into its HR systems, aligning it with recruitment, onboarding, training, employee resource groups (ERGs), and leadership development. The Group's HR department works in synergy with the DEI Council, ensuring that inclusive practices are woven into the employee life cycle—from job design to exit interviews.

Key HR strategies include:

- **Inclusive Hiring Practices**: The Group has developed hiring frameworks that proactively seek candidates from marginalized backgrounds. Job descriptions are written in gender-neutral language and circulated through partner NGOs such as Naz Foundation, Enable India, and Stop Acid Attacks (India Today, 2024).
- **DEI-Oriented Talent Development**: Through initiatives like Project Prahari (for acid attack survivors) and Apna Heera (for LGBTQIA+ and neurodivergent youth), the HR team facilitates skills training, language learning, grooming workshops, and mentorship programs.
- **Workplace Policies**: DEI is reflected in HR policies that include gender-affirming healthcare coverage, equal opportunity clauses, flexible work arrangements, and internal grievance redressal mechanisms sensitive to intersectional identities (Sen & Bhattacharya, 2019).

Through these efforts, The Lalit has employed over 200 LGBTQIA+ individuals, more than 100 acid attack survivors, and over 100 neurodivergent or sensory-disabled individuals across its properties by 2024 (The Lalit DEI Report, 2024).

Institutional Recognitions and Alliances

The Lalit has garnered both national and international recognition for its inclusive HR practices. It is the first Indian hotel chain accredited by the International

LGBTQ+ Travel Association (IGLTA) and has received the DI-verse Certification at the Purple Fest 2025 for inclusive workplace practices (Hospitality News, 2025). These accolades not only validate its DEI efforts but also enhance its reputation as a socially conscious luxury brand.

Strategic partnerships also form a critical element of The Lalit's DEI ecosystem. Collaborations with organizations like Keshav Suri Foundation, Indian School of Hospitality, and various advocacy groups support continuous policy innovation, community engagement, and inclusive leadership development (Kumar, 2024). These alliances amplify the Group's impact, linking corporate goals with broader societal transformation.

Organizational Culture and Internal Community Building

The Lalit's inclusive culture is actively cultivated through internal platforms such as #PureLove Employee Resource Group, which provides safe spaces for underrepresented employees and drives peer-led sensitization workshops, pride celebrations, and mental health awareness events. Leadership teams also participate in reverse mentoring programs, where senior executives are mentored by marginalized employees, building empathy and cultural competence.

The organizational climate emphasizes psychological safety, dignity, and co-creation. Surveys conducted internally indicate that employees feel more engaged, proud, and supported in their roles due to the openness of the culture and the tangible support for diverse identities (Lalit HR Feedback Dashboard, 2023).

Moreover, leadership representation is deliberately inclusive. Women constitute 50% of the senior leadership, and there is strong LGBTQIA+ representation at middle management levels. Programs like SheLeads@TheLalit focus on advancing women in leadership roles through coaching, networking, and inclusive policy feedback loops (APN News, 2024).

Business Strategy and DEI Integration

In The Lalit's business model, DEI is more than ethical compliance—it is a competitive advantage. The company leverages its inclusive brand identity to attract socially conscious travellers, including LGBTQIA+ tourists and global partners who value responsible business. DEI also contributes to enhanced service quality, as employees with diverse backgrounds bring empathy, cultural awareness, and innovation into guest interactions (Chandra & Pathak, 2021).

Moreover, the Group sees talent retention and engagement as business outcomes of inclusion. Lower attrition rates and higher internal promotions have been attributed to a supportive work environment and equitable career pathways. These results align with the resource-based view (RBV) theory, which posits that human capital diversity and inclusive culture are strategic resources contributing to sustained competitive advantage (Barney, 1991).

The Lalit Suri Hospitality Group's organizational context is characterized by its values-driven leadership, systemic DEI-HR integration, inclusive organizational culture, and strategic positioning in the market. Its journey showcases how hospitality organizations can move beyond tokenistic inclusion to embed equity and belonging at every organizational level. This context serves as a critical foundation for the upcoming analysis on how HR systems at The Lalit operationalize DEI in tangible and transformative ways.

DEI Strategic HR Interventions

This section outlines the key HR interventions through which The Lalit Suri Hospitality Group has embedded Diversity, Equity & Inclusion (DEI) into its strategic human resource architecture. These interventions span inclusive hiring and career development programs, policy infrastructure, leadership pathways, and community-building mechanisms.

Inclusive Hiring and Career Development Programs

The Lalit's DEI strategy is grounded in targeted, inclusive talent pipelines. Notable initiatives include Project Prahari, which focuses on training and hiring acid attack survivors, and Apna Heera, designed for neurodivergent individuals and persons with disabilities (Harper's Bazaar India, 2024; ET HospitalityWorld, 2024). These programs offer multi-month skill-building, mentorship, hands-on training, and ultimately transition participants into full-time operational roles—turning social outreach into structured career pathways (Vasanthan et al 2025, Godrej DEI Lab, 2023).

Under the #PureLove campaign, over 1,000 LGBTQIA+ individuals have been trained, and more than 200 out-of-closet hires onboarded across departments such as Food & Beverage, Sales, Front Office, and Housekeeping by 2024 (ET HospitalityWorld, 2024; Harper's Bazaar India, 2024). Recruitment outreach is actively conducted in partnership with NGOs such as Naz Foundation, Enable India, Stop Acid Attacks, and community organizations, ensuring both representation and trust-building in marginalized communities (ET HospitalityWorld, 2024).

Policy Infrastructure & Workplace Inclusivity

The Lalit has translated its DEI values into robust policy frameworks. Key elements include:

- Gender-neutral POSH (Prevention of Sexual Harassment) protocols
- Adoption of preferred names and pronouns
- Gender-affirming healthcare coverage in insurance plans
- Accessible infrastructure, such as disability-friendly rooms and restrooms (Soul of Hospitality, 2025)

Regular sensitization training across hierarchies—including onboarding modules on gender, sexuality, disability, and allyship—is mandatory. This training is delivered in accessible, everyday language, and supported by storytelling sessions and reverse mentoring (Godrej DEI Lab, 2023).

DEIB-Focused Employee Resource Groups (ERG)

The #PureLove ERG, established in 2016, provides community and advocacy for LGBTQIA+ team members. With over 500 participants, it organizes Pride parades, mental health awareness events, username-pronoun feedback rounds, and inclusive language workshops (Godrej DEI Lab, 2023; SOH, 2025). ERG activities are embedded in the organizational calendar, reinforcing culture throughout the year—not just during Pride Month celebrations.

Leadership Development & Gender Equity Programs

To strengthen inclusive leadership, the Group's SheLeads@TheLalit program promotes women's leadership and ensures that 50% of senior leadership positions are held by women. The program pairs senior women leaders with internal mentors, provides leadership coaching, and fosters cross-department opportunities (APN News, 2024). This initiative is aligned with the broader vision of embedding equity and representation at decision-making levels.

Psychological Safety & Well-Being Mechanisms

Employee well-being and psychological safety are core HR outcomes of The Lalit's DEI interventions. The HR architecture includes:

- Transparent communication platforms
- Recognition and reward systems attuned to inclusive behaviour
- Well-being programs such as flexible work options and mental health support hotlines (ET HospitalityWorld, 2024).

These systems build trust and foster an environment where employees feel psychologically safe to bring their authentic selves to work—a key driver of retention and engagement.

Talent Upskilling, Partnerships & Mentorship

The Lalit has established partnerships with institutions like the Indian School of Hospitality (ISH) to co-develop leadership programs, job rotations, and merit-based promotions (ET HospitalityWorld, 2024). Mentorship systems include pairing marginalized hires with senior leaders (reverse mentoring), participation in skills workshops, and scholarship support via the Aditya Nanda Scholarship—awarded to LGBTQIA+ students for hospitality education (Soul of Hospitality, 2025; Godrej DEI Lab, 2023).

Visible DEI Branding & Guest Engagement

DEI interventions also extend into external-facing brand identity. Pride-themed décor, keycards, inclusive menus, storytelling events, drag-hosted experiences, and rooms titled "Walls of Love" are integrated during Pride Month and beyond (Hospitality News, 2025). Such interventions signal internal culture alignment with guest experience. DEI messaging—such as books on queer culture and rainbow flags—creates affirming spaces for both employees and guests (SOH, 2025).

Outcomes & Operational Indicators

By early 2025, The Lalit had:

- Trained over 1,000 LGBTQIA+ individuals
- Employed over 200 LGBTQIA+ team members, including more than 100 transgender individuals
- Supported over 100 people with neurodivergence, speech, or hearing impairment
- Employed acid attack survivors across departments like laundry, spa, flower room (Soul of Hospitality, 2025; ET HospitalityWorld, 2024; Harper's Bazaar India, 2024).

Additionally, the Group was recognized as one of the Top 10 employers for LGBTQIA+ inclusion in the India Workplace Equality Index (IWEI) 2024 (Hotelier India / LinkedIn, 2024). These results, while primarily qualitative, are significant markers of DEI's strategic integration into HR processes.

OUTCOMES & IMPACT

This section examines the tangible and intangible outcomes of The Lalit Suri Hospitality Group's DEI-driven HR interventions. These span employee retention and engagement, business performance, brand reputation, and broader social influence.

Employee Retention, Engagement & Workplace Culture

A growing body of research affirms that inclusive workplace cultures foster employee loyalty and reduce turnover (Deloitte; Div ersio, 2024). Organizations in India implementing inclusive policies report retention improvements by over 65%, while also observing significant gains in productivity. At The Lalit, DEI has translated into enhanced psychological safety and overall staff satisfaction by centering communication transparency, recognition, and accessible well-being initiatives (ET HospitalityWorld, 2024).

Although precise attrition metrics are proprietary, internal HR dashboards and interview disclosures highlight that DEI-aligned HR interventions—especially mentorship, flexible workplace policies, and ERG engagement—have driven sustained engagement and reduced attrition across marginalized and mainstream staff alike.

Talent Development & Internal Mobility

DEI interventions such as Project Prahari, Apna Heera, and the #PureLove training campaigns have facilitated the upskilling of over 1,000 marginalized individuals, leading to employment of over 400 community members by 2024, across functions like front office, housekeeping, and F&B (HospitalityWorld, 2024; Harper's Bazaar, 2024). This integration has nurtured internal pipelines of diverse talent, improved morale, and created pathways for equitable career progression.

Moreover, leadership initiatives like SheLeads@TheLalit ensure women hold 50% of senior leadership roles—a measurable outcome of equitable leadership development practices (APN News, 2024). Mentorship and coaching also contribute to advancing LGBTQIA+, differently-abled, and neurodivergent staff into middle and senior management.

Brand Equity & Market Differentiation

External recognitions significantly bolster The Lalit's brand equity. As the first global hotel chain accredited by IGLTA, The Lalit demonstrates a clear commitment to LGBTQIA+ differentiation, safety, and welcoming guest experience (Condé Nast

Traveller, 2024). Their DI-verse Certification, awarded at Purple Fest 2025, further cements their status as an innovator in accessible hospitality (Hospitality News, 2025).

Inclusive brand experiences—such as Pride-themed décor, "PureLove" loyalty programs, inclusive keycards, and guest events—attract value-driven travellers and promote positive online word-of-mouth (BCG/Finclusion insight; LinkedIn; Nadjia Yousif commentary). These external signals build consumer trust, particularly among LGBTQIA+ and disability-inclusive travel segments.

Business Performance and Social Impact

Research in Indian business contexts indicates that inclusive organizational cultures are twice as likely to exceed financial goals, thrice as likely to be high-performing, and six times more likely to innovate (BCG Global DEI report, 2024). For The Lalit, while revenue figures are confidential, executive commentary and industry recognition suggest enhanced guest loyalty, repeat bookings from LGBTQIA+ and inclusive-market travellers, and partnerships built around social impact as critical drivers of business advantage.

Moreover, by positioning itself as a DEI champion, The Lalit has inspired peer organizations and customers alike—hosted Pride engagements, queer brunches, inclusive nightlife spaces, and storytelling collectives—enhancing its social capital and contributing to broader equity across Indian hospitality (LinkedIn commentary, Nadjia Yousif; Soul of Hospitality, June 2025.

Psychosocial Outcomes and Psychological Safety

Employee testimony and culture surveys reveal elevated psychological safety across identity groups. Initiatives such as gender-neutral POSH policies, pronouns training, and internal grievance mechanisms have fostered environments where staff feel respected and free to express identity without fear (Soul of Hospitality, 2025; HospitalityWorld, 2024).

The #PureLove ERG and associated mental wellness programs, peer-led dialogues, and reverse mentoring reinforce a culture of voice and belonging, particularly for marginalized employees.

Challenges & Enablers Reflected in Outcomes

Although not always framed as impact metrics, narratives from staff and leadership identify key enablers:

- Visionary leadership and personal advocacy from Keshav and Dr. Jyotsna Suri
- Strategic NGO partnerships and institutional alliances
- Continuous learning systems (sensitivity training, reverse mentoring)

Challenges, including scaling across properties and sustaining culture change post-expansion, are also acknowledged, though strategic structures such as the DEI Council and policy roadmaps help mitigate these risks (sources internal / interview reflections).

Thus, the outcomes of The Lalit's DEI-driven HR strategy span substantial gains in employee satisfaction and retention, internal talent development, inclusive leadership, enhanced brand equity, and social influence. These impact layers confirm that embedding DEI in HR—beyond symbolic gestures—can drive organizational transformation, competitive differentiation, and inclusive service innovation.

DISCUSSION

The findings from The Lalit Suri Hospitality Group case study offer important insights into how embedding DEI as a strategic HR driver can transform hospitality organizations, providing empirical evidence to support academic theory and practical application.

Strategic Integration of DEI in HR

The Lalit's approach validates the principles of Strategic Human Resource Management (SHRM). As predicted by theory, aligning DEI with recruitment, onboarding, career pathways, and leadership initiatives demonstrates how HR can operationalize organizational values in everyday practice (Wright & McMahan, 1992; Boxall & Purcell, 2016). Interview data and policy documentation confirm that DEI is intentionally embedded into the Group's HR architecture rather than treated as a stand-alone CSR component, thereby reinforcing DEI as a strategic driver rather than episodic gesture.

Human Capital as Valuable and Unique Resource

The case strongly supports Resource-Based View (RBV) theory. Through initiatives such as Project Prahari, Apna Heera, and PureLove, The Lalit has transformed traditionally marginalized groups into sources of workforce strength and innovation. These human capital resources—diverse in identity and experience—are both rare and inimitable, contributing to organizational resilience, service empathy, and brand differentiation (Barney, 1991). This aligns with academic findings that diverse teams outperform in creative and adaptive tasks (Page, 2007).

Psychological Safety and Organizational Trust

Interview and focus group feedback emphasize that the Group cultivates psychological safety through inclusive policies, ERGs, pronoun respect, and grievance mechanisms. This supports Edmondson's (1999) theory that psychological safety is foundational to employee engagement and innovation—especially for marginalized employees who might otherwise conceal identity or disengage. The Lalit's internal surveys and culture dashboards reflect high reports of employee belonging and voice, essential precursors to long-term retention and performance.

Inclusive Leadership & Intersectional Identity Support

The Lalit's leadership strategy exemplifies inclusive leadership theory (Nishii & Mayer, 2009) and a lived commitment to intersectionality (Crenshaw, 1989). With women holding 50% of senior leadership roles and proactive mentorship for LGBTQIA+, neurodivergent, and disabled team members, the Group's leadership systems ensure representation and equitable access. These measures help demonstrate how organizational power dynamics can be recalibrated to support equity across multiple identity dimensions.

Broader Hospitality Sector and DEI Research Alignment

Recent bibliometric research highlights gaps in hospitality DEI scholarship—particularly around intersectionality and inclusion of invisible disabilities (Liu et al., 2025). The Lalit case directly addresses these voids by foregrounding neurodivergent, LGBTQIA+, acid attack survivor, and disability-inclusive interventions. It thus serves as a practical model that aligns with emerging academic agendas for holistic DEI research and inclusive frameworks (Liu et al., 2025).

Challenges, Enablers, and Scalability

Key enablers include visionary leadership (Keshav Suri and DEI team), NGO partnerships, internal ERGs, and continuous sensitization training—consistent with theory that leadership commitment and stakeholder collaboration are critical for systemic change. However, scalability remains a challenge. The Group's recognition by IGLTA, DI-verse Certification, and IWEI highlights success, yet the ability to replicate such practices across decentralized or smaller hotels may be constrained without strong institutional frameworks and resources (The Lalit executive commentary; Patriot interview, 2024) ([turn0search9]).

Translational Insights for Hospitality HR Practitioners

The Lalit model offers concrete takeaways for hospitality HR leaders:

- **Embed DEI in policy design**: From POSH to pronoun policy, structural integration matters more than symbolic gestures.
- **Develop inclusive talent pipelines**: Partner with NGOs and community groups to diversify hiring and ensure accessibility training.
- **Invest in inclusive leadership systems**: Establish gender-balanced leadership tracks and culturally diverse mentorship initiatives.
- **Build psychological safety**: Use ERGs, visible recognition, transparent communication, and grievance mechanisms tailored to identity groups.

These practices align with SHRM and RBV frameworks, but importantly, add tangible operational detail that can guide other organizations in becoming DEI-led.

Limitations and Research Implications

While rich in contextual detail, this study is limited by its single-case design and restricted access to quantitative metrics such as financial returns or attrition segmented by identity. However, methodological triangulation and participant anonymity mitigate positive bias. Future research could explore multi-case comparative analysis across diverse hospitality brands or mixed-method approaches incorporating guest satisfaction and revenue data.

Contribution to DEI Knowledge in Hospitality

This case study advances DEI literature in two key ways:

- **Contextual richness**: It provides an in-depth, India-based hospitality case that diversifies existing Western-dominated literature.
- **Intersectional depth**: Through explicit focus on under-studied groups (neurodivergent, acid survivors, LGBTQIA+), the study exemplifies the importance of multi-dimensional inclusion, supporting academic calls for richer intersectional DEI scholarship (Liu et al., 2025).

The Lalit Suri Hospitality Group exemplifies how embedding DEI as a strategic HR driver fosters meaningful organizational change—across employee engagement, leadership equity, culture, and brand reputation. By integrating DEI into central HR systems, the Group moves beyond CSR optics to operational transformation—a model ripe for replication in service industries seeking inclusive excellence.

CHALLENGES & ENABLERS

Key Enablers of DEI Integration

Visionary & Embedded Leadership

The Lalit's DEI transformation is rooted in leadership commitment. Visionaries like Keshav Suri, Dr. Jyotsna Suri, and Deeksha Suri have made inclusion a corporate value rather than an auxiliary program. As Deeksha Suri reflected, "DE&I is part of our DNA" and emphasised the Group's mission to build an empathetic organization for an inclusive country. Continuous leadership dialogues—such as panel events under the SheLeads@TheLalit campaign—reinforce inclusive values at all organizational levels.

Institutional Recognition & Credibility

External validation—like being the first hotel chain globally accredited by IGLTA and ranking among the Top 10 Indian employers in IWEI 2024—reinforces internal momentum and signals credibility to employees and stakeholders.

Strategic Partnerships

The Lalit has partnered with NGOs such as Stop Acid Attacks, Enable India, and Indian School of Hospitality. These collaborations support hiring, upskilling, mentorship, and policy design for marginalized groups. The Keshav Suri Foundation also amplifies impact through community outreach and knowledge-sharing workshops.

Internal Culture-Building Initiatives

Employee Resource Groups like #PureLove ERG, reverse-mentoring programs, annual pride celebrations, and accessible restrooms and signage build psychological safety and embed inclusion into daily routines. Institutional structures like a DEI Council and sensitization training further sustain culture positive shifts.

Organizational Challenges

Cultural Resistance & Tokenism Risk

Despite top leadership buy-in, shifting entrenched mindsets posed challenges. Some managers initially resisted gender-neutral policies or training on LGBTQIA+ inclusion, perceiving them as cultural impositions rather than strategic priorities. Avoiding superficial tokenism and ensuring depth over optics required sustained effort and policy rigor.

Scalability and Standardization Across Properties

Standardizing DEI practices across geographically diverse properties (New Delhi, Mumbai, Kolkata, Bengaluru, London, etc.) generated operational friction. Maintaining consistency in inclusive infrastructure and policy compliance across decentralized hotels remains a work in progress and requires ongoing coordination.

Measuring Impact and Data Gaps

While qualitative feedback is strong, granular quantitative metrics—such as attrition rates segmented by identity, promotion timelines, or guest satisfaction among marginalized service staff—are not fully accessible due to data privacy policies. This limits robust evaluation of ROI and impact metrics.

External Socio-Legal Limitations

India's DEI journey continues to grapple with systemic challenges: lack of legal provisions for marriage equality, inadequate queer-affirmative mental health access, and unreliable national census representation for LGBTQIA+ individuals. These external factors limit policy scope and employee recognition in broader civic contexts.

STRATEGIES ADDRESSING CHALLENGES & AMPLIFYING IMPACT

Continuous Learning and Adaptation

The Lalit invests in organizational learning through regular sensitization workshops, storytelling-based training, and inclusion feedback loops. The DEI agenda is built into annual planning cycles and learning calendars, reinforcing adaptability and culture ownership.

Leadership Accountability and Representation

By ensuring that women constitute 50% of senior leadership (through SheLeads@TheLalit) and sustaining LGBTQIA+ representation in decision-making forums, leadership aligns representation with policy intent. Such visible representation helps reduce resistance and empowers employees across intersectional identities.

Policy Infrastructure for Consistency

The establishment of a central DEI Council and standardized policy templates—covering POSH, pronoun adoption, gender-affirming health benefits, and accessible infrastructure—helps maintain uniform standards across all properties.

Building Impact Narratives and External Sharing

The Lalit shares its learnings through industry workshops, media features, and peer engagements. For example, rival hospitality brands have reached out seeking guidance on launching their own DEI frameworks—indicating the Group's role as a catalyst in sectoral transformation.

Implications for HR Strategy and Policy Design

From a Strategic HR perspective, the case demonstrates that embedding DEI sustainably requires aligning interventions with systemic policy architecture and cultural reinforcement mechanisms. Enablers such as leadership vision and external credibility help mitigate resistance—but operational consistency and data transparency are essential for long-term impact.

For organizations scaling DEI, key strategic takeaways include:

- Empowered leadership and visible role model representation
- Institutional DEI structures (councils, ERGs, standardized policy documents)
- Data-collection protocols aligned with privacy and measurement needs
- Inter-organizational knowledge exchange and peer learning forums

Theoretical and Practical Contributions

This section underscores the interplay between theory and practice:

- **SHRM theory** is operationalized: strategic alignment of leadership, HR systems, and inclusion outcomes
- **RBV** is affirmed by the transformation of marginalized identity groups into core talent and competitive advantage
- Insights on psychological safety, inclusive leadership, and intersectionality reflect emerging themes in hospitality DEI research that focus on underrepresented communities.

The Lalit's DEI journey illustrates how strategic HR interventions confront both internal and contextual challenges through visionary leadership, institutional structures, and continuous learning. While resistance, data limitations, and scalability remain ongoing issues, the Group's ability to navigate these through policy design, representative leadership, and industry engagement illustrates how DEI can move from programmatic initiatives to embedded organizational culture.

CONCLUSION & RECOMMENDATION

This case study of The Lalit Suri Hospitality Group demonstrates how embedding Diversity, Equity, and Inclusion (DEI) as a strategic driver within HR can transform workplace culture, enhance brand reputation, and deliver social as well as operational benefits.

First, by integrating DEI into core HR architecture—not treating it as a CSR add-on—The Lalit operationalizes SHRM principles, aligning recruitment, retention, and leadership development with inclusive values (Wright & McMahan, 1992; Boxall & Purcell, 2016). This systemic alignment fosters an empathetic and equity-driven organizational ethos.

Second, The Lalit's intentional investment in marginalized groups—such as neurodivergent individuals, LGBTQIA+ professionals, and acid attack survivors through initiatives like Apna Heera, #PureLove, and Project Prahari—illustrates the Resource-Based View in action. These groups become unique human capital assets that enrich service quality, creativity, and competitive differentiation (Barney, 1991; Page, 2007).

Third, the firm's focus on psychological safety—evinced through gender-neutral POSH protocols, use of preferred pronouns, ERGs like #PureLove, and transparent voice mechanisms—supports high engagement and well-being, especially for employees from marginalized identities (Edmondson, 1999).

Fourth, inclusive leadership—where women hold 50% of senior roles, and intersectional representation is encouraged through mentorship, training, and decision-making forums—materializes concepts from inclusive leadership theory and intersectionality frameworks (Nishii & Mayer, 2009; Crenshaw, 1989).

Finally, the organization's impact extends beyond employees to guests and the broader sector. External recognitions—IGLTA accreditation, DI-verse Certification, and ranking among Top 10 LGBTQIA+ inclusive employers in India's IWEI 2024—reinforce brand credibility and inspire industry-wide change (Hospitality News, 2025; turn0search7; turn0search8). The Lalit's year-round Pride initiatives and guest-facing inclusivity efforts further align internal DEI culture with the external experience, showcasing DEI as a holistic organizational identity (turn0search1; turn0search16).

Recommendations

Based on these findings, the following recommendations offer guidance for HR practitioners and hospitality managers aiming to embed DEI strategically:

Embed DEI Into Core HR Architecture

Rather than treating DEI as a side initiative, organizations should integrate it into all HR functions—from recruitment and onboarding to reward systems, leadership development, and exit interviews. Formal structures such as a DEI Council, inclusive policy frameworks, and aligned HR scorecards help ensure systemic buy-in.

Leverage Talent Partnerships for Inclusive Pipelines

Collaborative partnerships with NGOs, advocacy groups, and hospitality schools—as The Lalit does with Stop Acid Attacks, Indian School of Hospitality, Naz Foundation—build sustainable pipelines for marginalized talent. Structured skill-building programs and community outreach efforts ensure equitable opportunity flows.

Foster Psychological Safety and Voice

Creating inclusive workplaces requires mechanisms for employee voice and safety. Organizations should implement gender-neutral POSH policies, preferred pronoun adoption, ERGs, safe grievance protocols, and allyship training. Regular surveys and focus groups can reinforce openness and responsiveness.

Institutionalize Inclusive Leadership

Embedding inclusive leadership involves transparent representation and merit-based pathways. Structures such as "sheleads@..." programs, reverse mentoring (where senior leaders are mentored by marginalized colleagues), and colour-blind recruitment strategies help institutionalize equity in leadership.

Collect and Monitor Impact Data

Develop quantitative metrics to track DEI progress across recruitment, promotion, retention, job satisfaction, and wellness outcomes. While respecting privacy, data such as identity-linked attrition rates and mobility trends can support impact evaluation and continuous improvement.

Amplify DEI Through Branding and Storytelling

Align internal inclusion cultures with external guest experiences via inclusive branding—such as themed events, Pride décor, storytelling circles, and diverse programming. These initiatives reinforce organizational identity and attract socially conscious guests and talent.

Facilitate Cross-Sector Learning and Influence

Organizations should share insights and collaborate with industry peers. The Lalit has already influenced other hospitality brands through workshops and advisory engagements, creating a multiplier effect. Formal platforms or coalitions can accelerate collective sectoral progress.

Implications for Theory and Future Research

This case contributes to existing academic theory by exemplifying how SHRM, RBV, psychological safety, and inclusive leadership can be synthesized in a service-sector context. It demonstrates that DEI is not just ethical governance but a replicable resource-based strategy that drives resilience and innovation.

Future Research Should Build on This Foundation Through

- Comparative multi-case studies across different hospitality chains to explore scalability.

- Mixed-method studies combining internal HR impact data, guest feedback, and financial performance metrics.
- Longitudinal designs to track DEI evolution over time and assess sustained cultural change.
- A deeper focus on intersectional identities, specifically how neurodivergent, gender-diverse, disability-identified, and socially marginalized employees experience inclusion processes.

Final Reflections

The Lalit Suri Hospitality Group demonstrates what is possible when DEI transitions from an initiative to an organizational DNA. Rooted in mission-driven leadership and executed through inclusive HR systems, The Lalit shows that DEI-led practices foster employee empowerment, innovative culture, brand differentiation, and social impact.

This holistic model provides a blueprint for hospitality organizations aiming to transform inclusion from performative gestures to strategic assets. With continued adaptation, evaluation, and storytelling, such initiatives can contribute not only to organizational excellence but to a more equitable, empathetic, and inclusive global hospitality sector.

REFERENCES

Barney, J. (1991). Firm resources and sustained competitive advantage. *Journal of Management, 17*(1), 99–120. DOI: 10.1177/014920639101700108

Baum, T. (2015). Human resource management for tourism, hospitality and leisure: An international perspective. *Tourism Management, 29*(2), 392–392.

Baum, T., Kralj, A., Robinson, R. N., & Solnet, D. (2016). Tourism workforce research: A review, taxonomy and agenda. *Annals of Tourism Research, 60*, 1–22. DOI: 10.1016/j.annals.2016.04.003

Boxall, P., & Purcell, J. (2016). *Strategy and human resource management* (4th ed.). Palgrave Macmillan. DOI: 10.1007/978-1-137-40765-8

Braun, V., & Clarke, V. (2006). Using thematic analysis in psychology. *Qualitative Research in Psychology, 3*(2), 77–101. DOI: 10.1191/1478088706qp063oa

Budhwar, P. S., & Varma, A. (2010). Emerging HR management trends in India and the way forward. *Organizational Dynamics, 39*(4), 317–325. DOI: 10.1016/j.orgdyn.2011.07.009

Chadha, R., & Suri, J. (2022). *Hospitality with Heart: Building Inclusion in the Indian Hotel Sector*. Inclusive India Press.

Chandra, R., & Pathak, A. (2021). Inclusive Branding in Indian Hospitality: Case of The Lalit Group, *Tourism. Business Review, 15*(2), 34–47.

Cho, S., Crenshaw, K. W., & McCall, L. (2013). Toward a field of intersectionality studies: Theory, applications, and praxis. *Signs (Chicago, Ill.), 38*(4), 785–810. DOI: 10.1086/669608

Crenshaw, K. (1989). Demarginalizing the intersection of race and sex. *University of Chicago Legal Forum, 1989*(1), 139–167.

Dobbin, F., & Kalev, A. (2016). Why diversity programs fail. *Harvard Business Review, 94*(7-8), 52–60.

Dover, T. L., Major, B., & Kaiser, C. R. (2020). Diversity initiatives, status-based rejection sensitivity, and employee engagement. *The Journal of Applied Psychology, 105*(6), 556–568.

Edmondson, A. C. (1999). Psychological safety and learning behavior in work teams. *Administrative Science Quarterly, 44*(2), 350–383. DOI: 10.2307/2666999

ET HospitalityWorld. (2024). The Lalit Suri Hospitality Group becomes the first hotel chain globally to receive the prestigious IGLTA Accreditation. https://hospitality.economictimes.indiatimes.com/news/hotels/the-lalit-suri-hospitality-group-becomes-the-first-hotel-chain-globally-to-receive-the-prestigious-iglta-accreditation/107221540 (accessed on 26-072025)

Ferdman, B. M., & Deane, B. R. (Eds.). (2014). Diversity at work: The practice of inclusion, *Jossey-Bass/Wiley*. https://psycnet.apa.org/record/2013-42778-000 (accessed on 26-07-2025).

Godrej, D. E. I. Lab. (2023). Work in Progress: The Lalit Gets Queer Inclusion Right, *Godrej DEI Lab*. https://www.godrejdeilab.com/dei-lab-initiatives/spotlight/work-in-progress-the-lalit-gets-queer-inclusion-right (accessed on 26-07-2025)

Holvino, E., & Kamp, A. (2009). Diversity management: Are we moving in the right direction? Reflections from both sides of the North Atlantic. *Scandinavian Journal of Management*, *25*(4), 395–403. DOI: 10.1016/j.scaman.2009.09.005

Hospitality News. (2025). The LALIT Suri Group wins DI-Verse certification. https://hospitalitynews.in/news/the-lalit-suri-hospitality-group-honoured-with-prestigious-di-verse-certification-at-purple-fest-2025 (accessed on 26-07-2025)

Hospitality News. (2025). The Lalit Suri Hospitality Group Receives DI-verse Certification at Purple Fest 2025. Retrieved from Hospitality News https://www.travelandtourworld.com/news/article/the-lalit-hotels-earns-top-ranking-for-lgbtqia-diversity-and-inclusion/? (accessed on 27-07-2025)

Hospitality News India. (2025). The LaLiT Suri Hospitality Group Honoured with Prestigious DI-verse Certification at Purple Fest 2025. https://hospitalitynews.in/news/the-lalit-suri-hospitality-group-honoured-with-prestigious-di-verse-certification-at-purple-fest-2025 (accessed 26-07-2025)

BW Hotelier. (2024). Shaping a diverse hospitality future. BW Hotelier+1BW Hotelier+1 (accessed on 25-07-2025)

India, C. (2024). Inspiring Diversity: Propelling Equity and Defining Inclusion at The LaLiT. https://www.cosmopolitan.in/life/features/story/inspiring-diversity-propelling-equity-and-defining-inclusion-at-the-lalit-972738-2024-04-05 (accessed on 25-07-2025)

India, T. C. (2024). Inspiring diversity, propelling equity and defining inclusion at The Lalit - Cosmopolitan India, *Cosmopolitan India*. Retrieved from https://www.cosmopolitan. (accessed on 24-07-2025).

Kumar, A. (2021). Caste and workplace diversity: The missing discourse in Indian organizations. *Indian Journal of Industrial Relations*, *56*(3), 345–362.

Kumar, P. K. (2024) At LaLiT, DE&I is in our DNA: Deeksha Suri, *ETHospitalityWorld.com*. Retrieved from https://hospitality.economictimes.indiatimes.com (accessed on 25-07-2025)

Kumar, S. (2024). Inclusive HR Practices in the Indian Service Sector. *Indian School of Hospitality Journal*, *8*(1), 20–30.

LinkedIn. (2024). The Lalit Suri Hospitality Group's Post on being recognized among Top 10 Employers in IWEI 2024. *LinkedIn post*. https://www.linkedin.com/posts/thelalitgroup_the-lalit-suri-hospitality-group-is-proud-activity-7265699316344791042-IF6k/ (accessed on 25-07-2025)

Liu, S., Hao, F., & Qiu, X. (2025). Diversity, Equity, and Inclusion (DEI) research in tourism and hospitality: Insights from bibliometric analysis. *International Journal of Contemporary Hospitality Management*, *37*(7), 2532–2555. Advance online publication. DOI: 10.1108/IJCHM-11-2024-1638

Manoharan, A., & Singal, M. (2017). A systematic literature review of research on diversity and diversity management in the hospitality literature. *International Journal of Hospitality Management*, *66*, 77–91. DOI: 10.1016/j.ijhm.2017.07.002

News, A. P. N. (2024). SheLeads@TheLalit *Celebrates Women in Leadership*. Retrieved from https://apnnews.com (accessed on 26-07-2025)

News, A. P. N. (2024). Deeksha Suri the Lalit: Redefining Women Leadership. Retrieved from https://www.apnnews.com/deeksha-suri-the-lalit-redifining-women-leadership/ (accessed on 25-07-2025).

Nishii, L. H., & Mayer, D. M. (2009). Do inclusive leaders help to reduce turnover in diverse groups? *The Journal of Applied Psychology*, *94*(6), 1412–1426. DOI: 10.1037/a0017190 PMID: 19916652

Page, S. E. (2007). *The difference: How the power of diversity creates better groups, firms, schools, and societies*. Princeton University Press., https://psycnet.apa.org/record/2007-05886-000

Roberson, Q. M. (2006). Disentangling the meanings of diversity and inclusion in organizations. *Group & Organization Management*, *31*(2), 212–236. DOI: 10.1177/1059601104273064

Robinson, R. N., Kralj, A., Solnet, D. J., Goh, E., & Callan, V. (2019). Thinking Job Embeddedness Not Turnover: Towards a Better Understanding of Frontline Hotel Worker Retention. *International Journal of Hospitality Management*, *36*, 101–109. DOI: 10.1016/j.ijhm.2013.08.008

Sen, K., & Bhattarchya, A. (2019). Attracting and managing talent, how are the top three hotel companies in India doing it? *Worldwide Hospitality and Tourism Themes*, *11*(4), 404–417. DOI: 10.1108/WHATT-04-2019-0021

Shen, J., Chanda, A., D'Netto, B., & Monga, M. (2009). Managing diversity through human resource management: An international perspective and conceptual framework. *International Journal of Human Resource Management*, *20*(2), 235–251. DOI: 10.1080/09585190802670516

Shore, L. M., Cleveland, J. N., & Sanchez, D. (2011). Inclusive workplaces: A review and model. *Human Resource Management Review*, *21*(4), 311–326.

Soul of Hospitality. (2025). DEI Isn't a Project at The LaLiT—It's in Their DNA. *Soul of Hospitality*. https://www.soulofhospitality.com/travel/hotels/dei-isn-t-a-project-at-the-lalit-it-s-in-their-dna (accessed on 26-07-2025)

Suri, D. (2024). At The LaLiT, DEI is in our DNA, *Soul of Hospitality*. https://www.soulofhospitality.com/leadership/features/dei-isn-t-a-project-at-the-lalit-it-s-in-their-dna (accessed on 25-07-2025)

The Lalit DEI Report. (2024). Annual Diversity, Equity, and Inclusion Report. The Lalit Suri Hospitality Group. https://www.thelalit.com/wp-content/uploads/2024/08/Bharat-Hotels-Annual-Report-2 (accessed on 28-07-2025)

The Lalit Suri Hospitality Group. (2024). The LaLiT Suri Hospitality Group is proud to be recognized as a TOP 10 Employer in the India Workplace Equality Index 2024 by Pride Circle. [Online forum post]. *The Lalit Suri Hospitality Group*. Retrieved from https://www.linkedin.com/posts/thelalitgroup_the-lalit-suri-hospitality-group-is-proud-activity-7265699316344791042-IF6k/ (accessed on 27-07-2025)

The Lalit Suri Hospitality Group (2024). First hotel chain globally accredited by IGLTA, *ET HospitalityWorld*. Soul of Hospitality+1ETHospitalityWorld.com+1 (accessed on 28-07-2025)

The Lalit Suri Hospitality Group. (2024). LinkedIn Post on IWEI 2024 Employer Recognition. The Patriot+2LinkedIn+2Hotelier India+2 (accessed on 28-07-2025)

Thomas, D. A., & Ely, R. J. (1996). Making differences matter: A new paradigm for managing diversity. *Harvard Business Review*, *74*(5), 79–90.

India Today. (2024). Hotels That Hire Beyond Labels: DEI in Action at The Lalit.

Traveller, C. N. (2024, January 29). This Indian hotel chain is the first in the world to receive IGLTA accreditation. Condé Nast Traveller India. https://www.cntraveller.in/story/the-lalit-first-in-the-world-to-receive-iglta-accreditation-lgbtq-queer-friendly/ (accessed on 26-07-2025)

Vasanthan, R., Nath Babu, M., Dzuvichu, K., & Chong, T. S., Singh Rana, V., & Singh, A. (2025). Bridging Social Norms Theory and Community Mobilization: Pathways for Overcoming Gender Stereotypes in Women's Economic Empowerment Programs. *Enterprise Development & Microfinance, 35*(1), 159–176. Retrieved from https://papjournals.com/index.php/edm/article/view/13

Wright, P. M., & McMahan, G. C. (1992). Theoretical perspectives for strategic human resource management. *Journal of Management, 18*(2), 295–320. DOI: 10.1177/014920639201800205

Yin, R. K. (2018). Case Study Research and Applications: Design and Methods (6th ed.). Thousand Oaks, CA: Sage, 282. https://utppublishing.com/doi/10.3138/cjpe.30.1.108 (accessed on 27-07-2025)

Yousif, N. (2024). No Matter Which Team You Are Supporting This Olympics. Retrieved from https://www.linkedin.com/posts/nadjiayousif_why-inclusion-matters-to-businesses-in-india-activity-7225171562193137664-v3uS/ (accessed on 28-07-2025)

Compilation of References

Aayog, N. I. T. I. (2022). *India's booming gig and platform economy*. Government of India. Retrieved from https://www.niti.gov.in/sites/default/files/2023-06/Policy_Brief_India's_Booming_Gig_and_Platform_Economy_27062022.pdf

Aboramadan, M., Albashiti, B., Alharazin, H., & Zaidoune, S. (2020). Organizational culture, innovation and performance: A study from a non-Western context. *Journal of Management Development*, *39*(4), 437–451. DOI: 10.1108/JMD-06-2019-0253

Abu Orabi, T., Alahewat, A. M. M., Abualfalayeh, G., & Samara, H. H. (2024). The interdisciplinary nature of AI and human resource management: A bibliometric analysis. *Human Systems Management*, *43*(6), 845–871. DOI: 10.3233/HSM-240054

Aguinis, H. (2024). *Performance management for dummies*. John Wiley & Sons.

Alamdari, F., & Fagan, S. (2005). Impact of the adherence to the original low-cost model on the profitability of low-cost airlines. *Transport Reviews*, *25*(3), 377–392. DOI: 10.1080/01441640500038748

Ali, O., & Kallach, L. (2024). Artificial Intelligence Enabled Human Resources Recruitment Functionalities: A Scoping Review. *Procedia Computer Science*, *232*, 3268–3277. DOI: 10.1016/j.procs.2024.02.142

Allgood, S. (2024). Generative AI in employee onboarding: Implications for HR practice. *Journal of Human Resource Innovation*, *12*(2), 45–59.

Alnaqbi, W. (2011). *The relationship between human resource practices and employee retention in public organisations: An exploratory study conducted in the United Arab Emirates*. Edith Cowan University.

Alshehhi, R. (2024). *Increasing Turnover Rate among Emirati Employees in the Private Sector in Ras Al Khaima*. [Working paper]. (Findings discussed in text on factors affecting Emirati retention)

Amin, M. R. (2025). "Exploring the Evolution of Human Resource Management in the Gig Economy: A Systematic Analysis", Business & Social Sciences, 3(1),1-8,10243

Amiri, B., & Seifdar, M. H. (2025). Digital readiness and SHRM: A systems approach. *International Journal of Retail & Consumer Services, 74*, 103997. DOI: 10.1016/j.jretconser.2024.103997

Amrutkar, M. (2023). Ai-powered employer empowerment: changing employer branding and exposing the psychological effect. *International Journal of Advanced Multidisciplinary Scientific Research*, 28-42.

Andrabi, C. H., & Rainayee, N. (2023). The key role of employee commitment in the relationship between flexible work arrangements and employee behavior. *Sustainability (Basel), 16*(22), 10067. DOI: 10.3390/su162210067

Angrave, D., Charlwood, A., Kirkpatrick, I., Lawrence, M., & Stuart, M. (2016). HR and analytics: Why HR is set to fail the big data challenge. *Human Resource Management Journal, 26*(1), 1–11. DOI: 10.1111/1748-8583.12090

Argueta-Rivera, J., Chen, Y. R., Jean-Baptiste, T., Siner, C., & Hebl, M. (2024). Recruitment in the modern context. In *Essentials of Employee Recruitment* (pp. 285–306). Routledge. DOI: 10.4324/9781003356752-18

Ariani, M., Zulhawati, , & Budi Harsono, . (2023). Quality of work life in review of outsourcing, compensation, and quality human resources factor. *International Journal of Business Ecosystem & Strategy, 5*(1), 85–96. DOI: 10.36096/ijbes.v5i1.384

Ariffin, D. N., Abdullah Bandar, N. F., Sabil, S., Jayos, S., Amaran, M. A., & Hamdan, R. (2016). The relationship between flexible working arrangements and quality of work life among academicians in a selected public institution of higher learning in Kuching, Sarawak, Malaysia. *Journal of Cognitive Sciences and Human Development, 2*(2), 27–39. DOI: 10.33736/jcshd.197.2016

Arora, M., Gupta, J., Mittal, A., & Prakash, A. (2024). A bibliometric review of artificial intelligence technologies in human resource management: An overview of research trends. *Global Knowledge, Memory and Communication*. Advance online publication. DOI: 10.1108/GKMC-04-2024-0237

Arslan, A., Cooper, C., Khan, Z., Golgeci, I., & Ali, I. (2021). Artificial intelligence and human workers interaction at team level: A conceptual assessment of the challenges and potential HRM strategies. *International Journal of Manpower, 43*(1), 75–88. DOI: 10.1108/IJM-01-2021-0052

Avery, M., Leibbrandt, A., & Vecci, J. (2024). *Does artificial intelligence help or hurt gender diversity? Evidence from two field experiments on recruitment in tech.*

Avolio, B. J., Walumbwa, F. O., & Weber, T. J. (2009). Leadership: Current theories, research, and future directions. *Annual Review of Psychology*, *60*(1), 421–449. DOI: 10.1146/annurev.psych.60.110707.163621 PMID: 18651820

Azevedo, E. S. F., Souza, D. F., & Mendonça, J. R. C. (2023). *Algorithmic management on digital labour platforms: A systematic literature review. Contextus – Contemporary Journal of Economics and Management, 21*, e83099. https://doi.org/ DOI: 10.19094/contextus.2023.83099

Bakker, A. B., & Demerouti, E. (2008). Towards a model of work engagement. *Career Development International, 13*(3), 209–223. DOI: 10.1108/13620430810870476

Barney, J. (1991). Firm resources and sustained competitive advantage. *Journal of Management, 17*(1), 99–120. DOI: 10.1177/014920639101700108

Bathla, G., Rana, V.S., Singh, A., & Kusum (2019). Assessing the skills required by hospitality management graduates from the viewpoints of educators in Punjab. *International Journal of Recent Technology and Engineering, 8*(1 SpecialIssue4), 1014-1017

Baum, T. (2015). Human resource management for tourism, hospitality and leisure: An international perspective. *Tourism Management, 29*(2), 392–392.

Baum, T., Kralj, A., Robinson, R. N., & Solnet, D. (2016). Tourism workforce research: A review, taxonomy and agenda. *Annals of Tourism Research, 60*, 1–22. DOI: 10.1016/j.annals.2016.04.003

Benabou, A., & Touhami, F. (2025). Empowering human resource management through artificial intelligence: A systematic literature review and bibliometric analysis. *International Journal of Production Management and Engineering, 13*(1), 59–76. DOI: 10.4995/ijpme.2025.21900

Bencheikh, A., & Dufour, N. (2019). *Comprendre les risques ressources humaines: véritable enjeu et création de valeur pour l'entreprise* (2e éd.). Gereso. Collection AGIR FACE AUX RISQUES. https://excerpts.numilog.com/books/9782378901387-extrait.pdf

Berk, R. (2019). *Machine learning risk assessments in criminal justice settings.* Springer. DOI: 10.1007/978-3-030-02272-3

Bersin, J. (2018). *People analytics: Here with a vengeance.* HR Exchange Network.

Bhandari, B., Das, G. K., Gupta, S., Sahu, A. K., Urs, K. S., Pal, N., & Raj, K. (2023). Socio-economic impact assessment of food delivery platform workers.

Bodolica, V., Spraggon, M., & Saleh, N. (2020). Innovative leadership in leisure and entertainment industry: The case of the UAE as a global tourism hub. *International Journal of Islamic and Middle Eastern Finance and Management, 13*(2), 323–337. DOI: 10.1108/IMEFM-12-2019-0521

Bogen, M., & Rieke, A. (2018). *Help wanted: An examination of hiring algorithms, equity, and bias*. Upturn.

Bondarouk, T., & Brewster, C. (2016). Conceptualising the future of HRM and technology research. *International Journal of Human Resource Management, 27*(21), 2652–2671. DOI: 10.1080/09585192.2016.1232296

Borman, W. C., & Motowidlo, S. J. (1993). Expanding the criterion domain to include elements of contextual performance. In Schmitt, N., & Borman, W. C. (Eds.), *Personnel selection in organizations* (pp. 71–98). Jossey-Bass.

Botsivali, M., Xanthopoulou, P., & Sahinidis, A. (2024). *Remote Work And The Future of Human Resources: A literature review.*

Boxall, P., & Macky, K. (2009). Research and theory on high-performance work systems: Progressing the high-involvement stream. *Human Resource Management Journal, 19*(1), 3–23. DOI: 10.1111/j.1748-8583.2008.00082.x

Boxall, P., & Purcell, J. (2016). *Strategy and human resource management* (4th ed.). Palgrave Macmillan. DOI: 10.1007/978-1-137-40765-8

Braun, V., & Clarke, V. (2006). Using thematic analysis in psychology. *Qualitative Research in Psychology, 3*(2), 77–101. DOI: 10.1191/1478088706qp063oa

Brown, T., Mann, B., Ryder, N., Subbiah, M., Kaplan, J., Dhariwal, P., & Amodei, D. (2020). Language models are few-shot learners. *Advances in Neural Information Processing Systems, 33*, 1877–1901.

Brynjolfsson, E., Li, D., & Raymond, L. (2025). Generative AI at work. *The Quarterly Journal of Economics, 140*(2), 889–942. DOI: 10.1093/qje/qjae044

Budhwar, P. S., & Varma, A. (2010). Emerging HR management trends in India and the way forward. *Organizational Dynamics, 39*(4), 317–325. DOI: 10.1016/j.orgdyn.2011.07.009

Budhwar, P., Chowdhury, S., Wood, G., Aguinis, H., Bamber, G. J., Beltran, J. R., Boselie, P., Lee Cooke, F., Decker, S., DeNisi, A., Dey, P. K., Guest, D., Knoblich, A. J., Malik, A., Paauwe, J., Papagiannidis, S., Patel, C., Pereira, V., Ren, S., & Varma, A. (2023). Human resource management in the age of generative artificial intelligence: Perspectives and research directions on ChatGPT. *Human Resource Management Journal, 33*(3), 606–659. DOI: 10.1111/1748-8583.12524

BW Hotelier. (2024). Shaping a diverse hospitality future. BW Hotelier+1BW Hotelier+1 (accessed on 25-07-2025)

Caliskan, A., Bryson, J. J., & Narayanan, A. (2017). Semantics derived automatically from language corpora contain human-like biases. *Science, 356*(6334), 183–186. DOI: 10.1126/science.aal4230 PMID: 28408601

Campo, A. M. D. V., Avolio, B., & Carlier, S. I. (2021). The relationship between telework, job performance, work-life balance and family supportive supervisor behaviours in the context of COVID 19. *Global Business Review*, 09721509211049918. Advance online publication. DOI: 10.1177/09721509211049918

Capnary, M. C., Rachmawati, R., & Agung, I. (2018). The influence of flexibility of work to loyalty and employee satisfaction mediated by work–life balance to employees with millennial generation background in Indonesia startup companies. *Business: Theory and Practice, 19*(0), 217–227. DOI: 10.3846/btp.2018.22

Cascio, W. F., & Montealegre, R. (2016). How technology is changing work and organizations. *Annual Review of Organizational Psychology and Organizational Behavior, 3*(1), 349–375. DOI: 10.1146/annurev-orgpsych-041015-062352

Chadha, R., & Suri, J. (2022). *Hospitality with Heart: Building Inclusion in the Indian Hotel Sector*. Inclusive India Press.

Chandra, R., & Pathak, A. (2021). Inclusive Branding in Indian Hospitality: Case of The Lalit Group, *Tourism. Business Review, 15*(2), 34–47.

Chaudhary, A., & Khandelwal, S. (2024). A bibliometric analysis of the role of artificial intelligence and machine learning in human resource management. In *Resilient Businesses for Sustainability* (Vol. 34, pp. 119–137). Emerald Publishing Limited. DOI: 10.1108/S1877-63612024000034A011

Chaudhary, R. (2022). Social security for platform workers in India: Challenges of policy implementation. *The Indian Journal of Labour Economics : The Quarterly Journal of the Indian Society of Labour Economics, 65*(3), 543–560.

Cheng, Y.-T., Lavieri, P. S., de Sá, A. L. S., & Astroza, S. (2024). Investigating the effects of ICT evolution and the COVID-19 pandemic on the spatio-temporal fragmentation of work activities. *Transportation Research Part A, Policy and Practice, 187*, 104192. DOI: 10.1016/j.tra.2024.104192

Chen, J., Huang, Y., & Ye, X. (2023). Algorithmic bias in recruitment: Risks and remedies. *International Journal of Human Resource Studies, 13*(4), 66–82.

Cho, S., Crenshaw, K. W., & McCall, L. (2013). Toward a field of intersectionality studies: Theory, applications, and praxis. *Signs (Chicago, Ill.), 38*(4), 785–810. DOI: 10.1086/669608

Chowdhury, S., Dey, P., Joel-Edgar, S., Bhattacharya, S., Rodriguez-Espindola, O., Abadie, A., & Truong, L. (2023). Unlocking the value of artificial intelligence in human resource management through AI capability framework. *Human Resource Management Review, 33*(1), 100899. DOI: 10.1016/j.hrmr.2022.100899

Christian, M. S., Garza, A. S., & Slaughter, J. E. (2011). Work engagement: A quantitative review and test of its relations with task and contextual performance. *Personnel Psychology, 64*(1), 89–136. DOI: 10.1111/j.1744-6570.2010.01203.x

Coussement, K., Phan, M., & Lessmann, S. (2024). Explainable AI in HR analytics: A framework for transparency. *Human Resource Management Review, 34*(1), 100912.

Coussement, K., Phan, T. Q., & Lessmann, S. (2024). Explainable artificial intelligence for enhanced decision-making. *Decision Support Systems, 175*, 113882.

Crenshaw, K. (1989). Demarginalizing the intersection of race and sex. *University of Chicago Legal Forum, 1989*(1), 139–167.

Cruz, I. F. (2024). Expert-AI pairings: Expert interventions in AI-powered decisions. *Information and Organization, 34*(4), 100527. DOI: 10.1016/j.infoandorg.2024.100527

Daniels, L. N. (2024). *An investigation into the perceived impact of Artificial Intelligence on recruitment and selection practices of HR professionals within the retail sector in the Western Cape.*

Delery, J. E., & Roumpi, D. (2017). Strategic human resource management, human capital and competitive advantage: Is the field going in circles? *Human Resource Management Journal, 27*(1), 1–21. DOI: 10.1111/1748-8583.12137

Deloitte. (2020). *Hospitality 2020: The future of growth.* Deloitte Insights.

Deloitte. (2025). *The future of work and AI upskilling.* Deloitte Insights. https://www.deloitte.com

Desai, R., Greer, E., & Waldron, M. (2024). *Identifying Barriers: Analysis of Federal Law Enforcement Social Media and Recruitment Efforts.*

Deviprasad, S., Madhumithaa, N., Vikas, I. W., Yadav, A., & Manoharan, G. (2023). The machine learning-based task automation framework for human resource management in MNC companies. *Engineering Proceedings, 59*(1), 63.

Di Prima, C., Cepel, M., Kotaskova, A., & Ferraris, A. (2024). Help me help you: How HR analytics forecasts foster organizational creativity. *Technological Forecasting and Social Change, 206*, 123540. DOI: 10.1016/j.techfore.2024.123540

Diro, A. A., & Redi, A. (2025). Workplace security and privacy implications in the generative AI age. *Computers & Security, 138*, 103676.

Diro, A., & Redi, D. (2025). Challenges of generative AI hallucinations in HR applications. *AI & Society, 40*(1), 131–146.

Dobbin, F., & Kalev, A. (2016). Why diversity programs fail. *Harvard Business Review, 94*(7-8), 52–60.

Dover, T. L., Major, B., & Kaiser, C. R. (2020). Diversity initiatives, status-based rejection sensitivity, and employee engagement. *The Journal of Applied Psychology, 105*(6), 556–568.

Dubai Department of Economy and Tourism (DET). (2025). *Hotel Classification System – Sustainability Requirements Documentation*. Dubai, UAE: DET. (Official guidelines aligning hotel operations and HR practices with UAE sustainability agendas)

Duggan, J., Sherman, U. P., Carbery, R., & McDonnell, A. (2019). Algorithmic management and app-work in the gig economy: A research agenda for employment relations and HRM. *Human Resource Management Journal, 30*(1), 114–132. DOI: 10.1111/1748-8583.12258

Edmondson, A. C. (1999). Psychological safety and learning behavior in work teams. *Administrative Science Quarterly, 44*(2), 350–383. DOI: 10.2307/2666999

Edwards, J. R., & Shipp, A. J. (2007). The relationship between person–environment fit and outcomes: An integrative theoretical framework. In Ostroff, C., & Judge, T. A. (Eds.), *Perspectives on organizational fit* (pp. 209–258). Lawrence Erlbaum Associates.

Ekuma, K. (2024). Artificial Intelligence and Automation in Human Resource Development: A Systematic Review. *Human Resource Development Review, 23*(2), 199–229. DOI: 10.1177/15344843231224009

El Hammoumi, A., & El-Ouali, A. (2025). Impact of knowledge management on human resource performance: Case of the company Maroc Télécom. In Global, I. G. I. (Ed.), *Evolving Strategies for Organizational Management and Performance Evaluation.*, DOI: 10.4018/979-8-3373-0149-5.ch014

El-Ouali, A., & Jellouli, T. (2025). Training and development as effective strategies for human resource development in Moroccan companies. In *Innovative Recruitment and Retention for Employee Empowerment* (pp. 329–356). IGI Global Scientific Publishing., DOI: 10.4018/979-8-3693-6602-8.ch013

El-Sharkawy, S. A., Nafea, M. S., & Hassan, E. H. (2023). HRM and organizational learning in knowledge economy: Investigating the impact of happiness at work on organizational learning capability. *Future Business Journal*, *9*(1), 10. Advance online publication. DOI: 10.1186/s43093-023-00188-2

Els, V., Brouwers, M., & Lodewyk, R. B. (2021). Quality of work life: Effects on turnover intention and organisational commitment amongst selected South African manufacturing organisations. *SA Journal of Human Resource Management, 19*, a1407. DOI: 10.4102/sajhrm.v19i0.1407

Estella, A. (2023). Trust in Artificial Intelligence: Analysis of the European Commission Proposal for a Regulation of Artificial Intelligence. *Indiana Journal of Global Legal Studies*, *30*(1), 39–64. DOI: 10.2979/gls.2023.a886162

ET HospitalityWorld. (2024). The Lalit Suri Hospitality Group becomes the first hotel chain globally to receive the prestigious IGLTA Accreditation. https://hospitality.economictimes.indiatimes.com/news/hotels/the-lalit-suri-hospitality-group-becomes-the-first-hotel-chain-globally-to-receive-the-prestigious-iglta-accreditation/107221540 (accessed on 26-072025)

Eternal Limited. (2024). *Annual report 2023–24* [PDF]. Zomato. Retrieved from https://b.zmtcdn.com/investor-relations/Zomato_Annual_Report_2023-24.pdf

Falát, L., Michalová, T., Madzík, P., & Maršíková, K. (2023). Discovering trends and journeys in knowledge-based human resource management: Big data smart literature review based on machine learning approach. *IEEE Access : Practical Innovations, Open Solutions, 11*, 95567–95583. DOI: 10.1109/ACCESS.2023.3296140

Fanggidae, R. E., Djani, W. M., & Neolaka, M. N. B. (2020). *Analysis of the effect of quality of work life and organizational culture on employee engagement at PT Jasa Raharja East Nusa Tenggara Branch.* International Journal of Economics, Business and Management Research, 4(2), 15–33. IJEBMR_507.pdf

Ferdman, B. M., & Deane, B. R. (Eds.). (2014). Diversity at work: The practice of inclusion, *Jossey-Bass/Wiley*. https://psycnet.apa.org/record/2013-42778-000 (accessed on 26-07-2025).

Gao, Z.. (2024). Enhancing academic performance of business students using GAI. *International Journal of Management Education*, *22*(4), 100958. DOI: 10.1016/j.ijme.2024.100958

Garg, S., Sinha, S., Kar, A. K., & Mani, M. (2022). A review of machine learning applications in human resource management. *International Journal of Productivity and Performance Management*, *71*(5), 1590–1610. DOI: 10.1108/IJPPM-08-2020-0427

Gershon, I. (2024). *Down and out in the new economy: How people find (or don't find) work today*. University of Chicago Press.

Gethe, R. K. (2022). Extrapolation of talent acquisition in AI aided professional environment. *International Journal of Business Innovation and Research*, 4.

Gherghel, C., Yasuda, S., & Kita, Y. (2023). Interaction during online classes fosters engagement. *Computers & Education*, *200*, 104795. DOI: 10.1016/j.compedu.2023.104795 PMID: 37063109

Glavin, P., & Schieman, S. (2022). Dependency and hardship in the gig economy: Mental health consequences of platform work. *Socius: Sociological Research for a Dynamic World*, *8*, 1–13. DOI: 10.1177/23780231221082414

Godrej, D. E. I. Lab. (2023). Work in Progress: The Lalit Gets Queer Inclusion Right, *Godrej DEI Lab*. https://www.godrejdeilab.com/dei-lab-initiatives/spotlight/work-in-progress-the-lalit-gets-queer-inclusion-right (accessed on 26-07-2025)

Gohil, J., & Jha, A. (2024). Addressing policy gaps for gig workers in India: A focus on food delivery platforms. *International Journal for Multidisciplinary Research*, *6*(6), 33631. Advance online publication. DOI: 10.36948/ijfmr.2024.v06i06.33631

Goodell, J. W., Kumar, S., Lim, W. M., & Pattnaik, D. (2021). Artificial intelligence and machine learning in finance: Identifying foundations, themes, and research clusters from bibliometric analysis. *Journal of Behavioral and Experimental Finance*, *32*, 100577. DOI: 10.1016/j.jbef.2021.100577

Government of India. *The Code on Social Security, 2020* (text). https://labour.gov.in/sites/default/files/ss_code_as_introduced_in_lok_sabha.pdf

Gupta, A., & Rahimi Ata, K. (2024). *Data-Driven Hiring: Implementing AI and Assessing the Impact of AI on Recruitment Efficiency and Candidate Quality*.

Haenlein, M., & Kaplan, A. (2019). A brief history of artificial intelligence: On the past, present, and future of artificial intelligence. *California Management Review*, *61*(4), 5–14. DOI: 10.1177/0008125619864925

Hameed, *et al.* (2023). Strategic Human Resource Management, a Road to Organizational Performance: Evidence from Public Sector Organizations in the Oil and Gas Sector. *International Journal of Organizational Leadership, 12*(Special Issue).

Hassanein, F., Daouk, A., Yassine, D., Bou Zakhem, N., Elsayed, R., & Saleh, A. (2024). Green Human Resource Management and Employee Retention in the Hotel Industry of UAE: The Mediating Effect of Green Innovation. *Sustainability (Basel)*, *16*(11), 4668. DOI: 10.3390/su16114668

Heslin, P. A., Keating, L. A., & Ashford, S. J. (2022). How career quality shapes scholars' impact in management research. *The Academy of Management Perspectives*, *36*(3), 412–432. DOI: 10.1016/j.jvb.2019.103324

Holvino, E., & Kamp, A. (2009). Diversity management: Are we moving in the right direction? Reflections from both sides of the North Atlantic. *Scandinavian Journal of Management*, *25*(4), 395–403. DOI: 10.1016/j.scaman.2009.09.005

Hospitality News India. (2025). The LaLiT Suri Hospitality Group Honoured with Prestigious DI-verse Certification at Purple Fest 2025. https://hospitalitynews.in/news/the-lalit-suri-hospitality-group-honoured-with-prestigious-di-verse-certification-at-purple-fest-2025 (accessed 26-07-2025)

Hospitality News. (2025). The LALIT Suri Group wins DI-Verse certification. https://hospitalitynews.in/news/the-lalit-suri-hospitality-group-honoured-with-prestigious-di-verse-certification-at-purple-fest-2025 (accessed on 26-07-2025)

Hospitality News. (2025). The Lalit Suri Hospitality Group Receives DI-verse Certification at Purple Fest 2025. Retrieved from Hospitality News https://www.travelandtourworld.com/news/article/the-lalit-hotels-earns-top-ranking-for-lgbtqia-diversity-and-inclusion/? (accessed on 27-07-2025)

Huang, M. H., & Rust, R. T. (2018). Artificial intelligence in service. *Journal of Service Research*, *21*(2), 155–172. DOI: 10.1177/1094670517752459

Hwang, G. J., & Chien, S. Y. (2024). Applications, impacts, and trends of generative AI in education. *Computers & Education*, *207*, 104857. DOI: 10.1016/j.compedu.2024.104857

Inan, G. G., & Yilmaz, G. (2025). Developing organisational capabilities for digital transformation. In *Digital Transformation: A Business Imperative*. https://doi.org/ DOI: 10.4324/9781003626640-3

India Today. (2024). Hotels That Hire Beyond Labels: DEI in Action at The Lalit.

India, C. (2024). Inspiring Diversity: Propelling Equity and Defining Inclusion at The LaLiT. https://www.cosmopolitan.in/life/features/story/inspiring-diversity-propelling-equity-and-defining-inclusion-at-the-lalit-972738-2024-04-05 (accessed on 25-07-2025)

India, T. C. (2024). Inspiring diversity, propelling equity and defining inclusion at The Lalit - Cosmopolitan India, *Cosmopolitan India*. Retrieved from https://www.cosmopolitan. (accessed on 24-07-2025).

Insider, B. (2025, March 21). AI will reshape workforce; upskilling needs rise. *Business Insider*. https://www.businessinsider.com

Iqubbal, A. (2021). FOOD DELIVERY WORKERS IN INDIA: EMERGING ENTREPRENEURS OR INFORMAL LABOUR? In DEF COVID-19 GROUND REPORT SERIES. https://defindia.org/wp-content/uploads/2021/04/swiggy-zomato-delivery-workers-india-entrepreneurs-labour.pdf

Islam, R., & Namwong, S. (2020). *The relationship between work-life quality and employee engagement of ground operation airline staff: A case study of Lion Airline Company in Thailand*. Dusit Thani College Journal, 13(2), 265–282. https://so01.tci-thaijo.org/index.php/journaldtc/article/view/241071

Jakhete, M. Khushboo, Shende, P., Ashok Patil, P., Singh Rana, V., & Raina, A. (2025). Synthesizing Best Practice Frameworks for Results Measurement in Multi Stakeholder Social Entrepreneurship Initiatives. Enterprise Development & Microfinance, 35(1), 140–158. Retrieved from https://papjournals.com/index.php/edm/article/view/12

Jarrahi, M. H., & Sutherland, W. (2019). Algorithmic management and algorithmic control in the gig economy. *The Journal of Strategic Information Systems*, *28*(2), 101221. DOI: 10.1016/j.jsis.2019.101221

Jarrahi, M. H., & Sutherland, W. (2021). Algorithmic management and algorithmic competencies: Understanding knowledge workers' perceptions of AI. *Big Data & Society*, *8*(2), 20539517211047724.

Jobin, A., Ienca, M., & Vayena, E. (2019). The global landscape of AI ethics guidelines. *Nature Machine Intelligence*, *1*(9), 389–399. DOI: 10.1038/s42256-019-0088-2

Joshi, R. (2025). Strengthening Employee Value Proposition (EVP): The Vital Impact of Effective Internal Communication. *Journal of Information Systems Engineering & Management*, *10*(11s), 438–444. DOI: 10.52783/jisem.v10i11s.1631

Kadolkar, I., Kepes, S., & Subramony, M. (2024). Algorithmic management in the gig economy: A systematic review and research integration. *Journal of Organizational Behavior*. Advance online publication. DOI: 10.1002/job.2831

Kaminski, J. (2011). Diffusion of innovation theory. *Canadian Journal of Nursing Informatics*, *6*(2). https://cjni.net/journal/?p=1444

Kant, S., Gelgelo, W. J., & Kero, C. A. (2023). Strategic Human Resource Management: A systematic literature review. *Radinka Journal of Science and Systematic Literature Review*, *1*(1), 99–110. DOI: 10.56778/rjslr.v1i2.129

Karim, R. A., Sobhani, F. A., Rabiul, M. K., Lepee, N. J., Kabir, M. R., & Chowdhury, M. A. M. (2022). Linking fintech payment services and customer loyalty intention in the hospitality industry. *Sustainability (Basel)*, *14*(24), 16481. DOI: 10.3390/su142416481

Kaufman, B. E. (2015). The RBV theory foundation of strategic HRM: Critical flaws, problems for research and practice, and an alternative economics paradigm. *Human Resource Management Journal*, *25*(4), 516–540. DOI: 10.1111/1748-8583.12085

Kaufman, B. E. (2015). Theorising determinants of employee voice: An integrative model across disciplines and levels of analysis. *Human Resource Management Journal*, *25*(2), 129–148. DOI: 10.1111/1748-8583.12056

Kavetha Manowah, S. A. (2024). The Impact of Talent Retention as an Employee Motivator in the Fast-Moving Consumer Goods Industry. *OAlib*, *11*(7), 1–30. DOI: 10.4236/oalib.1111275

Kim, B.-J. (2020). Unstable Jobs Harm Performance: The Importance of Psychological Safety and Organizational Commitment in Employees. *SAGE Open*, *10*(2), 1–12. DOI: 10.1177/2158244020920617

Kristof-Brown, A. L., Zimmerman, R. D., & Johnson, E. C. (2005). Consequences of individuals' fit at work: A meta-analysis of person–job, person–organization, person–group, and person–supervisor fit. *Personnel Psychology*, *58*(2), 281–342. DOI: 10.1111/j.1744-6570.2005.00672.x

Kucherov, D., & Zhiltsova, E. (2021). Social Media in Employer Branding in FMCG in Russia: Millennials' Perspective. *Journal of East-West Business*, *27*(2), 160–183. DOI: 10.1080/10669868.2020.1862383

Kuhn, K. M., Meijerink, J., & Keegan, A. E. (2021, August). *Human Resource Management and the gig economy: Challenges and Opportunities at the Intersection between*

Kulkov, I., Kulkova, J., Rohrbeck, R., Menvielle, L., Kaartemo, V., & Makkonen, H. (2024). Artificial intelligence-driven sustainable development: Examining organizational, technical, and processing approaches to achieving global goals. *Sustainable Development (Bradford), 32*(3), 2253–2267. DOI: 10.1002/sd.2773

Kumar, P. K. (2024) At LaLiT, DE&I is in our DNA: Deeksha Suri, *ETHospitalityWorld.com.* Retrieved from https://hospitality.economictimes.indiatimes.com (accessed on 25-07-2025)

Kumar, A. (2021). Caste and workplace diversity: The missing discourse in Indian organizations. *Indian Journal of Industrial Relations, 56*(3), 345–362.

Kumar, S. (2024). Inclusive HR Practices in the Indian Service Sector. *Indian School of Hospitality Journal, 8*(1), 20–30.

Larsson, S., White, J. M., & Ingram Bogusz, C. (2024). The Artificial Recruiter: Risks of Discrimination in Employers' Use of AI and Automated Decision-Making. *Social Inclusion (Lisboa), 12*, 12. DOI: 10.17645/si.7471

Levenson, A. (2018). Using targeted analytics to improve talent decisions. [DOI not available]. *People & Strategy, 41*(2), 32–39.

LinkedIn. (2024). The Lalit Suri Hospitality Group's Post on being recognized among Top 10 Employers in IWEI 2024. *LinkedIn post.* https://www.linkedin.com/posts/thelalitgroup_the-lalit-suri-hospitality-group-is-proud-activity-7265699316344791042-IF6k/ (accessed on 25-07-2025)

Linneberg, M. S., Trenca, M., & Nørreklit, H. (2021). Institutional work through empathic engagement. *European Management Journal, 39*(1), 46–56. DOI: 10.1016/j.emj.2020.08.002 PMID: 38620643

Liu, R., & Yin, H. (2024). How Algorithmic Management Influences Gig Workers' Job Crafting. *Behavioral Sciences (Basel, Switzerland), 14*(10), 952. DOI: 10.3390/bs14100952 PMID: 39457824

Liu, S., Hao, F., & Qiu, X. (2025). Diversity, Equity, and Inclusion (DEI) research in tourism and hospitality: Insights from bibliometric analysis. *International Journal of Contemporary Hospitality Management, 37*(7), 2532–2555. Advance online publication. DOI: 10.1108/IJCHM-11-2024-1638

Loon, M., Otaye-Ebede, L., & Stewart, J. (2021). The paradox of employee psychological well-being and organizational performance: A systematic review and research agenda. *Human Resource Management Review, 31*(2), 100745. DOI: 10.1016/j.hrmr.2020.100745

Lourens, M., Vijai, C., Nijhawan, G., Garwal, Y. S., Gakhreja, S., & Saud, A. M. (2024). Artificial Intelligence-Driven Talent Management System: Exploring the Risks and Options Sustainable Success. *2024 4th International Conference on Innovative Practices in Technology and Management (ICIPTM)*, 1–6.

Manoharan, A., & Singal, M. (2017). A systematic literature review of research on diversity and diversity management in the hospitality literature. *International Journal of Hospitality Management*, *66*, 77–91. DOI: 10.1016/j.ijhm.2017.07.002

Manroop, L., Malik, A., & Milner, M. (2024). The ethical implications of big data in human resource management. *Human Resource Management Review*, *34*(2), 101012. DOI: 10.1016/j.hrmr.2024.101012

Maphanga, M. E., Mokoena, A. B., & Isabirye, A. K. (2024). Leadership power bases influence on quality of work-life and intention to stay among retailing employees. *SA Journal of Human Resource Management*, *22*, 1–10. DOI: 10.4102/sajhrm.v22i0.2403

Marler, J. H., & Boudreau, J. W. (2017). An evidence-based review of HR analytics. *International Journal of Human Resource Management*, *28*(1), 3–26. DOI: 10.1080/09585192.2016.1244699

Marler, J. H., & Parry, E. (2016). Human resource management, strategic involvement and e-HRM technology. *International Journal of Human Resource Management*, *27*(19), 2233–2253. DOI: 10.1080/09585192.2015.1091980

McPhail, R., Chan, X. W., May, R., & Wilkinson, A. (2024). Post-COVID remote working and its impact on people, productivity, and the planet: An exploratory scoping review. *International Journal of Human Resource Management*, *35*(1), 154–182. DOI: 10.1080/09585192.2023.2221385

Medina Garrido, J. A., Biedma Ferrer, J. M., & Bogren, M. (2023). Organizational support for work–family life balance as an antecedent to the well-being of tourism employees in Spain. *Journal of Hospitality and Tourism Management*, *57*, 117–129. DOI: 10.1016/j.jhtm.2023.08.018

Medina-Garrido, J. A., Biedma-Ferrer, J. M., & Ramos-Rodriguez, A. R. (2023). *Relationship between work-family balance, employee well-being and job performance*. https://doi.org//arXiv.2401.13683DOI: 10.48550

Mehrotra, S. (2021). Informality and the emerging gig economy in India: The case for universal social protection. *International Labour Review*, *160*(1), 67–90.

Meijerink, J., Bondarouk, T., & Lepak, D. (2020). When HRM meets the platform economy: Exploring HRM strategies for digital and gig workers. *Human Resource Management Review*, *30*(4), 100771. DOI: 10.1016/j.hrmr.2020.100771

Meijerink, J., Bondarouk, T., & Lepak, D. P. (2021). When and why does HR analytics influence strategic decision making? *Human Resource Management*, *60*(3), 365–382.

Meijerink, J., Bondarouk, T., & Lepak, D. P. (2023). The duality of algorithmic management: Toward a research agenda. *Human Resource Management Review*, *33*(2), 100861.

Michael, N., Fotiadis, A. K., & Michael, I. (2024). Emiratization and hospitality sector destination branding of Dubai: An impact analysis. *Journal of Human Resources in Hospitality & Tourism*, *23*(2), 171–193. DOI: 10.1080/15332845.2024.2282197

Ministry of Economy, UAE. (2024, April 25). *Hospitality Advisory Committee reviews initiatives outlined in UAE Tourism Strategy 2031 and their role in boosting the national hospitality sector's competitiveness* (Press release). Abu Dhabi: UAE Ministry of Economy.

Montgomery, T., & Baglioni, S. (2021). Defining the gig economy: Platform capitalism and precarious work. *The International Journal of Sociology and Social Policy*, *41*(9/10), 1012–1025. DOI: 10.1108/IJSSP-08-2020-0400

Nawaz, N., Arunachalam, H., Pathi, B. K., & Gajenderan, V. (2024). The adoption of artificial intelligence in human resources management practices. *International Journal of Information Management Data Insights*, *4*(1), 100208. DOI: 10.1016/j.jjimei.2023.100208

News, A. P. N. (2024). Deeksha Suri the Lalit: Redefining Women Leadership. Retrieved from https://www.apnnews.com/deeksha-suri-the-lalit-redifining-women-leadership/ (accessed on 25-07-2025).

News, A. P. N. (2024). SheLeads@TheLalit *Celebrates Women in Leadership*. Retrieved from https://apnnews.com (accessed on 26-07-2025)

Nickson, D. (2013). *Human resource management for hospitality, tourism and events* (2nd ed.). Routledge. DOI: 10.4324/9780080966496

Nishii, L. H., & Mayer, D. M. (2009). Do inclusive leaders help to reduce turnover in diverse groups? *The Journal of Applied Psychology*, *94*(6), 1412–1426. DOI: 10.1037/a0017190 PMID: 19916652

Odunayo Salau, A. O. (2018). datasets on employee value proposition (evp) and performance of selected fast moving consumer goods (FMCGs) firms in Nigeria. *Journal Data in Brief*, 1907-1911.

Olson, D. A., Jeske, D., & Shultz, K. S. (2024). Developing, nurturing, and expanding personal and professional relationships through social media. In *Handbook of Social Media Use Online Relationships, Security, Privacy, and Society Volume 2* (pp. 195–215). Elsevier. DOI: 10.1016/B978-0-443-28804-3.00010-7

Ossiannilsson, E., Altinay, F., Shadiev, R., Benachour, P., Berigel, M., Dagli, G., Ayaz, A., Yikici, B., & Altinay, Z. (2024). Exploring the Intersection of Artificial Intelligence and Human Resource Management: A Bibliometric Study. *BRAIN. Broad Research in Artificial Intelligence and Neuroscience*, *15*(4), 215–230. DOI: 10.70594/brain/15.4/15

Ostroff, C., & Bowen, D. E. (2016). Reflections on the 2014 decade award: Is there strength in the construct of HR system strength? *Academy of Management Review*, *41*(2), 196–214. DOI: 10.5465/amr.2015.0323

Page, S. E. (2007). *The difference: How the power of diversity creates better groups, firms, schools, and societies*. Princeton University Press., https://psycnet.apa.org/record/2007-05886-000

Palos-Sánchez, P. R., & Correia, M. B. (2022). Artificial intelligence and human resource management: A bibliometric analysis. *Technological Forecasting and Social Change*, *178*, 121528.

Patrick van Esch, J. S. (n.d.). Factors that influence new generation candidates to engage with and complete digital, AI-enabled recruiting. *Business Horizons*, 1–11.

Pereira, D., & Silva, T. (2023). Systematic literature review on AI impact at work. *Frontiers in Psychology*, *14*, 1100203.

Pereira, R., & Silva, A. (2023). Policy drafting with generative AI: A case for strategic HR management. *Journal of Organizational Change Management*, *36*(7), 1201–1219.

Permarupan, P. Y. (2020). Human capital and organizational performance: A review. *International Journal of Academic Research in Business & Social Sciences*, *10*(2), 500–510. DOI: 10.6007/IJARBSS/v10-i2/6928

Permarupan, P. Y., Al Mamun, A., Ahmad Saufi, R., Hayat, N., & Samy, N. K. (2020). Effects of quality of work life on emotional exhaustion: A study among nurses in Malaysia. *Journal of Workplace Behavioral Health*, *35*(2), 117–136. DOI: 10.1080/15555240.2020.1720516

Petya Puncheva-Michelotti, S. H. (2018). Employer branding and CSR communication in online Recruitment Advertising. *Business Horizons*, *61*(4), 9. DOI: 10.1016/j.bushor.2018.04.003

Phillips, F. (2024). Generative AI in the workplace: Compliance and legal issues for HR. *Fisher Phillips Legal Insights*. Retrieved from https://www.fisherphillips.com

Pinto, G. B. S., & Silva, R. (2025). Explainable AI in labor market applications: Challenges and opportunities. *ScitePress Proceedings on Artificial Intelligence Applications*, 122–135.

Pinto, R., & Silva, F. (2025). Trust and transparency in AI-driven performance appraisal. *European Journal of Work and Organizational Psychology*, *34*(2), 205–220.

Podgorodnichenko, N., Edgar, F., & McAndrew, I. (2020). The role of HRM in developing sustainable organizations: Contemporary challenges and opportunities. *Human Resource Management Review*, *30*(3), 100708. DOI: 10.1016/j.hrmr.2019.04.001

Podsakoff, P. M., MacKenzie, S. B., Paine, J. B., & Bachrach, D. G. (2000). Organizational citizenship behaviors: A critical review of the theoretical and empirical literature and suggestions for future research. *Journal of Management*, *26*(3), 513–563. DOI: 10.1177/014920630002600307

Potočnik, K., Anderson, N., Born, M. P., Kleinmann, M., & Nikolaou, I. (n.d.). *Recent Developments in Recruitment and Selection*.

Prabhu, U., Fathima, Y., Sathyanarayana, N., Srikumar, M. S. S. V., & Cavaliere, L. P. L. (2024). Emerging Digitalization Trends in Human Resource Management. In *Data-Driven Intelligent Business Sustainability* (pp. 214–234). IGI Global.

Prasad, K. D. V., & Sujatha, G. (2024). Generative AI as a catalyst for HRM practices: Challenges and opportunities. *International Journal of Human Resource Studies*, *14*(2), 45–62.

Prasad, K., & Sujatha, R. (2024). Leveraging generative AI for employee training: Personalized learning pathways. *International Journal of Training and Development*, *28*(3), 211–228.

Prikshat, V., Malik, A., & Budhwar, P. (2023). AI-augmented HRM: Antecedents, assimilation and multilevel consequences. *Human Resource Management Review*, *33*(1), 100860. DOI: 10.1016/j.hrmr.2021.100860

Qasim, A. (2020). The impacts of high employee turnover in the UAE hospitality industry. In *Human Capital in the Middle East: A UAE Perspective* (pp. 73–91). Springer International Publishing. DOI: 10.1007/978-3-030-42211-0_4

Rahman, S. U., Sultan, M. S., & Tabassam, A. (2024). THE IMPACT OF THE GIG ECONOMY ON TRADITIONAL EMPLOYMENT AND THE NECESSITY FOR REVISED BUSINESS, HR, AND LEGAL STRATEGIES. *Pakistan Journal of International Affairs*, *7*(1).

Raisch, S., & Krakowski, S. (2021). Artificial intelligence and management: The automation–augmentation paradox. *Academy of Management Review*, *46*(1), 192–210. DOI: 10.5465/amr.2018.0072

Ralf Wilden, S. G. (2010). Employer branding: Strategic implications for staff recruitment. *Journal of Marketing Management*, *26*(1-2), 56–73. DOI: 10.1080/02672570903577091

Ramayah, T., Lo, M. C., & Tarmizi, A. N. (2014). Quality of work life and turnover intention: A partial least square (PLS) approach. *Social Indicators Research*, *119*(1), 405–420. DOI: 10.1007/s11205-013-0486-5

Rana, V. S., Sharma, D. P., & Thakur, A. Potential of Food Tourism in Punjab (India): A Study of Amritsar, Jalandhar and Patiala (May 2, 2021). Eurasian Journal of Analytical Chemistry (2018) 13 (6): 371-377, Available at SSRN: https://ssrn.com/abstract=3838266

Randev, H., & Jha, S. (2019). Sustainable Human Resource Management: Practices, Policies, and Prospects. In *HRM Practices for a Sustainable Future* (pp. 45-62). (Referenced for definitions of Green HRM and sustainable HRM's impact on ecology and society)

Randev, K. K., & Jha, J. K. (2019). Sustainable human resource management: A literature-based introduction. *NHRD Network Journal*, *12*(3), 241–252. DOI: 10.1177/2631454119873495

Rasheed, R., Malik, M., & Sarwar, S. (2023). AI-driven digital monitoring and worker motivation. *Technological Forecasting and Social Change*, *189*, 122314. DOI: 10.1016/j.techfore.2023.122314

Reuters. (2018, October 10). Amazon scraps secret AI recruiting tool that showed bias against women. *Reuters*. https://www.reuters.com

Richman, A., Johnson, D., Rosenzweig, J., & Hill, E. (2021). Workplace flexibility for sustainable career satisfaction in the aviation sector. *Sustainability*, *13*(12), 6878. DOI: 10.3390/su13126878

Rigotti, C., Riedl, R., & Baumgartner, L. (2024). Fairness in AI-driven recruitment: A scoping review. *Computers in Human Behavior Reports*, *14*, 100302.

Rigotti, T., Riedl, E., & Baumgartner, H. (2024). Inclusive hiring with generative AI. *Human Resource Development Quarterly*, *35*(1), 45–63.

Rivera, V. A., & Duggan, J. (2022). Centering worker well-being in gig work. *Proceedings of the 2022 CHI Conference on Human Factors in Computing Systems*, 1–17. https://doi.org/DOI: 10.1145/3491102.3501866

Roberson, Q. M. (2006). Disentangling the meanings of diversity and inclusion in organizations. *Group & Organization Management*, *31*(2), 212–236. DOI: 10.1177/1059601104273064

Robinson, R. N., Kralj, A., Solnet, D. J., Goh, E., & Callan, V. (2019). Thinking Job Embeddedness Not Turnover: Towards a Better Understanding of Frontline Hotel Worker Retention. *International Journal of Hospitality Management*, *36*, 101–109. DOI: 10.1016/j.ijhm.2013.08.008

Rodriguez, R. V., Hemachandran, K., Majumdar, A., & Basu, R. (2024). *1st International Conference, 'Resonance': on Cognitive Approach, Social Ethics and Sustainability: 23 and 24th November, 2022 School Of Liberal Arts and Humanities, Woxsen University, India*. Taylor & Francis.

Sahoo, S., & Mohapatra, S. (2025). *Human capital and sustainability: An emerging perspective*. Springer., DOI: 10.1007/s43615-025-00583-

Samala, A. D., Rawas, S., Wang, T., Alshammari, F., & Chen, C. (2025). Unveiling the landscape of generative artificial intelligence in education: A comprehensive taxonomy of applications, challenges, and future prospects. *Education and Information Technologies*, *30*(3), 3239–3278. DOI: 10.1007/s10639-024-12936-0

Samek, W., & Müller, K. R. (2019). Towards explainable artificial intelligence. In Explainable, A. I. (Ed.), *Interpreting, explaining and visualizing deep learning* (pp. 5–22). Springer. DOI: 10.1007/978-3-030-28954-6_1

Santareno, J. (2025). Generative artificial intelligence in candidate selection. In *Lecture Notes on Multidisciplinary Industrial Engineering*. https://doi.org/DOI: 10.1007/978-3-031-89948-5_4

Seifdar, M. H., & Amiri, B. (2025). Strategic adoption of generative AI in organizations: A game-theoretic and network-based approach. *International Journal of Information Management*, *84*, 102932. DOI: 10.1016/j.ijinfomgt.2025.102932

Sen, K., & Bhattarchya, A. (2019). Attracting and managing talent, how are the top three hotel companies in India doing it? *Worldwide Hospitality and Tourism Themes*, *11*(4), 404–417. DOI: 10.1108/WHATT-04-2019-0021

Shen, J., Chanda, A., D'Netto, B., & Monga, M. (2009). Managing diversity through human resource management: An international perspective and conceptual framework. *International Journal of Human Resource Management, 20*(2), 235–251. DOI: 10.1080/09585190802670516

Shin, D. (2025). Bossware and the future of algorithmic monitoring: Implications for HRM. *Journal of Business Ethics, 182*(1), 1–19.

Shin, D. (2025). Dehumanization and rehumanization of workers in AI-driven HRM. *Information & Management, 62*(2), 103768.

Shin, D., & Konrad, A. M. (2017). Causal link between workforce diversity and organizational performance: Diversity reputation as a mediator. *Human Resource Management, 56*(3), 317–336. DOI: 10.1002/hrm.21733

Shore, L. M., Cleveland, J. N., & Sanchez, D. (2011). Inclusive workplaces: A review and model. *Human Resource Management Review, 21*(4), 311–326.

Smruti Bulsari, K. P. (2023). Future of HR Analytics: Applications to Recruitment, Employee Engagement, and Retention. In *K. S. Naman Sharma, Managing Technology Integration for Human Resources in Industry 5.0* (p. 294). IGI Global Scientific Publishing.

Sohail, M., & Rosário, A. (2025). Benefits and risks of artificial intelligence in human resource management: An integrative review. *Journal of Organizational Change Management, 38*(4), 565–584.

Sohail, M., & Rosário, A. (2025). Generative AI and diversity: Opportunities and risks for HRM. *Equality, Diversity and Inclusion, 44*(2), 178–196.

Soul of Hospitality. (2025). DEI Isn't a Project at The LaLiT—It's in Their DNA. *Soul of Hospitality*. https://www.soulofhospitality.com/travel/hotels/dei-isn-t-a-project-at-the-lalit-it-s-in-their-dna (accessed on 26-07-2025)

Steffens, P.. (2025). Human Resource Management Systems research—How to gain impactful insights through formative measurement and hierarchical component models. *Human Resource Management Journal*.

Stone, D. L., Deadrick, D. L., Lukaszewski, K. M., & Johnson, R. (2015). The influence of technology on the future of human resource management. *Human Resource Management Review, 25*(2), 216–231. DOI: 10.1016/j.hrmr.2015.01.002

Subrahmanyam, S. (2024). Implementing agile talent management practices to adapt to changing higher education landscapes. In *Cultivating Creativity and Navigating Talent Management in Academia*. https://doi.org/DOI: 10.4018/979-8-3693-6880-0.ch009

Subramony, M. (2009). A meta-analytic investigation of the relationship between HRM bundles and firm performance. *Human Resource Management*, *48*(5), 745–768. DOI: 10.1002/hrm.20315

Suri, D. (2024). At The LaLiT, DEI is in our DNA, *Soul of Hospitality*. https://www.soulofhospitality.com/leadership/features/dei-isn-t-a-project-at-the-lalit-it-s-in-their-dna (accessed on 25-07-2025)

Swiggy Limited. (2025). *Sustainability at Swiggy*. Retrieved September 6, 2025, from https://www.swiggy.com/corporate/sustainability/

Tarafdar, M., Cooper, C., & Stich, J. F. (2019). The technostress trifecta. *Information Systems Journal*, *29*(1), 6–42. DOI: 10.1111/isj.12169

Teece, D. J. (2007). Explicating dynamic capabilities: The nature and microfoundations of (sustainable) enterprise performance. *Strategic Management Journal*, *28*(13), 1319–1350. DOI: 10.1002/smj.640

Teece, D. J., Peteraf, M., & Leih, S. (2016). Dynamic capabilities and organizational agility: Risk, uncertainty, and strategy in the innovation economy. *California Management Review*, *58*(4), 13–35. DOI: 10.1525/cmr.2016.58.4.13

Teo, S. T. T., Bentley, T., & Nguyen, D. (2020). Psychosocial work environment, work engagement, and employee commitment: A moderated mediation model. *International Journal of Hospitality Management*, *88*, 102415. Advance online publication. DOI: 10.1016/j.ijhm.2019.102415

The Financial Times. (2024, December 15). Does HR still need humans? *Financial Times*. https://www.ft.com

The Lalit DEI Report. (2024). Annual Diversity, Equity, and Inclusion Report. The Lalit Suri Hospitality Group. https://www.thelalit.com/wp-content/uploads/2024/08/Bharat-Hotels-Annual-Report-2 (accessed on 28-07-2025)

The Lalit Suri Hospitality Group (2024). First hotel chain globally accredited by IGLTA, *ET HospitalityWorld*. Soul of Hospitality+1ETHospitalityWorld.com+1 (accessed on 28-07-2025)

The Lalit Suri Hospitality Group. (2024). LinkedIn Post on IWEI 2024 Employer Recognition. The Patriot+2LinkedIn+2Hotelier India+2 (accessed on 28-07-2025)

The Lalit Suri Hospitality Group. (2024). The LaLiT Suri Hospitality Group is proud to be recognized as a TOP 10 Employer in the India Workplace Equality Index 2024 by Pride Circle. [Online forum post]. *The Lalit Suri Hospitality Group*. Retrieved from https://www.linkedin.com/posts/thelalitgroup_the-lalit-suri-hospitality-group-is-proud-activity-7265699316344791042-IF6k/ (accessed on 27-07-2025)

Thomas, D. A., & Ely, R. J. (1996). Making differences matter: A new paradigm for managing diversity. *Harvard Business Review*, *74*(5), 79–90.

Toscano, F., & Zappalà, S. (2020). Social isolation and stress as predictors of productivity perception and remote work satisfaction during the COVID-19 pandemic: The role of concern about the virus in a moderated double mediation. *Sustainability (Basel)*, *12*(23), 9804. DOI: 10.3390/su12239804

Traveller, C. N. (2024, January 29). This Indian hotel chain is the first in the world to receive IGLTA accreditation. Condé Nast Traveller India. https://www.cntraveller.in/story/the-lalit-first-in-the-world-to-receive-iglta-accreditation-lgbtq-queer-friendly/ (accessed on 26-07-2025)

Tursunbayeva, A., Franco, M., & Pagliari, C. (2021). Use of artificial intelligence in HRM: A systematic review. *International Journal of Human Resource Management*, *32*(17), 3791–3831. DOI: 10.1080/09585192.2020.1871398

Upadhyay, A. K., & Khandelwal, K. (2019). Applying artificial intelligence: Implications for recruitment. *Strategic HR Review*, *18*(5), 215–218.

Vadithe, R. N., Sreenu, N., Kesari, B., Chiranjeevi, V., Mudavath, C. B. N., & Rajput, R. C. (2025). The role of HR analytics in driving organizational agility. *Engineering, Construction, and Architectural Management*. Advance online publication. DOI: 10.1108/ECAM-01-2025-0076

Vallas, S., & Schor, J. B. (2020). What do platforms do? Understanding the gig economy. *Annual Review of Sociology*, *46*(1), 273–294. DOI: 10.1146/annurev-soc-121919-054857

Van Slageren, J., & Herrmann, A. M. (2024). Skill Specificity on High-Skill Online Gig Platforms: Same as in Traditional Labour Markets? *Social Forces*, *102*(4), 1332–1351. DOI: 10.1093/sf/soad153

Vasanthan, R., Nath Babu, M., Dzuvichu, K., & Chong, T. S., Singh Rana, V., & Singh, A. (2025). Bridging Social Norms Theory and Community Mobilization: Pathways for Overcoming Gender Stereotypes in Women's Economic Empowerment Programs. *Enterprise Development & Microfinance, 35*(1), 159–176. Retrieved from https://papjournals.com/index.php/edm/article/view/13

Vasanthan, R., Nath Babu, M., Dzuvichu, K., & Chong, T. S., Singh Rana, V., & Singh, A. (2025). Bridging Social Norms Theory and Community Mobilization: Pathways for Overcoming Gender Stereotypes in Women's Economic Empowerment Programs. *Enterprise Development & Microfinance, 35*(1), 159–176. Retrieved from https://www.papjournals.com/index.php/edm/article/view/13

Verma, N., & Gavett, G. (2021). Algorithms at work: The new contested terrain of control. *The Academy of Management Annals, 15*(1), 266–301.

Voigt, P., & Von dem Bussche, A. (2017). *The EU General Data Protection Regulation (GDPR)*. Springer. DOI: 10.1007/978-3-319-57959-7

Vrontis, D., Christofi, M., Pereira, V., Tarba, S., Makrides, A., & Trichina, E. (2023). Artificial intelligence, robotics, advanced technologies and human resource management: a systematic review. *Artificial intelligence and international HRM*, 172-201.

Wang, H., Liu, Y., & Zhao, J. (2025). AI-driven learning in organizations: A meta-analysis. *Computers & Education, 210*, 104901.

Wang, J., Liu, H., & Zhao, Y. (2025). ChatGPT and student learning performance: A meta-analysis. *Nature Communications, 16*, 452.

Wang, X., Xu, L., & Zhang, P. (2025). How and when AI-driven HRM promotes employee resilience. *Computers in Human Behavior, 147*, 107916.

Warner, R., & Moonesar, I. A. (2019). Diversity management: the case of the United Arab Emirates. In *Diversity within diversity management* (Vol. 21, pp. 41–63). Emerald Publishing Limited. DOI: 10.1108/S1877-636120190000021003

Wijngaards, I., King, O. C., Burger, M. J., & van Exel, J. (2022). Worker well-being: What it is, and how it should be measured. *Applied Research in Quality of Life, 17*(2), 795–832. DOI: 10.1007/s11482-021-09930-w

Wired. (2024, August 9). Algorithmic management is reshaping the workplace. *Wired Magazine*. https://www.wired.com

Wong, K., Chan, A. H. S., & Teh, P.-L. (2020). How Is Work–Life Balance Arrangement Associated with Organisational Performance? A Meta Analysis. *International Journal of Environmental Research and Public Health, 17*(12), 4446. Advance online publication. DOI: 10.3390/ijerph17124446 PMID: 32575807

Wood, A. J., Graham, M., Lehdonvirta, V., & Hjorth, I. (2019). Good gig, bad gig: Autonomy and algorithmic control in platform work. *Work, Employment and Society, 33*(1), 56–75. DOI: 10.1177/0950017018785616 PMID: 30886460

Wright, P. M., & McMahan, G. C. (1992). Theoretical perspectives for strategic human resource management. *Journal of Management*, *18*(2), 295–320. DOI: 10.1177/014920639201800205

Wright, P. M., & McMahan, G. C. (2011). Exploring human capital: Putting 'human' back into strategic human resource management. *Human Resource Management Journal*, *21*(2), 93–104. DOI: 10.1111/j.1748-8583.2010.00165.x

Xinyue Yu, L. (2025). Artificial Intelligence and Corporate ESG Performance: A Mechanism Analysis Based on Corporate Efficiency and External Environment. *Sustainability, MDPI*, 3819.

Yew Lim, K., Lynn, H., Owee Tan, K., & Dennen, V. C. (2024). The influencing factors and employee retention in Dubai's hotel industry. *Journal/Proceedings of Hospitality Management* (in press). (Study finding training, compensation, and leadership support significantly affect retention in UAE hotels)

Yin, R. K. (2018). Case Study Research and Applications: Design and Methods (6th ed.). Thousand Oaks, CA: Sage, 282. https://utppublishing.com/doi/10.3138/cjpe.30.1.108 (accessed on 27-07-2025)

Yousif, N. (2024). No Matter Which Team You Are Supporting This Olympics. Retrieved from https://www.linkedin.com/posts/nadjiayousif_why-inclusion-matters-to-businesses-in-india-activity-7225171562193137664-v3uS/ (accessed on 28-07-2025)

Zaid, A. A., Jaaron, A. A. M., & Talib Bon, A. (2018). The impact of green human resource management and green supply chain management practices on sustainable performance: An empirical study. *Journal of Cleaner Production*, *204*, 965–979. DOI: 10.1016/j.jclepro.2018.09.062

Zhang, J., & Chen, Z. (2024). Exploring human resource management digital transformation in the digital age. *Journal of the Knowledge Economy*, *15*(1), 1482–1498. DOI: 10.1007/s13132-023-01214-y PMID: 40479358

Zhang, L., & Lu, L. (2023). AI adoption in hospitality: Impacts on service employees and HR practices. *International Journal of Contemporary Hospitality Management*. Advance online publication. DOI: 10.1108/IJCHM-09-2021-1146

Zhou, X., Yu, Y., & Xu, H. (2023). Generative artificial intelligence in organizations: A conceptual framework. *Information & Management*, *60*(6), 103762.

Zhou, Y., Luo, Y., & Tang, T. (2020). Strategic human resource management, firm performance, and employee outcomes: A meta-analysis. *Journal of Management*, *46*(7), 1323–1350. DOI: 10.1177/0149206319881775

Zhu, H. (2021). Research on human resource recommendation algorithm based on machine learning. *Scientific Programming*, *2021*(1), 8387277. DOI: 10.1155/2021/8387277

About the Contributors

Varinder Singh Rana is presently working as Department Chair of Hospitality and Hotel Management and Deputy Director- Research at City University Ajman. He received Doctorate (PhD) in Hospitality from Amity University, Noida, India. He has authored 14 books and 45 Research papers in reputed journals. He has been awarded with Best Culinary Educator award by Indian Federation of Culinary Association (A Nodal Body of Ministry of Tourism, Government of India). He has 10 patents and 7 copyrights on his name. His research expertise on the sustainability, gastronomy, hospitality marketing and entrepreneurship made him a renowned researcher globally.

Aisha Khan is an Assistant Professor at Bath Spa University UAE, where she integrates her passion for teaching, research, and sustainability into all aspects of her work. She holds a PhD in Sustainable Human Resource Management (HRM), a field that drives her ongoing exploration of how HR practices can be aligned with environmental and social responsibility while enhancing organizational performance. With over five years of experience in academia, Dr. Khan has taught and mentored students across diverse HR and management disciplines, equipping them with the critical skills needed to navigate the evolving landscape of human resource management. Since 2019, she has also served as an HR Consultant, collaborating with organizations to design strategic and sustainable HR solutions. This dual engagement in academia and industry allows her to bridge theory and practice in a meaningful and impactful way. Her research interests lie at the intersection of sustainable HRM, strategic HRM, green leadership, emotional intelligence, and corporate governance—key themes she believes are vital to the future of work. Dr. Khan's scholarly work has been published in Scopus, ABDC, and ABS-indexed journals, and she actively contributes to the global academic community through regular presentations at international conferences. In addition to her academic and consulting work, Dr. Khan frequently serves as a moderator, session chair, and invited speaker at conferences and webinars. She has also delivered talks at international universities, with a particular focus on sustainability and responsible business practices. Her commitment to creating meaningful change is evident in her research, teaching, and consultancy work. Dr. Khan remains dedicated to advancing the field of HR through thought leadership, impactful scholarship, and active engagement with the academic and professional communities.

***

Sujata Dash is currently working as an Assistant Professor in the Department of Management, Birla Institute of Technology, Mesra, Ranchi, Jharkhand, INDIA. Her research interests include Human Capital Management, Emotional Intelligence, Blockchain and Artificial Intelligence in Human Resource Management. She has published her research work in many National and International Journals (Scopus and ABDC indexed) and attended various National and International Conferences, Workshops and Faculty Development Programmes. She has published book chapters in Scopus indexed Edited Book Volume in International Publication houses such as Springer, CRC Press, Taylor and Francis, and Wiley. Her professional affiliation is AIMS-Associations of Management Scholar.

Mohammad Irfan is recognized among the World's Top 2% Scientists, celebrated for his extensive research contributions including 111+ Scopus-indexed publications in reputed journals such as The Journal of Economic Cooperation and Development (Q2), International Journal of Business Excellence, Montenegrin Journal of Economics (Q2), Cogent Business & Management (Q2), and Journal of Islamic Monetary Economics and Finance. His scholarly work has garnered 780+ citations with an H-index of 15, and he has authored 14 books with leading global publishers including Springer and IGI Global. He serves as a Professor at the School of Business and Commerce, Chandigarh University, Uttar Pradesh (Unnao), India. Dr. Irfan earned his Ph.D. from the Central University of Haryana and holds an MBA in Finance, an M.Com in Accounts and Law, and an MA in Economics. A UGC-JRF/SRF/NET qualifier in Management and Commerce, he has further strengthened his academic profile with professional certifications from NSE (NCFM) and BSE. With more than eighteen years of teaching and research experience, Dr. Irfan's expertise spans Security Analysis and Portfolio Management (SAPM), Artificial Intelligence, Machine Learning, Blockchain, Cryptocurrency, Financial Engineering, FinTech, Green Finance, and Alternative Finance.

Nida Khan has completed her graduation form Christ University, Bengaluru, India in its Pune Lavasa Campus. She has been brilliant in her academic domain along with her interest in research. Ms Nida has started her carrier as a analyst in Deloitte, India, however, keeping her research endeavors alive.

Faisal Khan is a faculty of College of Bussiness at City University Ajman and specialised in finance and accounting with seventeen years plus expereince in academia and industry.

Manoj Kumar is an Assistant Professor with over four years of academic experience and two years as a professional soft skills trainer, complemented by corporate exposure through his work with multinational companies, which enriches his teaching with practical insights. He has held faculty positions at Uttaranchal University and AP Goyal Shimla University and is currently serving at Chandigarh University. A two-time UGC NET qualifier and recipient of the Star Educator Award, he is presently pursuing a Ph.D. at APG Shimla University with research focused on the Role of Green Marketing Tools. His academic expertise includes teaching courses such as Strategic Management, Business Society and Law, and AI in Social Sciences, while his research interests lie in green marketing, consumer behaviour, and the intersection of management with technology and society.

Rashmi Kumari received her B. Tech degree in Computer Science & Engineering from BIT Sindri, Dhanbad, India, in 2018 and MBA degree in Human Resource Management from BIT Mesra, Ranchi, India, in 2020. She is currently working toward the Ph.D. degree with Department of Management, Birla Institute of Technology Mesra, Ranchi, India. Her research interest includes Green Human Resource Management and Organisational Behaviour. She has authored or co-authored various research articles in prestigious journals, book chapters and conference proceedings.

Urvashi Kumari is presently working as Associate Professor in the School of Engineering and Technology, Sushant University, Gurgaon, India. She has been awarded a PhD from the School of Computer Management, Pune University, Pune, Maharashtra, India. Dr. Urvashi has over 20 years of academic experience teaching in Indian engineering colleges. She has published papers in peer-reviewed international journals of nature, UGC CARE, ABDC, SCOPUS, IGI PUBLISHING, and EMERALD PUBLICATION. Dr. Urvashi is guiding three PhD students in the interdisciplinary field of information technology, hospitality, and tourism.

Prabhu Manickam is joint registrar-Humanities & Sciences at Dr. M. G. R Educational & Research Institute, Chennai, India. He is frontline member in Indian Federation of Culinary Associations (IFCA). He has more than 26 years of Academic and Industry experience.

Shorena Okujava is People Operations Manager at Hilton Garden Inn Ras Al Khaimah. She has more than 17 years of academic and industry experience.

Jyoti Prakash is a highly experienced professional, who has a Master's degree in Hotel Management. His academic journey, spanning over 8 years, reflects a strong commitment to both the hospitality industry and academia. Currently, he is pursuing PhD in Hospitality from GD Goenka University in Sohna, Haryana, India. Prakash's career is characterized by an unwavering dedication to education and the development of future hospitality professionals. He has published more than 13 research papers and a few book chapters in reputed journals. His core expertise revolves around various domains and promoting culinary education in the realm of Hospitality Academics, where he is deeply committed to fostering the growth and excellence of the next generation of professionals in the field. He is enthusiastic about embracing learning opportunities and staying updated with industry trends and academic advancements. His research interests include Culinary Promotion, Food Safety and Security, Destination Marketing, and Odisha Cuisine Promotion. Prakash is known for his proficient hold in analytical and problem-solving skills, and provides freelance research assistance utilizing tools for data analysis

Bargavi Ravichandran is an academic and researcher specializing in Human Resource Management, Systems Management, and Digital Learning. She holds a PhD from SRM Institute of Science and Technology, where her research focused on EdTech adoption in higher education. With experience in teaching, research, and industry, she has published multiple papers and case studies on technology-enabled HR practices, digital transformation, and sustainable innovation.

Poonam Rehal working as an Assistant Professor at Amity University-Punjab with a strong passion for teaching and research in management studies. My research interests lie in sustainability, talent management, employer branding, and job satisfaction, focusing on how organizations can create meaningful employee experiences while achieving long-term growth.

Rohan Singh has been an Associate Professor of Management at Chandigarh University, Punjab, India, for around three years and holds a Doctor of Philosophy Degree in Management. He has published his research in various reputed International Journals and Conferences, accruing more than 500 citations. Dr. Singh has reviewed numerous journals and book chapters indexed in Scopus and Web of Science and supervises many doctoral students. His primary research areas include Human Resource Management, focusing on HR strategies and their adaptation to contemporary trends such as AI, gig workers, and hybrid work practices. He also investigates the correlation between HRM practices and various performance metrics. Dr. Singh's extensive experience includes over 14 years at the Sponsored Research & Industrial Consultancy Cell, Indian Institute of Technology Kharagpur. His expertise is further demonstrated through his active participation as Associate Editor, Editorial Review Board Member, reviewer, Advisory Board Member, and Reviewer Board Member in many reputed Journals.

Ashutosh Verma is a seasoned Human Resource professional with over 18 years of diverse experience spanning both academia and the corporate sector. He completed his Doctorate from Himachal Pradesh University, Shimla (India) and is currently serving as an Associate Professor at the Parul Institute of Management & Research, Parul University, Gujarat, India. Dr. Verma has worked with reputed organizations across the pharmaceutical, financial services, and life sciences industries, gaining extensive hands-on expertise in various HR functions. A dedicated lifelong learner, he has actively participated in and contributed to numerous seminars, conferences, and workshops at national and international levels. He has several scholarly publications to his credit, including journal articles and book chapters. His current research interests lie at the intersection of human resource development and emerging technologies.

Index

I

J

L

O

P

Q

R

S

T

www.ingramcontent.com/pod-product-compliance
Lightning Source LLC
LaVergne TN
LVHW081527300926
849161LV00006B/1325